D1593835

Parrots and Nightingales

THE MIDDLE AGES SERIES

Ruth Mazo Karras, Series Editor
Edward Peters, Founding Editor

A complete list of books in the series
is available from the publisher.

PARROTS AND NIGHTINGALES

Troubadour Quotations
and the Development
of European Poetry

Sarah Kay

PENN

UNIVERSITY OF PENNSYLVANIA PRESS

PHILADELPHIA

Published by
University of Pennsylvania Press
Philadelphia, Pennsylvania 19104-4112
www.upenn.edu/pennpress

Printed in the United States of America on acid-free paper
10 9 8 7 6 5 4 3 2 1

Library of Congress Cataloging-in-Publication Data
Kay, Sarah.
Parrots and nightingales : troubadour quotations and the
development of European poetry / Sarah Kay. — 1st ed.
        p. cm. — (Middle Ages series)
Includes bibliographical references and index.
ISBN 978-0-8122-4525-7 (hardcover : alk. paper)
    1. Provençal literature—History and criticism.
    2. Troubadour songs—History and criticism.
    3. Quotations in literature—History and criticism.
4. European poetry—Provençal influences—History and
criticism.   I. Title.   II. Series: Middle Ages series.
                PC3304.K39 2013
                849'.1009—dc23
                                    2013005804

CONTENTS

PART III. TRANSFORMING TROUBADOUR QUOTATION

NOTE ON REFERENCES, TRANSLATIONS, AND ABBREVIATIONS

Full references to all works cited in the notes using a shortened form of the title are listed in the bibliography. The bibliography also provides details of all the songs included in Appendices 1 and 2. Where there is more than one available edition, the one marked with an asterisk is the one referred to, unless otherwise indicated. The bibliography also indicates the spellings of troubadours' names adopted here. These names are listed in the conventional order established by Pillet and Carstens in their *Bibliographie der Troubadours*; Pillet-Carstens (PC) numbers are also used to identify individual songs.

My own quotations from editions follow the spelling conventions of the editors concerned, except that I modernize and bring in line with American usage the use of capital letters and the punctuation of direct speech; additionally, I use italics in quotations and the text in which they are embedded in order to identify words or phrases that are repeated from one to the other.

References to troubadour songs use PC numbers; thus, for example, 70.1, 33 means "line 33 of PC 70.1," this being the Pillet-Carstens identifier for Bernart de Ventadorn's song "Ab joi mou lo vers e·l comens." Passages quoted from the texts of songs are from the editions listed in the bibliography and are identified, in addition to their PC number, by their number in that edition.

All translations are my own, unless otherwise indicated.

The following abbreviations are used, primarily in the Appendices:

Ab	*Abril issi' e mays intrava* by Raimon Vidal
attrib.	attributed to, attribution
BEdT	*Bibliografia elettronica dei trovatori* (online resource)
Biographies	*Biographies des troubadours*, ed. Boutière and Schutz
ca.	approximately
cent.	century

DA	*Doctrina d'acort* by Terramagnino da Pisa
DVE	*De vulgari eloquentia* by Dante
ex.	example
GDole	*Guillaume de Dole* by Jean Renart
Leys 1341	Molinier's first prose redaction of *Las leys d'amors*
Leys 1356	Molinier's second prose redaction of *Las leys d'amors*
Mi	*Miralh de trobar* by Berenguer d'Anoia
PC	*Bibliographie der Troubadours* established by Pillet and Carstens
RaT	*Las Razos de trobar* by Raimon Vidal
ReT	*Las Regles de trobar* by Jofre de Foixà
Ri	Treatises from Ripoll
RS	Raynouard and Spanke
So (also *So fo* and *So fo e·l tems*)	*So fo e·l tems c'om era gais* by Raimon Vidal
unattrib.	unattributed

In addition, manuscripts are referred to by short, conventional *sigla* (see Appendix 17).

Introduction

Quotation, Knowledge, Change

Quotation—not a very promising subject, you might think. Like the footnote, with which indeed it shares a common history, quotation seems more of an academic obligation than a creative act.[1] Poets may allude to or imitate one another, but they will not repeat an earlier text except to pastiche it, as if repetition was in itself already faintly comic. The lyricist's emblem is the nightingale, not the parrot. In the twelfth century the prestige of poetic nightingales is at an all-time high.[2] Around the middle of the century, the troubadour Marcabru wrote a brace of parodic love songs in which a foolish lover sends a starling—not quite a parrot, but the point is the same—to deliver his message to a tart who then turns him down.[3] In an outrageous mock oration, which Marcabru surely knew, Ovid summons the world's birds, nightingale included, to mourn the death of his girlfriend's parakeet: the choice of bird implies both irony toward his theme and mimicry of Catullus's well-known lament for *his* girlfriend's loss of her pet sparrow.[4] Both Ovid and Marcabru come across as anti-parrot.

But parrots have always had their promoters, as we will see; and quotation has had its poetic high points too. One was in late antiquity when there developed the genre of the cento, a work put together entirely from fragments of classical texts.[5] Another was from the late twelfth to the early fourteenth centuries when, in a similar spirit, many new forms of writing prospered that centered on quotations from a literature that was fast assuming classical stature: that of the troubadours. With the exception of its best-known practitioner— no less a poet than Dante Alighieri—this "secondhand" deployment of troubadour song has been largely overlooked.[6] The task of documenting it has been relegated to editors' introductions and notes to the individual works concerned; and critical attention has been diverted to the related but distinct practice of lyric insertion that is typical of Northern French romance.[7]

Dante's troubadour quotations, however, are just a famous but fairly small-scale instance of an art that, by his time, had been flourishing for over a century. Appendix 1 records the presence in writings of this period of over 600 passages of quotation from more than 350 known poems by nearly 100 different troubadours, as well as from roughly 50 other unidentified compositions. That is, nearly a quarter of all known troubadours are quoted at some time; and about 15 percent of the corpus is quoted by other writers. The number of actual instances of quotation is of course higher than 600 but not by much since, as Appendix 1 also shows, the same troubadour passage is rarely quoted by more than one author or work. Almost all the works in question are in the same language as the troubadour lyrics they quote, a language I call Occitan.

No one questions the centrality of the troubadours to the development of European culture and, indeed, of European sensibilities; much has been written about the importance of their legacy. But this book is the first to re-store to visibility the phenomenon of troubadour quotation and to study it as a whole. The dozen or so lines that Dante quotes have not previously been set in this wider context. Nor has it been appreciated to what an extent the act of repetition on which quotation (like many other scholastic practices) depends is, paradoxically, an engine of change.[8] If troubadour poetry conveys knowl-edge of desire, quoting it exhibits desire for knowledge. This passage through the discourse of knowledge—or supposed knowledge—is, I shall argue, in-fluential in transforming desire from its various elaborations as *fin' amor* (or courtly love) in the Middle Ages to new and more learned formulations that culminate in what is often called the Renaissance.

This project has led me to revive a distinction that is not regularly upheld between citing and quoting. By citing, I understand referencing an author, a work, or an opinion. By quoting, I mean something much more textually precise: the verbatim repetition, in its original form, of a passage that can be anything in length from a complete line of verse to a sequence of several stan-zas. For my study, a core of at least a line must be accurately repeated, even if (as often happens) this core is accompanied by recapitulation of a more allu-sive kind, for a passage to qualify as a quotation. (I have set the minimum at a full line since the troubadours' stylized rhetoric abounds in reiterations of only a few syllables that may reflect convention more than intended allusion; and the network of connections between poets that this produces has been thoroughly studied by Jörn Gruber.)[9] Clearly it can happen that a text is quoted but not cited, as when a passage is repeated verbatim without any apparent markers of its provenance; and vice versa, a text can be cited without being quoted, for example, when a troubadour is named and an opinion imputed to him but no attempt is made to capture its verbal expression. Equally, a text may be both quoted *and* cited, as when an excerpt from a lyric is repeated, attributed to a celebrated poet, and hailed as an authoritative source of sound opinion. Differentiating in this way between quoting and citing makes it easier to grasp the extraordinary novelty of troubadour quotation. Whereas citation of Latin authorities is commonplace, Occitan lyrics are probably the first corpus in any language (including Latin) to be quoted at such length verbatim in medieval Europe.[10] The passages listed in Appendix 1 are all quotations in this sense.

Many twelfth-century troubadours allude to one another's songs, reprising phrases or rhyme schemes; they also reiterate material from their own songs, in *tornadas*, for example, or to link successive songs on the same theme together. But as far as I know, the earliest author to quote entire lines (or more) from troubadour songs is the Catalan poet and grammarian Raimon Vidal de Besalú, and the first work to contain quotations is his *Razos de trobar* (Rational principles of poetic composition). Dating from the turn of the twelfth to the thirteenth century, this, the oldest vernacular grammatical treatise-cum-art of poetry, quotes famous troubadour songs as models from which Raimon's fellow Catalans can learn to appreciate or compose lyrics themselves. There follow many other such treatises, some of them developments of the *Razos de trobar*, others independent. Raimon Vidal is also credited with the authorship of three short didactic verse narratives (*novas*), two of which are extensively peppered with quotations from troubadour lyric and were probably composed by 1209 or 1213. *Abril issi' e mays intrava* (April was ending and May beginning) is about how the successful *joglar*, or performer of lyric, can negotiate varying levels of connoisseurship in his audience; *So fo e·l tems c'om era gais* (It was at that time of merriment) dissects the rival claims of members of a love triangle.

In the first decades of the thirteenth century, new forms of troubadour quotation develop in the north of Italy too. Some or all were initiated by Uc de Saint Circ, a troubadour who took up residence in the Marca Treviziana, in the Veneto. Uc launched the genres of the *vida* and *razo*, short prose introductions to the lives of individual troubadours and explanations of how individual songs came to be composed. Only a few *vidas* contain quotations, but *razos* almost invariably quote at least the opening line of the song they accompany and may contain excerpts from several songs. This region and this period also sees the compilation of the first manuscript collections of the troubadours, known as *chansonniers*, which seemingly from an early date contained anthologies of excerpted stanzas (*coblas triadas*) alongside whole songs. Such collections have found their way into about a third of the surviving troubadour songbooks; there may have been many others that are now lost.[11] It is not easy to distinguish systematically between excerpted stanzas, stanzas that exist only in isolation (*coblas esparsas*), and truncated copies, but we do have the *vida* of one anthologist, Ferrarino da Ferrara, which credits him with extracting from whole songs the elements in them that are the most significant, thereby generating what has been called a "Sentenzensammlung"— a kind of lyric equivalent to a collection of Latin authorities.[12] In the manuscript that preserves the 226 extracts attributed to Ferrarino (the part of *chansonnier D* known as *Dc*), and in some others, these stanzas are accompanied by rubrics that clearly indicate their status as excerpts; and one, *chansonnier H*, even offers guidance on their meaning and potential application. The extracted stanzas are effectively being earmarked—or solicited[13]—as future quotations, the more structured the *florilegium*, the closer its foreshadowing of our modern dictionary of quotations. No other European poetry is explicated or anthologized in this way. Appendix 2 details the contents of six of these *florilegia*. Comparison with Appendix 1 shows that for some troubadours (like Folquet de Marselha, Raimon de Miraval, or the anonymous stanzas) there is a very close correlation between quoted passages and extracted stanzas, whereas for others (like Aimeric de Belenoi or Giraut de Bornelh), even though they are both extensively quoted and represented in collections of anthologized stanzas, there is less direct overlap between the actual passages concerned. If these excerpted stanzas are nevertheless regarded as quotations-in-waiting, and added to the count of actual passages quoted, the total more than doubles.

The treatment of Occitan quotations and anthologized stanzas in Italy and Catalonia provides a context in which to reconsider the troubadour passages inserted into the works of the northern French romancers Jean Renart (*Le roman de la rose*, more commonly known as *Le roman de Guillaume de Dole*, ca. 1210–1230) and Gerbert de Montreuil (*Le roman de la violette*, ca. 1230). Jean Renart has hitherto been studied as the inventor of lyric insertion; however, this "invention" might be better described as a response to lyric quotation (more on this distinction below). The practice of quotation may also shed light on the star role assigned to a parrot in an amusing verse *novas* of the mid-thirteenth century, the *Novas del papagai* (Tale of the parrot), and its possibly fourteenth-century successor, *Frayre de Joy e Sor de Plazer* (Brother of Joy and Sister of Pleasure).[14]

In the last third of the thirteenth century, we find lyric poets reaching for quotations in ways that have implications for the melodies of songs as well as their texts; I examine two examples of this practice, one Italian (Bertolome Zorzi) and one Catalan (Jofre de Foixà). Between 1288 and about 1292, Matfre Ermengau of Béziers writes the *Breviari d'amor* (Love's summary), a long verse encyclopedia describing the universe as emanating from God's love. One section of it is studded with over 260 lyric quotations, which Matfre interprets as a means to know the true nature of this love and so reverse our fall into carnal desire. The *Breviari* marks a high point in the work done by troubadour quotation to transform our relation to desire and knowledge. Unusually for the history of troubadour quotation, it is not only in Occitan, but composed in Occitania by an Occitan for Occitan compatriots. Although there is no evidence that Dante knew Matfre's text when composing his *Commedia*, there are striking similarities between the ambitious hermeneutic, cosmological, and theological frameworks in which the two authors place the troubadours. Dante certainly did know the Occitan treatises of grammar and poetics, and modeled on them his *De vulgari eloquentia* (composed between 1303 and 1305). It is because of this debt that I include the *De vulgari*, despite the fact that it is in Latin. (A few other Latin works of this period quote the troubadours but are not discussed in this study.)[15]

One of the last in date of the texts I consider is, like the first, an Occitan treatise of grammar and poetics, Guilhem Molinier's *Las leys d'amors* (The laws of love). This summa of poetic knowledge was compiled for the poetic academy in Toulouse that styled itself the *Consistori de la sobregaia companhia del gai saber* (Consistory of the most joyous company of the gay science), henceforth shortened to *Consistori de gai saber*. It went through various redactions between about 1323 and 1356, in the course of which quotations from the classical troubadours recede from prominence and new styles of quotation are established. Although the *Leys* and the activities of the Consistori inspired further Occitan works of grammar and poetics in both Occitania and Catalonia, and the practice of quotation continued sporadically in Catalonia into the fifteenth century,[16] I shall not follow these developments but instead end with Petrarch, in one of whose songs Occitan is quoted only in order to be superseded.

The overview I have just given indicates the trajectory of this book and the works covered in the individual chapters that follow. An opening group examines the pioneering forms taken by the scholastic address to troubadour poetry: the beginnings of troubadour quotation in the grammatical tradition (Chapter 1); the *translatio* of troubadour poetry to Catalonia in the *novas* of Raimon Vidal (Chapter 2); the role of quotation in *vidas* and *razos* in relation to the design of *chansonniers* (Chapter 3); and the influence of *florilegia* of excerpted stanzas (Chapter 4). Chapters 5 and 6 consider the reflections on quotation offered by Jean Renart's *Guillaume de Dole* and by the *Novas del papagai*, taken as representing, respectively, what I call the nightingales' way and that of the parrots. Chapters 7 to 11 deal with works written from the latter part of the thirteenth century onward. The pioneering days behind them, authors treat quotation ambitiously and self-consciously in works that progressively transform the preceding tradition. The playful use of lyric quotation in the lyric (Chapter 7) contrasts with the theological transformation of *florilegia* in the *Breviari* (Chapter 8). While Dante tends to occlude the earlier history of quotation, he nevertheless achieves with it some dazzlingly innovative effects (Chapter 9). Chapter 10 shows how the *Leys d'amors* goes further in this direction, wiping the slate clean so that vernacular poetry can begin again. This situation of semi-erasure of troubadour quotations is the starting point for Petrarch's "Lasso me." In Chapter 11, I contend that Petrarch's song illustrates how quotation has enabled the poetic subject to desire to desire differently. The Middle Ages of the troubadours are relegated to the past, and the birth is confirmed of a poetry that will sweep across Europe under the new banner of Renaissance. As an engine of change, quotation has revolutionized the first-person subject of poetry and with it the kind of poetry that can be produced and enjoyed.

The remainder of this introduction provides a general historical and theoretical framework within which to situate these chapters.

Quotation and the Troubadour Corpus

Appendix 1 is set out so as to show which troubadours, which songs, and which passages are quoted, using the standard Pillet-Carstens (PC) system of identifying authors and songs.[17] The most-quoted troubadours date from the third quarter of the twelfth century to the first quarter of the thirteenth, from

Bernart de Ventadorn to Aimeric de Peguilhan. The fact that the later troubadours simply have not yet begun their careers in time to be quoted by the earliest works containing quotations obviously affects the frequency with which they appear in this table; nevertheless, a kind of golden age seems to persist in the imagination of later writers, coloring which troubadours are perceived as most quotable at least to the early fourteenth century. The most prevalent genre to be quoted is the *canso*, or love song, which can be regarded as the canonical form of troubadour lyric even though *cansos* in fact make up only about 40 percent of the surviving corpus. Bernart de Ventadorn is the most popular troubadour, not only in terms of the number of passages and songs that are quoted but also in the variety of works that quote them. His "Ab joi mou lo vers e·l comens" (70.1) is the most quoted song in the corpus: not exactly a predictable winner, though it was certainly widely copied and imitated in the Middle Ages.[18] Arnaut de Maruelh, Folquet de Marselha, Gaucelm Faidit, Giraut de Bornelh, Peire Vidal, Raimbaut de Vaqueiras, and Raimon de Miraval are also all extensively mined. Alongside the *cansos*, the nonlyric verse *ensenhamens* of Arnaut de Maruelh ("Razos es e mezura") and Garin lo Brun ("El termini d'estiu") are widely aired, preparing a place for the similarly nonstrophic verse of the later At de Mons.

Some troubadours with long entries in Appendix 1 owe most of their apparent prominence to a single work or group of works that quote them. This is the case for Bertran de Born (because of the many *razos* devoted to his *sirventes*), Aimeric de Peguilhan (favored by the *Breviari*), and At de Mons (chief recourse of Guilhem Molinier in both redactions of the *Leys*). The emergence of a preferred troubadour is one of the hallmarks of the art of quotation; Dante's preference for Arnaut Daniel is as unique to him as Raimon Vidal's highlighting of Raimon de Miraval in *So fo e·l tems*, but the fact of having a favorite seems, by Dante's time, to be an established convention. While some troubadours are inevitably exploited more than others, the breadth of reference overall is impressive, with virtually every work reaching for some little-quoted poet or song. The tabular form of Appendix 1 makes it easy to see how little convergence in the choice of extracts there is. Quite the reverse: there appears to be a concerted effort at dispersal. One of the more amusing aspects of the authors' drive to personalize their selections is the tendency to slip in, alongside more celebrated songs, snippets of their own composition. Thus of Raimon Vidal's five lyrics, three are known only from self-quotations in *So fo*;[19] and Matfre Ermengau secures his own posterity as well as that of other troubadours in his family by quoting his own and their songs in the *Breviari*. The *Leys* contain verses likewise seemingly confected by Molinier himself, on an unprecedentedly large scale. Dante's predilection for self-quotation also indicates his adherence to earlier usage.

Despite the broad range of quotation, some troubadours seem noticeably absent or underrepresented in Appendix 1. The tiny number of quotations from the very early troubadours Guilhem de Peitieu, Jaufre Rudel, and Bernart Marti, and the total absence of Cercamon and Alegret, may not be surprising given their low profile in the *chansonniers*. More surprising are the very small number of quotations from Marcabru and the quasi absence of Peire d'Alvernha, since the lyrics of both troubadours circulated widely. The case of Peire is especially striking since his poems open a substantial group of Italian songbooks and his name features on lists of famous troubadours compiled by Dante and Petrarch. Another shortfall, which may go some way to explain the relative absence of Marcabru and Peire, affects songs we might classify as *clus* (composed in an obscure or hermetic style). As will be abundantly confirmed throughout this study, those who quote the troubadours tend to home in on nuggets of thought; they seek illumination from what is quoted, rather than aiming to throw light on *it*. Thus it is that, as well as Marcabru and Peire d'Alvernha, Raimbaut d'Aurenga, the hermetic poems of Giraut de Bornelh, and indeed the whole corpus of Arnaut Daniel are underrepresented in Appendix 1 in comparison with their standing in the transmission elsewhere.

An absence of a quite different kind is that of songs by women and dialogue songs, which perhaps do not seem sufficiently substantial or sententious. Women's voices make no appearance at all apart from the stanzas included within prose *razos*, the song attributed in manuscripts to Raimon Jordan (404.5), and the likely fictitious dialogue between Aimeric de Peguilhan and a lady (10.23). The fact that dialogue pieces are often composed for specific circumstances may also make them less mobile and transferrable than *cansos*. Songs by nonnative Occitans are also extremely rare, maybe because the grammarians, who inaugurate the practice of quotation, have scruples about linguistic authenticity (a notable exception is the showcasing of songs by Catalan poets in the Ripoll treatises).[20] With only minor differences of emphasis, the same generalizations hold true for the entries in Appendix 2.

Thus, amid the diversity of quotation, certain conventions develop and some of the ways in which quotations are used in earlier works—the early grammars, *novas*, *vidas*, *razos*, and early *florilegia*—are adopted by the later ones, including those of Dante.

Quotation and Literary Occitan

The fact that quotation, unlike citation, is constituted by verbatim repetition means that it promotes the troubadours' language as well as their poetry. And indeed, a striking feature of the list of works containing troubadour quotations is the dominance among them of treatises of Occitan grammar and poetics. Occitania is an area corresponding to roughly the bottom third of what is now France and extending down into the valleys of Piedmont. It comprises many regional dialects, but the Occitan of the troubadours is already fairly standardized in the twelfth century and is not identified with any one of them. The grammarians thus have an already poetic, to some extent codified, idiom with which to work. But they innovate decisively when, in a move mirroring the respect for its poetry that quotation enacts, they elevate this idiom to a grammatical language on the model of Latin. Indeed, it is noticeable that all the texts containing quotations, although divergent among themselves, have Latin analogues (treatises, didactic poems, debate poems, *accessus ad auctores*, hymns, encyclopedias), and that their use of quotation bears an edgy relation to the quotation by Latin authors of extracts from the Bible or from ecclesiastical or classical texts. Is such proximity to Latin broadly parodic, or merely a vernacular parallel? In any case, its effect is increasingly to consecrate Occitan as a kind of neo-Latin whose poets are authorities and to identify its literature as an opportunity to extend scholasticism to the vernacular. Scholastic models are likewise explored relative to vernacular texts by thirteenth-century authors from northern France (Henri d'Andeli, Gautier de Coinci, Richard de Fournival, Jean de Meun), but the mode of textual quotation is unique to writers in Occitan.[21]

It is striking that many of these Occitan writers are either Italian or Catalan, and/or have Italian or Catalan audiences and readers in mind, even though they all quote the troubadours in the original and, except Dante and Petrarch, adopt Occitan for all their known compositions. Only Matfre Ermengau and Guilhem Molinier are Occitans writing in Occitania seemingly solely for fellow Occitans, and even their works quickly give rise to Catalan traditions. Clearly, Occitan enjoys a status that today we would call "international," though the term is hard to justify at a time before the development of the modern nations. Perhaps the best way of describing it is as a mobile, literary standard. As such, Occitan has a significantly different status from other, emergent, vernacular literary languages in that it is not grounded in the political realm.[22] It was not and never has been the language of a nation or a people and in this respect again it has a quasi-classical status, resembling Latin, Hebrew, or Arabic more than do, for example, German and French.

Why did those who copied and repeated troubadour poetry assist in consecrating Occitan as such a language? And why was such a language so widely copied and repeated? In trying to answer these questions, I have been helped by Jacques Derrida's controversial assertion, in *Le monolinguisme de l'autre*, that culture as such is colonial. In his own experience of growing up as an Algerian Jew, Derrida recounts how French appeared as a prestige literary standard (albeit one with all too many political associations). One passage in particular suggests a parallel with the way literary Occitan seems to have attracted so many speakers. Here Derrida describes the seductive lure of identification offered by an alien, written language, even though the forms that promise a sense of identity by their very nature deprive one of it: "People always imagine that a man or a woman who writes must know how to say *I*. At any rate, the potential for identification must seem assured: both assured within language and assured of it."[23] In this respect, prestige languages are revealing of language in general: the effect of simultaneously finding a self and losing one's self within a foreign language is only the most visible instance of the inevitable impact of *any* language and of language as such: "This *I* would have formed itself, then, at the site of a 'situation' which cannot be located but instead is constantly referred on to somewhere else, to something else, to another language, to the Other in general. Its site would be in an experience of language as such, language in the broad sense of the word, one that cannot be situated."[24] Derrida's remarks can help us to figure why so many medieval speakers quote the first-person poetry of the troubadours. Assuming the prestigious discourse of the lyric promises to constitute an *I* that would enable them to situate themselves alongside other authors in that discourse; it beckons with the imaginary assurance of finding themselves at home in a language that, because it is a mobile standard, has no home; it offers to identify them in a language that, in itself, lacks identity.

Buoyed up by prestige and unencumbered by political or ecclesiastical baggage, literary Occitan offers the dream of a genuinely new, secular and lay, poetic subjectivity. Quotations from its poetry are like seeds from which a new, secular and lay poetry can grow.

Quotation as an Aspect of Troubadour Reception

Derrida's remarks help draw attention to one of the most fundamental properties of the Occitan first-person lyric: its capacity to inspire the desire to repeat it, to assume one's place in it, and to assume a personal relation to it, however self-defeating such a desire for identity may be. Repetition of this poetry takes many forms, of which quotation is just one. Viewing quotation in this wider context will help focus its significance.

In twelfth-century Occitania the troubadours are involved in intense interactions with one another, debating and reworking one another's songs. Probably the most elaborate technique of imitation devised in this period is contrafacture, a technique whereby a new song is modeled on the stanza form of an existing one and can be sung to the same music. Such formal and musical quotation is the counterpart of the textual quotation studied here, in which words are typically detached altogether from music. As if aware of this complementarity, some of the works that exploit textual quotation—like Raimon Vidal or Jofre de Foixà—seem playfully to pit it against contrafacture. Contrafacture enables troubadour song to percolate—not as text, but as form or melody—into the cultures of all the regions neighboring Occitania.[25]

Other ways of recycling the troubadours present different emphases from region to region. North of Occitania, in northern France and Germany, the closest form of repetition to be widely practiced is the translation of Occitan lyrics into German or French.[26] (Some are also translated into Italian by the Sicilian school, seemingly under the influence of the German Frederick II's Sicilian court.)[27] Literal quotation of the troubadours in the original Occitan is found only rarely in France, and the original is regularly Gallicized (that is, assimilated linguistically to Northern French). This is the fate of the troubadour songs quoted in *Guillaume de Dole* and the *Roman de la violette*, and also of the troubadour stanzas copied in manuscripts recording Northern French texts.[28] In France and Germany, and later in Sicily, the troubadours also serve as models for imitation by native poets in their own vernacular; the Occitan originals are rapidly absorbed into evolving domestic traditions. Because of this emphasis on recreation rather than verbatim repetition, I call this path the nightingales' way; the importance of the Sicilian school makes such a label preferable to defining this mode of reception as exclusively "northern."

Among the troubadours' immediate Mediterranean neighbors, in what are now parts of Spain or Italy, there is a much greater tendency for native poets to imitate troubadour poetry in Occitan.[29] Among the earliest examples of romance vernacular song from Aragon, Catalonia, and Italy are works of poets whose first language is Catalan and/or Italian, but who choose to compose using the language as well as the forms of the troubadours, and they are intended for readers or listeners whose first language is likewise Catalan and/or Italian. It is these same regions, and the Occitanian homeland in between, that give rise to the works studied in this book: works composed in Occitan that quote the troubadours very expertly likewise in Occitan. In these regions, then, the desire to repeat operates first of all at the level of language; either the troubadours are repeated verbatim, or more broadly their language is mastered so as to provide a recognizable subject position (Derrida's *monolangue*). Although this path does not exclude song, it tends to identify lyric above all as language and as text, and I call it the parrots' way.

One reason for the division between the two ways lies in Occitan political and cultural history. Occitania was not politically unified, since most Occitan-speaking territories were nominally held either from the French king or the Empire, and all were relatively autonomous both from their overlords and from one another. Their strongest cultural ties were with Iberia and Italy, and these are also the regions the languages of which Occitan most resembles; it is especially close to Catalan and indeed may not always have been distinguished from it. Iberian courts were among the very earliest to extend patronage to troubadours, followed by those of northern Italy in the late twelfth century; troubadours had far less direct contact with northern France.[30] Alfonso II, king of Aragon from 1162 to 1196 and also, as the count of Barcelona, ruler of Catalonia, adopted Occitan as the literary language of his court in order to bolster his claim to Provence.[31] Catalonia was an important sea power with aspirations to dominate the northern Mediterranean; the Crown of Aragon helped to diffuse Occitan, and with it troubadour culture, across Catalan-held territories, which included at different times Sardinia, Sicily, Naples, and the Balearics.

If Catalan imperial ambition boosts the status of Occitan, in other respects the prominence of troubadour parlance beyond the Alps and the Pyrenees seems rather to result from the vulnerability of Occitania. By the end of the twelfth century the troubadours were frequent visitors to both regions, but their presence seems to have increased in the thirteenth in response to the Albigensian Crusade of 1209 to about 1229. Begun as a holy war against Cathar heretics in the Midi, this war was rapidly interpreted by the Occitans as a campaign for the closer control of the south by the kingdom of France. The crusade's impact on troubadour poetry has often been overstated; it may not have precipitated widespread literary decline;[32] nevertheless it resoundingly confirmed Occitania's propensity always to be more intimately involved with its southern neighbors than with its northern overlords. Troubadours like Uc de Saint Circ relocated in the Veneto at a time when French barons were seizing control of southern lands, exiling native landholders, and introducing the Inquisition. The survival of a hitherto primarily oral culture may have seemed precarious, the need correspondingly urgent to compile and preserve it in writing.

Quotation, then, forms a strand in troubadour reception that is influenced by both cultural and political factors. It takes its place among a whole complex of modes of recycling that range from contrafacture to compilation, but of which different forms predominate in different regions. The main differences overall are that the parrots' reception emphasizes the Occitan language (and, concomitantly, grammatical and textual expertise in Occitan works) and that it stresses the value as knowledge, sententious or revelatory, of the troubadours, whereas the nightingales' reception is more interested in assimilation, affect, and song. The differences between these two ways are epitomized by the point at which they are closest to one another: in the practice of lyric insertion as compared with that of lyric quotation.

Lyric Quotation and Lyric Insertion

The importance and interest of lyric insertion have been brilliantly demonstrated in recent years.[33] Inaugurated in northern France in the early thirteenth century, the art of including lyrics within a longer work is traced from Jean Renart through the thirteenth century to the great *dits amoureux* of the fourteenth and on. Some of the lyrics that are inserted could, indeed, also be said to be quoted. But while, for example, Jean Renart identifies some of his inset pieces as having been composed by others, he leaves the origins of others deliberately opaque (see Chapter 5). And by the fourteenth century, rather than quoting other people's poetry, northern French authors like Guillaume de Machaut insert their own *formes fixes* in their mesmerizingly sophisticated *dits*. Although the authorship of these lyric pieces is sometimes attributed to characters within the fiction, there are very few cases where they are clearly the work of anyone other than the poets of the *dit* concerned.[34] In some cases the presence of the same songs in the lyric sections of the same manuscripts as the *dits* further dispels doubt as to their authorship.

An important implication of this development toward single authorship in lyric insertion is the assurance of having distanced the memory and authority of the troubadours, of having created one's own tradition. The creative skill and poetic versatility of the nightingales' way can be dazzling. In the parrots' way of quotation, by contrast, not only are excerpts from other poets carefully preserved and repeated, but the sense of a multilingual environment is fostered, since in the majority of cases the authors and implied readers of the works that quote them are speakers of Catalan and/or Italian. If lyric insertion aspires to a national culture, quotation is exiled, diasporic, and cosmopolitan.[35]

Lyric insertion is found from the start in texts that are largely narrative (though they may have a didactic dimension), whereas verbatim quotations occur in texts that are more instructive or moralizing in character, and often in what are straightforwardly treatises. Insertion serves various narrative functions but the most typical, as Maureen Boulton shows, is to reflect or voice emotion; songs are also sung to jollify social occasions or to accompany social activities (such as women's work).[36] By contrast, as I have already said, quotations tend to home in on the moral, reflective, or other sententious aspects of troubadour poetry, inscribing it less in the field of affect than of knowledge. While lyric insertion typically imports songs into a fictional world where they are sung by characters within the narrative, accompanying their dancing or needlework, most Occitan texts that quote troubadour lyrics more closely resemble compilations of diverse voices. The differences between insertion and quotation are well exemplified by Dante. His own lyrics are inserted in *Vita nuova* and are a far cry from the lists of first lines from other poets reeled off in *De vulgari eloquentia*. (The fact that Dante uses both techniques confirms that the nightingales' way is not exclusive to a particular region; the parrots' way is less widely diffused.)

Boulton pinpoints the distinctiveness of lyric insertion when she observes that "the heart of the device seems to lie less in quotation or in borrowing than in combining genres."[37] Although the earliest examples seemingly involve only short excerpts (stanzas or refrains) set in verse narrative, the practice becomes more and more flamboyantly heterogeneous as entire lyric poems are included, they become increasingly intricate formally, and/or prose is chosen for the surrounding narrative (as in the *Prose Tristan* and the *Perceforest*). Up to the *dits* of Guillaume de Machaut, inset lyrics are also usually represented as sung, and seemingly were intended actually to be so; they would thus stand out in performance from the remainder of the work, which would be recited or read aloud. In Jean Renart's *Guillaume de Dole*, characters behave as if they were in a karaoke bar, delivering spirited if not always convincing performances of recent hits. The hybrid nature of texts with lyric insertions is reflected in their transmission, with many manuscripts including musical notation or marking the lyrics off from their narrative setting in some other way.[38]

Lyric quotations, by contrast, are usually assimilated to their context as much as possible. They seem never expected to be sung except when they are found in other lyrics. Formally, they tend to be treated by didactic poets as if they were passages of didactic verse; authors of prose treatises often opt for quotations of a single line, that is, of a passage so short that its metrical form is hard to detect in the surrounding prose. This tendency also persists in transmission. Manuscripts of works in rhyming couplets usually set out quotations in the same format as the rest of the text, in columns and line by line; and manuscripts of prose texts include the quotations within the flow of the prose.[39] The influence of Latin practice in calling attention to quotations is found in *razos* in some *chansonniers* where quoted incipits (first lines) are written in red ink, and in some *Breviari* manuscripts where the name of cited troubadours may be underlined or copied in colored ink.[40] But none of the texts I have looked at adopts the more flagrant signaling of quotations found in some Latin manuscripts, where the whole of a quoted passage may be underlined (often in red), overlined (by a pen stroke, often red, through the middle of the words concerned), or picked out by a column of *diples* (little *s*-like marks) in the adjacent margin.[41] If lyric insertion involves a poetics of disruption, as Boulton aptly calls it,[42] the poetics of quotation is rather one of *mise en abyme* in the basic sense defined by Lucien Dallenbach of "any insertion grounded in a relation of similarity to the work which contains it."[43]

Such similarity gives rise to indeterminacy in identifying the limits of quotation. In fact, as already suggested, quotation in general plays with expectations of knowledge and recognition, whereas lyric insertion speaks more to the expressive qualities of the lyric text. Focusing on recognition (in quotation) or expressivity (in lyric insertion) has implications for subjectivity in the texts concerned. The first person implied by lyric insertion is typically a subject of desire—for love or for social involvement—identified as a character within the fiction. This subjectivity, strung between the discursive poles of narrative and lyric, invites analysis in terms of the relations between these respective genres. How successfully do romance and lyric discourses combine to constitute a single subject? Do they complement or ironize one another? By contrast, in the more academic climate of the Occitan texts, we find not a single subjectivity defined (or not) between several genres, but rather a discourse of knowledge that connects together a network of potential subjects—minimally the one who quotes, the one who is quoted from, and the reader trying to fathom what is going on. While the concept of intertextuality is obviously still relevant,[44] it offers less critical leverage here, I think, than that of intersubjectivity, by which I mean the relations forged between and thereby constituting subjects. When a writer chooses to quote some troubadours and not others, for example, he indexes a position relative to other subjects (including the troubadours he quotes and his readers) in a supposed knowledge community in which every subject is potentially both connected to and differentiated from the others. Subsequently, as Anthony Grafton has wittily shown, footnotes similarly found an economy of acknowledged and unacknowledged knowledge that is understood differently by different subjects.[45]

French lyric insertion exhibits the same innovative brio as the trouvères when they recreated troubadour lyrics in the langue d'oïl. The dynamism of this nightingales' way seems to guarantee its future success. And yet the kinds of lyric verse that are essayed in lyric insertion sputter out in the sixteenth century, when the tide of taste turns in favor of Petrarchan models imported from Italy. The parrots' way, although less glamorous than the nightingales', wins out in the end. Lyric quotation is not of course solely responsible for this success; but it contributes to it by helping to keep alive a sense of poetry's value as a mode of knowledge as well as of desire. The troubadours are mined for their insights by the authors who quote them; quotations test readers' competence to recognize them; and the whole practice of quotation identifies troubadour poetry as something worth knowing *about*. For over 150 years before the Consistori at Toulouse decided to test candidates' mastery of poetics and award them degrees and diplomas for it, writers emulated one another in exhibiting their command of the Occitan lyric tradition, its poets, their lives and opinions, as well as their actual words. The Occitan lyric corpus is at once deferred to as a *source* of knowledge and displayed as a culturally desirable *object* of knowledge.

It is in the interplay between intersubjectivity, desire, and knowledge that I believe the answer lies as to why quotation helps to produce subjective and cultural change.

Enabling Change: Transference and the Subject Supposed to Know

From the very beginning, troubadour lyrics intertwine desire and knowledge. They express desire; they lay claim to knowledge of desire; they inspire, in different proportions in different listeners, the desire to desire and the desire to know; these in turn fuel the desire for lyric as both a vehicle and an object of knowledge; and a discursive field is created in which different subjects of desire/knowledge are supposed. This introduction has already spoken of the knowledge conveyed by quotations, the knowledge displayed by those who quote, and the challenge to knowledge that quotation poses to the reader or audience. Here I would like to sketch the transferential framework as a result of which these cognitive exchanges generate change, understood as a new alignment of the subject with the symbolic fabric that enables a new articulation of knowledge and desire.

I have proposed that the challenge to recognize quotation differentiates it from other forms of textual repetition. Similarly, Herman Meyer suggests that we distinguish between borrowing from a work and quoting it because, unlike quoting, "borrowing . . . has no referential character."[46] He means, I take it, that quoting inevitably involves referencing the extract's origin in some way. How, though? Derrida's well-known essay "Signature événement contexte" suggests that the answer is more elusive than we realize: "Every sign . . . can be quoted, put between quotation marks; in so doing it can break with every given context, engendering an infinity of new contexts. . . . This quotability, this duplication or doubleness/duplicity [*duplicité*], this repeatability of the mark is not an accident or an anomaly. . . . What would a mark be that could not be quoted? And whose origin could not be lost en route?"[47] Given that any utterance is indefinitely repeatable and hence indefinitely quotable, we cannot rely on there being a stable origin that can be "referenced." Perhaps we should say, then, that what characterizes quotation is that it foregrounds this repeatability (what Derrida calls its doubleness/duplicity [*duplicité*]), and provokes the reader to recognize it?[48] Quoting will always be perilously close to other procedures of writing that rely on iteration;

to differentiate it from other kinds of copy, a quotation will depend only on this tantalizing supposition that it has an original (or at least a second) home. Responding to quotation requires an act of recognition that—Derrida implies—is always only provisional and liable to misprision, since all these other forms of repetition are also capable of manifesting their own doubleness, or of having it variously recognized by different readers.

When it comes to recognizing the original home of a quotation, the instability of medieval texts creates particular difficulties. Quotation typically involves partiality, in the sense both of division and of preference. Troubadour songs are not long, but it is exceptional for them to be quoted in full. Different works have different preferred lengths of quotation: in the *novas* it is the stanza, in *razos* the incipit (first line); the *Breviari* and the *Leys* are alone in including long extracts from didactic poems. Antoine Compagnon has baptized "solicitation" this capacity of a text to differentiate itself internally in such a way that a part of it calls out to be removed from its context and redeployed in another.[49] His vocabulary of seduction softens what others have identified as a more violent process. "To quote a text is to break into it, to 'tear' something out of it," writes Marjorie Garber.[50] Yet how can we know that a passage is indeed a part when the notion of "whole" is problematic?

In some cases, the effect of internal division is undoubtedly important. While a portion of the text is manifest in the quotation, the remainder is latent alongside it. This is so when what is quoted is an opening line since the incipit doubles as a title, and so stands for the whole work from which it is taken, it is both part and whole (see below). Isolated excerpts can likewise require supplementing with other material from the same song, as I contend happens in Raimon Vidal de Besalú's *novas* (Chapter 2) or Dante's use of Arnaut Daniel (Chapter 9). On the other hand, quotations were not always hewed purposively from whole songs; as we have seen, they might be found ready-made in *cobla* collections (Chapter 4). Readers of these anthologies may well have been unaware of the rest of the songs from which they were taken and unable—as we are—always to be able to distinguish *coblas triadas* (excerpted stanzas) from *coblas esparsas* (freestanding stanzas).[51] Manuscript copies, in any case, preserve shorter and longer versions of individual songs. In sum, it is virtually impossible to specify the exact outlines of the original context of any given quotation (supposing such an original existed) or to assess how much knowledge needs to be assumed to supplement it. This uncertainty is not only experienced differently by different subjects, it also actively fosters the idea that there are other possible subjects possessing a different level of knowledge.

Another difficulty in the way of recognizing quotations is grammatical. Verbatim quotation is closely related to direct speech, what we call "quotation marks" being used in modern punctuation to identify both. The way manuscripts usually signal the beginning and end of quotations, with enlarged initials or paraphs or touches of red ink, corresponds with how direct speech is marked in other vernacular texts, rather than with how quotations are marked in Latin ones.[52] The persistence, or the shadow, of the unquoted around that which is quoted means, however, that pragmatically quotation is closer to free indirect discourse, in which two different discourses—the one quoting and the one quoted—are so superimposed as to make it difficult to establish the boundaries between them, or between the subjectivities involved.[53]

Quotation therefore plays with expectations of knowledge and recognition; it summons subjects of knowledge and recognition into existence; but it does not necessarily ratify them. In trying to get to grips with this phenomenon, I have adopted Jacques Lacan's concept of "the subject supposed to know" ("le sujet supposé savoir"), because it means both that knowledge presupposes a series of subjects that are difficult to locate, and that subjects are supposed to have knowledge that is difficult or impossible to specify. Contending that everything we call "knowledge" is articulated against the background of the unknown of the primary repression and designed to protect us against whatever that unknown contains, Lacan postulates the subject supposed to know as the condition of all symbolic transactions and the reason why they are shot through with so much confusion and deceit. In particular, he views it as a crucial part of the psychoanalytical transference, where the subject supposed to know is both a necessary vehicle for the exchanges between analyst and patient and that which makes it possible for the patient to benefit from therapy. By observing the feints and displacements of the subject supposed to know, the patient is enabled to see that the subject *as such* is merely supposed, hypothetical; this perception enables him or her to disconnect from the symbolic web in which all subjects are entangled and experience a transforming interval of radical freedom before reconnecting to it once more, potentially in an altogether new way. Outside the domain of therapy, this book contends, the same cycle of repetition, (mis)recognition, freedom, and reconnection can also enable subjective change: the rearticulation of the subject of poetry from medieval courtly lover to Petrarchan poet.

I will not repeat here the theoretical complexities of this argument, which I have worked through elsewhere (and see Chapter 8).[54] Instead I exemplify how knowledge and subjects are supposed in quotation, and how such suppositions can be transformative, in the case of a particular form of quotation—that of an incipit—which we will encounter many times in the following chapters.

The Love of Beginnings

The principal use of the incipit, in an age when works did not usually have titles, was to act as one. In many cases the incipit effectively became the title (e.g., Genesis, meaning "in the beginning"), or one of several alternative titles. D. Vance Smith observes that a commonly quoted incipit is "In principio" (In the beginning), the opening words of the Gospel of Saint John, and thus, like the Genesis example, an incipit that is itself about the act of beginning.[55] Medieval scholars were expected, then, to recognize a text *by* its beginning and to identify it *with* its beginning. This gives the incipit enormous symbolic value, both as inaugurating something and, at the same time, as being that which is inaugurated.[56]

In addition to acting as titles, incipits were also used to introduce quotations in an abbreviated form. Well-known texts such as biblical passages could be quoted by their opening words alone, and readers would be expected to supply the remainder from their own knowledge. Here the incipit is not a fixed beginning like "In principio," but a mobile one whose position depends on where in a text the decision to start quoting falls. The implication of quoting from within a text by means of an incipit is that the text is replete with beginnings—that it could begin again at any point. The challenge thrown down by quotation of an incipit is that of recognizing and being able to recall (enough—how much?—of) what follows. For D. Vance Smith, an incipit is not so much a point in time when something starts as the opening up of an enigma.[57] Quite literally, incipital quotation is an invitation to begin again: to initiate (even if one appears to repeat it) a symbolic realm. Edward Saïd has identified this initiation as a specifically secular form of innovation. "Beginnings," he writes, "inaugurate a deliberately *other* production of meaning—a gentile (as opposed to a sacred) one. It is 'other' because, in writing, this gentile production claims a status *alongside* other works: it is *another* work, rather than one in a line of descent from X or Y."[58] Saïd does not write from a psychoanalytic standpoint but his formulation captures exactly the mechanism of rupture and potential alteration that I have just described.

Closer to Lacan, psychoanalyst Jean-Bertrand Pontalis focuses on the potentially transformative value of inauguration when he takes as the title of his autobiography the "love of beginnings" (*L'amour des commencements*). As a therapist, his aim is precisely to help people to change (get better); to do so, their existing relation to reality needs to be temporarily suspended so that they can reconnect to it in a new way. As Pontalis puts it, "When words fail, it is because, without realizing it, one is about to touch a different earth."[59] A beginning institutes a break with what precedes, and it is this break where "words fail" that makes it possible to start afresh, "touch a different earth." Fresh starts precipitated by moments of doubt and hesitation are what make up all lived experience, making "the love of beginnings" a fitting title for an autobiography.

Incipital quotation, the quotation of a beginning, creates the chance to "touch a different earth" because its demands provoke the momentary hesitation that enables the subject to begin again.[60] It supposes a text that the one who quotes it knows; it supposes a knowledge enshrined in the text that is thereby supposed; it supposes knowledge of that text on behalf of the one who quotes, and it further supposes an act of recognition on the part of those who read it. In Saïd's word's again, "such a beginning authorizes; it constitutes an authorization for what follows from it."[61] If the incipit is attributed to a well-known author, then the fact that he is supposed to be knowledgeable enhances the value of the quotation; at the same time, quoting that author supposes that he is recognized as an authority, and helps to confirm him as one. But the fact of reaching for this quotation also supposes that the one who quotes is also an authority, one who commands the field of knowledge, not just the isolated incipit but troubadour poetry in general. It lies in the power of such an expert to make or break a poet's authority and canonical status. Authority is supposed as being transferred away from the one quoted to the one who quotes. But this authority must be supposed to be recognized at least by some readers. Without a third person to do this at least some of the time, authority collapses, and so this third knowing subject has to be supposed. It can be supposed to such an extent that, even if the quotation appears banal or vapid, or not to mean quite what it is implied it means, it still carries weight.

Thus the reader is lured in by what Roger Dragonetti calls, in his book of the same title, "the mirage of the source": "To recognize an author, praise him and take him as one's guide may be an elegant means of creating an empty space behind the stage set of the source."[62] Incipits may be quoted and never expanded, as happens with those inserted into the biographical sequences in *chansonnier N².*[63] The incipit quoted in Garin d'Apchier's biography in *IK* is from a song that is found nowhere else. This supposition that there may or may not be a knowing subject elsewhere infuses the act of quotation with suspicion. What looks like quotation could just as well be a fabrication, or it could be a misremembering or a misrepresentation to a point that could be called a suppression. Response to an incipital quotation is equally capable of mangling the text to which it might be supposed to refer.

All such exchanges mean that incipital quotation is capable of transforming the meaning of the text from which it is taken. Passing to and fro between incipit and the supposed expanded text does not stabilize interpretation but sends it spiraling. Concomitantly, a subject's own position can veer dramatically. He or she need no longer be subject to the suppositions of others but recognize them as the suppositions that they are. Encountering supposed knowledge in its supposed form, a subject is free to forge his or her relation to it in a new way. Subjectivity changes as it passes through the detours of (supposed) knowledge. The following chapters will trace the paths of this detour, as a result of which the symbolic relation to desire is reforged.

Parrots and Nightingales

The idea that the act of quotation is transformative was put forward some time ago by Umberto Eco. Using a sartorial metaphor, Eco shows how medieval Latin writers, when quoting their forebears, perennially succeeded in refashioning them, even though they always cut their garb from old cloth.[64] Although the tailoring metaphor is undoubtedly medieval, in Old Occitan parrots are a better emblem of quotation. Despite being seemingly disadvantaged relative to nightingales by a supposed lack of creativity, medieval parrots have the capacity to sing as well as talk, whereas nightingales can only sing, they cannot speak.[65] Thus parrots embody the fundamental human capacity for mimesis.[66] Although nightingales' mastery of song is natural, parrots have the advantage of being able to learn. Moreover, while they may learn to repeat what they have heard, parrots may also know what they are saying; in the Middle Ages some writers even attribute them "with [a] miraculous command of language and [a] fully developed human consciousness."[67]

According to bestiaries, though some parrots are foolish and representative of sin, others are so wise and noble that they exemplify to human readers the qualities of a spiritual life.[68] In both Occitan *novas* featuring parrots, the bird is considerably more resourceful and in some ways more human than the other protagonists. An exotic bird, the parrot is also an apt representation of the otherness of Occitan to the Catalan and Italian contexts of most of the works I examine. Their words may have an uncanny relation to the desires they seem to voice.

I do not intend my opposition between parrots and nightingales to be taken as discrediting nightingales, more as rehabilitating the kinds of imitation associated with parrots. Nor, in choosing to speak of nightingales' way and a parrots' way do I mean to insist too literally on the avian images. Nevertheless the central section of this book suggests that there were moments in the thirteenth century when writers did indeed resort precisely to the image of parrots and nightingales in order to characterize what was by then a divergence in the reception of troubadour poetry between northern France and the Empire on the one hand—represented in *Guillaume de Dole* (Chapter 5)—and Catalonia and northern Italy on the other—represented in various ways by the *Novas del papagai* (Chapter 6).[69]

This book is primarily about the parrots' way. At its core is a practice of quotation, by which I mean not only verbatim repetition, but a repetition that calls into play a supposed act of recognition of a supposed act of knowledge, which, by supposing anchorage in anterior subjects, enables subjective renewal and hence, potentially, subjective change. It is this transformation of the lyric subject by means of quotation that I will now follow over roughly a century and a half, in Occitania, Catalonia, and Italy.

PART I

Pioneering Troubadour Quotation

## CHAPTER I

Rhyme and Reason

Quotation in Raimon Vidal de Besalú's *Razos de trobar* and the Grammars of the Vidal Tradition

One of the remarkable features of Occitan culture is its precocious production of vernacular treatises on vernacular grammar and poetics. The earliest, the *Razos de trobar* by the Catalan Raimon Vidal de Besalú, dates from around the end of the twelfth century, two hundred years before anything equivalent appears in French.[1] The word *razos* has many meanings, including "explanation," "theme," "speech," "proportion," as well as "reason";[2] but I believe we should take the reference to "reason" seriously and understand his title to mean "Rational principles of poetic composition." Such a conjunction of *razos* with *trobar* may have struck Raimon's contemporaries as provocative, even oxymoronic. Attributing rationality—*razo*—to a courtly diversion—*trobar*—paradoxically precipitates it to the status of an "art" in the scholastic sense of the word.[3] Of the many treatises subsequently produced in Catalan- and/or Italian-speaking territories through the thirteenth and into the early fourteenth century, several are grouped by John H. Marshall in what he calls "the Vidal tradition" because of their debt to the *Razos*.[4] In the overview of surviving treatises up to 1356 given in Appendix 3, all the entries before Dante fall within this tradition except for the *Donatz proensals* of Uc Faidit.

The *Razos de trobar*, composed so far as we know in Catalonia, is preserved in four manuscripts of which three (*BCL*) were copied in Italy and the fourth (*H*) is Catalan (Figure 1 shows a folio of *L*).[5] The permeability that this suggests between Catalan and Italian domains is continued in the late thirteenth century by Raimon Vidal's two principal imitators whose work I discuss in this chapter. The Italian Terramagnino da Pisa writes his *Doctrina d'acort* (Instruction in rhyme), preserved only in the Catalan grammatical compilation *H*, in Sardinia.[6] Raimon's fellow Catalan, Jofre de Foixà, composes the *Regles de trobar* (Rules of poetic composition) for the Catalan court of Sicily and it too is subsequently compiled in Catalan manuscripts (*HR*).[7] Clearly, both texts and authors journeyed back and forth across the Mediterranean, the best copies of the *Razos*, which originated in Catalonia, being found in Italy, whereas conversely the only copies of *Doctrina* and the *Regles* are Catalan, even though they were composed in what is now Italy.[8]

Although early grammars of French are also associated with travel, their aim is to help nonnative French speakers transact commercial or diplomatic business in francophone territories. By contrast, the Occitan grammars transmit Occitan as a language of poetry, marshaling grammatical information with a view to enabling their readers to compose or appreciate lyric. The grammarians of the Vidal tradition concentrate almost exclusively on flexion (thus "grammaticalizing" Occitan on the model of Latin); they claim, explicitly or implicitly, that their rationale for this focus is to help their readers achieve or recognize correct rhyme (thus identifying vernacular poetry with rhyme); and in this way they create a new disciplinary hybrid of grammar-cum-poetry, which I have elsewhere called a "science of endings."[9] In addition, the Vidal grammarians resemble Latin ones in harnessing language learning to the study of the *auctores*, providing extracts from troubadour songs to serve as illustrations and models. It is remarkable to see the troubadours being treated like Classical poets as early as 1200.[10] These quotations contribute to the grammarians' bid to extend Occitan from a regional poetic standard to a more universal one and, by the same token, to found their innovative grammar-cum-poetry as an art.

The plan of Raimon Vidal's *Razos de trobar* is broadly followed by the *Doctrina d'acort* and the *Regles de trobar*. A longish preamble distinctive to each author advances claims about the importance of Occitan and its poetry. Then comes the statement, standard in Latin grammar, that there are eight parts of speech. Coverage of these occupies most of the rest of each treatise, but is unequally proportioned. Nouns and nominal morphology take up about half the space, rather less is given to verbs, and the remainder is shared by other topics. One reason for devoting relatively more attention to nouns, as Jofre de Foixà explains, is that literary Occitan still has a case system that distinguishes nominative from other forms, whereas that of Catalan has been lost (*Regles de trobar*, *H* text, 172–86). So has that of Italian; similar instances of teaching being slanted to help Catalans and Italians avoid the pitfalls of Occitan are found elsewhere in these grammars. Nevertheless the Vidal grammarians' heightened attention to nouns is surprising in view of the greater difficulty posed by the complex Occitan verbal system, a difficulty they acknowledge when they find errors of conjugation in the very troubadours they most promote as models for imitation by their readers.

Preambles: Grammar, Poetry, *Razo*

At the beginning of the *Razos de trobar*, Raimon declares that his aim is to enhance appreciation of the art of *trobar* by discriminating between better and less good models; in turn, he encourages others to identify faults and omissions in his own text. In promoting his topic he stresses that *trobar* is valued and aspired to by people from all walks of life; and that the troubadours knew how, through rhyme, to render moral truths memorable:

> Et tuit li mal e·l ben del mont sont mes en remembransa per trobadors. Et ia non trobares mot [ben] ni mal dig, po[s] trobaires l'a mes en rima, qe tot iorns [non sia] en remembranza, qar trobars et chantars son movemenz de totas galliardias. (*Razos de trobar*, B text, 27–31)

> And all the good and evil things of the world are made memorable by the troubadours. And you won't find a well-expressed or badly expressed idea that, once a troubadour has set it to rhyme, will not be remembered forever. For composition and song are what move all exceptional bravery.[11]

Ill-informed listeners who condone second-rate poetry are as reprehensible as the poets who produce it; by honing their linguistic sensibilities, Raimon undertakes to educate connoisseurs who will keep standards from slipping.[12] The strength of Limousin as a poetic medium is that, while a "natural" vernacular (a language one is born into), it shares the structures of *grammatica*: "for the Limousin idiom both is acquired naturally, and expresses itself by means of case, number, gender, tense, person, and word class, as you will be able to hear if you listen properly" (B text, 83–89, "car tota la parladura de Lemosyn se parla naturalmenz et per cas et per [nombres e per] genres e per temps e per personas e per motz, aisi com poretz auzir aissi si ben o escoutas").

Inflection, Raimon continues, distinguishes what he calls "substantive" and "adjective" words from all the other word classes, which he terms "neutral" (*neutras*, B text, 99–103). The difference between "substantive" and "adjective," he goes on to explain, is between words designating substances and those that predicate them:

> Las paraulas adiectivas son con *bons, bels, bona, bella, fortz, vils, sotils, plazens, soffrenz, am, vau, grazisc, en[e]gresisc*, et cant a o qe fa o qe suffre; et son appelladas aiectivas car hom no la[s] pot portar ad entendement si sobre substantius no las geta.
>
> Las paraulas substantivas son aisi come *belezza, boneçza, cavaliers, cavals, dopna, poma, ieu, tu, mieus, tieus, sui, estau*, et toutas las autras del mont qe demostron substantia visibil o non visibil; et per so an nom substantivas car demonstran substantia et sostenon las aiectivas, aisi com qi dizia *rei[s] sui d'Aragon*, o *ieu sui rics homs*. (*Razos de trobar*, B text, 104–12)

Adjective words are such as *beautiful* [m.], *good, beautiful* [f.], *strong, cheap, subtle, pleasing, patient, I love, I go, I thank, I grow pale*, and whatever possesses or acts or suffers; and they are called adjectives because they cannot be rendered intelligible unless they are "thrown upon" substantives.

Substantive words are those such as *beauty, goodness, knight, horse, lady, apple, I, you, mine, yours, I am* [ontic], *I am* [stative], and all the others in the world that show substance visible or invisible; and they are called substantives because they show substance and support adjectives, as for example if someone were to say *I am the king of Aragon* or *I am a powerful man*.

Raimon is here echoing Latin grammatical theory, which analyzed the cognitive and logical capacities of language in light of contemporary philosophical preoccupation with universals.[13] He seems to be contending that the presence of inflexion in Occitan makes it not only "grammatical" in the sense of sharing Latin paradigms, but also universal in the sense of mirroring the relation of substance and predication. Substantive words convey what exists (*essentia*, or substance); adjective words tell us about the attributes of substance; their combination enables the formulation of intelligible claims and the advancement of rational understanding.

At the risk of crediting these borrowings from contemporary thought with more coherence than they in fact possess, we can discern the following logic to the seemingly disjointed statements in Raimon's preamble:

The love of *trobar* is universal: why?

Because rhyme makes moral insights memorable.

In Limousin rhyme is inseparable from inflecting forms.

Inflecting forms manifest substance and its predicates; they enable one to form propositions through which one can achieve rational understanding.

Therefore the moral insight made memorable by rhyme is, at the same time, a form of rational understanding.

That is, poetry defined by rhyme [*trobar*] is an expression of reason [*razo*].

The idea that troubadour poetry could be a privileged distillation of reason is formulated a little more clearly in the equivalent discussion in the *Doctrina d'acort*. Terramagnino praises Limousin as "better than all reasoned forms of speech" ("sobre totz razonatz parlars," 30) because "it is as though it reasons in a manner similar to good Latin" ("quays se razona / con la gramatica bona," 33–34); mastery of all the various kinds of flexion, he promises, "holds open its pathway to speech that is reasoned with certainty" ("te lo sieu cami ubert / del parlar razonat per cert," 49–50). The thrust of this opening passage is admirably formulated in *H*'s initial rubric: "the beginning of the Provençal *Instruction* regarding true and reasonable expression" ("començament de Doctrina provincial de vera e rahonable locucio").

In a more ambitious preamble than Raimon Vidal's, Jofre de Foixà similarly lends support to the view of poetic Occitan as somehow opening a pathway to rational understanding. He begins by surveying what he calls the nine *causas* (first causes, prerequisites) of *trobar*. They include agreement in number and gender, sequence of tense, rhyme, case, and the use and inflexion of articles. First among them, however, is *razo*, which here could mean simply "theme" but which seems, in addition, to take on the more philosophical coloring of "reason." This is due in part to the quotation from Aimeric de Peguilhan, which precedes it, to which I return at the end of this chapter; and in part to Jofre's reprise, at the end of his preamble, of Raimon Vidal's account of word classes in a way that shows he has grasped the logical and cognitive implications of his model, even if he expresses them in different terms. Unlike Raimon, Jofre does not consider verbs at all in this particular discussion, but instead focuses on two categories of *nomen* (name/nominal form), one of which renders the category of substance, the other various forms of accident:

> totes les causes qui son nomenades e han sustancia, axi com *Deus, angles, reys, comtes, duchs, cavallers* . . . , et d'altre motz qu'en hi a sens nombre, cove a far que aquestas coses, les quals son appellades nomen, haien alguna natura o algun acte o algun accident o alcuna causa qui lo[r e]s aiustada; aquella es axi matex appellada nomen. (*Regles de trobar*, H text, 218–24)

> all things that are named and have substance, like *God, angel, king, count, duke, knight* . . . and other such words ad infinitum—all such things, which are called "names" [*or* "nominal forms"], need to have some nature or some act or some accident or some other thing that is added to them. And this thing is also called a name [nominal form].

This second name/nominal form must agree with the first,

> car aquests nomens, segons que son accident, en la maior part no poden esser sens lo nomen primer. Per que lor coven a sseguir llur natura, car ell non han sustancia, ans los coe esser en los noms qui hansustancia—en axi co *bells, bos, blanchs*, e mantz d'autres, car beutatz ni bondatz ni blanquesa ni bellesa no podon esser sino en los noms qui han sustancia. (*Regles de trobar*, H text, 226–31)

> for these names/nominal forms, insofar as they are accidents, for the most part cannot function without the first one. Therefore they must follow their own nature: for they do not have substance but must accompany names/nominal forms that do; thus it is with *beautiful, good, white*, and many others, for beauty or goodness or whiteness cannot exist except in names/nominal forms that have substance.

This enables Jofre to return to his favorite topic: agreement. But we can also see how recasting Raimon Vidal leads him to focus attention almost exclusively on nominal forms as those most apt to render what is rational about song: its capacity to make substance and its accidents materialize in the language of poetry. Where Jofre differs most significantly from Raimon is in detaching the study of inflexion from Latin, confident in the independence and universality of vernacular art since one no longer requires "the art of *grammatica*" ("la art de gramatica," *H*, 6) in order to access it.

These preambles help to explain why, in the examination of the parts of speech that follows in each of these treatises, more attention is paid to nouns than verbs. Nouns map poetic substance, whereas the verbs that predicate them are subject to caution.

Uses of Quotation in the Vidal Tradition

Following their preambles, the grammarians' presentation of the parts of speech is illustrated with reference to the troubadours. Appendix 4 provides a breakdown of which passages are quoted at what point in each treatise. The majority of quotations, it shows, divide between discussion of two major categories, nominal forms (including adjectives) and verbs. By grouping adjectives together with nouns, the grammarians retreat from the subject-predicate distinctions drawn in their preambles. But their progression from nouns to verbs nevertheless evokes sentence formation, or, from a logician's standpoint, the passage from term to proposition.

The kinship between the treatises is apparent in the way they illustrate the same grammatical forms, sometimes indeed with the same words. Yet it is remarkable how little overlap there is in their choice of excerpts. All three authors like to extract a succession of quotations from the same song or the same troubadour, but each privileges different sources. Raimon Vidal favors Bernart de Ventadorn and Giraut de Bornelh, taking almost half his quotations from them. Terramagnino da Pisa most often names Folquet de Marselha (though not always, as it happens, correctly),[14] and Jofre quotes most from Gaucelm Faidit and Aimeric de Peguilhan. In their quotations from poets other than these favorites, the effort at diversity is also palpable. The three grammarians further introduce unattributed examples that may be their own compositions, as if to insinuate themselves into the company of distinguished troubadours. For each of them, independent knowledge of Occitan poetry and a personal relationship to it are ways of staking out their individual authority. Conversely, their reliance on quotations has the odd effect of turning the troubadour corpus into a compendium of grammatical lore, a body of knowledge to be tapped. This lore is entirely divorced from music.[15] Quotations in all three treatises are introduced by forms of *dire*, which, although not so narrow in meaning as English "say," does nothing to indicate that these texts are (or once were) songs (although Terramagnino, author of the only rhymed treatise, has the interesting eccentricity of referring to the troubadours' language as *chant*, "song").

Raimon Vidal pioneers two different forms of quotation that are taken up in the later grammars.[16] One is the self-contained example, usually one or two lines long, chosen to illustrate a point of grammar. In the older *B* redaction this practice is justified by the claim that nominal forms are best acquired from troubadours familiar with the *parladura* ("spoken idiom"), the poetic language that Raimon elsewhere calls Limousin:

> Et per so qe ancaras n'aias maior entendement, vos en trobarai senblan dels trobadors, aisi con o an menat sobre·l nominatiu cas singular et sobre·l nominatiu plural et sobre·l vocatiu singular et sobre.l plural, per so car aqest qatre cas son plus de leu per entendre a cels qe an la parladura. . . . En Bernartz del Ventedor dieis:
> Bien s'escai [a] dompna ardimenz. (*Razos de trobar*, *B* text, 172–85)

> And so you can have a better grasp of it I'll find models among the troubadours of how they used the nominative singular case and the nominative plural and the vocative singular and plural, because these four cases are easier to grasp for those who know the spoken idiom. . . . Sir Bernart de Ventadorn said: "Boldness befits a lady well."

Bernart's line (70.1, 33) is quoted "materially," as contemporary grammarians termed it,[17] not for its meaning but for its formal expression, in this instance the correct form of the nominative singular noun *ardimenz*. In the *Regles de trobar*, Jofre reinforces the quotations' exemplary value by introducing them with the formula "per eximpli," as when he says that masculine nominative forms are lengthened in the singular and shortened in the plural by addition or removal of flexional –*s*: "for example, as Bernart de Ventadorn said, 'Now advise me lords'" ("e per eximpli axi com dix Bernat de Ventadorn: 'Ar me conselatz, senyor,'" *Regles de trobar*, *H* text, 384–86; 70.6, 1). The grammatical form addressed by each quotation is identified in Appendix 4.

In the section of Raimon Vidal's treatise devoted to verbs a second form of quotation surfaces. Before reproducing an example "materially," he may situate it by providing the incipit (opening line) of the song in which it appears. The first instance occurs when he criticizes Bernart de Ventadorn, previously hailed for his instinctive mastery of nouns, for saying (*re*)*trai* when he should have said (*re*)*trac* (Appendix 4, *RaT*, #14–#17; 70.25 and 70.7):

> Pero En B. del Ventedor mes la terza persona per prima en dos cantars. L'uns ditz *Ara can vei la fuella ios dels arbres cazer*, et l'autres ditz *Era non vei luzer soleill*. Del primier cantar fon li falla en la cobla qe ditz:
> > Escontra·l dampnatge
> > e la pena q'ieu trai.
> . . . En l'autre cantar fon li falla en la cobla qe ditz:
> > ia ma dompna no·s meravelh . . .
> > contra la foudat q'i[eu] retrai. (*Razos de trobar*, B text, 360–70)

But Sir Bernart de Ventadorn put the third person for the first in two songs. One goes, "Now when I see the leaf / fall from the trees" and the other goes, "Now I cannot see the sun shine." In the first song, the error was in the stanza that says: "In the face of the harm / and suffering I endure." . . . In the other song the error was in the stanza that says: "Let my lady not be astonished . . . at the crazy things I say."

In such cases quotation of the incipit names the song as well as reproducing part of it; it has no exemplary function in itself, but enables the reader to contextualize the example that follows.

There are striking differences in the distribution both of quotations and of types of quotation between the sections of these treatises devoted to nominal forms and those that deal with verbs. The grammarians take more pains in the former than the latter. In its nominal section the *B* text of the *Razos* contains about a dozen quotations, the *CL* redaction slightly more.[18] None of the same quotations reappears among the twenty-four with the same remit in the *Doctrina d'acort* and only one is reused among the five in the *Regles*. With one exception, Raimon Vidal selects examples where the form in question is at the rhyme, and all Jofre de Foixà's examples follow suit, thereby tacitly confirming that the need to study inflexion in the first place stems from the fact that Occitan lyric depends for its structure on rhyme (the forms in bold in Appendix 4 are rhyme words). Terramagnino da Pisa initially adopts the different strategy of choosing extracts that helpfully show the same word, *amic*, variously inflected for number and case, though not at the rhyme;[19] but his subsequent nominal examples are mostly rhyme words.

Raimon's preference for the Limousin poets Bernart de Ventadorn and Giraut de Bornelh chimes with his claim that speakers from this region instinctively know best how to combine grammar and rhyme. Jofre's quotations in his noun section are all from troubadours referred to at some point in the *Razos de trobar*, but Terramagnino's examples display a real effort at innovation; he quotes from twenty songs and fifteen poets including several (such as Rigaut de Berbezilh) who are not quoted at all by Raimon Vidal, and others who are unknown or unidentified (Andrianz del Palais, Uc). Terramagnino also prefaces quotations with expressions of admiration for the troubadour concerned, for example, "As Andrian, a good and true troubadour, said" (200–201, "Con dis Andrianz del Palais. / Trobayre bos e verays"), a trait found in Raimon Vidal's *novas* but not in his grammar.

When Raimon Vidal moves on to verbs, he provides the incipits of four of the eight songs excerpted in the *B* text.[20] Two are the Bernart de Ventadorn songs quoted above; the others are Giraut de Borneil's "Gen m'aten" (242.34) and Folquet de Marselha's "Ai! quan gen vens et ab quan pauc d'afan" (155.3). Distinguishing between incipits and examples shows that Raimon's verb section contains markedly fewer illustrations than the section on nouns, and this asymmetry is reproduced by Jofre de Foixà, who provides only two verbal examples to five nominal ones. Terramagnino da Pisa's zeal for quotation continues to outstrip both of the others, but once examples are distinguished from contextualizing incipits it becomes clear that he too provides many fewer illustrations for verbs than nouns. Like Jofre de Foixà, Terramagnino seems less invested in this part of his treatise than in the earlier section on nominal morphology. Whereas his nominal quotations were markedly original, here he is satisfied with quoting the same songs and even the same lines as Raimon.[21]

The most striking and unexpected development from Raimon's treatment of nouns to that of verbs is that now almost every example alerts his readers to alleged errors in the great Limousin troubadours—the very ones who had figured so positively in the previous section.[22] The forms that he stigmatizes are all found at the rhyme; most involve forms of *traire* and *creire* (see Figure 1). Whereas Jofre parts company with Raimon Vidal on this point and urges acceptance of troubadour usage, Terramagnino continues the pur-

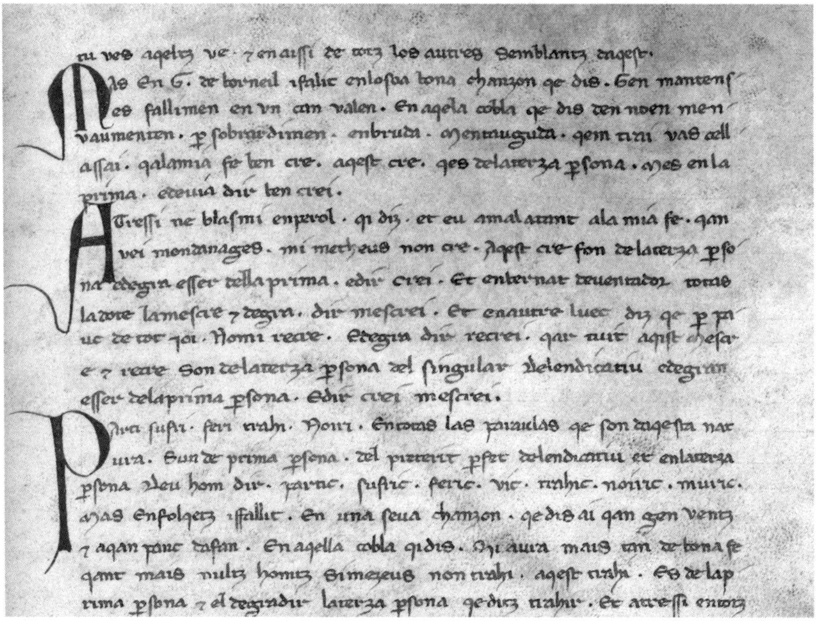

Figure 1. Quotations in Raimon Vidal's *Razos de trobar*, New York, Pierpont Morgan Library MS M 831 (grammar manuscript *L*), fo. 6r. This figure contains quotations corresponding with Appendix 4, ##18–24, which illustrate errors of conjugation committed by famous troubadours. In the first section: incipit and commentary on the form *cre* in Giraut de Bornelh 242.34 ("Gen m'aten"). In the second section: the quotations are from Peirol 366.21 ("Mout m'entremis de chantar voluntiers") and Bernart de Ventadorn 70.43 ("Can vei la lauzeta mover"), with attention again directed to the form *cre* for *crei*. The final section (beginning with the enlarged P) repeats the process with reference to the conjugation of the verb *traïr* in Folquet de Marselha 155.3 ("Ai! quan gen vens et ab quan pauc d'afan"). Note how the scribe adapts the punctus, used following the convention of *chansonniers* to mark the ends of metrical lines, also to mark potential linguistically correct rhyme words. The text in this image corresponds with J. H. Marshall's edition of the *CL* text, lines 354–84.

ism of his model, proliferating instances of supposedly incorrect forms of *creire* just as, in the previous section, he had accumulated examples of *amic*. In this section, Terramagnino also follows Raimon in placing examples at the rhyme. By focusing on rhyme words, Raimon and Terramagnino are simultaneously stigmatizing the poetic and the linguistic competence of the authors they quote. The *Doctrina d'acort*'s expressions of admiration now ring distinctly hollow: "Mas En Ffolquetz, trobayre fis, / I fallic en son chan e dis . . ." (*H* text, 645–66, "But Sir Folquet, true poet, erred in his song and said . . .").

I see the practice of providing the incipits of many of the songs that they criticize as furnishing these two grammarians with the authority for their critique. Used as a title on the model of Latin works, the incipit connotes learnedness (see Introduction). Their mastery of the entire song implicitly justifies the grammarians' presumption in correcting the great troubadours— the very ones whom they themselves are promoting to the status of *auctores*. (Conversely, perhaps it is because Jofre de Foixà does not try to correct troubadour usage that he does not use incipits to contextualize any of his quotations; or maybe he is just less eager than his predecessors to assume the trappings of scholasticism, since part of his aim is to free the study of the vernacular from the yoke of *grammatica*.)[23]

A strange consequence of Raimon's and Terramagnino's use of quotations is the impression they convey that troubadour poetry is distinguished by well-formed nouns and adjectives but marred by badly conjugated verbs. Whereas the good nouns feature in the context only of single lines or small groups of lines, the bad verbs are introduced by the incipits as belonging within whole poems; this wider frame presents verbs as marking the passage from noun to sentence, or from topic to theme (*razo*). The words exemplified in the two sets of quotations linger in the mind to create bizarre combinations. The nominal examples highlight core elements of troubadour vocabulary; thus Raimon Vidal's excerpts foreground positive adjectives like *genz* (beautiful), *pros* (worthy), *presanz* (estimable), *gentil* (noble), and nouns that include *ardimenz* (boldness), *cavaliers* (knight), *senhor* (lords), and *amors* (love); Terramagnino da Pisa's highlighted words include *amic* (friend, lover), *domna* (lady), *valor* (worth), *sabor* (relish, savor), and *chansos* (song)—not to mention *razon*;[24] and Jofre contributes *douçor* (sweetness) and *merces* (favor, mercy) to the mix. Such quotations convey the sense of touring obligatory landmarks in the ideological landscape of *cortezia*. But these values appear compromised, in the *Razos* and *Doctrina d'acort*, as a result of the failures implied by the vocabulary enshrined in the verbal quotations. Here things are experienced (*tray*), recounted (*retray*), believed (*cre*), reneged on (*recre*) or betrayed (*trahit*), in all cases ineptly, and mostly in the first person. The combination of *amic* (friend, declined correctly) with *cre* (believe, conjugated wrongly) is especially insistent in Terramagnino. The substance of troubadour poetry, we feel, is beyond reproach; but its articulation and its predication are wanting. If all good and bad things are memorialized by troubadour rhymes, as the introduction to the *Razos* asserts, then the bad (or at least the erroneous) seem to have the last word.

Rhyme, Reason, and the Future of Poetry

Allusions to philosophical grammar in the Vidal tradition may represent less a thoroughgoing conceptualization of the Occitan language than an intellectual veneer adopted to attract amateur enthusiasts. Nevertheless, the grammars' association of rhyme with reason offers the possibility that vernacular poetry could encapsulate understanding. The pessimistic trajectory from nouns to verbs of the *Razos de trobar* and the *Doctrina d'acort* implies that this aspiration is yet to be fulfilled. Illustrations in these treatises are equivocal since some are to be followed and others eschewed.

By contrast, Jofre de Foixà's presentation of *trobar* is more sanguine. He also provides the sole example in the Vidal tradition of quotation functioning as a genuine means of understanding: the stanza from Aimeric de Peguilhan's "Mangtas vetz sui enqueritz" (10.34) quoted at the beginning of the *Regles de trobar*. Neither a grammatical illustration nor a contextualizing incipit, this stanza is repeated for the sake of its content; that is, it introduces a third, justificatory form of quotation into the grammars. Jofre has just stated that he is writing so that laymen ignorant of *grammatica* can recognize and acquire the skill (*saber*) of writing poetry. He continues, adapting Raimon's prefatory exhortation to his readers to identify faults and omissions in the *Razos* (in the text and translation below, as throughout this book, italics are used to highlight an overlap between quotation and context):

> E si alcuna causa de repreniment hi ha ques eu non entenda, a mi platz fort que la pusquen esmenar *segons rayso; car N'Aymerich de Peguila m'o ensenya* en una sua cançó dient en axi:

> > Si eu en soy desmentitz
> > c'aysso no sia veritatz,
> > no n'er hom per mi blasmatz
> > si per ver m'o contreditz;

> ans vey sos sabers plus grans
> entre·ls pros, e·ls meus mermans,
> Si·m pot venser d'ayso *segons rayso,*
> *qu'eu no say ges tot lo sen Salamo. (Regles de trobar,* H text, 15–26)

And if there is in it any grounds for criticism that I am unaware of,
I'd be very glad for them to amend it *in accordance with reason; for
Sir Aimeric de Peguilhan taught me this* in one of his songs, saying in
this manner: "If I am found not to be speaking the truth, I won't
blame anyone who truthfully opposes what I say. On the contrary, I
see his skills as great among the worthy and my own as diminishing,
if he can do this better than me, *in accordance with reason; for I do
not possess all the wisdom of Solomon.*"

This engaging modesty device, in which Jofre admits to learning from Aimeric who confesses to knowing less than Solomon and both submit to higher
reason, uses repeated phraseology and syntax (in italics above) in order to fuse
Jofre's thinking with that of the quoted text.[25] The effect of the fusion is effectively to retract the declaration of modesty in the very act of making it, since
by insinuating his community of outlook with Aimeric, and placing both
barely a peg lower than Solomon, Jofre seems rather to assert his own authority. The vaunted reason and wisdom of the quotation serve the grammarian's
claim to professional knowledge. They also affirm the value *as* knowledge of
the poetry he expounds. When Jofre passes immediately afterward to a consideration of *razo,* its usual sense of "theme" cannot help but be affected by
the reiterated *segon rayso* of the preceding lines and assume the meaning of
"reason" too. Here, quotation exemplifies and contributes to the intellectual
substance of the treatise, confirming the capacity of *trobar* to transmit *razo.*

Although such substantive use of quotation is not found in the *Razos de
trobar,* it is seemingly inaugurated by Raimon Vidal in the verse *novas* he is
thought to have composed shortly after. Indeed, the *novas* quote six of the
same lyrics—though not the same passages—as the *Razos.*[26] Three are songs
that Raimon had criticized from a grammatical standpoint, but he can nevertheless draw wisdom from them. Despite Giraut's faulty conjugation of
creire in "Gen m'aten," Raimon quotes from it to support his argument:

> E car hom per esgardamen
> val may ades n'estatz membratz

qu'en Guiraut dis als acabatz
per esfortir lur bon captenh:
 "Ni no tenh a dan si·m destrenh
 amors ni·m deschay
 c'una vetz n'auray
 man bon esdevenh."
                    (*Abril issia*, 1545–52)

And since through reflection a man is worth more, remember what Sir Giraut said to people of refinement in order to strengthen their good conduct: "Nor do I see it as a setback if Love torments me or brings me low because one day I shall get many a good outcome from it all."

The narrator's emphasis on improvement through intellectual effort is more clearly expressed in his own than in Giraut's words, but this does not mean that the song has not provoked and justified this reflection. As an articulation of rhyme with reason, song can serve as a tool of thought.

When Raimon Vidal claims that poetry makes understanding memorable, then, he is not claiming that its only role is to perpetuate the past. Memory enables understanding to progress, so that the past can be improved on in the future. As we will see in Chapter 2, in *Abril issia* Raimon Vidal both remembers and misremembers Giraut de Bornelh as a means for developing his own thought. His grammar, by the associations it forges between rhyme and reason, lays the groundwork for the substantive use of quotation found in later works. His treatise, and those of the tradition it inspired, consist only partly in documenting the achievements of the classical troubadours. They also project a future for Catalan- or Italian-authored Occitan poetry in which troubadour lyric will both continue and begin anew.

## CHAPTER 2

Quotation, Memory, and Connoisseurship in the *Novas* of Raimon Vidal de Besalú

In the opening lines of *Abril issi' e mays intrava* (April was ending and May beginning) its first-person narrator, whom we take to be Raimon Vidal, is alone in the square of Besalú when a young *joglar* approaches. The young man wants his older colleague's advice because, he complains, today's courts are so much less receptive to troubadour poetry than those of the past. He launches into a rather rambling anecdote about the hospitality he enjoyed at the court of the poet and patron Count Dalfi d'Alvernha (ca. 1160–1235), into which is set another tale, told to him by Dalfi, illustrating how values have declined. The narrator then advises his young companion to take heart. Many courts are still welcoming, and an astute performer who knows how to adapt to his audience can extract rewards even from the ill-mannered or ignorant; he too recalls happy days spent with a patron, Alfonso II of Aragon (ruled 1162–96). All the speakers pepper their discourse with quotations from the troubadours, star billing going to Arnaut de Maruelh, Giraut de Bornelh, and Raimon de Miraval (see Appendix 5). The excerpts found in the *joglar*'s exchanges with Dalfi are mainly about merit finding its due reward; those in the narrator's recommendations are more about discerning where merit is and having the wit to succeed even when it is lacking.[1]

All this instruction makes the text more didactic than narrative, perhaps conveying above all its narrator's own credentials as a teacher.[2] As author of the *Razos de trobar*, Raimon Vidal was, after all, an expert on troubadour poetry. His expertise shines through in another verse *novas* that contains even more quotations, *So fo e·l tems c'om era gais* (It was at that time of merriment). More novella-like than *Abril issia*, and probably composed slightly later but within the same time frame of circa 1199–1209, *So fo* is harder to summarize because, whereas *Abril issia* is transmitted only by troubadour *chansonnier R*, *So fo* appears in several manuscripts in a variety of longer and shorter formats.[3] It opens, like *Abril issia*, in the first person. The narrator recalls an anecdote from the Limousin about a knight spurned by the *domna* (married lady) he has been faithfully courting. The knight turns for advice to a *donzela* (unmarried lady), who at first urges him to persevere and even intercedes with the *domna* on his behalf. But when the *domna* responds unfavorably, the *donzela* herself begins to experience interest in the knight and eventually he declares his love for her. Shortly afterward the *donzela* marries; now a *domna*, she and the knight become exemplary courtly lovers. The first *domna*, when she sees the knight's reputation prosper in this way, repents her hard-heartedness and asks him back, but he refuses. The version of the story found in *chansonniers L* and *N* ends at this point. In *R*, the story continues with the first *domna* confronting the second (formerly the *donzela*) and demanding that she give up the knight. Again she meets with refusal. The two ladies' competition for the knight's affections is referred via a *joglar* to the Catalan poet and patron Uc de Mataplana (ruled 1197–1213); the narrator is present when the *joglar* arrives and so witnesses what ensues. Uc's verdict is that the second *domna* should relinquish her claim to the knight and, even if he chooses not to return to the first *domna*, dismiss him from her affections because he will have shown himself unforgiving and fickle in love. This ending is in turn reversed by some 180 additional lines found only in manuscript *a²*, which present the second *domna*, when she hears Uc's verdict, refusing to obey. As in *Abril issia*, only more so, the narrator and all of the characters quote the troubadours at every turn, in this case primarily to justify their views on the proper way to behave in love. Raimon de Miraval is the most quoted troubadour, followed by Bernart de Ventadorn, Folquet de Marselha, and Giraut de Bornelh (see Appendix 5).

This more complex transmission of *So fo* has led Hugh Field, Raimon's editor, to hypothesize three stages of composition, whereby the text found in *LN* would be by Raimon de Miraval and only the continuation in *R* by Raimon Vidal.[4] However, it is characteristic of Italian manuscripts like *L* and *N* to abbreviate or excerpt Occitan narratives that are preserved in full in the Occitan source *R*; the transmission of the *Novas del papagai* presents a similar picture (see Chapter 6).[5] Since I do not find Field's arguments persuasive, this chapter will be about the texts of both *novas* as they appear in *R*.[6]

Both *Abril issia* and *So fo* are composed in octosyllabic rhyming couplets and use the same techniques of quotation, which will be subsequently imitated by Matfre Ermengau in the *Breviari* (Chapter 8). The speaker claims to remember (*membrar*), or invites his listeners to remember, the words of a famous troubadour, identified by name and praised for his wisdom;[7] the excerpt is then introduced by the verb *dire* with no suggestion that it might be sung;[8] quotations seem chosen for their content; and they are assimilated metrically as far as possible to the surrounding text. For example, at the beginning of *Abril issia*, the first sight of the little *joglar* reminds the narrator of lines from Giraut de Bornelh's "Per solatz reveillar" (242.55, 41–44):

> e membret mi qu'en Guiraut dis
> que tan se fes a totz prezar:
>   "Eu vi per cortz anar
>   us joglaretz petitz,
>   gen caussatz e vestitz,
>   sol per donas lauzar."
> E si·m fos natural de far
> aisi·m volgra estar tostemps.
>   (*Abril issia*, 94–101)

And I recalled what my lord Giraut said who won so much esteem from all: "I saw groups of little *joglars*[9] going from court to court elegantly shod and clothed, for the sole purpose of praising ladies." And I would have liked to have stayed standing like that forever, so naturally it came to me to do so.

Giraut is cited as an authority worth remembering on account of his universally acclaimed merit. His lines are shorter than Raimon Vidal's but their rhyme scheme is absorbed into his, the first line of the quotation forming a pair with the line preceding it, and the last line of the quotation with the line following it, so that the onward march of couplets continues without a halt. The transcription of the *novas* in *R* reflects this compromise between marking the distinctness of quotations and integrating them to the surrounding verse. Their beginnings are marked by capitals and their ends by paraphs. Throughout *Abril issia* the quoted extracts are set out line by line exactly like the rest of the text. In *So fo*, however, this layout is used for only fourteen of the thirty-nine quotations. The remainder are set out as prose

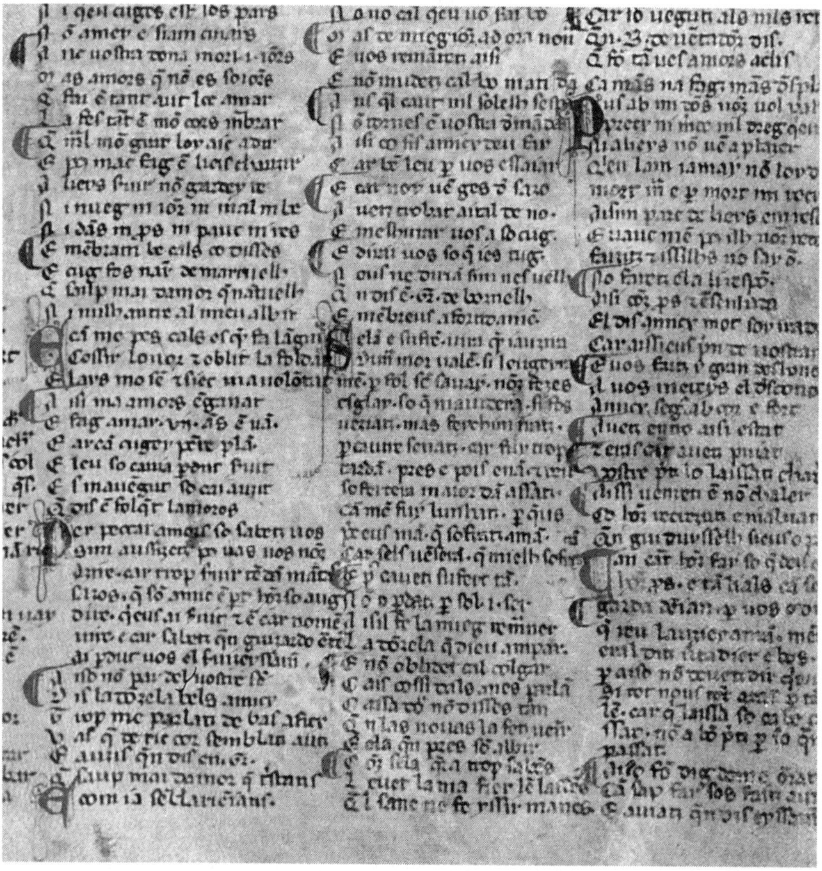

Figure 2. Quotations in Raimon Vidal's *So fo e·l tems c'om era gais* in Paris, BnF, français 22543 (*chansonnier R*), folio 131r. Bottom right-hand section of the page, showing how the scribe comes to integrate the layout of the lyric quotations to that of the narrative verse frame. In the inner (left-hand) columns, the narrative is set out line by line with the initial letter offset from the rest of the line, whereas the quotations are copied according to lyric conventions—as prose paragraphs occupying the full column width, with a punctus at the end of each verse; the start of the lyric excerpts is marked by an enlarged initial, whereas paraphs mark the resumption of the narrative and progression within it. In the outermost (right-hand) column, however, the scribe stops offsetting the initial letter of the narrative verse, and adjusts the width of the lyric quotations to better match the surrounding narrative. Compare at the bottom of the inmost (left-hand) column the long quotation from Folquet de Marselh 155.1 (*So fo*, ed. Field, lines 248–54; Appendix 5, #7), beginning "Per q'er pechat, Amors," with that from Bernart de Ventadorn 70.43 (433–40; #14) that starts "Pos ab midonç no·m pot valer" on the far right column. The last quotation in this column, Gui d'Ussel 194.19 (455–62; #15), though it starts with an enlarged initial T ("Tant cant hom fal"), is interrupted two lines later by a paraph like the narrative. The distinction between quoted and quoting text has become almost invisible. Reproduced by permission of the Bibliothèque nationale de France.

paragraphs with a punctus marking the ends of verses, like stanzas in the older *chansonniers*. Initially, this gives the text a more hybrid appearance. However, from line 373 (the last column on fo. 131r), the scribe stops setting the initial letter of the octosyllabic couplets apart from the rest of the column; the lyric passages immediately blend in with the rest of the text, even when they are copied as prose paragraphs, because both lyric and narrative occupy the full width of the column (see Figure 2).

Like the quotations in the *Razos de trobar*, those in both *novas* are, I shall argue, remembered in order to school connoisseurship and ensure the future of the lyric, even at the cost of breaking with the past.[10] The relation between memory and connoisseurship proves surprisingly complex, in ways already hinted by the *Razos*, since it is often necessary to remember more (or remember differently) than what is seemingly remembered by those who quote. It can be difficult to know what there is to know, and by whom; this creates a web of supposition to negotiate. By examining quotations from three troubadour songs, one each by Giraut de Bornelh, Raimon de Miraval, and Bertran de Born, it will become apparent that the *novas* both memorialize existing troubadour poetry and disavow it, thereby subtly shifting connoisseurship from Occitania to Raimon's native Catalonia.

Giraut de Bornelh's "Per solatz reveillar" (242.55) and the Narrator's Memory

The first quotation in *Abril issia* refers, as we have just seen, to *joglars* going from court to court praising ladies. It is from stanza V of "Per solatz reveillar," the remainder of which presents the poet wondering why this no longer happens:

> Ar no·n auzem parlar
> tant es lor pretz delitz!
> don es lo tortz issitz
> d'ellas malrazonar?—
> Non sai!—de cals, d'ellas o dels amans?—
> Eu dic de toz, que·l pretz n'a trait l'enianz.
>   (Song 74, 45–50)

No words of praise do we hear now, so completely is their reputation in ruins! Who is to be blamed for speaking ill of them?—I know not!—Whose is the blame, theirs or their lovers'?—I call them all guilty, for it is deceitfulness that has stolen away their fair renown.[11]

These lines—the lines *not* quoted by Raimon Vidal—develop the song's central theme of lament over social decline. Stanza I opens with Giraut complaining that he has tried hard to rouse *solatz* (social enjoyment) from its torpor but finds his efforts defeated and his distress worsening. Stanzas II and III deplore the degeneration of chivalry; stanzas IV and V follow these complaints with others about the falling standards of court life, specifically the way minstrels are no longer welcomed as they once were. In stanza VI, Giraut fumes at his fallen fortunes in a world where a random anecdote about Bremar's goose is as well received as "a fine song about splendid deeds and the march of time and the years" (59–60, "us bons chanz / dels rics affars e dels temps e dels anz"): the kind of song, presumably, that he himself would sing.

Although the narrator of *Abril issia* has elected not to quote any of these stanzas of "Per solatz," retaining only the relatively trivial description of the minstrels' appearance, its stanzas I–VI are the germ of the young *joglar*'s entire harangue on the decline of courts. Stanza VI, additionally, anticipates the narrator's solution. Much as he deplores the passing of better days, Giraut discreetly insinuates that their values live on in himself. He even, in stanza VII, concedes the need to compromise with the times; his lady should avoid giving him grounds for complaint since words of censure, from a man prepared to praise less than estimable men when the need arises, would be extremely damaging to her.[12] Giraut's oblique presentation of himself as the answer to social decline and his pragmatic bid for success in spite of it furnish uncanny parallels with the recommendations of the *novas*' narrator. In short, the parts of "Per solatz" that the narrator omits to quote are the blueprint for the whole of *Abril issia*, but the only clue to this function is its quotation of four innocuous-seeming lines. By framing the whole *novas* as an unacknowledged reprise of such a well-known song, Raimon Vidal concedes that complaints about decadence were always already inscribed in the troubadour tradition, and remedies for survival proposed. The young *joglar*'s jejune hand-wringing over the good old days is just another instance of nostalgia for a past that maybe never was. Far from sympathizing with his young colleague's complaints, the canny older *joglar* promotes his own agenda for success.[13]

If Giraut is the key to the *novas*, what does the *novas* tell us about quotation? Raimon Vidal praises the great troubadour, but the only borrowing he acknowledges is the trivial one of the *joglars'* portrait: the tip of an iceberg of unacknowledged debt. Has the substance of Giraut's song been so thoroughly memorized as to become fused with Raimon Vidal's own thoughts? Or has Raimon Vidal, disavowing his source, set out to displace Giraut as the speaker of these thoughts? Or again, is he testing his audience to see if they have remembered what he appears to have forgotten? Such questions point to knowledge as a set of complex intersubjective negotiations in which hypotheses and suppositions are exchanged about what is known by whom.

These negotiations, playful in *Abril issia*, take on a harder tone in *So fo*, a tough school in connoisseurship especially for the ladies of Limousin.

Raimon de Miraval's "Tals vai mon chan enqueren" (406.42) and the Ladies of Limousin

The characters in *So fo e·l tems* constantly quote troubadour songs as though trying to work out how to feel and act in conformity with some ideal model. In the middle of the text, when the *donzela* has become a married *domna*, is still loved by the knight, and they are hailed as the perfect couple, their diligence seems to have paid dividends:

> Mot lo tenon tug per cortes
> lur fag donas et cavaier,
> et dizon que anc tan entier
> no·l viron ni tan benanan.
> 　　(*So fo*, R text, 560–63)

Ladies and knights all thought their conduct extremely courtly and said they had never before seen any so perfect or so fitting.

When the first *domna* returns to the scene, however, their ideal identities unravel. Quotation fails to provide the disputants with a solution and they seek recourse instead to a variant of the "court of love." Uc's judgment, judiciously supported by more snippets of troubadour song, puts the clock back to the starting point of the *novas* by reuniting the knight with the first *domna* and recommending patience and fidelity in love, just as the *donzela* had done at the outset. The whole of the central part of the *novas*, despite having been guided by the wit and wisdom of the troubadours, appears to have gone down a series of blind alleys. Perhaps the authority of the songs is ambiguous. But perhaps, since most of the quotations are placed in the mouths of women, female ears are less comprehending of the troubadours' teaching than they might be; perhaps even, since this part of the tale is set in Limousin, its courtly class generally lacks appreciation of the poetry for which the region is famous.

The troubadours certainly lend themselves to amusingly diverse interpretations. Bernart de Ventadorn initially provides a model for the knight's love for the first lady (Appendix 5, *So fo* quotation #1); and then her grounds for fending him off (#5); and then his reason for despairing of her (#14); and finally his justification for transferring his courtship to the *donzela* (#19). Even more than Bernart de Ventadorn, Raimon de Miraval is used to justify every twist of the plot. He is quoted both to endorse the knight when he perseveres with the first *domna* (#4), and by the *donzela* to woo him over to her instead (#17). Subsequently he is quoted on both sides in the spat between the knight and the first *domna* as to whether he was or was not justified in leaving her (##21, 23, 25, 26). The lady then quotes him while she is trying to persuade the *donzela* to let the knight come back to her (##27, 30); and he makes a final appearance in Uc de Mataplana's verdict (#38).

Just as "Per solatz" is both present and absent in *Abril issia*, so Raimon de Miraval, Raimon Vidal's contemporary, is the troubadour whose didacticism is simultaneously exploited and masked in *So fo*. "Tals vai mon chan enqueren" (406.42) is quoted by both the knight and the first *domna* at the point where the *domna*, seeing the knight's reputation soar, regrets her earlier indifference and tries to win him back (Appendix 5, *So fo* quotations 25 and 26). The knight defends himself against the lady's reproaches by countering that she dismissed *him*, he did not abandon *her*. In response, the *domna* claims she was putting his patience to the test and he failed; she backs her claim with stanza V:

> Mas si fossetz tan ensenhatz
> ni tan cortes ni tans vassalhs,
> —aisi com dis en Miravalhs—
> degratz entendre [joy][14] valen:
> "Greu pot aver jauzimen
> en dreg d'amor drut biays

> qui er se det et huey s'estrays.
> Mas qui ben ser et aten
> e sap selar la folia,
> sos pros en ai' e·ls enbria,
> ans que·ls tortz sidons aplanh,
> aquel es d'amor companh."
> (So fo, 690–701)

But if, as my lord of Miraval said, you had been well-bred, courtly, and valiant enough, then you could have expected a worthy joy: "An inconstant lover who gives himself one day and takes himself off the next is hardly going to gain enjoyment in love; but one who is good at serving and being attentive and can keep his impulsiveness under control, may he get what he wants and more, even before his lady softens her injustice toward him, for such a man is love's companion."

The knight is unconcerned by her intended rebuke because he is now committed to the *donzela*. So he sarcastically compliments the *domna* on her choice of author and quotes another stanza (stanza IV) from the same song:

> Avetz trobat reyre cosselh,
> c'anc mentre·us fuy en apparelh
> aital vos no·m volgues amar;
> per qu'aiso vos no·m vuelh tornar,
> ans faray so que·l meteys dis
> (en Miravalhs!), que tan fon fis
> e francx et de bon chauzimen:
>   "pus midons m'a en coven
>   c'autr' amic non am ni bays,
>   ja Dieu no·m sia verays
>   si ja per nulh' autra·l men."
> (So fo, 705–15)

You have found precious counsel, given that while I was in a similar situation vis-à-vis yourself, you chose not to love me! That is why I don't want to come back to you. Instead I will do what he himself— my lord Miraval—said, who was so true, noble, and discerning: "Since my lady has promised not to love or kiss another lover, may God not be true to me if I betray her with any other woman."

This marks his definitive rupture with the lady. Each, then, is using Miraval's song to contrary effect: the lady to recommend patient loyalty to her, the knight to congratulate himself on having found love elsewhere.

Such a split in the song's reception is warned of in its opening lines:

Tals vai mon chan enqueren
per so qu'en s'emble plus guays
que d'autre part s'irays
quan au mos digz e·ls enten;
tals n'i a per gelozia,
e drut que no segon via
que a bon' amor s'atanh
conosc que meinhs son estranh.
(Song 23, 1–8)

There are some who seek out my song intending to go away cheered by it but instead leave upset when they hear and pay attention to my words. In some cases the problem is their jealousy; in others, they are not following the right path to good love, and these I would see as less deviant.

According to circumstances, then, Miraval's song will strike its audience differently; only those with their hearts properly attuned to *bon' amor* will rejoice at his words. In the next stanza he identifies ladies in particular as needing his instruction (11–12). Stanza III then warns them not to be swayed from sound judgment of potential lovers:

Que ja per chastiamen
neguna son miels non lays;
pus conoys quals es savays
o quals es pros issamen,
quals es fis ni quals gualia
e s'adoncs so miels non tria,
Dieu li do so don se planh,
dona, pus sa valor franh.
(Song 23, 17–24)

For let no *domna* leave what is best as a result of the admonitions of others. Once she recognizes what is base and, likewise, what is meritorious, which man is sincere and which deceiving, then if she doesn't choose what is best may God reward her in a way she will regret.

These three stanzas show that, as with the quotation from Giraut's "Per solatz" in *Abril issia*, what is omitted from Raimon de Miraval's song is as important for *So fo* as what is quoted. In the initial context, when the *domna* introduces the song in a bid to win back the knight but is, instead, crushed by him, the omissions provide a rationale for her failure (indeed, she seems unaware that the very lines she quotes in her defense censure women's waywardness [*So fo*, 700]). The *domna* may be counted among those who, the song predicts, will suffer distress from hearing it, since her jealousy toward the *donzela* makes her one of the worst listeners of all (stanza I). As a woman she needs teaching anyway (stanza II); and so she is punished for not recognizing or rewarding a true admirer (stanza III).

Uc's judgment will suggest that the knight and the second *domna* too have strayed from what stanza I calls the "right path." Uc rules that a lover should not fail in constancy to his lady (compare stanza V, quoted by the first *domna*); and that since the knight did not merit the second *domna*'s fidelity she must give him up. The *novas* directs Miraval's *ensenhamen* (teaching) against the second *domna* even more than the first, since she ends up with nothing. As a woman she has been a *donzela*, a wife, and the knight's lady, but none of these female identities secures her lasting success. Although she controls the major developments of the plot as she switches from (1) adviser to the knight to (2) intercessor with the first lady to (3) seducer of the knight and finally (4) rival to the first lady, all her initiatives are undone and her intentions frustrated. Since she justifies each of her successive roles with quotations from the troubadours, her understanding of their poetry is shown up as defective. The crucial opening stanzas of Raimon de Miraval's "Tals vai," which predict the song's misinterpretation and denounce women listeners in particular, may be omitted from the text of the *novas*, but they are resoundingly present in the verdicts it reaches.[15]

As with the quotation from "Per solatz" in *Abril issia*, then, the quotations from "Tals vai" in *So fo* are part of Raimon Vidal's wider strategy to exploit the knowledge in and of the unquoted portions of Miraval's song. In both *novas*, sentiments and quotations are caught up in an intricate web of intersubjective interactions in the course of which knowledge is remembered, forgotten, affirmed, disavowed, assimilated, displaced, produced, or found wanting. In the case of Giraut's "Per solatz," the process broadly affirms the narrator's credentials, and thereby Raimon Vidal's. In the case of Raimon de Miraval's "Tals vai," it seems rather to censure fictional characters, primarily female consumers of troubadour lyric from the Limousin who, for want of memory and connoisseurship, contribute to poetry's decline. My final example concerns a listener of a different order: the patron.[16]

Bertran de Born's "S'abrils e fuoillas e flors" (80.38) and the Patron's Connoisseurship

Uc de Mataplana's judgment in the *R* version of *So fo* has been interpreted by Field as grounds for seeing the *novas* as resulting from two stages of composition, one by Miraval and the other by Raimon Vidal. *So fo* seems to be related to a group of satirical exchanges between Uc de Mataplana and Raimon de Miraval, which begins when Uc criticizes the troubadour for being unfaithful to his wife, and Miraval responds in a *contrafactum* (formal imitation), accusing Uc of being "totz moilleratz" (totally married) and too Catalan to interfere (!).[17] Field rightly emphasizes that Uc upholds fidelity to one's original partner in both the poetic exchange and the *novas*. It is less clear why he would conclude that the composition of *So fo* echoes that of the poetic exchanges, with Miraval responsible for the core of both. Miraval's situation in the songs is moreover not analogous to that of the knight in the *novas*, since the knight is not married. I believe Uc's verdict owes more to "S'abrils e fuoillas e flors" (80.38) than to his own exchange with Raimon de Miraval, and that the important role of Bertran's song in both *novas* confirms the hand of Raimon Vidal. In each, the song is quoted by a prominent patron and amateur poet, Dalfi d'Alvernha in *Abril issia* and Uc de Mataplana in *So fo*. And like the other examples discussed here, elements of the song persist in both *novas* outside the words that are actually quoted. This combination of absence and presence provokes questions about the location of knowledge that are particularly acute for figures whose position would appear ideally to constitute them as "subjects supposed to know" (see Introduction for this term).

In *Abril issia*, four lines of Bertran's "S'abrils e fuoillas e flors" (Gouiran edition, Song 8, 85–88)[18] are placed in the mouth of Dalfi whose words are then transmitted by the *joglar* to the older poet who subsequently, in his role of narrator, recalls them to the audience. (This constant filtering of knowledge through a variety of personal and temporal perspectives is typical of the *novas*; their multiple embeddings confirm the indissolubility of knowledge from memory but leave the effectiveness of its transmission in doubt.) Dalfi quotes the lines as he discourses, by way of an anecdote about a Moorish sultan, on the good old days when merit was rewarded:

> Be fazian so qu'en Bertrans
> del Born dis en .i. sirventes
> a far *ricx homes* pus *cortes*
> e pus *francx* et pus *donadors*,
> que sian *ses tortz faire*, elitz,
> e adretz e *francx e chauzitz*:
>   "Ad aiso fon pretz establitz
>   c'om guerrejes, e so fortmens
>   et a caresma et avens
>   e fezes soudadiers manens."
>   (*Abril issia*, 462–71)

They did indeed what Bertran de Born said in one of his *sirventes* to make *powerful men* more *courtly*, *noble*, and *liberal with their gifts*, so that *without committing injustic*e they would be outstanding, skill-ful, *noble*, and *discerning*: "For this purpose valor was established: that one should make war, and do so vigorously, in both Lent and Advent, and make mercenaries rich."

Field's observation that the lines Dalfi quotes are much less relevant to his position than words and expressions from earlier in the same song, is borne out by a comparison between this passage from the *novas* and Bertran's entire stanza. Although Dalfi quotes only its last four lines, the sense of the preced-ing lines together with much of their phraseology have saturated his speech. The words and phrases in italics are the same in both Dalfi's pronouncements and Bertran's stanza:

> *Ric home*, vuelh qu'ab amors
> sapchon cavalliers aver
> e que·ls sapchon retener
> ab befag et ab honors
> e c'om los truep *ses tort faire*,

francx e cortes e chautitz
e larcx e bos *donadors,*
qu'aissi fon pretz establitz
qu'om guerreyes ab torneys
e Quaresmes et Avens
fesson soudadiers manens.

> (Song 8, 78–88)

I wish that *powerful men* knew how to have knights through giving them their love, and how to keep them through giving them lands and benefits, so that we could find them *noble, courtly, and discerning*, generous and *liberal with their gifts, without committing injustice,* for this is how merit was established: by making war in battles, while [even] Lent and Advent made mercenaries rich.

They confirm that Raimon Vidal does not necessarily quote those parts of his source texts that have most informed his own; he both remembers and forgets the knowledge they contain, both attributing it to an *auctor* and retaining it for himself.

Dalfi's quotation also poses textual problems, as witness the divergences between Bertran's lines as quoted in *Abril issia*, 468–71 and in Gérard Gouiran's edition. In Gouiran, Bertran is advocating that magnates should inspire fidelity in their mercenaries first by their valor in war, and then by continuing to pay them even when the Peace of God prevents them from fighting. Gouiran is skeptical about the meaning imputed to Bertran in *Abril issia*: "Raimon Vidal's text," he says, "would have us believe that Bertran is calling on the *rics omes* to make war in Lent and Advent, that is to say, during the periods proscribed by the Peace of God."[19] Is the quotation placed in the mouth of Dalfi d'Alvernha a deliberate distortion of the original text?[20] If so, Bertran's voice is buried so deep in the embedded layers of *Abril issia* that it is difficult to assess the significance of the distortion. Dalfi quotes Bertran to the *joglar*, the *joglar* repeats Dalfi's words to the narrator, and then he narrates the *joglar*'s anecdote to us. Are we to surmise that Dalfi misunderstood Bertran and thought he was recommending warmongering despite the Peace of God, or that the *joglar* misrepresents Dalfi, or that the older poet misheard what the *joglar* said? Has a copyist intervened in this flawed chain of transmission to set the record wrong? The point, in any case, is that in the intersubjective maze of this text, the seemingly remembered lines of Bertran's text may well misrepresent his likely meaning whereas the ostensibly forgotten but in fact repeated ones, which form the aura of the quotation, more truly convey his thought, since they call on powerful men to act generously and eschew injustice. In other words, what seems to have been remembered contains an element of forgetting, whereas what seems to have been forgotten persists as a true memory. There is ample scope for misprision in the interaction between *joglar* and patron.

Bertran's song is cited again at the end of the *R* version of *So fo e·l tems*. This scene is a *mise en abyme* of the entire work since the ladies' dealings with the knight are referred to Uc, in the narrator's presence, by a *joglar* who describes his account as a *novas* (1141). After deliberating, Uc determines that the *donzela* behaved well in taking care of the knight but the time now has come for her to give him up.

> Et enquer may li membrara
> si bona via vol seguir,
> so qu'en Bertran dis al partir
> de lay on fon gent aculhitz:
> > "E sel que manten faizitz,
> > per honor de si meteys,
> > e·n fa bons acordamens,
> > absol los afizamens."
> . . . .[21]
> a dona qu'en pren autr' amic;
> per qu·l prec e·l cosselh e dic:
> absolva·l cavayer ades.
> > (*So fo*, *R* text, 1403–14)

And now she [the former *donzela*] will remember, if she wishes to follow the right path, what Bertran [de Born] said when departing from the place where he had been so well received: "And she who supports exiles for the sake of her own honor enables good reconciliations to be reached and annuls the oaths that bound them." [It appears a deficit and a lack of sense] in a lady who takes another person's *amic*; so let her release the knight at once.

As with Dalfi's quotation from this same song, though for different reasons, Uc's meaning is somewhat opaque; again we need to look at the excerpt in context to grasp its meaning. Here, in stanza II of "S'abrils," Bertran assures his lady that, although he has been received by another, he is not unfaithful; he affirms his devotion and leaves his temporary home. The lines "and she who supports an exile . . ." refer to the way a second lady, who took him in when he was estranged ("exiled") from his first lady, now releases him from any commitment so that he can be reconciled with the first lady. (This stanza forms the basis of the subsequent *razo* to the song, which is discussed in Chapter 3.)

Uc's verdict that the knight should leave the former *donzela* and be reconciled with the first *domna* matches Bertran's return to his original lady.[22] Correspondingly the knight's situation in the *novas* resembles Bertran's tug of love between two *domnas* more than it does the scenario of the Uc-Miraval exchanges in which Miraval is advised to return to the wife he had abandoned. Indeed, strategically positioned as the final quotation in *So fo*, "S'abrils" could be seen as resuming the whole *R* version of this *novas*, much as Giraut de Bornelh's "Per solatz," the inaugural quotation in *Abril issia*, is the matrix from which that whole *novas* emerges. And as with "Per solatz," the excerpt of Bertran de Born that is quoted by Uc demands excellent recall of the rest of the song if its significance is to be appreciated. This example confirms that what is at stake in Raimon Vidal's use of quotations is not just what knowledge is transmitted by the troubadours, but what knowledge other people—and not just those who quote them—have of their poems.

The reason why Uc's quotation is opaque is therefore unlike the difficulty surrounding Dalfi's quotation of the same poem. Dalfi is associated (though perhaps not by his own fault) with a likely misquotation that requires independent knowledge of the song to rectify. Uc relies on independent knowledge of the song to confirm that the use he has made of it, though allusive, is spot on. Dalfi and the young *joglar* combine to get Bertran wrong, whereas Raimon Vidal and Uc together demonstrate their expertise in getting him right. As poet-patrons, Dalfi and Uc may both be supposed to be connoisseurs of troubadour lyrics, but Uc emerges with greater credit. Raimon Vidal endorses the present and its ongoing transactions with troubadour culture. The role of memory is not to preserve but to improve upon the potentially flawed knowledge of the past. More especially, Raimon Vidal confirms Catalan connoisseurship and the sense that, in the more discerning Catalan courts, the future of the Occitan lyric is in safe hands.

## CHAPTER 3

Starting Afresh with Quotation
in the *Vidas* and *Razos*

By 1219 Uc de Saint Circ, troubadour and scholar, had left his home in the Quercy to live in the Marca Treviziana in the north of the Veneto. Although he may have paid several visits to the Midi over the next decades, he remained active mainly in the north of Italy and was last heard of there in 1257.[1]

It is fair to say that no one cared much about Uc's whereabouts until recent scholarship revealed the importance of his Italian activity. His forty-four or so songs of various genres had never struck anyone as better than stilted, and he was otherwise known only for putting his name to a few prose biographies.[2] But studying the transmission of the troubadours in Italy has resulted in Uc becoming a magnetic figure to whom ever more texts can be attached and ever more achievements credited. Many if not all of what are termed *vidas* (lives) and *razos* (expositions)[3] of the troubadours are now ascribed to him, he is believed to have compiled the song collection drawn on by the oldest surviving *chansonnier* (*Da*, 1254), he is in contention for most of the contents of another (*H*, also third quarter of the thirteenth century), and he is sometimes attributed with the authorship of the *Donatz proensals* of about 1240, a grammatical treatise ascribed to Uc Faidit, or "Uc in exile."[4] In short Uc de Saint Circ is now seen as almost single-handedly responsible for creating the paradigms for the written reception of the Occitan lyric in Italy and thus as the inventor of "the troubadours" as we now know them.[5]

This chapter is about the way quotations are used in *vidas* and *razos*— short prose biographical works that Uc inaugurated even if he did not write them all and that recount the circumstances behind the composition of songs

and/or the lives of individual poets. These forms met with international success, since though the majority of *chansonniers* that contain them are of Italian origin, they are also found in some Iberian and Occitan manuscripts;[6]
they continue to thrive over time, giving rise to distinctive developments in
later manuscripts such as *P* and *N²*. Uc is believed to have composed his inaugural cycle of over twenty *razos* for Bertran de Born's political songs either
just before or shortly after his first arrival in Italy in 1219.[7] His other *razos*
followed in the period circa 1227–30, while his *vidas* date to the 1220s generally. Both forms are related to Latin introductions to the lives and works of
Latin authors (*accessus ad auctores*) that were used in grammar teaching in
medieval schools, since "grammar is not simply a matter of learning how to
write and speak well . . . ; it also has as its proper task the explication and
study of the authors" (Thierry of Chartres).[8] They are thus part of the same
impulse as Raimon Vidal's *Razos de trobar* and subsequent treatises to grammaticalize (or make more like Latin) the language of troubadour poetry.

Uc de Saint Circ's treatment of this poetry nevertheless differs from
Raimon Vidal's. *Abril issia* is about the hunt for audiences capable of appreciating troubadour songs in performance. *So fo* presents local courts peopled by
troubadour aficionados who trade quotations in a kind of courtly game. The
Razos de trobar seems calculated to encourage such enthusiasts and refine their
tastes. Raimon Vidal represents knowledge as oral and memorial rather than
as bookish. Even though Uc de Saint Circ's biographies may originally have
been intended for live performance alongside songs, his context is more
avowedly writerly than Raimon Vidal's. The *Donatz proensals* (supposing he
wrote it) is a more technical manual than those of the Vidal tradition and,
once equipped with a Latin interlinear translation, could only have been sat-
isfactorily accessed in written form. It might have been used for practical,
writing-related purposes, for example, as a bilingual dictionary.[9] If not under
Uc de Saint Circ's direction, at least in the same milieu, the early troubadour
chansonniers evolve a complex *ordinatio* that acts as an archival supplement
to memory. As forms of commentary, *vidas* and *razos* belong together with
other core scholastic activities of copying and compiling that combine to
preserve troubadour songs in writing for posterity. Moreover they overlap in
interesting ways with *chansonnier* rubrics and indices to signpost how a
manuscript's contents are organized, with the result that their status hovers
between that of text and paratext. A particularly concrete instance of this
overlap is that the biographies predominantly quote the incipits of songs, the

very lines most likely to feature in indices or rubrics. This chapter concentrates on incipital quotations, especially in relation to the other devices of inauguration that accompany the onset of the troubadours' written transmission, relating them to the love of beginnings discussed in my introduction.

Vida, Razo, and Quotation

Although they are authentic Occitan words, *vida* and *razo* have become generic labels only in modern usage. The distinction between the two is not hard and fast, and a significant number of biographical texts are borderline cases that could belong in either (or neither) category.[10]

Quotations, however, do offer a way of differentiating the commonest forms of these two narrative types.[11] In the edition of the prose biographies by Jean Boutière and A. H. Schutz, texts classed as *razos* quote at least the opening line of the song they explain, usually at the end of the narrative.[12] They may additionally quote a whole skein of excerpts linking together a group of songs into a narrative cycle.[13] Others, notably the *razos* contained in *chansonnier H*, embed *coblas* that may be shortened versions of songs we have lost (for example, that of Tibors), or may be freestanding *coblas* (like those in the exchanges involving Dalfi d'Alvernha). Since it is impossible to distinguish between isolated *coblas* and excerpted *coblas*, all the *coblas* embedded in *razos* are included in Appendix 1, where they account for all of the quotations from women troubadours.[14]

By contrast, only nine of the hundred or so texts that Boutière and Schutz label *vidas* contain quotation. Most are lives of prominent twelfth-century poets: Arnaut Daniel, Arnaut de Maruelh, Bernart de Ventadorn (version B, found only in the very late manuscript N^2), Marcabru (version A), Peire d'Alvernha, Peire Rogier, and Raimbaut d'Aurenga (this last only with a so far unidentified quotation, likewise in N^2).[15] To have a *vida* containing quotation(s) is thus an unusual distinction for a poet. Since *accessus* to Ovid were more likely to incorporate quotations from the works they introduce than those to other *auctores*, it is seemingly on them that the *vidas* containing quotations are most closely modeled, implying the quasi-Ovidian status of the troubadours concerned.[16] Unlike with *razos*, not all the quotations in *vidas* are incipits; they can be *tornadas* (Arnaut Daniel) or late stanzas (Marcabru) or indeed extracts from different troubadours (Bernart de Ventadorn, in whose *vida* the poets quoted are Peire d'Alvernha, Arnaut de Maruelh and Gui d'Ussel). Another formal difference is that quotations in *vidas* do not typically occur at the very end of the prose text but are embedded in the middle of the narrative.

Within *chansonnier* manuscripts, the quotations in these biographical texts can be seen as distinguishing them generically in another way. When the passage quoted is from an immediately adjacent lyric, and serves to key the prose exposition to it, we have the classic *razo* pattern that is standard in the thirteenth-century *chansonniers I* and *K*, and in the Bertran de Born section of *F*. Conversely, where a biographical text contains quotations that are not necessarily from an adjacent lyric, and that serve to introduce a selection of lyrics by an individual troubadour rather than one lyric in particular, it makes more sense to see the text as a *vida*. This usage is found in *vidas* in *ABIK*, and in *a*[1], a late paper copy of an early, probably thirteenth-century *chansonnier*. The biography of Raimon Jordan is a *vida* in this sense in *ABIK*, even though it is classed as a *razo* by Boutière and Schutz.[17] Conversely, what Boutière and Schutz present as the *vida* of Bertolome Zorzi functions as a *razo* in *IK* since it is placed between the two songs, one by Bertolome (74.10) and the other by Bonifaci Calvo (101.7), of which it quotes both incipits.[18]

Quotation, from this perspective, would be an indicator less of the narrative form of the prose text than of its relationship to its surroundings in the *chansonnier*; it draws attention to the ambiguous status of the biographies as between texts and paratexts. The difference between *vidas* and *razos* would then relate to their different function in a manuscript's *ordinatio*, *vidas* signaling the start of major sections, *razos* having the lowlier role of accompanying particular texts, though in the capacity of being themselves texts too. Only in some later, fourteenth-century manuscripts such as *EPR* are biographical texts found grouped together apart from songs, and thus in another relation to the codex entirely.[19] The most remarkable arrangement is that of *N*[2]. Here the *vidas* and *razos* of individual poets are compiled to form biographical sequences into which are intercalated lists of incipits of the songs by the troubadour in question. The blurring between quotation, index, and rubric is here complete.

We cannot know how Uc envisaged the layout of his biographical works, or indeed if he anticipated their being incorporated into large codices, because only one *chansonnier* survives that dates to his lifetime and it contains no biographies.[20] But we might take the format of *chansonniers I* and *K* as the best available evidence of early practice, if not of Uc's actual intentions. These two closely related manuscripts were both copied in the Veneto in the third or fourth quarter of the thirteenth century. They are among the oldest song-books to contain biographical texts; they preserve the largest number of them of any *chansonniers*; and their text of the Bertran de Born *razos* is now thought to be the closest to Uc's original.[21] Boutière and Schutz edit biographical texts from *I* wherever possible.[22] In his edition of Bertran de Born, Gouiran favors the transmission of *K* especially. *I* and *K* are thus obvious choices for study.[23]

These *chansonniers* visibly inscribe a difference between *vidas* and *razos*. *Razos* are transcribed like any other text in ordinary dark ink, whereas *vidas* are written in red. *Vidas* thereby appear as a kind of expanded rubric or title, but *razos* are introduced by rubrics of their own. In both *I* and *K*, the Bertran de Born section begins: "from here on, those *sirventes* of Bertran de Born that have *razos* are copied, the *sirventes* and then the *razo*, one after the other" (de ci en auan son escrit del siruentez den bertran de born lo cals an la rason per qual fon faitz lo siruentes e la rason. lun apres lautre).[24] In the index of *K*, though not of *I*, the incipits of *razos* are listed alongside those of the songs; *vidas* are not indexed in either manuscript. It seems that in *I*, and even more in *K*, *razos* have the status of texts but *vidas*, being part of the system for signposting texts, are paratexts.[25] On the other hand the fact that the quota-tions in *razos* are sometimes copied in red makes them look like a rubric to the songs they accompany.

This interplay between quotation, rubric, and index in the *IK vidas* and *razos* draws attention to the proximity between quoting and other forms of copying. The following reflections will be guided by their common element, the incipit, and the act of symbolic inauguration and thus of the potential for change that it represents (see Introduction).

The Love of Beginnings in *I* and *K*

In oral performance, nearly all of the significant effects of troubadour song are clustered around endings. The rhyme scheme is borne by the ends of lines and frequently emphasized by musical settings more likely to ornament the conclusion of a phrase than its beginning. The sequence of rhyme words will often provide a key to the song's substance, a rapid mapping of its contents, sometimes a more profound indication of its import. The final full stanza usually contains a song's most explicit appeal to its addressee, while *tornadas*

are the likeliest source of information about its authorship and historical audience. All this concentration of interest on endings is put into reverse by the
veritable fanfare of beginnings that marks the transition to writing.

In *I* and *K* in particular, disposition, design, and color combine to front-
load effects of all kinds. The opening folios of both *chansonniers* present long
tables of incipits, which act as lists of contents for the various sections of each
codex. These tables institutionalize the beginning as the principle of organization and retrieval of the volumes' contents. The first index heading in *I* is
typical of the wording of the others, including those in *K*: "From here on are
written the beginnings of the songs that are in this book" (Dissi enauan son
escrig li comenzamen de las cansos qui son en aquest liure). The incipits follow in ordinary ink, prefaced by the names of the troubadours in red. The
promotion to quasi-technical status of the Occitan word *comenzamen* (beginning) is striking; the equivalent in the lists of incipits in *D* is the Latin
inceptiones.[26]

Both *I* and *K* open with a large collection of *cansos*, putting the most
prestigious genre first. Troubadours are ordered at least partly in descending
order of importance; in both, the first twelve are Peire d'Alvernha, Peire Rogier, Giraut de Bornelh, Bernart de Ventadorn, Gaucelm Faidit, Peire Vidal,
Arnaut de Maruelh, Perdigon, Aimeric de Peguilhan, Peirol, Folquet de
Marselha, and Arnaut Daniel.[27] The *canso* selection for each author of any
distinction is prefaced by a *vida* copied in red ink, which thus appears as an
extended form of prefatory rubric. After each *vida*, the enlarged initial at the
start of the opening song contains an author portrait, larger in *K* than in *I*.[28]
Each song is prefaced by the poet's name, in red, together with a numeral
indicating its position in that section. With all this information flashed up
above the start of the song there is no need to scour the *tornada* for clues to
authorship. The poems are copied so as to fill out the two columns per page
of the writing block, the ends of the verses being marked only by a discreet
punctus; the rhyme scheme having become invisible, what stand out instead
are the enlarged initials at the beginning of each stanza. The *canso* section in
I and *K* is followed with one of dialogue poems where many of the same troubadours resurface with further marks of beginnings in the form of rubrics,
new numbering, and a sprinkling of new *vidas*. Afterward comes the least
valued genre of the three, the *sirventes*, where the *razos* for Bertran de Born
appear.

The concerted privileging of beginnings in *I* and *K* is overwhelming. It is
as though the first editors and scribes were aware of inaugurating a new phase

in the history of troubadour song, one where beginning a song meant not beginning to sing it, as it does in countless troubadour exordia, but beginning
to write it down—beginning, that is, to *copy* it.[29] This very act of copying, of
course, is profoundly transformative;[30] and one of its chief sites of change is
the incipit.

Incipital quotation of troubadour songs is introduced into Occitan by
Raimon Vidal de Besalú in the *Razos de trobar* and used with increasing
regularity in later grammars. As we saw in Chapter 1, one of its functions is
to create an aura of authority for the grammarian, effectively promoting him
to a subject supposed to know. Transposing to the vernacular the usage of the
Latin schoolroom, it also helps to conjure into existence the troubadours'
"grammaticality." Only exceptionally quoted in other lyrics (see Chapter 7),
incipits are not quoted in Occitan works that stage speech. Characters in
novas may argue over the meaning of an individual song, as do Matfre and
his interlocutors in the *Breviari d'amor*, but they never identify it by its opening line, preferring periphrases such as "and he himself says in the same
song."[31] Still less will they evoke a significant passage such as a *cobla* by means
of its opening words, as happens in *H* (see Chapter 4). Although quotations
in the *novas*, and to some extent the *Breviari*, test recognition of what is not
quoted, they do not do so using the very particular synecdoche that is the
incipit.

It is in the written environment of songbooks and in their commitment
to writing, copying, and hence repeating, that incipital quotation thrives.
The convergence between index, rubric, quotation, and copy as creatures of
writing raises the specter of indefinite iterability evoked by Derrida in the
essay already quoted in my introduction: "Every sign . . . can be quoted, put
between quotation marks; in so doing it can break with every given context."[32] However, as Derrida continues, reiteration can be inherently transformative, "engendering," as he puts it, "an infinity of new contexts." *Chansonnier*
manuscripts might be thought the ideal medium to resolve this challenge, on
the assumption that these quotations are truncated forms of texts that it is
the codex's remit to provide elsewhere copied in full. A rubric consisting of
an incipit may directly preface an *in extenso* copy. Or an effective retrieval
system in the form of an index of incipits may prove the exact counterpart to
the puzzle of incipital quotation, and its prospective solution. However, as
pointed out in my introduction, not all incipits are expanded in the texts that
contain them (notably those in the biographical sequences in *chansonnier N²*,
and the Garin d'Apchier *razo*). The last sections of this chapter examine the

challenge and the impetus to transformation posed by incipital quotations in
the *IK vidas* and *razos*.

Quotations in the *IK* Bertran de Born *Razos*

The Bertran de Born *razos* in *I* and *K* usually contain only one quotation, the
incipit of the song they explicate. Often it is distinguished from the text by
being copied in red ink or prefaced by an initial paraph. This makes it in-
stantly obvious that the quotation has a different status from the surrounding
prose: it represents the commentator's object, a discourse he will explicate
with discourse of his own. Whereas, as we will see, in the *vidas* the quotations are subsumed into the same discourse as the biographer's, in the *razos*
the discourse of the commentator remains distinct from that which is com-
mentated on.

When the quotation is in red at the very end of the *razo*, it also looks like
a rubric flashing up the incipit-as-title of the *sirventes* to which it relates, and
this is indeed how it functions in *F*. This impression is misleading, however,
in *I* and *K*, since both of these (alone among *chansonniers*) place each *razo*
after the *sirventes* it comments on, not before; the incipit is the rubric not of
the song following, but of the one that precedes. In light of both manuscripts' emphasis on inauguration, *I* and *K* present the song as initiating the
commentary, not the other way around; the concluding quotation operates
retrospectively, challenging readers to recall what they have just read. I say
"recall," but "reconstruct" or even "reinterpret" might be more accurate since,
with their understanding of the song shaped by the commentary, they may
rather be supposed to recover it in an altered form. This is a clear instance
where incipital quotation involves a break that may be followed by a change:
after reading the *razo*, and then looping back to the song, its words no longer
mean the same, even when repeated verbatim. In the course of this return,
what Compagnon calls, by analogy with the "work of mourning," "the work
of quotation" takes effect. As a form of beginning, the incipital quotation
provokes the whole song to begin again and thus to begin otherwise. To quote
Saïd once more, "Beginnings inaugurate a deliberately *other* production of
meaning" (*Beginnings*, 13).

Bertran's *razos* situate him among the most blue-blooded and red-handed
in the land, while at the same time expanding into a series of novelettes his
hints at sexual imbroglios. These aspects combine in the *razo* to "Rassa, tan

creis" (80.37), which imagines Richard Lionheart, Geoffrey of Brittany, and Alfonso of Aragon as Bertran's rivals in his love affair with Maheut de Montaignac. In both *I* and *K* the stanza quoted from the song in the middle of the *razo* is copied in red, as is the final incipit. The *razo* to "S'abrils e fuoillas e flors" (80.38), a song quoted by Raimon Vidal in both *novas* discussed in Chapter 2, interprets it as another chapter in Bertran's liaison with the same Maheut, creating a detailed scenario involving two other women to whose existence the song gives little or no clue. As Bertran's political reflections play no part in this exposition, the *razo* is closer to Uc de Mataplana's treatment of the song in *So fo* (where it is understood as resolving a love triangle) than to Dalfi's in *Abril issia* (which recognizes its discourse as political even if it appears to misrepresent it). The *razo*, that is, does not so much "explain" the song as enter into contention for its interpretation. The incipit (flagged by a paraph but not a change of ink in *K*, and not marked at all in *I*) directs its readers to a quite specific reconstruction of its meaning.

Quotations in the *Vidas* in *IK*

The *vidas* in the *IK canso* section contribute to these codices' general inflation of beginnings. Any troubadour worthy of consideration is afforded a *vida*, which, copied in red ink, appears as an extended form of introductory rubric.[33] That the *vidas'* presence has more to do with inaugurating a selection than with glorifying or explicating authorship as such is indicated by the fact that both codices are primarily organized by genre, not by author. Moreover, repetition of the same format to introduce all the troubadours insinuates similarity rather than difference between them, the more as the narrative pattern of each *vida* is quite predictable.

Four *vidas* among those for the first twelve troubadours in the *canso* section of *I* and *K* contain quotations: those of Peire d'Alvernha (two quotations), Peire Rogier, Arnaut de Maruelh, and Arnaut Daniel (one apiece).[34] There is thus a noticeable concentration of quotations at the beginning of both codices, an inevitable consequence of the fact that they accord priority to the more distinguished early troubadours whose *vidas* are most likely to adopt what has been identified (see above) as an Ovidian model. All four troubadours dignified in this way were clerics at some stage of their careers; perhaps this education helps to qualify them for the status of *poeta*. Quotations in three of these four *vidas* are from the openings of songs. The accumulation of markers of inauguration in *I* and *K* is thus compounded, near the beginning of both codices, by the quotation of beginnings. Except for Arnaut Daniel's, none of the *vidas* is followed immediately by the song(s) from which it quotes; as with the *razos* a pause is marked between quotation and (the copy of the) song. Moreover, Arnaut Daniel's *vida* builds in a pause too, though by different means since it quotes the *tornada* of the song following (see Chapter 9 for discussion of this quotation).

Beginning, rupture, and change are clearly at issue in the incipit quoted in the *vida* to Arnaut de Maruelh. We learn that Arnaut was in love with the wife of the count of Béziers. He would read aloud to her but could not admit to authorship of his songs because he was afraid to declare his love.[35]

> Mas si avenc c'amors lo forsa tant qu'el fetz una canson, la quals co-mensa:
>
> [30.15]   La franca captenensa.
>
> Et en aquesta canson el li descobri l'amor qu'el li avia. E la comtessa no·l esquiva, ans entendet sos precs e los receput e los grazi. (*Biographies*, VII, 32)

> But then it happened that love overwhelms him so forcefully that he composed a song which begins "The noble demeanor." And in this song he disclosed to her the love he had for her. And the countess does not refuse him (it) but rather heeded his (its) prayers and received and welcomed them.

A copy of "La franca captenensa" follows later, coming second (*I*) or third (*K*) in the selection of Arnaut's songs, but for now readers have only its opening line to go on, barely amplified from its appearance in the index a few folios earlier. As in the index, the phrase "una canson, la quals comensa" posits the incipit as a synecdoche for the whole; readers are challenged to recognize the song and if possible supply its contents from memory.[36] In case they cannot do this, or until they reach the full copy, they have as a mysterious surrogate the interpretation marvelously performed on their behalf by the countess. The biographer does not specify what this interpretation is, saying merely that the song uncovered (*descobri*) what was hitherto hidden: an act of disclosure that, from the point of view of a reader equipped only with the incipit, is actually only a further act of concealment. As the countess was the original target of Arnaut's extreme discretion, the fact that she perceives the song's meaning, while the *vida*'s readers remain in the dark, colors her portrayal; the "noble" or "generous and open" (*franc*) character attributed to her in the incipit is enhanced by her virtuosity. Readers are maneuvered into regarding her as the "subject supposed to know" the song's true content.

An aspect that may be transformed by the countess's reception is the song's second stanza, which in R. C. Johnston's edition reads:

> Ses geing e ses faillensa
> vos am, e ses cor var,
> al plus c'om pot pensar;
> d'aitan vos puosc forsar
> part vostres mandamens.
> Ai! dompna cui desir,
> si conoissetz ni·us par
> que sia faillimens
> car vos sui benvolens,
> sofretz m'aquest falhir.
> (Song 3, 11–20)

> I love you without deceit or wrongdoing and with an unswerving heart, the most one can imagine; on this account, I am capable of forcing you beyond what you command. Ah lady whom I desire, if you recognize or if it seems to you that it is a failing in me to be so fond of you, allow me this failing.

As Johnston's embarrassed note confesses, it is hard not to understand this stanza as Arnaut fantasizing about forcing himself sexually on his lady and asking her to condone his fantasy. The problematic line 14 containing the verb *forsar* (coerce, rape) is anticipated in the lead-up to the quotation in the *vida*. The biographer explains Arnaut's inspiration using the same verb ("amors la forsa tan," "love impels him"), but the force in question has become Arnaut's compulsion to compose the song, declare his love, and so make the moment of disclosure inevitable. Disguising rape behind the persuasions of poetry may, indeed, be the biographer's way of gesturing toward this uncharacteristically Ovidian moment in Arnaut de Maruelh's otherwise genteel corpus. The countess's accommodating reception could then be interpreted precisely as her condoning his violent desires—an "open and generous" reaction in the circumstances—again, perhaps as an expression of Ovidian cynicism on the biographer's part. Alternatively, the application of the word *forsa* to poetic energy may just be a way of preemptively eliminating the issue of rape. This is certainly what happens when this song is quoted elsewhere: the problematic stanza consistently disappears in favor of other preoccupations (see Chapter 4). As with the *razos*, the separation between the *vida* and the poem creates room for the hesitations and suppositions generated by the incipit to transform reception of the song concerned so that, when its copy begins, it also starts afresh.

In the opening *vida*, the very first quotation in *IK* presents the incipit in its most mysterious guise. We learn of Peire d'Alvernha that

> trobet ben e cantet ben, e fo lo premiers bons trobaire que fon outra mon et aquel que fez los meillors sons de vers que anc fosson faichs:
> [323.15]   De josta·ls breus jorns e·ls loncs sers.
> Canson no fetz, qe non era adoncs negus cantars appellatz cansos, mas vers. (*Biographies*, XXXIX, 263)

> he composed and sang well, and was the first good troubadour there ever was beyond the Alps [i.e., in France], and the one who composed the best ever melodies for *vers*, "Alongside the short days and the long evenings." He did not compose any *cansos*, because at that time no song was called a *canso*, but a *vers*.

The reader's prospective encounter with "De josta·ls breus jorns," the third song in the Peire d'Alverhna selection in *IK*, is dissimulated by the biographer's syntax, which presents it not as a title or a quotation, still less a reminiscence of the recent index, but merely as an adverbial phrase modifying "composed the best ever melodies." (When did he compose them? Alongside the short days and long evenings.)[37] Nor is it betrayed by the scribe of either codex, who give no indication that this is a quotation. It is only the bizarreness of the phrase itself that sticks out and triggers hesitation.

When the song is eventually reached, its puzzling opening stanza develops the riddle of the incipit through a contrast between the springtime of knowledge (*saber*) burgeoning and bearing fruit in the poet's head and the darkening air and thinning trees around him. We understand that, in reality, wintertime is approaching at the same time as, in his imagination, the singer is leaving it behind; the reason for the odd choice of adverbial phrase is to enable him to be "alongside" winter in both directions, both nearing and departing from it. As he enters the imaginary springtime of his song, still in the first stanza, real birds disappear in the face of the real winter:

> Per que·s retrai entre·ls enois e·ls freys
> lo rossignols e·l tortz e·l guays e·l picx.
>   (Song 12, 6–7)

> And so amid the torments and the cold, the nightingale, the turtle-dove, the jay, and the woodpecker withdraw.

Two songbirds identified with love, nightingale and dove, are followed by the noisily imitating jay, a term liable to confusion with "popinjay" or parrot, and the woodpecker with its tuneless tapping. The song was composed in the mid-twelfth century, at a time when troubadours promoted nightingales and depreciated parrots. From Peire's viewpoint, then, this enumeration descends from the most to the least amorous or musical of the birds, and from the least to the most mechanically repetitive. Its bathos is intended to undermine the value of the poet's new, inner season of enlightenment; and we soon discover that the love that preoccupies him is proving equally disillusioning. As the song continues, and Peire apes—parrots—the theme of "love from afar," he does indeed self-mockingly concede the presence, in his song, of repetitive jays or woodpeckers where we might have expected only rapturous turtledoves and spontaneous nightingales. "De josta·ls breus jorns" does, then, raise the specter of the parrots' way, if only to deride it.

The incipit's presence in the *vida* refocuses the problematic, since its context is that of a copy—that of the manuscript—which is a good deal more literal and mechanical than the recycling of poetic tropes to which Peire draws attention. The line "Alongside the short days and the long evenings," which is both quoted and dissimulated, serves to situate Peire as "the one who composed the best ever melodies for *vers*." To what extent can the troubadour as nightingale survive in the world of copying that is the *chansonnier*? If he can already concede that love and song are merely repetitive, what about quotation, and what about the labor of the scribe? What is the significance of calling attention at the very beginning of large and prestigious codices like *I* and *K* to the fineness of the line between composing, quoting, and simply copying? What is the impact on subjectivity of such enmeshment in repetition? Perhaps the point is precisely to underline the value of beginning, and beginning again; to point to the opportunity for freedom in the very act of repeating.

A poet who benefits from this moment of freedom is Dante. In *De vulgari eloquentia* (2.13), he asserts that one of his *rime petrose*, "Al poco giorno e al gran cerchio d'ombra," takes its form from Arnaut Daniel's "Si·m fos Amors de ioi donar tant larga" (29.17). The assertion is doubly provocative, since in professing this implausible debt Dante dissimulates two real ones: one to Arnaut's *sestina* "Lo ferm voler" (29.14), which is the formal point of departure for "Al poco giorno"; and the other to the troubadour hailed by his *vida* as the first great vernacular artist, whose melodies were composed "dejosta.ls breus jorns e.ls loncs sers."[38] The wintry chiaroscuro of Peire's mysterious incipit, precisely because it is unencumbered in the *vida* by the rest of the song, can be reworked by Dante as he in turn explores the tug between clarity and obfuscation, between fixity and mobility, and the inescapable complicity between copying and starting afresh.

## CHAPTER 4

Soliciting Quotation in *Florilegia*

Attribution, Authority, and Freedom

Master Ferrarino, an early fourteenth-century lawyer from Ferrara, boasts of consigning to oblivion the parts of songs that he does not select for inclusion in his anthology, confident that a song's essential *sentenças* can be captured in only a few of its stanzas.[1] A 226-item *florilegium* based on his collection makes up the section of *chansonnier D* known as *Dc*.[2] His *vida*, preserved solely as a preface to this anthology, explains his procedure: "He made a selection from all the songs of the best troubadours in the world and from each *canso* or *sirventes* he drew one or two or three stanzas that carried the meaning of the song and had the most carefully chosen words" ("E fe[s] un estrat de tutas las cançzos des bos trobador[s] del mon; e de chadaunas cançzos o serventes tras .i. cobla o .ii. o .iii. aqelas qe portan la[s] sentenças de las cansos e o son tu[i]t li mot triat," *Biographies*, CI, 581).[3]

Nancy Washer points out the double burden this formulation places on the excerpted stanzas, which both "replicate the meaning of and replace the complete songs."[4] In thus identifying the core meaning of a song, the anthologist puts himself, in Maria Luisa Meneghetti's words, "in a position of antagonism vis-à-vis the poet,"[5] effectively declaring much of the troubadour's composition redundant. Such comments recall the qualification, in the Introduction, of quotation as an act of violence, whether in the form of aggression toward the original author, mutilation of his text, or defiance of the reader.[6] Ferrarino has already performed this violence on behalf of users who may subsequently decide to quote the extracted passages. But at the same time, the fact that he has reduced songs to bite-sized morsels preempts the process of solicitation (to evoke Compagnon's more seductive term) whereby only *parts* of texts appeal to us as quotable.[7] If selection is the first step toward quotation, it is here, thanks to Ferrarino, a *fait accompli*. The *coblas* he elects to copy are already, in some degree, quoted by him and are offered up as inviting quotation by others.

In *Dc* the process of excerption is rendered palpable by the use of incipits as rubrics to introduce the selected stanzas (except in rare cases where the first stanza itself forms part of the excerpt): the incipits, written in red ink, underline the incompleteness of the following text and raise the specter of other lines and stanzas that the anthologist has chosen *not* to include. The same format of incipits plus selected stanzas is followed by the shorter *florilegium* in *chansonnier F* (170 items on folios 13r–62r of *F*, referred to as *Fa*), and in the more recently discovered fragment *Cm* (13 items, all by Raimon de Miraval and Arnaut de Maruelh, from what was clearly an anthology on at least the scale of *Fa*).[8] The way all three anthologies *CmDcFa* make visible the labor of extraction confirms the readiness for quotation of the selections they propose.

Since their entries are organized troubadour by troubadour, with attributions to named poets (also in red) heading almost every entry, these anthologies are, moreover, collections of "authorities" that can be cited by name as well as quoted. The process of excerption interestingly reveals that an authority should not be identified with what an author actually wrote. Rather, it is what another person (the anthologist) deems worth preserving and acknowledging in that author. As happens likewise in citation, the notion of attribution here offers a useful alternative to that of "authorship." Attribution implies less that a given opinion originated in the mind of an earlier author than that it can be ascribed to one; it involves a direction *to*, not a movement *from*, the author in question. If authorship implies that an author is to be credited with responsibility for what is written, attributing a quotation also ratifies what the person quoting already thinks by referring the opinion to someone else; the conservation of a recognizable name is valuable primarily as a means of underwriting ideas (*sentenças*, in the terminology of Ferrarino's biography) to which one wishes to give currency. As I shall argue in the last section of this chapter, such a concept of authority is far more enabling than it is constraining, since it licenses the exploration of different concepts and affects under the flag of a well-known name and exposes the multiplicity— and hence the contingency—of the positions that a textual "I" may hold (see also Chapter 11).

In what is probably the earliest surviving copy of a *florilegium*, item #167 on folios 47–49 of *chansonnier H* (third quarter of the thirteenth century), it is even clearer that the compiler has both culled extracts from songs and earmarked them as future quotations.[9] The format of #167 is unique to this manuscript. It consists of twenty-six entries each comprising a prose rubric followed by one or more excerpted *coblas* (thirty-seven of them all told) grouped according to the lyric from which they were taken, and cut back to the *coblas'* opening line (though for items <3> and <25> the entire strophe is provided).[10] Typically the prose rubrics issue directives as to what contexts the abridged stanza or stanzas are appropriate for, and who their author is. Since the copyist used black ink only for the actual troubadour verses, which are less extensive than the rubrics, the folios containing #167 are more red than black; their hectic appearance matches their somewhat hectoring manner. Modern critics usually call these prose rubrics *razos*, but they are the diametrical opposite of the biographies referred to by that term. Whereas biographical *razos* anchor the composition of individual songs in the specifics of their authors' experiences, the *H razos* prescribe the broad applicability of the extracted stanzas to a range of contexts. The *coblas* cease being expressions of a particular individual's feelings and become instead generic reflections or commonplaces. While this gesture frees them up for general use, the fact that they are abbreviated to just their incipits is conversely restrictive. The reader of #167 is challenged to summon up the knowledge necessary to supply the omitted lines with no more helpful prompt than a curt "etc."[11] Users are put in the strange position of being informed what purpose each stanza might serve while being denied access to most of its text. Their situation is thus very different from that of readers of *florilegia* like *Dc*, who are assured that there is no need for them to know any more of the songs than the anthologist has selected for them. More explicitly than those anthologies, however, the arrangement of *H* attributes to known troubadours opinions that have been formulated by its compiler; even more than them it may provoke its users to respond to and experiment with its materials.

Appendix 2 documents the contents of the *CmDcFaH florilegia*. In addition, it includes those of the anthologies in *chansonniers G* and *J*, which observe different principles again.[12] (These manuscripts were chosen because of their connection with *H*, signaled by Maria Careri,[13] and because they transmit the *Novas del papagai* discussed in Chapter 6.) Instead of reproducing what are clearly excerpts from multi-stanza works attributed to named troubadours, they contain single *coblas* that are either isolated stanzas or extracts from longer songs—though without indicating which. The *GJ* anthologists are similarly noncommittal about attribution: many of the *coblas* they single out are anonymous, but even those that are by known troubadours are copied anonymously. In these two *florilegia* the practice of quotation has effectively merged with copying *tout court*, a convergence commented on in Chapter 3. Even if scholarship reveals that some of the single stanzas in *GJ* are identical to excerpted ones in *CmDcFa*, *G* and *J* present them as copies of self-contained compositions (*coblas esparsas*), or as copies that accidentally became truncated in transmission: nothing marks the intention to select, or the specter of a larger whole of which the extracted stanzas would form a part. As instances of authority these stanzas are entirely free-floating and available, with neither constraints nor recommendations as to their potential use.

It is difficult to determine when these anthologies came into existence. Over the course of the thirteenth century they evidently circulated in considerable numbers since interconnected compilations are found in at least *CmDcFaGHJNPQT*. The Italian origin of all of these manuscripts except *J* strongly implies that the practice of compiling *florilegia* began in Italy. Probably, as Meneghetti proposes, there were originally two anthologies: a courtly one best preserved in *Dc* and a more scurrilous one best represented in *GQ*.[14] As a result, *Dc* and its relatives read like an abridgment of one of the big Italian *chansonniers* (such as *ABDIK*), while the *GQ* type of *florilegium* seems more like a raucous supplement to such a codex. The ordering of columns in Appendix 2 from *Dc* on the left to *G* on the right reveals the variations and permutations between these two poles. They are already fused in *H* #167, which shows that the two underlying types of anthology were thoroughly interwoven well before the end of the thirteenth century, and certainly long before Ferrarino da Ferrara's biographer attempted to give him credit for having invented the anthology form. In the next section of this chapter I give reasons for thinking that collections of *coblas triadas* date back as early as the pioneering forms of quotation discussed in Chapters 1–3.

As Meneghetti notes, anthologized stanzas become increasingly freestanding over time, the pattern of *J* and *G* resurfacing in *N*, *T*, and especially *P*.[15] But the older and seemingly better defined *florilegia* in *DcFa* already contain a slippery mix that includes a few unattributed freestanding *coblas*, abridged copies, inset entire songs, and even what may be entire songbooks of lyrics by less well-known troubadours. Meneghetti thinks that, paradoxically, one of Ferrarino's contributions to the *florilegium* he reworked may have been to increase the number of whole songs.[16] Even in the ruthlessly abbreviating *H* an exchange of *coblas esparsas* between the Count of Rodez and Uc de Saint Circ (185.3 and 457.33) has crept in among the otherwise clearly flagged *coblas triadas*, though presumably without forming part of the anthology.

Consequently, of all the practices considered in these first four chapters, those of the *florilegia* are the hardest to generalize about, especially with regard to how they relate part to whole and quotation to other forms of iteration. Meneghetti may, however, be right to say that there is little value in attempting to categorize anthologized *coblas* in terms of their putative origins, and that instead of asking whether they are accidentally truncated, deliberately excerpted, or self-contained, we should concentrate on their common availability as handy gobbets of troubadour lore.[17] That the terms *esparsas* and *triadas* were not opposed for medieval readers is indicated by a rubric in *R*, which introduces a section with the words "Aiso so coblas triadas esparsas de[n] B[er]tr[n] carbonel de marselha" (112v; Here are selected isolated stanzas of Bertran Carbonel of Marselha). Whereas copies of whole songs are instances of curatorship that monumentalize the troubadours, copies of isolated or selected stanzas are pragmatically oriented. They are ready for use by those who quote, even if they are not all equally designated as being already quotations. I would go further and suggest that anthologies *solicit* quotation because they preselect authorities and enable maximal flexibility as to their use.

The next section of this chapter surveys the overlap between anthologization and quotation. In the final section, I examine two songs that are both anthologized and quoted, showing the freedom to experiment with different conceptual or affective stances to which their reduction to snippets of authority gave rise.

Anthologized Extracts and Troubadour Quotations: An Overview

Florilegia do more than signal quotability. Comparing Appendices 1 and 2 shows that the contents of anthologies coincide with actual quotations. Before the extent of this overlap can be assessed, however, two provisos need to be borne in mind.

First, since Appendix 2 includes only some of the existing anthologies, the extent of the shared material between anthologized stanzas and passages quoted is probably greater than shown here. Second, how one compares Appendix 1 with Appendix 2 depends on how the information provided by Appendix 2 is read. I chose the stanza as the basic recording unit throughout Appendix 2 for several reasons: to facilitate comparison with Appendix 1, given that most of the correspondences between it and Appendix 2 occur at or below the level of the stanza; because the stanza is the basic unit of the *JG florilegia* and also, for the most part, of *H*; and because, while the same songs sometimes occur in *CmDcFa*, they are not usually represented by the same stanzas. Thus, for example, the distribution over four rows in Appendix 2 of Folquet de Marselha's "Per Dieu, Amors, ben sabetz veramen" (155.16) makes it apparent that (material from) stanza I appears in *DcFa* and the *Breviari*; that (material from) stanza II is repeated in *DcFaH* plus *So fo* and the *Breviari*; that stanza III occurs in *FaH*; and that stanza V is excerpted only in *Dc*. But it takes a closer look to see that in *Dc*, stanzas I, II, III, and V all form part of a single anthology item, #29, and that in *Fa*, the incipit and stanzas II–III similarly constitute item #53. This is because, as already explained, the rubrics in *CmDcFa* itemize their contents with reference to an entire song, whether they record one stanza from it or many. Consequently, the *CmDcFa* columns in Appendix 2 risk giving the impression that these manuscripts contain many more items than is indicated by the *florilegia* themselves. For instance, Guilhem Augier Novella's "Per vos, bella dolz amia" (205.4a), all five stanzas of which are copied in *Fa* but none of which is anthologized or quoted elsewhere to my knowledge, is presented in Appendix 2 as five potential stanza-length sources of quotation, as much as it is as the single anthology item *Fa* #137. Calculating the contents of Appendix 2 gives different results according to what one counts: the stanza-by-stanza *ordinatio* modeled by *GJ* produces a total of around 1,200 stanzas, the song-by-song disposition typified by *CmDcFaH* results in a count of 365 songs, and the author-based arrangement that *H* more or less shares with *CmDcFa* yields seventy-four troubadours plus thirty-two anonymous pieces. Each of these outcomes compares differently with its counterpart in Appendix 1. Following a stanza count, Appendix 2 contains about twice as many units up to a *cobla* in length as Appendix 1. Starting from the numbers of songs or of troubadours, however, reverses this result, making Appendix 1 (with about 383 known songs, including anonymous ones, and ninety-four named poets) the richer of the two.

These provisos about the way Appendix 2 is compiled mean that, heuristically, it makes more sense to start with the quotations recorded in Appendix 1 and see how many of them also appear in the anthologies I have analyzed, than to begin from Appendix 2. Essentially, that means counting the number of entries in Appendix 1, and the number of positive correspondences between those entries and those in Appendix 2 as indicated in the last column of

Appendix 1, and comparing the results. Only identifiable quotations (i.e., those from known troubadours or from anonymous songs attested elsewhere) are worth including in this comparison, since unidentified ones by definition have no PC number and no known equivalent in any other source.

The calculation reveals a striking degree of correspondence. Of the 589 rows in Appendix 1 that represent identifiable quotations, 188, or 32 percent, correspond with passages excerpted in the *florilegia* documented in Appendix 2. The overlap is especially marked in the cases of Arnaut de Maruelh, Cadenet, Folquet de Marselha, Gui d'Ussel, Peirol, Pons Fabre d'Uzes, Raimon de Miraval, Uc Brunenc,[18] and the anonymous songs. For many other troubadours a high proportion of the passages quoted are also anthologized: Aimeric de Peguilhan, Guillem de Montanhagol, Peire Rogier, Perdigon, Pons de Capdoill, and Raimbaut de Vaqueiras. Certain well-known ones, notably Bernart de Ventadorn, Gaucelm Faidit, Giraut de Bornelh, and Peire Vidal, feature extensively in both appendices, yet with less overlap in the actual passages figuring from one to the other. The two appendices also coincide in many of their omissions. The early troubadours from Guilhem de Peitieu to not only Jaufre Rudel but also Peire d'Alvernha[19] are almost completely absent from both, as are the *trobairitz*.[20] Italian and Catalan troubadours make little appearance in either appendix, though they are more common as anthology pieces than as regular quotations—witness, for instance, the entries in Appendix 2 for Lanfranc Cigala and Sordello.[21] Dialogue pieces are also more commonly anthologized than quoted, but they remain relatively underrepresented in both appendices. There is, then, an overall high level of convergence between the passages quoted and those anthologized.

Turning now to the major contexts in which quotations are found, one might expect the *vidas* and *razos* to overlap the most with the anthologies. These biographical texts are found in *chansonniers* such as *ABDIK*, which, like the *florilegia*, are Italian and are organized troubadour by troubadour with better-known poets higher up the order, as happens in *CmDcFa* and to some extent in the anthology in *H*. However, of the 130 quotations in the biographies, only 33 (about 25 percent) correspond with the *coblas* inventoried in Appendix 2.

Consequently, if surprisingly, there is more convergence between the contents of *florilegia* and the quotations found in non-Italian texts. Maria Careri and Elizabeth Poe have demonstrated the overlap between the excerpted stanzas in *H* and the passages quoted in the later *Breviari d'amor*, which, like the *florilegia*, favors the stanza as its unit of quotation.[22] The *Breviari* also imitates the anthologist's sense of extracting the essential argument from a song, though Matfre Ermengau's interpretations go well beyond the courtly or satirical limits of *florilegia*, highlighting instead the songs' potential for theological enlightenment (see below and Chapter 8). Of some 264 quotations from troubadour lyrics in the *Breviari*, 92 or 35 percent) are the same as, or overlap with, anthologized stanzas, and Matfre also quotes from nine songs that are represented in *florilegia* though his choice does not fall on the same stanzas as those that are anthologized.

Even more surprising is the high proportion of overlap between quotations and anthologized stanzas in the *novas* and grammars that originate in Catalonia and date from the turn of the twelfth to the thirteenth century onward. The very earliest treatise, the *Razos de trobar*, possibly composed before 1200, contains twenty-nine quotations, twelve (41 percent) of which overlap with excerpted stanzas. Its author, the Catalan Raimon Vidal, was also the first to deploy, as a sign of scholarly mastery, the technique also found in *CmDcFa* of quoting a song's incipit and then a selection of its content (see Chapter 1). And of the forty-seven identified passages quoted in *Abril issia* and *So fo e·l tems*, twenty-four (51 percent) overlap with material in excerpted stanzas, while a further seven come from songs that are mined by compilers of *florilegia*, even if different stanzas appear in the *florilegia* from in the *novas*. Like the *Breviari*, the *novas* are more inclined to favor the stanza as a unit of quotation, and this is another respect in which they resemble anthologies, especially those in *CmDcFaH* since like them the *novas* (and the grammars too) regularly include attributions (though unlike grammars, the *novas* do not quote incipits). Moreover the *H florilegium*, while sharing very few actual passages with the *novas*, inserts its excerpts within generic situations involving men and women, a trait that gives it common ground with the short story. Indeed, some of the *H* extracts are linked together in a narrative arc in a way that seemingly overrides its poet-by-poet disposition; for example, <16>–<18> form a sequence of adventures and misadventures. At one stage of working on this book I amused myself by inserting all the *H* prose *razos* in order into a *novas*-like tale in which a noble patron steers unsteadily between two ladies, helped and occasionally hindered by his *joglar*. The fact that this was quite easy to achieve shows that *H* #167 could conceivably be material for, or the remnants of, a short story.

The relatively high proportion of shared material between Italian *florilegia* and Occitan and Catalan texts dating back to the early thirteenth century is remarkable. It cannot simply be explained by the prevalence, from an early date, of copies of certain songs, given that the same passages of those songs are both quoted and anthologized. Could it be that the Italian compilers of *florilegia* were influenced by the Catalano-Occitan vogue for quotation, more than they were by quotations in the biographical genres? Or should we rather conclude that collections of excerpted stanzas arose much earlier than previously appreciated and circulated more widely than in Italy, even though that is where the surviving copies originated? Whatever the answers to these questions, it is clear that collections of excerpted stanzas belong together with the pioneering forms of quotation outlined in this first part of my book, despite the relative lateness of their manuscript attestation.

In the final section of this chapter I examine excerpts from two songs that, between them, are anthologized in *CmDcFa, H,* and *J,* as well as parodied in *G,* and quoted in every pre-1300 Occitan genre that includes quotation: grammars, *novas,* biographies, the *Breviari,* and the lyric. These examples thus provide a link between the pioneering modes of quotation explored in Chapters 1, 2, and 3, and their elaboration considered in Chapters 7 and 8. The variation in the treatment of the excerpts is striking and suggests that the solicitation on the part of *florilegia* to quote their authorities did not restrict freedom so much as define it.

Anthologized Authorities and the Freedoms of Quotation

The quotation of the incipit to "La franca captenensa" (30.15) in *IK*'s *vida* of Arnaut de Maruelh was discussed in Chapter 3. Arnaut, says the biographer, composed the song for a countess to whom he could not otherwise admit his love; her capacity to discern its meaning makes her a surrogate for the reader of the *chansonnier* who has not yet reached the copy of the song's text. In addition to the incipit, the *vida* may allude to the second stanza of the song in which Arnaut fears he may be tempted to *forsar* (coerce) his lady, euphemizing Arnaut's unsavory thoughts of assault into an unimpeachable urge to sing to her of his love.

I noted in my discussion of the *vida* that this second stanza is not alluded to or anthologized elsewhere. Like the *vida,* the *florilegia* in *Dc* and *Cm* both reproduce the song's incipit, but in order to situate their inclusion of stanzas IV and V. The opening line of stanza IV is quoted in *H* following a brief prose *razo.* The *Breviari d'amor* also quotes this same stanza IV; the line introducing the quotation ends with the rhyme word *captenensa* (30836) in a reminiscence of *CmDc*'s practice of prefacing quotation of this stanza with the incipit. Of greatest interest to medieval readers, clearly, was this fourth stanza, which in Johnston's edition reads:

> Dompna, per gran temensa,
> tant vos am e·us teing car,
> no·us aus estiers pregar.
> mas plus fai ad honrar
> us paubres avinens
> que sap honor grazir
> e·ls bes d'amor celar,
> c'us rics desonoissens,
> cui par que totas gens
> lo deian obezir.
>
> (Song 3, 31–40)

> Lady, I dare not implore you otherwise than in great fear, so much do I love and cherish you. But a poor, agreeable man who knows how to appreciate the honor done to him and conceal the benefits of love is to be honored more than an undiscerning magnate who imagines it is everyone's duty to obey him.

Stanza V expresses the hope that success in love will reward fortune and wit ("astres et sens," 49) more than it does wealth.

In both *Dc* and *Cm* the anthology item consisting of the incipit and two stanzas is placed among other extracts from the same troubadour and conforms to the image they compile of Arnaut as a courtly supplicant. Whereas in the *vida* the incipit purports to reference the original context of the song, in these anthologies it acts as a title and gestures toward an absent, complete copy. Neither *Dc* nor *Cm* furnishes it with any commentary. By contrast, the contexts in which stanza IV is inserted in the *florilegium* in *H* and in Matfre Ermengau's *Breviari d'amor* use it to essay utterly divergent meanings.

H prefaces the stanza's opening line with this *razo*: [23]

> Aqesta si·s fan a mandar a dompna c'om no aussa pregar d'amor. Per q'ella dei soffrir los precs e entendre la dolor e·l pensamen e·l desir coral de l'amic. E con a lei no notz et el prec si refrain la dolor e

mostra qe plus deu hom far donar ad un paubre auinen qe ad un ric maluatz. Qe·l maluatz desconoissens cre c'om li deia far honor per sa ricor.

Arnautz de Miroill

[D]ompna per gran temenza etc. (*H* #167<21>)

This one is made to send to a lady whom one dares not beg for her love, because she ought to permit the prayers and heed the pain and sorrow and heartfelt desire of the lover. And how it does her no harm and how, in expressing his prayer, his pain is lessened; and it shows how one should cause more to be given to a poor, pleasing man than to an evil rich one. For the ignorant rich man believes he should be honored for his wealth.

Arnaut de Maruelh

Lady with great fear etc.

Such play on disclosing and withholding is typical of *H* and resembles the *vida* more than it does *CmDc*. The absence of text following the opening line of the stanza provides an opportunity for its meaning to be determined afresh, and the intimidating use of "etc." holds readers accountable for doing so; but at the same time the compiler preempts the absent stanza, paraphrasing it and thereby introducing significant changes of emphasis. Arnaut's text stresses the need for a poor man to be agreeable, grateful, and discreet if he is to win honor from his lady. The *H razo*, however, sidesteps any such demands on the lover to concentrate exclusively on what is required of the lady: she must hear the lover out and be answerable for his pain, obligations that are not voiced in the song. While in the *vida* interpretation is vested in the song's original recipient who responds to it with grace, in *H* it is potentially transferrable to a host of new antifeminist contexts.[24] In the *vida*, readers are assured that the lady understands the poem when they have only its first line and the barest indications of her thoughts, but here they seemingly benefit from the anthologist's command of its import. Readers of the *vida* are unlikely to find their memories in overt conflict with the countess's, or at least they are not provoked to conflict to the same extent as readers of *H* who, if they are capable of recalling Arnaut's text, may well notice a lack of fit between the compiler's paraphrase and the stanza in question. The contingent, hypothetical nature of the subject supposed to know is thus particularly exposed in *H*. And yet the *H razo* coincides uncannily with the *vida* in that both fantasize a lady's capitulation to her lover's desire—even though the knowledge imputed to the subject (and to women) is different in the two cases.

The same stanza of "La franca captenensa," which in *H* tasks women with responding to their lovers, promotes in Matfre's advice to ladies an exchange of virtuous love that is uncorrupted by worldly concerns (*Breviari* #135, 30837–46).[25] In the lines preceding the quoted stanza, but before announcing it as such, Matfre rehearses its key vocabulary. He warns that lovers can be foolish and haughty on account of their rank (*riqueza*, 30819), which makes them undiscerning (*desconoichen*, 30820) toward women, incapable of appreciating the favor (*grazir lo be*, 30824) they receive from them, or of being discreet (*celar*, 30825). But ladies should love a man who is truly appreciative and also timid (*temeros*, 30828), even if he lacks all wealth (*ricor*, 30832). Having presented these views as if they were his own, Matfre proceeds to name Arnaut de Maruelh and repeat his words verbatim. Whereas the *H* compiler warned against the propensity for abuse in love, Matfre, without changing anything in Arnaut's text, ultimately counsels that through humble, reciprocal love the soul will find its true identity. Both *H* and Matfre defer announcement of the troubadour's name until after they have given their own version of the stanza's contents, but Matfre does not even announce the fact that he is quoting until after this summary, thereby giving the impression that the troubadour agrees with *him*, rather than the other way round. Thus where *H* both compiles and preempts the troubadour, Matfre presents himself as his spokesman. The logic of attribution is essential to the freedom each enjoys to ascribe his own convictions to Arnaut de Maruelh, thereby constituting him as an "authority" and enjoying the return of that authority upon themselves.

Similar slippages are observable in ways in which songs of Folquet de Marselha are both extensively anthologized and quoted; I shall focus here on "Amors, merce: non mueira tan soven" (155.1), discussed in more detail by Nancy Washer.[26] This song is quoted by incipit in *DcFa* and by Jofre de Foixà in his song "Be m'a lonc temps menat a guiza d'aura" (304.1). In *Dc*, the incipit prefaces the anthologized stanzas II and V; in *Fa*, only stanza V is excerpted. Stanza II is quoted by Raimon Vidal in *So fo e·l tems* and lines from it appear in the *Doctrina d'acort*. Stanza V, meanwhile, also appears in anthologies *H* and *J*, and two lines from it are quoted by Matfre in the *Breviari*, while a parody of it figures among the *coblas esparsas* in *G*. The most comprehensive exploitation of this song is therefore *Dc*, with two more specialized usages emerging from it. One of these is broadly Vidalian (a *novas* by Raimon

Vidal himself, a grammatical treatise in the tradition of the *Razos de trobar*, and the poem by Jofre de Foixà who was also the author of another Vidalian treatise) and the other broadly clerical-satirical (the anthologies *JGH* and the spiritually edifying *Breviari*).

The song is one of wry complaint against Love, as summarized in the incipit ("Have mercy, Love! Let me not die so many times over!"). The potential humor of this line is amplified in its quotation by Jofre de Foixà as line 35 of his own song, when he accuses love of repeatedly killing and resuscitating him, so that his sufferings are worse than if he were to die once and for all ("qu'ieu trac piegz d'ome del tot moren," 33; see Chapter 7). Folquet then proceeds to reflect ironically, in stanza II, on service and, in stanza V, on discretion. In Paolo Squillacioti's edition, stanza II reads:

> Per qu'er peccatz, Amors, so sabes vos,
> si m'auzizetz, pos vas vos no m'azire;
> mas trop servirs ten dan mantas sazos,
> que son amic en pert om, so aug dire;
> qu'ie·us ai servit et encars no m'en vire,
> e quar sabetz qu'al gizardon n'aten,
> ai perdut vos e·l servir eissamen.
> (Song 5, 8–14)

> You know it would be wrong of you, Love, to kill me for being unable to rebel against you; but too prolonged a service often causes harm, for it makes one lose one's ally, so I have heard; for I have served you and still remain unswerving, and because you know that I hope to be rewarded for it, I have both lost you and wasted my effort.

Diverging from the usual trope that service breeds dissatisfaction in the one who serves, the stanza plays instead with the idea that it produces disenchantment in the one served, who is put off by prolonged, self-interested attention (13–14). I see lines 10–11 as anticipating this conclusion (*amic* referring to the ally thus served who, wearying of the role, ceases to be one), but they could also be understood as introducing the more familiar, converse situation, that the devotee (*amic* referring to the one serving) grows disillusioned with his long wait and gives up.

The stanza following continues the military metaphor of an impasse between the lover and Love by asking the lady to intervene forcibly to resolve it. In stanza IV the speaker is amazed at her long resistance to his desire, but dares not complain to her of his suffering: can she not simply read it in his eyes? This leads to the other widely excerpted stanza, stanza V:

> A vos volgra mostrar lo mal qu'ieu sen
> et als autres celar et escondire;
> qu'anc no·us puec dir mon cor celadamen;
> donc, s'ieu no·m sai cubrir qui m'er cubrire?
> ni qui m'er fis s'ieu eis me sui traire?
> qui se non sap celar non es razos
> que·l celon cill a cui non es nuls pros.
>
> (Song 5, 29–35)

I wish to show my suffering to you, and conceal and deny it to others. For I could never keep it secret when telling you what is in my heart, and if I cannot cover my feelings, who will cover for me? Who will be faithful to me if I betray myself? If someone doesn't know how to keep a secret, it's not reasonable to expect others who have no interest in doing so keep it so for him.

As Washer observes, in *Dc*, which includes both stanzas II and V, the sense of stanza V is changed by the absence of the intervening stanzas, since it appears to be about the singer's difficulty speaking to Love rather than to his lady.[27]

Jofre is the only author to quote "Amors, merce" who does not attribute the borrowing to Folquet de Marselha; perhaps its incipit was famous enough for that to be unnecessary. The whole of stanza II is repeated by the frustrated knight in *So fo* (248–54, Appendix 5, #7). His bitterness at his lady's indifference now that he has served her for seven years implies that his use of Folquet is close to the way I understand the stanza: as meaning, that is, that the very person who ought to be moved to reward his service has in fact been put off by it. Whereas Folquet struggles with his distress, however, the knight almost immediately takes up with the *donzela* to whom he quotes these lines. Uc de Mataplana's verdict in the version of the *novas* discussed in Chapter 2 rules that the knight should return to the hard-hearted lady. This judgment in turn implies that the knight was wrong to assume that he was entitled to a reward for his service—wrong to attribute, that is, to Folquet's authority the behavior that he himself supposed Folquet's words to justify. Perhaps this is another instance where Uc is represented as a greater connoisseur of Occitan lyric than the knights and ladies of Limousin.

The medial lines 10–11 of this same stanza are quoted by Terramagnino da Pisa (#10, *DA*, 225–26) as the last in his list of examples of passages modeling forms of the noun *amic* and, by implication, the behavior that love poetry supposes in a lover (see Chapter 1). It seems from this context that the grammarian understood the lines more conventionally than Raimon Vidal, identifying the *amic* as the lover who serves unrequited for so long that he eventually quits. Folquet's authority is supposed in order to uphold the grammarian's knowledge of the subject of love in troubadour song.

There is more divergence in the uses made of Folquet's stanza V. The obscene parody that occurs in *G* is not a quotation in the sense I define the word (though as a *contrafactum* it may reiterate Folquet's music); it appears in a cluster of similarly transgressive reworkings of well-known courtly songs.[28] In *J* the stanza appears in the company of other courtly didactic *coblas*.[29] In *H*, where it directly follows Arnaut de Maruelh 30.15, it is accompanied by this directive:

> Aquet auia uolontat de mostrar a sua dompna los mals q'el sentia per ella, e a totas cobrir e escondire. E mostra qe qi no sap si cobrir, qe mal lo cobrira autre. E cel qe si trais, greu l'er autre fis.
> Folqet de Marselha
> [A] uos uolgra mostrar lo mal q'eu sen. (*H* #167<22>)

> This one wanted to reveal to his lady the ills that he suffered on her account and to conceal them from all other women. And he shows that he who does not know how to conceal for himself will not be well concealed by anyone else. And if someone betrays himself, another will scarcely be true to him.
> Folquet de Marselha
> I wish to show my suffering to you.

The compiler's purported recapitulation strikingly omits the opening lines where Folquet protests that he cannot fail to express his sufferings to his lady. Instead of the dilemma of a lover caught between the need for discretion and the incapacity for dissimulation, the stanza becomes a sardonic comment on the politics of concealment. In the *Breviari*, however, lines 34–35 of this same stanza are quoted to exemplify the need to maintain discretion in the face of those who would betray it (#236, 33514.2–3). Resisting indiscretion (*decelar*) will help to safeguard the virtues of the biblical tree of knowledge of good and evil, which Matfre has shown are equivalent to the qualities of divine Love voiced by troubadour song. In the *Breviari* the subject of knowledge of troubadour song is ultimately God himself, an authority to trump all others who alone is supposed to know what Folquet was supposed to have meant.

The practice of compiling anthologies of *coblas* feeds into that of troubadour quotation and may also be nourished by it. *Florilegia* perform on behalf of those who quote the acts of mutilation and solicitation that are intrinsic to quotation, especially in *CmDcFa* and *H* where the process of excerption is highlighted. The presence of attributions in these same manuscripts also parallels the usage of most authors who quote; their use of incipits finds an echo both in grammars and in *vidas* and *razos*; and their focus on whole stanzas gives them common ground with quotations in *novas* and the *Breviari*. As with Latin compilations of exempla or authorities, there is immense freedom in the uses to which the materials in all *florilegia* can be put. Anthologization is not a mode of confinement but a means of releasing the textual subject from entrapment in its original context. While the *H* compiler appears the most prescriptive, his combination of misleading paraphrase with ruthless abridgment in fact makes visible the adaptability of quotations to new contexts. The different experimental stances authorized by the same excerpts underline the paradoxical connection that exists between repetition and the freedom to adopt new subject positions.

Part III of this book examines the developments in quotation and sensibility to which this freedom gives rise from the second half of the thirteenth century. Before that, Chapters 5 and 6 reflect on what I have called the nightingales' way and the parrots' way, showing how these notions are to some extent inscribed in thirteenth-century texts. Chapter 6 returns to the *florilegia* in *G* and *J*, showing by a different path how quotation and anthologization interact.

PART II

Parrots and Nightingales

## CHAPTER 5

The Nightingales' Way

Poetry as French Song in Jean Renart's *Guillaume de Dole*

Jean Renart's *Guillaume de Dole*, also known as the *Roman de la rose*, boasts the innovation that within it are included numerous lyric pieces.[1] The Introduction compared this practice of lyric insertion, typical of Northern French romance, with that of lyric quotation found among Occitania's Mediterranean neighbors. The comparison is important, because lyric insertion is the point where the nightingales' way comes closest to the use of quotation on that of the parrots. This chapter exploits their proximity to bring out their difference.

In the nightingales' mode of lyric reception, the desire to repeat the first person of troubadour poetry operates above all at the level of affect and musical performance; troubadour song is adapted by poets into their native language and integrated to evolving indigenous traditions; in northern French contexts, Occitan linguistic features are assimilated to the langue d'oïl. The previous four chapters have illustrated the very different procedures of the parrots' way, which is characterized by philological mastery and by the intersubjective interactions that are generated by knowingly modulated repetition. We have seen quotations act to map logic, test memory and recognition, inaugurate forms of writing, and redeploy authorities; even slight linguistic differences (for example, between Catalan and Occitan) are scrupulously observed; there is an endless play with supposed knowledge and the subject positions supposed to possess it.

Many critics have written about lyric insertion, but obviously they could not consider it from the viewpoint of its divergence from troubadour quotation because this has not previously been studied as a practice in its own right. I propose reading *Guillaume de Dole* less as innovating lyric insertion than as reacting to lyric quotation; in mapping the nightingales' way, I suggest, Jean Renart offers his perspective on the parrots' way. This chapter consequently differs from others in that it describes the path *not* followed by the texts that they discuss. It argues that Jean Renart's promotion of poetry as song embraces practices that are the obverse of the scholastic validation of the troubadours, except that he succumbs to the lure of substituting French for Occitan as a cultural *monolangue*, thereby offering the parrots a kind of backdoor return. Focusing on northern France and Germany, it is intended to be read in tandem with the next chapter, which traces the parrots' way through the Mediterranean regions contiguous with Occitania.

As his pseudonym "foxy one" suggests, Jean Renart is a slippery writer, and describing the verse insertions in *Guillaume de Dole* poses a number of difficulties that are exacerbated by the fact that it survives in only one manuscript (Vatican, Reg. Lat. 1725). Apart from the excerpt from a chanson de geste all the insertions appear to be either short self-contained lyric pieces or else the opening stanza or stanzas of longer songs; at the most generous count they total forty-eight; they represent a wide range of forms and probably also of distinct genres; many of them are narrative in cast, most obviously the epic excerpt, but also several of the lyrics such as *pastourelles*; some are used as dance tunes; and three (##16, 41, and 45) are extracts from the troubadours (see Appendix 6).[2] All the insertions are represented as being sung within the fiction and perhaps were also intended actually to be sung when the romance was performed, but that is less certain since the manuscript contains neither musical notation nor spaces in which it might have been copied.[3] Since the romance itself is in rhyming couplets, the whole ensemble is something of a showcase for the French verse of its period.

The plot centers on the relationship between Conrad, emperor of Germany, and Guillaume de Dole, his favorite knight. Conrad hosts great parties and, with Guillaume, organizes a spectacular tournament, but *noblesse oblige*; his position demands that he marry and have heirs. Who better to wed than his best friend's sister, whom he has heard praised even though he has never met her? This seemingly heaven-sent solution is derailed, however, by the unscrupulous scheming of Conrad's seneschal, the very person entrusted with the administration of justice at his court. The seneschal visits Guillaume's home in Dole, worms his way into his mother's favor, and discovers that the promised sister, Lienor, has a rose-colored, rose-shaped birthmark on her thigh. Although he has not seen her any more than Conrad has, the sene-schal uses this intimate secret about Lienor's body as evidence that he has taken her virginity. The sexual experience that mention of the rose purport-edly represents passes from mouth to mouth in what amounts to a process of social rape, and the wedding is abandoned.[4] But resourceful Lienor bril-liantly regains her reputation, purity, and desirability as Conrad's bride by publicly acting out the role of rape victim and planting evidence to incrimi-nate the seneschal. When he protests his innocence, and proves it by ordeal, she is correspondingly exculpated; and the romance concludes with wedding bells. Thanks to Lienor, Conrad and Guillaume de Dole can live together happily ever after. The characters keep breaking into song throughout; if the songs actually *were* performed when the romance was read, it would sound something like a modern musical.

Most scholars date the romance somewhere between about 1210 and 1230,[5] later than Raimon Vidal's grammar and *Abril issia*, and probably also after the composition of *So fo* and Uc's earliest *razos* and *vidas*. Its inclusion of troubadour quotations acquires additional resonance from the fact that its probable date range coincides with that of the Albigensian Crusade (1209–ca. 1229). This campaign, initially proclaimed against the Cathars, gradually be-came less a holy war and more a campaign for the political annexation of the south of France by northern French barons and their English allies. From 1212 some southern courts pass under the control of northern French lords, in 1213 the southern forces are humiliated at the battle of Muret, and from 1229 the Inquisition is established in Toulouse in order to root out the Cathar heresy. Depending whether it was composed earlier or later in the range of 1210 to 1230, *Guillaume de Dole* coincides either with the early years of the crusade or with the progressive subjection of much of the Midi by the French crown.[6]

The Albigensian campaign is not the only frontier war that coincides with the romance's probable period of composition. An exceptionally successful king, Philip Augustus also increased the prestige of the kingdom of France at the expense of England and the Empire (based in modern-day Germany). The decisive battle of Bouvines in 1214 saw the French triumph over both. The English king John Lackland failed in his bid to regain the lands in France he had lost in 1204, and French victory also led eventually to the ending of the Ottonian emperors and their replacement by the Staufer (also called Ho-henstaufen). Historian John Baldwin has read *Guillaume de Dole* as sympa-thetic to the deposed Otto, whose Welf (or Guelf) family predominated in the territories of Belgium and western Germany represented in the romance.[7]

But Jean Renart may have been equally interested in the successful Staufer contender for the imperial throne, Frederick II, who, as king of Rome and Sicily, upheld the imperial (or Ghibelline) cause in Italy.[8] In any case, it is clear that the French domain was expanding at its neighbors' expense, and that what was meant by "France" was changing rapidly, during the period when *Guillaume de Dole* was composed. Caught up in these changes, how does the romance's treatment of the troubadours respond to their reception by France's neighbors and her foes?

Poetry as Song in *Guillaume de Dole*

In contrast to the southern practice of quoting the troubadours as texts, the inset pieces in *Guillaume de Dole* are almost always explicitly described as sung;[9] eleven are performed by (or together with) professional minstrels,[10] twenty-three by miscellaneous courtiers,[11] and the remainder by the principal actors—Conrad, Guillaume, Lienor, and the mother. Performances by courtiers appear somewhat impromptu, and often overlap or interrupt one another's, a pattern established as early as the opening four insertions. This superimposition of voices is one reason why Michel Zink casts doubt on the traditional view that performance of the romance included actual singing, not just its representation.[12] Although some songs are described as being finished, far more are said to begin than to end. We are also left uncertain how much of a particular song might be thought of as performed: the stanzas contained in the manuscript could be all that is intended to be sung, but they could also be prompts that readers or performers could extend ad lib.

The romance appears, then, as a kind of anthology not dissimilar to those examined in Chapter 4.[13] But it differs from troubadour *florilegia* in providing a narrative frame, in the foregrounding of musical performance (none of the *florilegia* is notated), and in favoring opening stanzas. Occitan anthologies typically select medial *coblas* in which, as the biography of Ferrarino da Ferrara indicates, the reflective content of lyrics is concentrated. By contrast, the exordia overwhelmingly chosen in *Guillaume de Dole* are those most likely to highlight songs' status as song. Its selection of *grands chants*, the French genre most imitative of the troubadours, obsessively repeats variants of the nature opening, especially birdsong, combined with an irrepressible urge to sing. The first (#11 in Appendix 6), for instance, offers four reiterations of *chanter* or *chanson* reinforced by analogy with birds' singing:

> Et si chantent ceste chançon
>   en l'onor monsignor gasçon:
> "Quant flors et glais et verdure s'esloigne
> que cil oisel n'osent un mot soner
> por la froidor chascuns crient e resoigne
> tresqu'au biau tens qu'il soloient chanter.
> E por ce chant, que nel puis oublier . . ."
>   (*Guillaume de Dole*, 844–50)

And they sing this song in honor of Gace Brulé: "When blossom and gladiolus and greenery depart, so that birds dare not sing a word on account of the cold that each fears until the good weather when they sing again, yet then I sing: because I can't forget the good love . . ."

Only eighty lines later, the next *grand chant* (#12) presents the text's first literal nightingale, again with repeated *chanson/chanter*:

> A comencié ceste chançon:
> "Li noviaus tens et mais (et violete)
> et roissignox me semont de chanter;
> et mes fins cuers me fet d'une amorete
> un doz present que ge n'os refuser . . ."
>   (*Guillaume de Dole*, 922–26)

He began this song: "The new season and May [and the violet] and nightingale summon me to sing and my true heart makes a sweet gift for me of a love affair that I dare not refuse . . ."

Trouvère poetry is thus cast as the art of song and compared with nonverbal, nonhuman, natural sound.[14]

Nancy A. Jones has observed that the songs in *Guillaume de Dole* function like patches of color against the narrative background, much like the repeated mentions of the rose that stands out on Lienor's thigh.[15] The romance's plot is insistently marked by the never seen but always imagined imprint of this rose, a visual stain that the characters repeatedly tell one another about in hushed tones. The rose both draws attention to sexual enjoyment and makes it easier not to see it: not in the shameful abyss of Lienor's feminine sexuality (since in the end we are reassured that it was not sexual, let alone shameful), still less in the rampant eroticism and homoeroticism of Conrad's court. Jean Renart's deft, ironic narrative voice weaves around these moments of indecency, highlighting them but also ultimately avoiding them, in a spectacular combination of knowingness with understatement. Lienor's rose, then, acts as a kind of blot on the imperial landscape of Conrad's domains: it marks where fantasies of sexuality and femininity have been blotted out, and thus also draws attention to them.

Similarly, Jean's prologue invites us to see the actual or imagined singing within the romance as the auditory equivalent of a blot or stain. It is described as comparable to a scarlet tincture or dye in a bizarre passage where, as Jones observes, Jean Renart does not say—as one might expect him to—that his text has been dipped in dye so as to be evenly transformed in color, but instead says that dye has been applied to the text. He might mean that the text is uniformly colored, but the wording suggests that the songs are so many blots of color upon it, similar to the patches of embroidery with which the songs are also compared. If we take seriously this analogy between the insistent stain of the rose, the blots of dye, the patches of embroidery, and the coloration effected by the lyrics, we can see the moments of song as points where the text becomes dense with sexual or social affect without necessarily assigning it meaning, just as the rose both stains the text with the scandal of sex and blots it out.[16]

Many critics have suggested that there are ironic discrepancies between the emotions expressed in the songs and the cruder maneuverings or urges of the characters who sing them, producing what Caroline Jewers calls "a discordant rupture of sound and sense."[17] Just as the rose acts as a visual euphemism for women's sex, the nightingales' way of song would then conceal, from the very characters who sing about their desire, its uglier and more compromising aspects. In particular, song disguises these aspects behind the melodious but not necessarily meaningful songs of birds, the sounds of the natural world, or, failing those, behind the formulaic conventions of courtly love and the good life. Indeed, the two forms of blot, Lienor's rose and song, converge with one another in their parallel patterns of repetition, so that when the rose is finally established as an image of decorous innocuousness, it seems to be freshly plucked from the world of the lyric *reverdie*.

This effect of meaning being blotted out is especially marked in the three troubadour extracts, where birds are evoked alongside moments that are emotively expressive but semantically opaque.[18] Distant and half-heard (or

even unheard) birdsong in a heavily Gallicized Jaufre Rudel (#16; 262.2)[19] is
followed by the nightingale in the linguistically mangled Daude de Pradas
(#41; 124.5), and then by Bernart de Ventadorn's lark in an obscure rendition
of his famous "Can vei la lauzeta mover" (#45; 70.43). This last is sung after
Lienor has proved her innocence and the plot is being wrapped up. It interrupts, and is then sung concurrently with, a more popular *romance* (#44); it
appears that both are performed through to the end, even though the manuscript contains only the first two stanzas of each. Immediately following,
another song is begun, a French *grand chant* by Gautier de Soignies (#46), in
which birdsong also features. Several factors conspire together, then, to make
the meaning of Bernart's text evaporate into pure song. Since Félix Lecoy's
edition emends extensively the way Bernart de Ventadorn's text appears in
the manuscript, I reproduce it here from Regina Psaki's transcription. The
parentheses in my translation mark the points at which it becomes unintel-
ligible; the italics highlight the passages I shall comment on below, contending that they increase the emotivity of Bernart's original text at the cost of its
coherence.[20]

> **Q** uant voi laloete moder de goi.ses ales
> contre el rai.que sobete lesse cader par
> la doucor q'el cor li vai.ensi grant en
> vie mest pris de ce que voi.a ma grant
> *miravile est que vis del sens ne coir do[n]t*
> *desier non fou.* ha las tant cuidoie savoir
> donor et point n'en sai.pas on damar
> non pou tenir celi dont ja prou ne nau[ra]i
> tol mei lor cor et tol meismes.et soi mees
> me et tol le mon.et por tant el *ne moste*
> *rent fors desier et cor volon.* —oooo—
> (*Guillaume de Dole*, 5212–27)

When I see the lark move with joy its wings in the sunbeam, which
(?) itself, lets itself fall, because of the sweetness that penetrates its
heart, just such envy has seized me for that which I see. *It is a marvel
that completely out of my mind (I do not burn? Do not run?) from
which desire (was not? does not melt?).* Alas I imagined I knew so
much about honor and I know nothing. I cannot keep (?) from loving her from whom I will never have any benefit. She takes away my

heart and she takes herself and myself and she takes the world and then *she (?) gives but desire and a longing heart.*

The first of the italicized passages represents the last lines of the song's opening stanza as edited by Lazar: "Meravelh es quar desse / Lo cor desirier no·m fon" (Song 31, 7–8; It is a marvel that, at once, my heart does not melt with desire). The Occitan adverb *desse* (at once) has no equivalent in French and is replaced by an approximate homonym in the langue d'oïl, *del sen* in the phrase "vis del sen" (utterly out of one's mind, beside oneself). This phrase makes sense in itself and raises the emotional stakes of Bernart's text, but at the cost of a complete collapse in intelligibility in the line following. The second passage coincides with the closing lines of the stanza following: "E qant se·m tolc, no·m laisset re / Mas desirier e cor volon" (Song 31, 15–16; And when she takes me from herself, she leaves me nothing but desire and a longing heart). The version in *Guillaume de Dole* substitutes for the Occitan noun *re* the virtually homonymous French verb *rent* (gives), implying a swirl of emotion but also, as in the earlier passage, precipitating a breakdown of the ensuing grammar. Overall, what remains of Bernart's text is a series of expressions of intense feeling that are incoherently strung together. Jean Renart may have intended a less corrupt version of the song than that recorded in the manuscript. But what we have is an extreme case of song as blot: high on affect, low on intelligibility.

The insertion is worth comparing with Raimon Vidal's quotations from the same song. In the *Razos de trobar* he cites a later line, "totas las dot et las mescre" (I fear and mistrust all women) because it features the verb *creire* at the rhyme (Appendix 4, *RaT* #21). Where *Guillaume de Dole* garbles Bernart's text, Raimon reproaches it for construing the verb erroneously, taking the first person singular indicative to be *cre* when it should be *crei* (Chapter 1). The philological hypercorrectness of the parrots' way is the total opposite of the nightingales' grammatical incoherence, just as Raimon's emphasis on textual knowledge, his and the troubadour's, is the counterpart to Jean Renart's emotional hype.

Textual knowledge extends to include amorous understanding in Raimon Vidal's other quotation from "Can vei," in the *novas So fo*. The knight, unhappy with the response he has so far obtained from the lady he has served, quotes stanza VII to his confidante, the young lady (lines 49–56; Appendix 5, #14).[21] Unlike in the romance, in the *novas* the lines are quoted knowledgeably and in their original language, with no indication that they were ever intended to be sung. Whereas Jean Renart quotes the song anonymously, Raimon attributes it to Bernart de Ventadorn, identifying him as an authority on matters of love. The insertion of opening stanzas in the romance emphasizes song, but the knight's choice of a medial stanza places the emphasis on argument. In fact, it is by means of the quotation that the protagonist understands how he has been treated and how he should react. Even if Jean Renart did not intend the content of the Occitan stanzas that he quotes to be as opaque as it has become, he never seems concerned with using lyric insertion to pinpoint the finer points of a lover's experience.

Perhaps the most telling difference between these quotations from "Can vei" is that in the French romance the troubadour lyric is sung in competition with another song, but in the *novas* attention is so focused on "Can vei" that a summary of the stanza that is about to be quoted makes itself heard in the run-up to the actual quotation (see the passage in italics).

> Car sel que sos cors fon iratz
> *Car ab sidons no·l val servir*
> *Ni lonc atendre ni blandir,*
> *Ni ac un jorn no·n valc merces,*
> Li dis: "Amia, mal m'es pres,
> E pieitz aten, e pietz aten
> Car on pus ab mi dons m'aten
> Ni mays la prec ieu, may y pert,
> E mens y truep de bo sufert
> E avols ditz e peiorz faitz,
> Car son vengutz als mals retraitz,
> C'en B[ernartz] de Ventadorn dis,
> Que fon tan ves amors aclis,
> C'a mans n'a fag mans desplazer:
> 'Pus ab mi dons no·m pot valer . . .' "
> (*So fo*, R text, 419–33)

For the man whose heart was grief-stricken *because his service to his lady did him no good and nor did patient waiting, nor attentiveness, and never on any day did mercy avail him*, said to the young lady, "Friend, ill has overcome me, and I expect more ill, and more again, because the longer I wait with my lady, the more I beseech her, the more time I waste, and less reward do I get, but vile words and worse acts, for

I have now met with her complete withdrawal, like Bernart de Ventadorn spoke about who was so submissive to love, which causes much
displeasure to many: 'Since of no avail to me with my lady . . .'"

Where Jean Renart's narrative drowns out the troubadour's words, Raimon
Vidal opens his to receive them. The effect of solidarity between Raimon and
Bernart is strengthened by the metrical integration of the quotation to the surrounding text; the first and last lines of the stanza quoted form rhyming couplets with lines of Raimon's. This is the opposite of the French romance, where
the song is not integrated metrically but stands apart as an extraneous element.[22] If the parrots' way raises questions of knowledge, it does so because it
represents poetry as continuous with other forms of love discourse; the nightingales' way forecloses these questions by perpetuating its origins as song,
where song is conceived primarily as vocal expressivity and musical *sound*.

The Frenchness of Song in *Guillaume de Dole*

Jean Renart is concerned not with the Celtic *merveilles* that preoccupy many
other romancers but with France's current geographical, political, and linguistic frontiers, which he highlights in various ways; for example, the par-
ticipants at Conrad's tournament are patently selected to represent different
regions and countries. He also plots distinctly the home territories of his
protagonists—those who sing the songs in the romance—against the places
of origin of the songs themselves. The divergence between the two sets of
names draws attention to the frontier(s) between them. Only six of the inserted lyrics are assigned a geographical origin within *Guillaume de Dole*, but
these toponyms form a line that crosses France from the southwest to the
northeast, from the Auvergne and Poitou up to Sablé-sur-Sarthe (near Le Mans),
then Chartres, Reims, and at its most northern point, Soignies in Hainaut.[23]
Most of the places along this line fall in the heartland of the French kingdom
in the Ile de France and Champagne, while its two most extreme lie on contested frontiers: the northeastern one with the Empire, the southwestern one
with Occitania.

The three troubadour songs each receive different treatment. Bernart de
Ventadorn's is said to be anonymous and Poitevin (although Bernart was in
fact from the Limousin), one is presented as anonymous and Auvergnac (the

song is thought to be by Daude de Pradas, who actually came from the Quercy), and the third (by Jaufre Rudel of Blaye, on the Gironde) is quoted entirely without attribution. This disparate treatment has the effect of dismantling the unity of Occitan culture and implying that, instead of a single language, troubadours composed in various regional dialects of French. Since the other songs that Jean formally attributes to authors are all by poets from Maine northward, the "French" of Poitou and the Auvergne is clearly some way from the imputed center of French poetry. Its marginality is reinforced by the hybridized *scripta* used to record it.

Jean Renart's vagueness about the songs' origins may be strategic, an instance of his slippery ways. In the prologue, the narrator claims both that the songs are included in order to preserve their memory and that they have been inserted so seamlessly as to make one think that he himself composed them. The two claims seem to be at odds with one another: why would one view an original composition as preserving the memory of a previous one, or conversely, why would one view a remembered text as an original composition? These discrepant postulates converge, however, in a bid to put the songs' authorship in doubt and render authorship itself problematic. Taken together, the claims may imply that Jean Renart is *not* the author of the inset lyrics, however much their expert integration gives the contrary impression. Alternatively, they may together imply that, although the songs he includes may *recall* earlier songs, Jean Renart himself is their author, either literally, or by virtue of having so skillfully integrated them to his own work. Given how Jean Renart elsewhere ingeniously dissimulates his authorship,[24] we can take this playful equivocation as to whether the songs are by him as deliberate. Of the forty-eight inserted songs, only eight are explicitly conceded to other authors, so Jean Renart could indeed pass himself off as the author of the other forty, at least to a reader ignorant of the lyric tradition. And since only thirty of the inserted pieces are attested elsewhere, he could truly be responsible for nearly half of them (see details in Appendix 6). The staining or embroidering of his text with songs involves, then, yet another kind of opacity: that of their uncertain authorship.

One possible reason for this indeterminacy is to enable Jean Renart to conjure into existence a body of French poetry while at the same time giving the impression that it has authentic roots deep in French culture—in the France, that is, which lies to the west of the German Empire and the north of Occitania, and is lightly traversed by the snaking line of place names acknowledged as having produced French song.[25] This conjuring trick is especially effective in regard to the songs scholars call "popularizing" as opposed to those termed "courtly." Popularizing songs have a strong narrative cast, commonly have refrains, are typically sung at social events, and often involve dance and maybe a chorus in addition to the solo voice. They are generally anonymous when they are found in other manuscripts and all the roughly thirty examples in *Guillaume de Dole* are inserted without attribution; sometimes they are seemingly improvised by the characters who sing them, and almost half of them are unattested elsewhere (details in Appendix 6). Is Jean Renart the author of these otherwise unknown songs, or at least some of them? He would in that case be the creator of a pseudo-folk literature, a bit like those nineteenth-century forgers who set out to invent an authentic national tradition. Or is he exploiting the convention of anonymity in order to allow his audience to infer, should they so choose, that this body of song preexists his text? This "mirage of sources," as Dragonetti calls it, would be another way in which Jean Renart dyes or embroiders his text with "Frenchness" as the previously unsymbolized or unrecorded fund of popular song. Refrains, because they are transferrable from song to song, could especially be seen as a popular, French, performed, musical equivalent of quotation.

Such songs populate France (or "France") with characters with good French names like Gui, Alis, Doe, or Aiglentine. Another of their features is that many are gendered feminine (whether or not they are sung by women). Thirteen feature female protagonists;[26] five stage a female voice;[27] several imply a female subject position and a female voice.[28] In thus boosting the representation of women's roles, women's voices, and women's perspective, Jean Renart may have been less concerned with giving voice to women than with underlining the vernacular character of song, its association with the maternal vernacular, and the female body. French song appears as a "rose on the thigh" of France. Although all of the songs in *Guillaume de Dole* that are attributed with an author or other origin fall on the courtly side of the courtly-popular divide, at least half of these courtly songs, like the more popular ones, are unattested elsewhere and/or are performed anonymously. The impression is thereby given that most of the *grands chants* form essentially the same tradition as this body of French vernacular song—with one important exception, the song said to have been composed by Conrad (#31), to which I return.

Consequently, *Guillaume de Dole* implies a very different literary history from others that were current in Jean Renart's day. Collectors and commentators of troubadour poetry organize it following a hierarchy of genres that always privileges the *canso*, almost always classified by author, starting from the troubadours regarded as the most prestigious. Trouvère *chansonniers* also proceed author by author, giving the place of honor to the *grand chant* and typically starting with Thibaut de Champagne, who makes no appearance in *Guillaume de Dole*. Jean Renart is unique, indeed perverse, in making popular and women's song the determining matrix, both as the implied point of origin of French poetry, and as the frame in which it is to be viewed. An obvious effect of this new maternal origin is to deny to the troubadours any role as originators of the romance lyric. Indeed, what may well be the most contemporary song to be inserted is #41, by the troubadour Daude de Pradas (the so-called Auvergnac), whose known period of activity is from 1214 onward. It is an odd choice of song to quote, and it suggests that Jean Renart is actively interested not only in the cultural subordination and linguistic appropriation of Occitan song but also in representing the annexation of Occitania as current. Poitou and the Auvergne may also be named because they were areas annexed to the royal domain by Philip Augustus.

And what of the text's northeastern border, that between France and the Empire? Poets' names count for little in this romance compared with performers' names: those of the characters and the territories they are associated with, which all fall outside the kingdom of France.[29] Some, like Guillaume, Lienor, and their household, are from Dole in Burgundy, an area that speaks a Romance tongue, though one very different from Jean Renart's Francien. Others are from parts of the Empire that speak what we would now call German or Dutch. Although within the romance's fiction all the major characters and events take place in French, there are passing references to Dutch being spoken at Conrad's court (2169, 4664), to typically Flemish names being called out (Boidin, Wautre, 2168) and Germanic greetings exchanged ("'Wilecome!' et 'Godehere!'" 2595). The line of origin of the songs traverses France from southwest to northeast, with its heartland in the Ile de France and Champagne, but the place names associated with singers describe a crescent just outside France's eastern periphery, from Dole up to Liège. If Jean Renart had taken a highlighter pen and drawn it up France's eastern border he could not have made this frontier more evident. Just as evident is the representation of France's cultural dominance. Now that Occitan has been reclassified as regional French, it becomes evident that everyone in the Empire, whatever language he or she may speak, sings in French.

The paradoxical outcome is that what, from the standpoint of the romancer and his French audience, is a nightingales' way is, in Jean Renart's representation of the Welf dynasty, another version of the parrots' way: one in which the Empire imitates French song, as opposed to Occitan texts. Although Jean Renart negates the Occitan lyric by repositioning it on the margins of France, he also reaffirms it as a model for cultural hegemony.

The Welfs and French Song

Conrad's Germans and Burgundians repeat French songs adeptly, in the way that courts in Catalonia and Italy (including Staufer courts in Italy) repeat the poetry of the troubadours, although Conrad's entourage exclusively *sings* them. The widespread impression that there is an ironic distance between the characters' situation and the songs they sing is not surprising, then: the singers really are distanced from the lyrics because they are texts in a foreign tongue, moreover a *mother* or *female* tongue that expresses a mythic "French" *Volk*.

A prime example of this opacity of song to the singer is the *grand chant* that is described as being composed by the Welf emperor Conrad himself. He is in Cologne, far from the French border, whether imperial or linguistic. Seemingly inspired by the birdsong that he hears around him, Conrad spontaneously sings a lyric in the first stanza of which all of the features of the *grand chant* are assembled: *reverdie*, rose, nightingale, and the torments of love:

> Quant de la foelle espoissent li vergier,
> que l'erbe est vert et la rose espanie,
> et au matin oi le chant conmencier
> dou rossignol qui par le bois s'escrie,
> lors ne me sai vers amors conseillier,
> car oncques n'oi d'autre richece envie
>   fors que d'amors,
> ne riens [fors li] ne m'en puet fere aïe.
>   (*Guillaume de Dole*, 3180–87)

When the meadows grow thick with leaves, and the grass is green and the rose in full bloom, and in the morning I hear the nightingale's song that begins to cry through the woodland, then I don't know what to do with regard to Love, for I never envied anyone else their wealth except in love, and nothing [but Love] can help me now.

Conrad's composition in faultless French resembles Occitan imitations of troubadour lyrics by Italians or Catalans and contrasts with the garbling of Occitan in the French manuscript.

To what extent does the emperor know what he is singing? He will later show himself to be motivated by concerns other than love: rank and honor count for more, and when Lienor's "rose" comes under suspicion he abandons her at once. Conversely his listener, the treacherous seneschal, accepts the lyric at face value, but fails to show any respect for French courtly emotion. His accidentally overhearing it makes him jealous and provokes the visit to Dole that results in Lienor's being temporarily dishonored. Does the uneasy fit between the song's words and the practices of Conrad and his court stem from the melodious blotting of the nightingales' way or unwitting subjection to the *monolangue* of the parrots? Whatever the answer, the Germans' plot cannot progress without French song.

This chapter began with the difficulty of dating *Guillaume de Dole*. Although I have not brought forward new historical evidence, the literary context I have adduced for it is consistent with placing the romance after Raimon Vidal's *Razos de trobar* and *novas*, that is, after 1209 or 1213; and probably after the French humiliated the Occitans at Muret (1213) and the German and English forces at Bouvines (1214), at the time when the known period of activity of Daude de Pradas began (1214).

Situating *Guillaume de Dole* in this way nuances the traditional view of it as inaugurating French lyric insertion. Jean Renart's mapping of the nightingales' way now appears as much a reaction to the parrots' way as it does a novel treatment of French song. The enthusiastic scholarly attention paid to the troubadours' texts by their immediate neighbors can be seen as motivating his diametrically opposite promotion of song as song, as color and blot, as emotive if incoherent, as popular and maternal, and as exclusively French. Emulation of the success of literary Occitan at the Italian Staufer courts, however, may be responsible for his imagined imposition of French as a *monolangue* on the Welfs of the northern Empire where his romance is set.

## CHAPTER 6

The Parrots' Way

The *Novas del papagai* from Catalonia to Italy

If *Guillaume de Dole* maps the nightingales' way, two hilarious Occitan short stories can be read as a response to the issues raised by the parroting on which the Mediterranean transmission relies. *Las novas del papagai* (Tale of the parrot) and *Frayre de Joy e Sor de Plazer* (Brother of Joy and Sister of Pleasure) both present a male protagonist largely overshadowed by a talking bird, which serves as his factotum, especially in situations requiring diplomacy and courtship. The parrot that sweet-talks a lady into an erotic rendezvous with the knight Antiphanor in the *Papagai* (ca. 1250) may cut a less heroic figure than his master but is more resourceful. In the possibly later *Frayre de Joy*, parroting serves far-reaching (including spiritual) ends. Here a *jeai*—most likely a shortened form of *papagai*, or "popinjay" (parrot)—is given to Frayre de Joy by Virgil, who, in accordance with medieval tradition, is a master magician.[1] The *jeai* restores the hero's sleeping-beauty beloved to consciousness by magic, eloquently exonerates his master from blame for having made her pregnant while she was still asleep, ingeniously extricates itself from temporary capture, appeases the girl's understandably upset parents, persuades them to allow the hero and heroine to marry, and hobnobs with the pope while arranging the baby's baptism. This *jeai* is always in some sense a factotum following orders, yet its words are inspirational and transformative.[2]

The agency attributed to a parrot—as opposed to a nightingale—in these tales is both comic and unsettling.[3] By turns subordinate and managerial, merely repetitive and wildly imaginative, the bird provides the main lines of communication in both stories and is the essential vehicle without which their plots could not advance. The parrot's well-known capacity for mimicry turns a spotlight on the various forms of repetition that characterize the southern mode of reception, especially quotation. A bird's supposed lack of reason may trouble the dividing lines between speaking, quoting, repeating, and merely copying, distinctions that, as we have seen, are none too assured.

Suzanne Thiolier-Méjean has shown how fictional parrots often display knowledge of foreign languages, especially Occitan; her conclusions confirm the parrot's suitability to represent the verbatim percolation of Occitan through the multilingual Catalano-Occitano-Italian zone.[4] But the bird's purported multilingualism also manifests the *monolangue* as conceptualized by Jacques Derrida in *Le monolinguisme de l'autre*. By monolingualism, Derrida does not mean having only one language, even though some of the most moving parts of his book are those where he talks about the suppression of every language but French from his North African upbringing.[5] He means more fundamentally that any language, once one is speaking it, both defines the speaker and yet is other to him—hence the expression "monolingualism of the other" (see Introduction, above). The effect of speaking a language is always uncanny because it is the only home one has, and yet one is never at home in it. Language is, in the words of Derrida's subtitle, "a prosthesis of origin" in the sense that, while it appears the source of identities of all kinds, it is also an alien appendage, a contrivance that comes from without. As a mobile literary standard and language of culture, Occitan is prosthetic in this sense. Not only was it extensively used by Catalans and Italians; it also to some extent had to be learned even by troubadours from Occitan-speaking areas, being remarkably standardized regardless of their region of origin and not entirely native to any. As exotic birds, parrots are an apt representation of the otherness of literary Occitan to those who compose in it. They raise the possibility that all troubadours are parrots, not just those writers who explicitly imitate, copy, or quote from troubadour poems.

The Transmission of the *Papagai*

I focus on the *Novas del papagai*, the more relevant of the two stories since it is unquestionably parrot-centered and mid-thirteenth century. Five manuscripts transmit it, the divergences between them exhibiting both the kind of textual variation associated with the fabliaux[6] and the tendency of Occitan narrative verse to assume longer and shorter versions (see Chapter 2).[7] Such variations presumably reflect the tastes or expectations of different communities of readers within the Catalano-Occitano-Italian zone. In particular they offer rather different reflections on the nature and function of quotation.

Four of the five manuscripts that transmit the *novas* are the troubadour *chansonniers R, J, G,* and *Da* (the oldest section of *D*). The fifth stands apart: Florence Riccardiana 2756 is a late thirteenth-century Italian manuscript of Latin didactic works, at the end of which have been transcribed, as though they were prose, twenty-seven lines of Chrétien's *Cligés* and some forty-two lines of the *Papagai*; I shall call this manuscript *π*.[8] While *π* is the most marginal copy, the four *chansonniers* between them represent different strands of troubadour transmission. *R* is from Occitania, and seemingly reflects the prominence of Toulouse as a center of troubadour expertise in the fourteenth century.[9] The *Novas del papagai* is found in the nonlyric section of *R* that also transmits three Occitan *novas* by the Catalan savant Raimon Vidal de Besalú, and an epistle by another Catalan, the troubadour Guillem de Berguedà.[10] François Zufferey sees the presence of otherwise unaattested works by Catalans among these nonlyric pieces in *R* as a reflection of the literary links between Catalonia and Toulouse that developed during the fourteenth century when the Consistori de gai saber, based in Toulouse, vigorously promoted a troubadour revival.[11] By contrast, *D* and *G* are both northern Italian *chansonniers*. The fourth, *chansonnier J*, though apparently copied in eastern Languedoc, has much in common with the Italian transmission, particularly with *G*, and seems to have been compiled from primarily Italian sources.[12] Between them, the five manuscripts define the arc of territory in which Occitan is used, copied, and quoted; ordering them from west to east, we have *R*, then *J*, and then *G* and *D*, along with the non-*chansonnier* manuscript *π*. If *R* evokes Occitan as the *monolangue* in relation to Catalan, in *J* and *G* it becomes the *monolangue* in preference to Italian; while in *D* and *π* it coexists with other languages as well: French in the case of *D*, since the text comes shortly after three French *salut*-like texts and a little before the trouvère *chansonnier H*, which is bound into the same codex as *D*; Latin and French in that of *π*. In its various manifestations along this arc, the *novas* illuminates the parrots' way of the troubadours' Mediterranean reception.

The two manuscripts containing the longest, and probably complete, versions of the *novas* are those from Occitania, *R* and *J*; in all of the manuscripts originating in Italy the text is preserved in a shorter and perhaps fragmented form (Appendix 7 represents the different versions diagrammatically). *R* is the only copy to include an author's name, Arnaut de Carcassès. The surname suggests an origin either in the immediate region of Carcassonne, or else in a village thirty kilometers to the south of it:[13] in either case, in territories that were ruled by the Crown of Barcelona-Aragon until 1276 and that lay close to the linguistic frontier between Occitan and Catalan, probably just on the Occitan side of it. This chimes with the Catalano-Toulousain flavor of the nonlyric pieces in *R*. Moreover, since the *novas* in *R* is copied alongside other *novas* by Raimon Vidal, who was the first author to quote the troubadours (see Chapters 1 and 2), the *R* version of the *Novas del papagai* may also appear to address this literary vogue and its Catalan associations.

Da, *G*, and *J*, by contrast, all *chansonniers* with Italian roots, also share the common feature that they all contain collections of *coblas esparsas* or *triadas* from the troubadours. The *florilegium* in the *Dc* section of *D* consists mainly of well-known courtly songs that have been drastically reduced to *Reader's Digest* proportions (see Chapter 4), but as these are copied in a different part of the manuscript from the *Papagai* I shan't press for a relation between them and the *novas*. In *J* and *G*, however, the *novas* appears adjacent to the *coblas esparsas*, which are less courtly, and more humorous and satirical, than those in *Dc*, and are, moreover, similar in both manuscripts, since thirteen of the thirty-three *coblas* anthologized in *G* are also found among the seventy-four in *J* (see Appendix 2). The parrot in these manuscripts' versions of the *Novas del papagai* also points to the practice of quotation, but—in *G* especially—the *novas* itself now appears as a text that can be excerpted, and therefore potentially quoted *from*. Thus, from one standpoint, we have an Occitan transmission (*RJ*) that favors longer texts versus an Italian one that favors shorter ones (*GDπ*). But from another, we have an emblematic parrot that in *R* reflects the practice, originating in Catalonia, of *containing* quotations from the troubadours; and one that in G, and to some extent also in *JD* and *π*, also recalls the practice, originating in Italy, of copying and excerpting works so that they can *become* quotations.

The plot begins in the same way in the versions found in both *chansonniers R* and *J*. The narrator overhears a parrot in a garden wooing a lady on behalf of its master, the knight Antiphanor, son of a king. The lady refuses all his advances on the grounds that she has a husband whom she loves, but the parrot, by means of a bravura rhetorical performance, wins her over. At the point where the lady consents to return Antiphanor's love the versions diverge. In *J* the parrot goes back with the good news to his master and hurries him off to the garden. Briefly affirming their love for one another, lover and lady kiss and "took their solace" (*J*, 167; feron de lor solatz) until the parrot returns to warn them of the husband's return. Compelled to separate, they promise to meet again, Antiphanor pronouncing a 56-line oath swearing to love the lady faithfully. So long a speech is surprising, given the husband's threatening proximity, and feels disproportionate in a text that is, in total, only 245 lines long. In this version, then, the parrot speaks first, setting up the subsequent love scene in which the human beings speak about and perform their love, represented as a form of *fin' amor*.

In *R*, the narrative is more focused on the parrot and more fabliau-esque. When the lady has agreed to requite Antiphanor's love, she entrusts it with love tokens for its master, which the parrot duly conveys. It then urges Antiphanor to seal the deal and meet the lady. A good way to distract the husband's attention, the parrot suggests, would be to set fire to his castle; Antiphanor agrees and sends the parrot back to the lady to confirm the details of their rendezvous. The parrot then executes its cunning plan, flying to the castle carrying Greek fire in a cauldron clutched in its little toes. The castle blazes merrily, the lovers meet in the garden, but the fire is eventually put out and the parrot warns them they must part. The lady exhorts Antiphanor to be valiant and he departs cheerfully with the parrot. The narrator signs his name and declares he composed this tale as a warning to husbands who try to lock up their wives. As compared with the version in *J*, the *R* text reduplicates meetings between the lovers and the parrot, and records almost no exchanges between the lovers themselves. Less courtly than in *J*, the lovers' meeting in *R* is humorously paralleled by the burning castle and, when the "fire" has been put out, they seem quite content to separate with no thought of a future meeting.

The way the story develops in *R* is more familiar to modern readers since *R* is the base of most editions, but the *J* version is better represented in medieval copies. In *G*, the tale ends just after the parrot's return to Antiphanor with the expectation that the lovers will meet; the motif of the gifts is absent, aligning *G* with *J*. In *G*, furthermore, Antiphanor's long address to the lady, which forms the end of the story in *J*, is copied as a separate text a few folios *before* the beginning of the tale. As this passage is entirely in the first person, when severed from the *novas* it is a completely freestanding text, like a *salut*. Indeed, some scholars believe it to be an originally independent "address to a lady," or *domnejaire*, that was appended to the *novas* in *J*, rather than an originally integral part of the *novas* that was excerpted in *G*; its potential existence as a poem in its own right is acknowledged in the award of its own PC number, 461.VI.[14] The same extract or *domnejaire* is copied as a freestanding item in *D*, which otherwise contains none of the rest of the *novas*. The short extract in the only non-*chansonnier* manuscript, π, corresponds to the first eighty or so lines of the common beginning, but is closer to *J* and *G* than to *R*.

Most scholarship on these variant versions is preoccupied with identifying the original form of the tale. My approach, however, is not chronological but geographical, as I trace the insights of the different copies into the reception of troubadour poetry along the parrots' way, as it stretches from Catalonia, via Occitania, to northern Italy. Since all versions of the *Novas del papagai* share the first panel constituted by the parrot's persuasion of the lady, this common element will be considered first.

Parroting the Troubadours

Our entire knowledge of Antiphanor in this first part of the text comes from the parrot's representation of him as the best knight in the world who has, the parrot claims, already fought to demonstrate his love for the lady. Initially the parrot is represented as the mere intermediary of a message that allegedly originated with Antiphanor: "I am a messenger . . . Antiphanor . . . sends you greetings . . . and asks you through me" (Messatje soy . . . Antiphanor . . . vos tramet salutz . . . e prega·us per mi; *R*, 8–16; *JG*π).[15] Antiphanor is, says the parrot, sick with love that only the lady can heal (this last motif is more extensively elaborated in *JG*π), a message hardly striking for its originality. Soon, however, the parrot starts embroidering independently:

Encara·us dic may, per ma fe
per que·l devetz aver merce:
car, si·eus play, morir vol per vos
may que per autre vieure joios.
(*R* text, 19–22; *J*π)[16]

And I tell you further, by my faith, why you should have mercy on him: for if it pleases you [or *perhaps rather*: thus I pledge to you, <*plevir*], he prefers to die for you rather than to love happily through someone else.

Only at this point does the lady respond, and clearly she is impressed: "You seem to me extremely/excessively good at arguing" (*R*, 26, "Trop me paretz enrazonatz"; with less reservation in *JG*, "molt mi pares enrazonatz"). Now that the lady has been drawn into argument, the parrot is forced to continue improvising. To each rhetorical sally the lady responds with humorous admiration. The parrot is so eloquent, she says, that if only it were a knight it would have no shortage of girlfriends! But she still has no intention of betraying her husband. Finally, the parrot delivers its winning speech (*R*, 66–90; *JG*),[17] a virtuoso performance that begins with reformulations of some of its previous inducements, then continues with new ones fired off in a rapid salvo: loving Antiphanor in secret need not prevent the lady loving her husband in public, she is obliged to have mercy on a love-struck suitor (both these arguments have been made before); she should take heed of the exemplary love of Blanchefleur, Iseut, and Thisbe; it will do her no good if Antiphanor pines away, on the contrary the god of love will punish her, and it, the parrot, will blacken her name as much as it can.[18] The parrot here acts as a jongleur-troubadour, capable of reciting songs of courtship, but also in command of a repertoire of narrative works and a satirical tongue that it would not hesitate to use against her. In the face of this rhetorical barrage, the lady gives in, repeating her earlier admiration for the parrot's eloquence and even repeating some of its words as she does so: "And I tell you further that I am amazed you know how to woo so well" (Encara·us dic que·m meravelh / car vos tan gent [sabetz] prejar; *R*, 92–93; *JG*). She is explicit that the parrot's wooing is the reason for her love: "As a result of your entreaty I will love him and never leave him" (pels vostres precx, l'amaray / et ja de luy no·m partiray; *R* 102–3; *JG*).[19] The clichés in this episode are pronounced as much by the characters as by the parrot, and the whole of this opening panel confirms what Paul Carter says in his study *Parrot*: "We persist in thinking that parrots merely mimic us, when their mimicry is a way of telling us that we are mimics."[20]

A relation between the parrot and quotation is forged in this, the common stock of the *novas* in the various versions. But these versions diverge in their representation of the parrot's role and of the concept of "parroting," following the arc from west to east described starting with *R* on the Catalano-Occitan side, and then moving on to *J*, *G*, *D*, and finally *π*.

The Parrots' Way in *Chansonnier R*

The development of the second half of the story in *R* begins with a delicious display of the parrot's proverbial skill as a mimic. The lady entrusts it with traditional love gifts:

E portatz li·m aquest anel
qu'el mon non cug n'aya pus bel,
ab sest cordo ab aur obrat,
que·l prenga per m'amistat

(R text, 104–7)

So take him this ring for me, which I don't believe can be bettered
anywhere in the world, together with this cord worked with gold,
for him to take out of friendship for me.

The parrot duly delivers them, repeating word for word "And I give you this
ring . . .":

E tramet vos aquest anel
qu'el mon non cug n'aya pus bel,
ab sest cordo ab aur obrat,
que·l prendatz per m'amistat.

(R text, 136–39)

Such exact repetition indicates that this version at least might be guying
the Catalan author Raimon Vidal's *novas* with their scholarly, verbatim quotations from the troubadours. However, if the lady gives the parrot full instructions for it to repeat, the material Antiphanor gives his factotum to
communicate back to the lady is much less polished. All he can say is, "Go
back and talk to her again and tell her these things we have spoken about."

Tornatz prymier al parlamen
a lieys parlar, si a vos platz,
doncx sestas razos li mostratz.

(R text, 153–55)

Antiphanor's speech relies on earlier speech and in particular his phrase "sestas razos" refers back to the parrot's own suggestion that it could set fire to
the husband's castle so as to create an opportunity for the lady and Antiphanor to meet. Antiphanor's commission, then, adds strictly nothing to
what the parrot has already said: the parrot has no one to quote but itself, and
Antiphanor, as the name may imply, is merely the parrot's echo, or anti-
phon.[21] Keen to avoid any slip-up on the part of these unimaginative human

beings, the parrot spells out how Antiphanor can benefit from the proposed diversion:

> E can lo foc er abrassatz,
> poiretz intrar per espatz,
> ab vostra dompna domenjar
> e lieis tener et abrassar.
> (R text, 148–51)

And when the fire is set alight you can easily get in, pay court to your lady, and hold and kiss her.

It is even more explicit with the lady, giving her step-by-step instructions on how to admit Antiphanor to the garden and take pleasure with him in a bed.

In the passage just quoted (lines 148–51), the parrot not only plans to fire the castle, it also establishes the fire as metaphor for the lover's sexual activity by means of the pun on *abrassatz*, meaning first "set alight" and then "embrace." The resulting identification of *fin' amor* with arson is hilarious. Is it even possible that the much repeated word *foc*, in the succession "metre foc" (253, 259), "Al foc!" (260), "E·l foc fo totz adormatatz" (275), "que·l foc es mortz" (283), recalls the verb *fotre*? In any case insistence on the sequence "set fire" "fire!" "the fire receded," "the fire was dead," with its exact parallel in the actions of the lovers, all too manifestly mimics the successive phases of their encounter. The parrot in the *R* version of the *Novas del papagai* not only repeats and dictates the words of the characters, it shapes their desires, leads them to perform them, and exhibits what is most intimate about them in a farcical external display. Muscle-bound and inarticulate, Antiphanor in particular has his identity shaped by the parrot as his prosthesis, monolinguist, and comic double.[22]

The Parrots' Way in *Chansonnier J*

In the *J* version of the *novas*, the immediate consequence of the opening scene in which the parrot woos the lady is the encounter between the lovers. This might lead us to expect that the model of real human courtship in the second would expose as a mere copy the courtship performed by the parrot, but such an expectation would be disappointed. Although the parrot claims to be simply a messenger, the feelings and attitudes of both humans turn out to be heavily mediated by *it*. The lady opens her meeting with Antiphanor by telling him that, if she has formed an excellent impression of him, it is thanks to the parrot:

Gran tems ha, non ui caualier,
tan mi plagues, si dieu mi sal,
per uostre papagai uos ual,
car hieu uos uei tan plazentier
pero, quar es tan ben parlier,
e per lo be que·m di de uos,
e quar es tan bel e tan pros
farai uostre comandamen.

(*J* text, 136–43)

I've not for a long time seen a knight who pleased me as much, so save me God, you have your parrot to thank for this, that [*or* for?] I see you so agreeable, and so, because you are so eloquent, and because of the good things it told me about you, and because you are so handsome and valiant, I will do your command.

The syntax of this passage is left somewhat floating in Stengel's punctuation, but it appears that the knight's pleasing looks were sculpted in the lady's mind by the parrot ("per uostre papagai uos ual / car hieu uos uei tan plazentier") before they could be confirmed by her observation ("quar es tan bel e tan pros"), whereas the parrot's eloquence in speaking well of his master ("per lo ben que·m di de uos") was first of all an attribute of Antiphanor himself ("quar es tan ben parlier"). Antiphanor declares he will love the lady loyally and offers to swear to that effect. This convinces her enough to dispense him from further oaths, because she has already decided that he is "courtly, wise and valiant" (cortes, sauis, e pros; *J* text, 162), another phrase that rings as a *redite*, this time of her earlier recognition of his qualities as communicated by the parrot. We may know in theory that all discourse is pervaded by citationality, but having its effects concentrated in a parrot that alternates between the roles of ventriloquist and dummy so that one can no longer tell which is which, delivers that recognition with a shock of laughter. The oath that ends this version of the tale, but is found elsewhere as an independent text, expresses the fidelity that Antiphanor earlier offered to swear, but did not;

postponing it allows the lovers to kiss and embrace in the little time that re-mains before the parrot calls a halt on the grounds of the husband's return. Unlike in *R*, where consummation leads to what looks like a definitive sepa-ration, the parrot in *J* leads the *fin aman* to embrace constancy in hopes of further meetings, sentiments expressed in the long quasi-lyric address by the knight to the lady. In this version of the *Novas del papagai*, the parrot evokes less the formal act of quotation than the infinite recyclability of troubadour love discourse and the endless sublimation it performs.

Another difference from *R* is that whereas in *R* the *novas* forms part of an Occitano-Catalan nonlyric cluster, in *J* it is the only narrative in the *chanson-nier*. It is copied immediately after a series of *cansos* grouped by author and shortly before its concluding collection of isolated stanzas, from which it is separated by two lyrics of different genres: a widely copied parodic wish-fantasy *sirventes* by Pistoleta (372.3), listing all the things he would like and doesn't have, and a silly *tenso* between Gaucelm Faidit and Perdigon on the question of which is more reprehensible, a husband who guards a beautiful wife or one who polices an ugly one (167.47 = 370.12). The opening *coblas* in the *florilegium* likewise promote courtly behavior and condemn adultery. The desire for wisdom like Solomon's features as a shared theme in a stanza of Pistoleta's song and in the third of the isolated *coblas*, a much-copied anony-mous anthology piece (461.154). The *Novas del papagai* thereby appears as a fulcrum tipping between love songs and scraps of rueful wisdom regarding love. Its dialogue form, opposing an initially faithful lady and a corrupting parrot, may also chime with its position close to the *tenso* about adultery. The parrot's involvement in iteration in the *J* version of the *novas* is paralleled by the way the text leads on to excerpts and the courtly knowledge they may bring, but the *novas* does not itself yet figure as a quotation.

The Parrots' Way in *Chansonniers G* and *D*, and the π Text

In the Italian manuscripts *D*, *G*, and π, however, the "parrot factor" takes a new turn as the "lover's oath" part of the *novas* is itself excerpted—that is, unless we see the text in *J* as originally comprising independent texts that have been joined together.[23] In *G* the tale is found, as in *J*, almost immedi-ately before a collection of *coblas triadas*. In *J* the *novas* is the only nonlyric work, but *G* places it in a small group of *ensenhamens* and *saluts* that has been inserted between its main lyric corpus and the *florilegium*. (This nonlyric section of texts in rhyming couplets has some overlap with that of *R*, but without the Catalan reminiscences; conversely in *R* there are no Italian-style *coblas triadas*.) The most striking feature of *G* is its separation of the *J* text into two parts. The *domnejaire*, or closing monologue, of the *Papagai* (sixty-four lines) is copied anonymously and without rubric on folio 120r following Arnaut de Maruelh's *ensenhamen* "Razos es e mezura" (30.VI) and his *salut* "Donmna genser q'eu no sair dir" (30.III).[24] It is followed on folios 120v–127v by two more *saluts* (Falquet de Romans' "Dompna eu pring conjat de vos," 156.I, misattributed here to Pons de Capdoill, and Raimbaut d'Aurenga's "Donna, cel qe·us es bos amics," 389.I) and by Garin lo Brun's *ensenhamen* "El termini d'estiu" (163.I).[25] Then, beginning on folio 127v, the first part of the *Papagai* is copied in a form shortened from *J*'s 110 lines to 98 by the omission of most of the lady's protestations of fidelity to her husband, and ending with her agreeing to receive Antiphanor. It appears, then, as a short dialogue between a lady and a parrot in which the parrot easily persuades the lady to betray her husband. It is followed by a satirical two-*cobla* exchange between Blacatz and another troubadour (?Peire Pelisiers), asking which of three thieves received the worst punishment for his theft (97.3 = 353.2), and a scurrilous two-stanza celebration of *un fotaire* (461.241). In short, *G* represents the *domnejaire* part of the *novas* as a freestanding *salut* alongside other *saluts*, and then tilts the opening dialogue with the parrot toward satire. In their abridged form vis-à-vis other manuscripts, these two parts of the *novas* appear as anthology pieces, and thus on the way to themselves becoming quotations, especially given their proximity to the *G florilegium*.

The last part of the *novas* in *J* is also found as a self-contained *domnejaire* at the end of the section of *D* known as *Da*, thought to be the oldest *chansonnier* in existence. At some distance from *Dc*, the *florilegium* of Ferrarino da Ferrara, the *domnejaire* in *Da* is not explicitly connected to excerption. It does, however, share the courtly didactic quality of the *Dc* anthology more than the scurrilous orientation of *JG*, since it follows directly after a short encyclopedic text (Peire Corbian's *Tezaur*). Charmaine Lee underlines the preference on the part of Italian audiences, already suggested by other scholars, for courtly didacticism and their tendency to shy away from narratives of adultery,[26] and this may explain why, in this pioneering *chansonnier*, only the most anodyne part of the *novas* is included: the parrot and its wily seduction are gone.

They reappear, however, in *π*, the least monolingual of all the manuscripts, since the extract found there, copied in a space at the end of a compilation of Latin and French didactic texts, is juxtaposed with the excerpt from

Cligés in such a way as potentially to draw attention to their common use of Greek protagonists (Antiphanor is a Greek name). Indeed, the text of the π excerpt is itself distinctly hybrid, the parrot's first words to the lady being full of Italianisms: "Donna, Dieu vu sal, / messagier sum, ne vu sia mal; / del miglior cabbaler cum fus" (π text, Wesselofsky, lines 7–9). Antiphanor's prosthesis has lost touch with the refined literary standard of the other manuscripts, producing a mishmash resembling other examples of parrot talk identified by Thiolier-Méjean.[27] Unlike in other copies of the *novas*, the parrot's memory in π is certainly not of the best. The extract tails off in the course of the bird's attempts to persuade the lady by reminding her of famous literary lovers. Alas, these memorable tales prove too much for it to remember; both text and meter seem to drift out of control (the editor does not even attempt line divisions):

> Domna de vus me meravil, che de bom cor non ll'amez, Nel vu remembre de Flur et de Blanceflur, d'Isotto c'amo Trittan,
>
> E de Tisbe co al* pertus   *MS alal
> Ala parleva Perannus? (π text, Wesselofsky, p. 329)

> Lady, I am amazed at your not loving him with a good heart. Don't you remember Floire and Blanchefleur, Iseut who loved Tristan, and Thisbe who, at the hole, went and spoke to Pyramus?

A Pyramus crossed with perennial is frankly not *that* perennial. In this manuscript, so distant from the *chansonnier* tradition, the parrot and the Occitan love discourse that it represents have lost their standing to the prestige *monolangue* of Latin.

In conclusion, then, the parrot in the *Novas del papagai* epitomizes the parrots' way that stretches across the northern Mediterranean from Catalonia to northern Italy. In Derrida's terms, the parrot, as it directs the speech and actions of the characters it allegedly serves, is a prosthesis embodying the colonializing otherness of language to the speaker, the fabrication in language of identities and desires, and the repetitions it involves whether it is explicitly quoted or not. The manuscript context of the *novas* promotes interaction between the parrot and various modes of textual repetition—especially quoting and being quoted—but also reveals differences between the dominant modes of repetition in different areas. The version in *R*, copied alongside the two *novas* of Raimon Vidal that contain quotations from the troubadours, is the only one in which the parrot literally quotes verbatim; it seemingly pokes fun at quoting the troubadours as potentially incendiary; the attribution to Arnaut de Carcassès strengthens reference to the specifically Catalan use of Occitan. In *J* the parrot is caught up in recycling courtly discourse without, however, there being any formal quotation; the *novas* forms a bridge between lyric texts and a satirical *florilegium*. *G*'s version places the knight's monologue among other *saluts*, pares down the narrative core to a *tenso*-like dialogue about adultery, and makes both segments function as anthology pieces anticipating its collection of *coblas triadas*. The courtly value of excerption is clearest in *D* where, however, the parrot is absent. In *π*, the parrot loses its credibility in proximity to the primarily Latin compendium. While the *novas*' content laughs at our uncanny relation to language and desire, its diverse manuscript situations discreetly evoke the troubadour diaspora and the plurilingualism of the northern Mediterranean.

PART III

Transforming Troubadour Quotation

## CHAPTER 7

Songs Within Songs

Subjectivity and Performance in Bertolome Zorzi (74.9) and Jofre de Foixà (304.1)

The chapters that make up the final part of this book study texts in which the use of quotation elaborates and transforms the pioneering models explored in Chapters 1 to 4 (and reflected on in Chapters 5 and 6). This chapter is about quotations from the troubadours in other Occitan lyrics.

Although it is not uncommon for songs to reprise elements of other songs and to quote parts of lines from them, especially their incipits,[1] verbatim quotation of a whole line or more is rare. In *Die Dialektik des Trobars*, his exhaustive study of allusions between troubadours, Jörn Gruber identifies only seven examples of which two are the songs examined in this chapter. Bertolome Zorzi's "Mout fai sobrieira folia" (74.9) cannibalizes Peire Vidal's "Quant hom es en autrui poder" (364.39) by incorporating the first four lines of each of the seven stanzas of Peire's *canso-sirventes* as the last quatrain of each stanza of his own (the texts of both songs are given in Appendix 8). And Jofre de Foixà's *canso* "Be m'a lonc temps menat a guiza d'aura" (304.1) quotes the incipit of a well-known troubadour love song as the final line of each of its six stanzas and its *tornada*. The incipits thus recycled are Arnaut de Maruelh's "Las grans beutatz e·l fis ensenhamens" (30.16) and "Si·m destreignetz, dompna, vos et Amors" (30.23) (stanzas I and II); Perdigon's "Ben aio·l mal e·l afan e·l consir" (370.3) and "Ir' e pezars e dona ses merce" (370.8) (stanzas III and IV); Folquet de Marselha's "Amors, merce: non mueira tan soven" (155.1) (stanza V); Gaucelm Faidit's "Mon cor et mi e mes bonas chansos" (167.37) (stanza VI); and Pons de Capdoill's "Humils e francs e fis soplei ves vos"

(375.10) (*tornada*; for details and the complete text of Jofre's song, see Appendix 9).

The uniqueness of these two songs, with their extraordinary OULIPO-like construction, leaps out when they are compared with Gruber's other examples of lyrics containing full-line quotations (the quoted song is the first of each pair):[2]

Giraut de Bornelh 242.40	Iois e chanz / e solatz / E cortesia·m platz	(*canso*)
Anonymous 461.142a	Jois e chans e solatz E amors certana E cortesia·m platz	(*descort*)
Raimon Jordan 404.7	Per solatz e per deport Mi conort	(*canso*)
Guillem de Salaignac 235.2	Per solatz et per deport Me conort[3]	(*descort*)
Peire Guillem de Luzerna 344.3	En aquest gai sonet leuger	(*sirventes*)
Anonymous 461.104	En aquest gai son e leugier	(*descort*)
Cadenet 106.10	Be volgra, s'esser pogues	(crusade song)
Guiraut d'Espanha 244.1a	Ben volgra s'esser pogues	(*dansa*)[4]
Bernart de Rovenac 66.2	D'un sirventes m'es grans volontatz preza	(*sirventes*)
Luquet Gatelus 290.1a	D'un sirventes m'es grans volontatz preza	(*sirventes*)

Whereas both Bertolome and Jofre quote extensively, these songs merely repeat the incipit from one other song. The lyrics composed by Bertolome and Jofre are both forms of the *canso*, but the other five quoting songs are from more marginal genres. Most of the songs they quote are relatively marginal, too, or at least are not quoted elsewhere.[5] By contrast, the troubadours whose lines are redeployed by Bertolome and Jofre are among the best represented in Appendices 1 and 2, and most of the eight songs in question are quoted elsewhere and/or anthologized, some of them several times.[6] The incipits included in Jofre de Foixà's song are sufficiently familiar to evoke a spectrum of other contexts: Arnaut's "Si·m destreignetz," for example, is quoted in a grammar, a *novas*, a *razo*, and the *Breviari*, and anthologized in *CmDcFa*; passages from Folquet's "Amors, merce" appear in a grammar, a *novas*, and the *Breviari*, and are excerpted in *DcFaHJ* (see discussion in Chapter 4). And although Bertolome's wholesale plundering is unprecedented—no one else systematically excerpts *half* stanzas, nor pillages precisely *half* of an existing text, discarding the other half—his choice of Peire Vidal's "Quant hom es en autrui poder" similarly places him in the mainstream. Five of its seven stanzas are also quoted in the *Breviari d'amor*, and it is further quoted in the *Doctrina d'acort* and excerpted in *DcFa*; in addition to evoking other quotations of this same troubadour, Bertolome's radical diminution of Peire's song seems to reference the rigorous scaling down of lyrics in *florilegia*. It is safe to infer that, in integrating the words of other troubadours verbatim into their own texts, Bertolome and Jofre are knowingly engaging with practices with which they are familiar from elsewhere than within the lyric. In the other five cases identified by Gruber it is much less clear that there is any such reference to the practice of quotation at large.

On the other hand, Gruber's five other cases present some illuminating similarities with the songs by Bertolome and Jofre. None of the quoting troubadours cites his source (though Bertolome does so indirectly) but simply assumes another's line(s) as his own, thereby making the fact of quotation unusually challenging to recognize. Because the quoted words are in the first person, their utterance blurs the subject position of the one quoted with that of the one who quotes. The effects of this coalescence will vary, but it is noticeable that most of Gruber's quoting poets are, like Bertolome Zorzi and Jofre de Foixà, non-Occitan poets redeploying the works of Occitan troubadours who are far better known than themselves, as if to gain a share in their prestige and a stake in their linguistic patrimony. All these examples, that is, illustrate a desire to claim a subject position in the *monolangue*.

Gruber's examples also all have implications for music and performance. Troubadour quotation is normally the opposite of *contrafactum*: in the first, the words are quoted without the melody; in the second, the melody is quoted without the words. But when a line from a song is quoted within another song, either its original tune is retained (and textual quotation coincides with musical quotation), or else it acquires a new melody in its new context (and the relation between quotation and *contrafactum* shifts).[7] Either way, the divorce of words from music found in other quotations is resisted. The practice of quoting one song within another therefore extends the technical range of both lyric and quotation, in what Adrian Armstrong, adopting the concept of "virtuous circle" in economics, has called a "virtuoso circle": a knowing accumulation of poetic resources resulting from poets' interactions one with another.[8]

However, both Jofre and Bertolome stand apart by their topsy-turvy positioning of quotation. Instead of reusing another poet's first line as their own, they invert the quoted material from the beginning to the end of a stanza. This affects musical performance, since the quoted lines, which were originally set to opening cadences, are now sung to closing ones. In a culture where incipits and explicits are the keys to defining and recognizing works, transforming one into the other is a subversive gesture. The love of beginnings that informs the inauguration of a self-consciously written culture for the troubadours undergoes a remarkable twist at the hands of Bertolome and Jofre, and may even be countered head on.

A Song of Three Halves: Bertolome Zorzi's "Mout fai sobrieira folia"

A Venetian merchant and diplomat, Bertolome Zorzi's known period of activity as a troubadour is circa 1266 to 1273; between 1263 and 1270 he was held prisoner by the Genoese during their war with Venice.[9] His corpus of eighteen songs, preserved only in *AIK*, contains several that build on the same form as songs by other composers.[10] A political strain runs through many of them, and stanzas I–IV of "Mout fai sobrieira folia" seem to follow suit since they progressively mount a veiled attack on an unidentified person (see Appendix 8).

In the *tornada* of his song, Bertolome describes it as playing with revelation and concealment, at which his editor, Emil Levy, complains that "the disguise of its meaning has been only too successful."[11] Line 64 identifies the work as a *dimei chant* (half song), the formulation referring presumably to the half that Bertolome actually composed himself. But the term clearly draws attention to the song's other half, the seven half stanzas by Peire Vidal that Bertolome annexes for his own purposes; and beyond that, to its *other* other half, those parts of Peire's text that Bertolome has excised. Bertolome's boast about his *gran sciensa* (66, great learning) may allude specifically to his knowledge of Peire Vidal's song, his mastery of which has enabled him to borrow from it only what serves his apparent nonsense, and thus veil the sense that would emerge more plainly if the remainder were recalled to mind.

Certainly, Bertolome edits "Quant home es en autrui poder" in such a way as to reorient the satirical content of stanzas I–IV toward his own concerns and divert the love theme to the very end of his own song; although both lyrics are *canso-sirventes*, they thus differ in their dosage of *canso* and *sirventes* components. (Note that in Avalle's edition of "Quant home es en autrui poder" the relevant stanzas are in fact I, II, III and V, stanzas V and IV having been transposed either by Bertolome himself or in his source.)

The theme of love that opens Peire's song disappears at the beginning of Bertolome's into general reflections on power and the need for dissimulation. Bertolome's stanza II encapsulates the contention that meaning is best conveyed in concealment, since it quotes from Peire Vidal the need for diplomacy and even hypocrisy if one is to avoid giving offense to others, but then omits to reiterate his advice to seize the opportunity to harm one's oppressor when it arises. Bertolome's suppression of Peire's very particular reference in stanza III to the power of the Genoese inevitably calls to mind the Venetian troubadour's seven years as a prisoner in Genoa,[12] where he was indeed "en autrui poder" (in someone else's power). Peire's railing in stanza IV (Avalle's stanza V) against nobles who subordinate courtly to fiscal concerns, is effaced in favor of the rather unspecific reproach of someone who should have assisted him but failed to do so. Only in the concluding stanzas does Bertolome cease alluding, via Peire, to his own rancor and bring his song into sync with the love theme in the corresponding stanzas of his model.

The sense that this is a literary joke as much as a satirical polemic is built by the first stanza. Peire Vidal's reputation, fostered by the troubadour himself and cemented by his biographers, was that of a near lunatic. In defying anyone to call Peire mad (1–2), Bertolome is therefore taking on the whole Peire Vidal legend. His endorsement of Peire's "great natural judgment" (3) plays with the convention of affirming the authority of an author one is about to quote—paradoxically given Peire's reputation, and also parodically since the only evidence Bertolome offers for the wisdom of quoting Peire is that he does so himself (4–5). Much of the humor of these opening stanzas derives from systematic equivocation between *dire* meaning "compose" and "repeat." If it was true, pace the legend, that Peire Vidal showed sense in composing these verses, does Bertolome make it truer by repeating them? The more the text of "Mout fai" uses the word *dire*—and it does so frequently (see lines 2, 4, 10, 14, 19, 20, 23, 46, and 58)—the less one knows who is speaking (and there is no sign in the manuscript copies that some of these words are quoted).[13] This evasion is at its most comic in stanza III which announces that, contrary to what the enemy of the speaker (which speaker?) may have thought, he (who?) knows what is best for him (whom? 24–25) and can (who can?) interpret other people's behavior (what others? 26–27), in short he (who?) is thoroughly trustworthy (21) and without a shred of deceit (23)! Whereas elsewhere quotation brings about a strange cohabitation of voices, Bertolome's self-presentation as Peire Vidal constitutes a veritable drag act that draws attention to citationality as the motor of poetic production.[14]

The ambiguity of a *dire* that is always already a *redite* must also have been inscribed in the musical performance of this song. The melody of "Mout fai sobrieira folia" does not survive, but three manuscripts (*GRW*) transmit music for "Quant hom es en autrui poder." The *G* and *W* versions are more similar to one another than either is to *R*,[15] but in all manuscripts the melody concludes on middle C, while line 4, the midpoint of the stanza, perches unresolved on the G above. This note of expectation is overturned in Bertolome's drag act that transforms Peire Vidal's opening sallies into conclusions for his own thoughts, quoting selectively so as to eliminate as much concrete meaning as possible from Peire's text in favor of a shadow play of remainders and an echo of unheard song.

"Mout fai sobrieira folia" both retains and overturns the love of beginnings as it transforms beginnings into endings and as techniques associated with the schoolroom are travestied in a kind of comic writing that is rarely found in Occitan lyric.

Jofre de Foixà's "Be m'a lonc temps menat a guiza d'aura" and the Force of Song

The Monk (*monge*) of Foissan, as Jofre de Foixà is called in *chansonnier* rubrics, was a Catalan whose dates of known activity range from 1267 to 1295, a little later than Bertolome Zorzi's but overlapping with them. Jofre seems to have been what we would now call a troubleshooter: he was entrusted with a series of delicate assignments, such as reforming the management of religious houses, which he apparently carried out with exceptional skill.[16] First a Franciscan friar, then a Benedictine monk, Jofre's services were not confined to these orders. His *Regles de trobar*, a treatise in the Vidal tradition written for the Catalan court in Sicily between 1289 and 1295, contains snippets of unattributed verse that may be by him. In addition, he is assigned four *cansos* whose date is unknown but which are assumed to be youthful works composed in Catalonia prior to the *Regles*; they are transmitted solely in *C* and *R*.[17] Jofre's "Be m'a lonc temps menat a guiza d'aura" is remarkable for the way it condenses many songs within its compass, most obviously because of its inclusion of the incipits from seven golden age troubadour songs, but also because it reprises Northern French and Latin poetry. The result is that, like Bertolome's "Mout fai," it echoes densely with the Occitan lyric, while also engaging comically with Latin schoolroom practices of composition and quotation.

Jofre's contribution to the Occitan grammatical tradition sheds interesting light on his treatment of incipits. We have seen how quoting a first line to stand for (some or all of) the rest of a song typifies the scholastic turn taken by courtly poetry in Catalonia and Italy, especially the tendency in grammars and in the organization of *chansonniers* to grammaticalize troubadour poetry (Chapters 1 and 3). Already there are more instances of contextualizing incipits in the *CL* text of the *Razos de trobar* than in the earlier *BH* redaction. Beyond the Vidal tradition, grammarians' recourse to incipits only increases. In the two poetic treatises from Ripoll, first lines stand in for all the songs referenced, a usage also adopted by Dante in *De vulgari eloquentia*; in his *Mirall de trobar* the early fourteenth-century Catalan Berenguer d'Anoia systematically introduces his examples by quoting the incipit of the song from which they are taken (see Appendix 13). Given the establishment of this norm, it is surprising that in his *Regles de trobar* Jofre should quote only one first line, that of Bernart de Ventadorn's "Era·m cosselhatz, senhor" (70.6), using it moreover not in lieu of a title but as a self-contained example illustrating the form *senhor*.[18] This, in conjunction with the extreme infrequency of verbatim quotation of full lines within lyrics elsewhere, makes the presence of seven incipits in "Be m'a lonc temps menat a guiza d'aura" utterly unexpected. It is as though Jofre de Foixà took stock of what everyone else was doing—at least within the Occitan tradition—and then did the exact opposite. Is "Be m'a lonc temps" actively mocking and transforming the scholastic usage of the incipit, which the later treatise merely resists?

The song that scholars agree must have served as Jofre's immediate model helps direct our answer to this question and, as it does so, provides a novel, external perspective on the parrots' way. The northern French trouvère Gilles de Viés-Maisons is thought to have composed "Se per mon chant me deüse aligier" (RS 1252) around 1200. It survives in two versions, one of four stanzas each concluding with an incipit and another of six stanzas of which only the first two end in this way. Holger Petersen Dyggve argues convincingly that the first of these versions, preserved in trouvère *chansonnier C*, is closer to the original.[19] Its opening stanza ends with the first line of an extremely well-known song by the Chastelain de Couci (RS 40); subsequent stanzas have as their final lines two incipits from Gace Brulé (RS 42, 1102) and one from Blondel de Nesle (RS 1227). According to Dyggve, all three *trouvères* are Gilles's contemporaries and belong in the same patronage milieu.

Gilles's skill in quotation is well displayed in this first stanza. The singer hopes that song can lighten his mood where nature fails to do so, but his distinction between art and the world falters on the delicious ambiguity of the closing line:

> Se per mon chant me deüsse aligier
> de l'ire grant ke j'ai en mon couraige,
> mestier m'avroit, car a moi leecier
> ni mi valt riens, ne ne mi rasuaige
> fuelle ne flors, chans d'oisiax per boscaige;
> plus seux iriés quant plux oi coentoier
> *la douce voix dou roisignor savaige.*
> ("Se per mon chant," 1–7)[20]

If, from the great distress in my heart, I could lighten my mood by my singing, that would be useful, for nothing cheers or consoles me, neither leaf nor flower nor birdsong in the groves; I just feel worse the more I hear merrily singing "the sweet voice of the wild nightingale."

"J'oi coentoier" (I hear merrily singing) announces both a literal referent (the annoying nightingale) and an incipit (from the Chastelain's apparently equally annoying song); it barely matters which, since Gilles's mood is so bad that listening to either makes it worse. Given that nightingales epitomize the spontaneity and integrity of the lyric subject, it is especially piquant to find one at the very point in the stanza where a meta-discourse opens out and where the subject position equivocates between Gilles and the Chastelain. In each of the three other stanzas of this version, the same ambiguity is wittily replayed between quoting a famous lyric and simply completing what comes before.

István Frank proposes a possible antecedent for Gilles in Latin *versus cum auctoritate*, also called *chansons glosées* (glossed songs), a form probably invented by Walter of Châtillon and common in Latin goliardic or student poetry, which consists of quatrains each concluding with a well-known quotation from a Classical poet or else from the Bible.[21] Such verses are humorous distortions of hymns that quote, at the end of each stanza, the incipits of famous earlier hymns, whereas in *versus cum auctoritate* the quoted line that the rest of the stanza purports to gloss can come from anywhere in the "authority." Given the insistence on incipits in "Se per mon chant," Gilles may actually be imitating the liturgical archetype directly. Frank singles out as a likely model the twelfth-century Cistercian hymn "Corusca Sion inclitis / ornatibus, cum gloria," which includes among its seven quotations two incipits by Venantius Fortunatus plus another by Sedulius Scotus, and is also set to the music of an Ambrosian hymn.[22] Similar liturgical compositions abound through the thirteenth and into the fourteenth century; Gruber claims to have identified over a hundred of them.[23]

Whereas Bartolome Zorzi's travesty of Peire Vidal turns on the question "Who is speaking?" I suggest that Gilles's song is rather leading its audience to ask, "What am I hearing?" The song as a whole offers its listeners the option of hearing its unsung but nevertheless potentially present Latin models, liturgical and/or goliardic. Each stanza extends the possibility of either hearing or not recognizing the trouvère incipit that it quotes. Each incipit, once recognized, allows the audience the choice mentally to hear out, or not to entertain, the rest of the song from which it is taken. And aside from words that may or may not be heard, the song confronts the listener with music heard and unheard given that, alongside Gilles's own melody (notation for which survives in all copies except *CI*), the musical settings of the four songs quoted would also be evoked, making "Se per mon chant me deüsse aligier" a kind of virtual motet.

The question "What am I hearing?" is even more appropriate to Jofre de Foixà's "Be m'a lonc temps menat a guisa d'aura," which draws on Gilles's example while also exceeding it at every turn. For example, Jofre follows "Corusca Sion inclitis" more faithfully than Gilles, like it, including seven incipits where the trouvère supplied at most four. The spectacle of the troubadour in his monk's habit singing a secular love song modeled on a popular style of hymn must have been quite delicious to contemporary audiences.

In addition Jofre de Foixà, even more than Gilles de Viés-Maisons, capitalizes on the celebrity of Gace Brulé's "Tant m'a mené force de signorage."

This song enjoyed an astonishingly wide diffusion. The Swiss *Minnesänger* Rudolf von Fenis composed a German imitation (though probably not a *contrafactum*), which Jofre may have known since, somewhat like his own song, it recasts various troubadour songs.[24] The same form as "Tant m'a mené force de signorage" is also found in Gaucelm Faidit's "Pel messatgier que fai tan lonc estatge" (167.46).[25] This song in turn has a series of formal equivalents in Occitan including, amusingly, a *tenso* between Albertet (de Sestaro?) and a certain Monge (16.17 = 303.1) on the question whether the French or the Catalans are nobler, in which the Monk—as though anticipating the interest in the trouvères of the future Monk of Foissan—takes the side of the French.[26] Jofre de Foixà's "Be m'a lonc temps menat a guiza d'aura" is another member of this extensive, multilingual family of nightingale-style recreations.

Gilles de Viés-Maisons's "Se per mon chant" explicitly acknowledges Gace's influence, since his incipit "Tant m'a mené force de signorage" is quoted at the end of Gilles's second stanza (in the form "Trop m'ait greveit force de signoraige"). Both French *grands chants* have stanzas of seven decasyllabic lines arranged in *coblas doblas* with just two rhymes per stanza pair. Gilles, however, does not retain Gace's distribution of masculine and feminine rhymes, a'ba'bba'b, instead inverting it to produce the schema ab'ab'b'ab'. By contrast, the Occitan poems—Jofre's "Be m'a lonc temps menat," together with Gaucelm Faidit 167.46 and the Albertet-Monge *tenso*—retain the same versification as Gace. Jofre too signals his debt to Gace, since he alludes to the trouvère's incipit "Tant m'a mené force de signorage" in his own opening line.[27]

Assuming that Jofre adopts Gace's melody as well as his form, audiences who heard "Be m'a lonc temps menat" performed might be quite forcibly reminded of the text of "Tant m'a mené force de signorage." It is tempting, then, to speculate what the effect might be of hearing Gace's closing melodic phrase displace the opening cadence of all the famous troubadour songs that Jofre quotes. Notation for "Tant m'a mené force de signorage" is given in trouvère *chansonniers KLMNOTVX*, among which *KLMNOX* share essentially the same melody, *T* resembles the majority group in its first section but develops differently, and *V* has a third distinct melody.[28] All begin with an ABAB structure, which parallels Gace's a'ba'b rhyme scheme, and in the majority of manuscripts (*KLMNOX*) the final melodic line, E, ends with a recapitulation of the closing notes of the B melody, which also chimes with the return, in the final line, of the b rhyme. If "Be m'a lonc temps menat a guiza d'aura" were sung to this most widely copied version of Gace's melody, not only would the incipits of the famous songs quoted at the end of each stanza lose their own melody, they would resonate musically with the second and fourth lines of their new context, and their integration to its versification would by the same token be reinforced.

Whatever the musical realization of "Be m'a lonc temps menat a guiza d'aura," the way it inserts the final incipits does differ interestingly from the model offered by Gilles. The French trouvère scrupulously holds open two alternative readings, in one of which the incipit is allowed to be recognized as such, and thus as evoking the voice of its author, whereas in the other it simply completes the ongoing utterance in the voice of Gilles. The "I hear merrily singing" of the first stanza is followed by "I have heard said and witnessed" (line 13; j'ai oï contier et tesmoignier), "reminds me of" (20; me fait remenbreir), and "consoles me" (27; me fait reconforteir). Jofre's skill, by contrast, lies in effacing all traces of the rhetoric of quotation from his stanzas so that there is no sense whatever of any gap between the other troubadours' discourse and his own. (This is also true of its copies, since C and R do not distinguish the quoted verses from the others.) As Frank observes in his commentary on "Be m'a lonc temps menat a guiza d'aura," the lines preceding each quotation are marked by intricate syntax together with enjambment and *rejets*, which together enable a line that originally opened another troubadour's song to fall seamlessly into place at the end of the stanza in question.[29]

The effect can be extremely witty. In stanza III, in preparation for the last line, Perdigon's "May the suffering and anguish and longing be rewarded," the speaker wavers between the drawbacks and advantages of suffering, and jestingly asserts that he would willingly die for his lady if only it would not prevent him ever enjoying her love! But the seamless integration of the quotations also has important consequences for subjectivity. I have elsewhere sketched a theoretical reading of how a subject supposed to know plays out in "Be m'a lonc temps menat,"[30] so a brief example of my argument will suffice here: the quotation from Gaucelm Faidit at the end of stanza VI. Even in its original context, the line "My heart and me and my good songs" casts the first person in a somewhat alien and uncanny light. Now that it has been assimilated to a new textual "I" with its own (different?) heart, its own (separate?) "me," and who knows what songs, the line becomes a complex *jeu d'esprit* that casts doubt on the very existence of a subject of utterance.

Theorizing quotation from a modern perspective, Mary Orr draws attention to how "quotations invite onward transmission"; there is, she suggests, a vibrancy about quotable expressions that exceeds any context in which they are repeated and ensures that they remain more memorable than it.[31] An impulse toward their own reiteration can be discerned in the lines Jofre chooses, since so many of them are quoted elsewhere. In their case, "incipit," literally "it begins," could be understood psychoanalytically with the "it" (or "id," as Freud's *Es* is usually translated in English, French opting for the straightforwardly equivalent *ça*) taken in the psychoanalytic sense of an unconscious drive. "It begins" would then designate a form of repetition compulsion where the drive is not only to repeat, but to begin again and thus potentially to change. "Be m'a lonc temps menat" can be thought of as the plaything of such a drive. Although the song sometimes sounds like a plea for something or a complaint against something, it seeks above all for song to be constantly renewed. In the *tornada*, for instance, where the singer seemingly humbles himself before his lady, his reprise of Pons de Capdoill's humbling himself before *his* lady effectively redirects the act of reverence away from one lady or the other and toward poetry as such—toward the symbolic structure in which alone the subject's objects, and his supposed knowledge and love of them, can be essayed.

As treated by Jofre de Foixà, this drive constantly to begin again remains resolutely tied to music. The net effect of detaching each quoted incipit from its own melody is to make the song's symbolic texture extraordinarily polyphonic. Condensed within it are Latin sung traditions associated with both church and tavern, a French *grand chant* by Gilles de Viés-Maisons, another by Gace Brulé, and a series of formally identical songs in Occitan by Gaucelm Faidit, Albertet and his monkish interlocutor, as well as potentially a Swiss song. All this makes "Be m'a lonc temps menat" the expression not just of an ineluctable drive to keep beginning but also of a drive to keep singing that seems all the more vibrant for having been so long divorced from quotation in the Occitan tradition. In thus calling attention to song, Jofre's "it begins" reconnect the parrots' way to that of the nightingales' way in a playful but also significant renewal of the earlier Occitano-Catalano-Italian practice.

I do not believe there is any mutual influence between the two songs by Bertolome and by Jofre. Both react independently to the well-established practice of troubadour quotation and seek to reinsert what has become a purely textual usage back into the domain of song. In so doing they are turning the dominant mode of quotation on its head. If Bertolome sets out to conceal in full view the stanza openings of a single, well-known song, Jofre's strategy, with its ludic inversion of that scholastic shibboleth the incipit, draws a series of songs by well-known troubadours into relation with quoting practices from outside Occitania, all of which (like his own song) involve music. Whereas Bertolome does not question the parrots' way, Jofre approaches it from the perspective of the Chastelain de Couci's and Gilles de Viés-Maisons's northern French nightingales. The Monk of Foissan raises the stakes of quotation and expands the virtuous circle more than any other poet to quote from other lyrics, and this is no doubt why Petrarch later chose his song as a model for his own "Lasso me" (see Chapter 11).

## CHAPTER 8

Perilous Quotations

Language, Desire, and Knowledge in Matfre Ermengau's *Breviari d'amor*

Like Raimon Vidal counseling the young *joglar* in *Abril issia*, a text he certainly knew since he quotes from it,[1] Matfre Ermengau presents himself as writing at the request of his fellow troubadours in Béziers. But Matfre's response when asked to explain the true nature of love is on a different scale from Raimon's on court performance. His misleadingly named *Breviari d'amor* (Concise compendium of love) is one of the most ambitious vernacular texts of the Middle Ages, a vast verse encyclopedia about God, creation, and the nature of humankind, which remains unfinished at around 35,000 lines. Its unifying theme is the doctrine that God is love and that there is no being (*essencia*) other than his; God's creatures exist only by virtue of participating in divine love and manifest, however palely, aspects of their divine origin. All being can thus be represented as a great interconnecting tree of love.

Early in the text Matfre describes this tree, which is both a means of mapping the various species of being and the plan of his book. Most manuscripts at this point provide a magnificent whole-page illustration of the tree. One of its two branches consists of all animate creatures, defined by the form of love that is common to them all: that between male and female. From this branch forks the other, that of humankind who, as well as loving sexually, are also capable of loving and serving God. As long as God's creatures are true to their divine nature they are virtuous and fruitful. To represent this potential for virtue, Matfre posits two additional growths grafted on each of the two branches of the tree of love. On the side of human love sprouts the tree of life, one of the trees in Eden according to Genesis 2:9. Its leaves are the theological and cardinal virtues and its fruit is eternal life. A second, smaller tree represents the virtues arising from a proper concern for temporal goods and its fruit, enjoyment, is likewise proper to humanity. The branch constituted by all animate creatures supports a small graft bearing, as its fruits and leaves, the qualities arising from parenthood, but the major growth grafted into it is the other tree named in Genesis 2:9, the *albre de saber*, or tree of the knowledge of good and evil.

After treating God, the angels, and the creation of the physical world, Matfre expounds the doctrinal and moral topics that constitute the branch of specifically human love. His treatment of the second branch, that of the love of all animate beings, begins at line 27255 with the rubric "Of the love of male with female" (D'amor de mascl' ab feme). After a short introduction this branch has three main parts. First, the perilous treatise (*perilhos tractat*, 27791–31933) addresses the dangers of sexual love in a series of lawsuits (*plags*) against love brought by its opponents, and in advice (*conselhs*) given to ladies and their lovers.[2] Second, the tree of knowledge of good and evil (*albre de saber*, 31934–33881), although still identified as the biblical tree that brought about original sin, is now represented as a source of secular, life-enhancing virtues and their opposing faults; its fruit is offspring conceived in matrimony. And third, the remedies against love's madness (*remedis*, 33882–34539) advise on avoiding love's excess. A final section, which would have dealt with the other graft on this branch, love for one's offspring, peters out after only fifty-five lines.

A remarkable feature of Matfre's exposition throughout the *perilhos tractat*, the *albre de saber*, and the *remedis* is his quotation and discussion of troubadour lyrics. With impressive scholarly expertise, 267 passages are quoted from sixty-five named troubadours, many anonymous ones, and some French trouvères, making this part of the *Breviari* the single largest contributor to Appendix 1.[3] Appendix 10 summarizes its structure and indicates the distribution within it of quotations using the numbering in Ricketts's edition, which is explained in Appendix 11 (I use the same numbering to identify *Breviari* quotations in this chapter). But while the quotations index the extent of Matfre's knowledge and serve as a repository of a *savoir* of their own, they are quoted primarily to enable the reader to change—to escape eternal damnation, no less. In no other work examined in this book are supposed subjects of knowledge appealed to more with more therapeutic intent than in the *Breviari*.

The knowledge Matfre and the troubadours are supposed to possess is a knowledge of love: both of desire as it is experienced in human sexual love, and of love's essence as God himself. Matfre's complex knotting of knowledge with desire is very like Lacan's, except that the psychoanalyst eschews theology in favor of a secular perspective. Similarly to Matfre, Lacan postulates a knowledge that is irretrievably lost, though in Lacan's case this is because it is unconscious as a result of repression, because, as Lacan puts it, this knowledge is "the price of renouncing enjoyment" (le prix de la renonciation à la jouissance).[4]

By this formulation, Lacan means that forfeiting knowledge is the condition of subjectivation. The subject is by definition a being deprived of *jouissance* (an immediate, prelinguistic intimacy with sexuality and the body), and in order to become a subject he must surrender all knowledge of this bliss. However, this same payment, by making him a subject in the symbolic order, also enables him to acquire knowledge in the sense we understand the term. Thus the "price of renunciation" refers to knowledge not only as the price we *pay*, but also as the price we *get*. This abyss at the heart of knowledge between the sold and the purchased is one cause of the confusions surrounding supposed subjects of knowledge. In the clinical transference, discerning these confusions is therapeutic because it can draw attention to the split in the knowledge of supposed subjects and help the patient to acknowledge the truth of his own contingent relation to the symbolic.

Matfre posits a similar split in the field of knowledge. The Fall caused Adam and Eve to be cut off forever from their Edenic intimacy with God, and cost them their knowledge of this particular form of enjoyment; but in return they received the *savoir* paid to them—the knowledge of good and evil conveyed by the tree of that name, together with awareness of sexual love and desire. By depicting the biblical tree of knowledge as grafted into the branch of sexual love of the *albre d'amor*, Matfre insists on the intricate connection, as well as the abysmal distance, between human sexual desire and divine love. Are we to see the requirement to lead sexual lives as the result of Adam and Eve eating the fruit, or was sexuality the reason for their fall? Is moral knowledge achieved through desire, or is it something that desire causes us to lose?[5] In either case, the dual nature of knowledge is echoed in human desire, which can restore human beings to harmony with their lost, divine origin, but which is unfortunately much more likely to ensnare and corrupt them.

Matfre does not share Lacan's view of the human subject as purely contingent and hypothetical, but this does prevent him from using quotations in a way that can be characterized as transferential. Quotation exposes the moral divide in his readers' knowledge of desire, between whether it returns them to God's law or hurtles them onward to damnation. And it has the capacity to reform radically their relationship to this knowledge, reawakening them to a love that is free from guilt, retroactively transforming the lethal fruits of the tree into life-giving virtues, and "pointing the way to salvation" (34534; mostran la via de salut). The stakes of quotation have never been so high.[6] This chapter considers the different ways quotation is used in the successive parts of Matfre's argument.

Introducing the "Love of Male with Female"

In setting up this section of his encyclopedia, Matfre outlines the problematic relations between desire, language, and knowledge. His motive for discussing sexual desire is to instill its rightful use (27291–384): one that is free of vice and that promotes virtue, in particular the fruits of marriage and children. Matfre candidly concedes the contradiction whereby the *albre de saber* is both the biblical death-bearing tree and a source of secular life-enhancing virtues (27540–48). In an astonishing move, he orders people not to read the text that follows since, like the forbidden fruit in Eden, it will put their immortal souls at risk (27611–50). Devils will seize unwary readers (27631–40), a warning rendered graphically in the illustrations of some manuscripts (Figure 3). However, if readers can realign their desire in accordance with God's love, the food that formerly brought them death will make them flourish (27655–70).

Since intent determines sin, and the impulse to sin is inflamed by language (27609–10), it is necessary to shape intent with a language of pure desire. This is where the troubadours come in: misread, their poetry puts the soul in peril, but if it is interpreted as preserving traces of of divine love, it can yield "good doctrine, sound reason, good judgment, and virtuous qualities and behavior" ("bonas doctrinas, . . . /e bonas razos e bos sens, / bos aibs e bells captenemens," 27786–90). Matfre therefore aims to retrieve from the troubadours meanings the poets themselves had lost before they even knew they had them; they are subjects supposed to possess a knowledge that is truly beyond their recall. Thanks to Matfre's mediation, quotations from their poems arouse in the *Breviari*'s readers knowledge of a desire necessary for their salvation, one that will make good the knowledge of God's love that they had in Eden, now irrecoverably lost.[7]

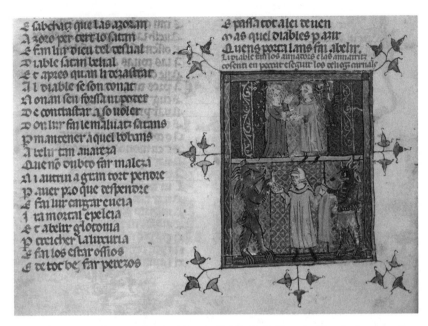

Figure 3. Vienna, Österreichische Nationalbibliothek, Hs 2583 (*Breviari* manuscript *G*), fo. 196v. Unlike some *Breviari* manuscripts, *G* does not here have a full-page painting of the devils that lurk in courtly activities, only this miniature occupying the foot of column *B*, just before line 27507, and headed "Li diable fan los aimadors e las aimatritz cosenti [*sic*] en peccat e seguir los deliegz carnals" (Devils cause lovers and ladies to consent to sin and follow carnal pleasures). In the upper register: a man and woman talking, demons whisper in their ears on either side. In the lower register: a man puts on new clothes, flanked by demons on either side. Note the face on the backside of the one on the left, who resembles the demons appearing in the margins next to quotations in the *perilhos tractat*.

One technique whereby Matfre "regenerates" (to use Valérie Fasseur's term)[8] these lost meanings is to preface a quotation with his own summary, thereby preempting the reader's understanding of it.[9] Formally, his insertion of extracts resembles Raimon Vidal's in his *novas* (see Chapter 2), since Matfre similarly integrates the troubadours' words metrically and discursively into their new context and stresses the wisdom of those he quotes. But he also shares extracts with the *florilegia*, and proceeds on a comparable scale; the way Matfre shapes interpretation is especially reminiscent of the compiler of the anthology in *H*, even though their intentions are utterly dissimilar (see Chapter 4).

Matfre also insists, however, that it is pointless to accumulate a discourse of knowledge around quotations. His opening quotation from Aimeric de Belenoi declares:

Qui vol apenre d'amor
   amar li cove,
que ja per esenhador
   no·n apenra re.
   (*Breviari*, 27821–24)

Whoever wants to learn from love must love: he will never learn anything from a teacher.

Aimeric's authority as a subject supposed to know derives from a knowledge of love that can never be communicated to those who don't already share it (27833–38). So although language shapes our knowledge of desire, desire also determines the capacity of our use of language to achieve knowledge. Matfre does not explain how he thinks this circularity can be changed, but his practice suggests that quotation operates by modeling different examples of its cycle so as to enable readers to make the leap from whatever pattern they are enmeshed in to a more salvific one.

Defensive Circularity: Aimeric de Peguilhan in the *Plags*

The four *plags* that open the *perilhos tractat* are ordered so as to work first from the side of language (the slanders of love's detractors, the complaints of poets), and then from that of sentiment (the laments of lovers and their complaints against women). Only after this does Matfre intervene in the lives of lovers (giving them advice in the *conselhs*). The *perilhos tractat* is a complex purifying plant in which the corruptions—linguistic, mental, affective—of human desire can, as far as possible, be addressed, preparing readers for the moral clarity of the *albre de saber* and thence, for a final refining round, to the *remedis*. Matfre's first move, then, is to lead readers into the position of defending pure love.

In each of the *plags* Matfre has the last word. The quotations in his final defense of each suit are selected to nail his argument. In his closing address to love's detractors he quotes passages that criticize those who slander love. His concluding words against the troubadours quote other troubadours who stigmatize the folly of attacking love. As regards lovers' grievances, Matfre quotes songs that do exactly what he is doing: complain against lovers who complain against love. And when finally dismissing lovers' attacks against ladies, he quotes from songs in which women are lavishly praised. These suits appear increasingly challenging for him, and perilous for the reader, as Matfre resorts to progressively larger numbers of quotations from more and more troubadours in his final defense of each. One poet—Aimeric de Peguilhan—appears especially frequently. Of the twenty-four extracts from thirteen of his songs that appear in the *Breviari*, twenty occur in the *perilhos tractat*, eleven of them in the speeches concluding individual *plags*; his support is particularly crucial in the two middle *plags*.[10]

Francesca M. Nicholson sees evidence for a bond between Aimeric de Peguilhan and Matfre from as early as the first Aimeric quotation, an extract from "Per razo natural" (10.40, #10, 28034–39), because it is immediately preceded by Matfre's first excerpt from a lyric of his own (297.5a, #9, 28020–27).[11] Matfre's song says that the virtuous are inevitably vilified but should not on that account cease their good work. Aimeric's stanza confirms the need to resist slanderers, for they are confined in their own malice:[12]

> Ges no falh quan s'ave
> qui ditz so que·ilh cove,
> que fals failh ver dizen
> e·l leials failh menten,
> qu'atressi failh fals leialtat menan
> cum le leials quan la vai desvian.
>
> (*Breviari*, 28034–39, #10)

> A man does not err when it comes about that he says what is fitting. For the false man errs when he speaks the truth and the man of his word errs when he lies. For the false man errs just as much when he acts with uprightness as the man of his word does when he goes astray.

The tortuous *adnominatio* of this stanza seals its circularity. Effectively Aimeric places the upright in a different symbolic universe from the false, each group knowing only its own truth. The stanza bolsters Matfre's affirmations that language, desire, and knowledge are all mutually determining; confronting this circularity might be the best way to enable the reader to change from a negative to a positive form of it. Aimeric's editors praise his poems for their decorum and high-mindedness,[13] qualities that provide Matfre with a perfect screen both in the sense that they shut out anything even faintly lecherous or sensual (hence perilous), and because they provide a surface receptive to his defensive (salvific) arguments.

Matfre is especially likely to anticipate the contents and phraseology of the quotations he takes from Aimeric. In the concluding section of the second *plag* he creates the impression of a solid front against backsliding troubadours by prequoting all of his witnesses.[14] Where Aimeric is concerned, such prequoting precedes the announcement of the following quotation, enabling Matfre always to present the troubadour as being in agreement with himself. The closing sequence Aimeric (249.1, #42)[15]–Matfre (297.5, #43)–Aimeric (10.15, #44)[16] consolidates their unison. Together Matfre and Aimeric declare that people are wrong to blame love when it is individuals who behave reprehensibly, their consensus epitomizing the preceding discussion and indeed the *plag* in general:

> Que per sso no fasso clamor
> ni cumplancha lunha d'amor,
> *quar cell qu'ab amor guereja*
> *majormen a tort foleja.*
> Et enaichi o digs tot pla
> ·l bos Aymericz de Pegulha,
> don digs, reprenden la error:
> > *Cell qui s'irais ni guerej' ab amor*
> > *ges que savis no fai,* al mieu semblan.
> > (*Breviari,* 28779–87, #44)

that they should not lodge any claim or complaint against love, for the *person who wars on love is committing a major and unjustifiable act of folly,* and the good Aimeric de Peguilhan said just this openly when he said, reproving the error, "*The person who wars on love is not acting wisely in the least,* it seems to me."

When Matfre begins his conclusion to the next *plag* he quotes the same phrases again (29080–86), this time to preface a song by Folquet de Marselha (155.21, #60, 29087–94) in which, however, the parallels are only rather general. It is hardly surprising that Folquet does not more precisely echo Matfre anticipating Aimeric; but the way Folquet's stanza is introduced nevertheless maximizes the impression of unison.

Despite Aimeric's generally bland high-mindedness, even his songs can benefit from regenerating as is shown by the knot of quotations ##74, 75, and 77 in the conclusion to this third *plag*. All are stanzas from Aimeric's "Anc mais de joy ni de chan" (10.8),[17] quoted by Matfre against the lovers' charge that love is overwhelmingly painful. Matfre counters that lovers have no one to blame but themselves if their hearts are inflamed: the motif of the eyes exciting the heart simply illustrates what the Bible reproves as "the lust of the eye."[18] Unfortunately for his argument, Aimeric's song quite specifically celebrates the eyes as the means to love and "interpreters of the heart" (drogoman / del cor).[19] In order to extract from it a condemnation of how the eyes incite dangerous passions, Matfre quotes the song selectively, modifies its argument by changing the stanza order, and surrounds quotations with commentary that inflects the way they are read.

As transmitted in the *chansonniers*,[20] "Anc mais de joy" starts with Aimeric extolling in general terms the need to be responsive to love's preeminence; he then submits to its power and hails the birth of true love from harmony between eyes and heart; in conclusion, Aimeric gratefully commends both eyes and heart to his lady. Matfre omits these final stanzas and works backward from the eyes' collusion in desire (III and IV) through to praise of love (II). He frames the first quotation (#74, stanza III) as an instance of Aimeric "gravely reproving lovers" (29374; reprenden mout los aimadors). As this is part of a passage (29368–402) conceding the importance of the eyes, it gives the impression that Aimeric is criticizing rather than welcoming the eyes' mediation. Quotation #75 (stanza IV) is capped by an endorsement that ostensibly reinforces Aimeric's words:

> Ben es vers senes falhensa,
> segon quez a dig N'Aimerics
> que fo tengutz entre·ls antics
> trobadors per un dels melhors,
> que, per obra d'ueilhs, est' amors,
> maintas vegadas, s'escompren
> (*Breviari*, 29403–8)

It is true without the least mistake as Sir Aimeric said, who was regarded as one of the best of the troubadours of old, that this love often catches fire through the eyes.

Yet by omitting from this summary Aimeric's eulogy of love born of the gaze—"then true love acquires its power" (29339; adoncas pren verai' amors valensa)[21]—Matfre makes the song appear neutral rather than approving toward desirous looks. Finally, the way Matfre quotes Aimeric's stanza II reinforces his point that lovers who complain at love should first examine their own conduct. Repositioned in this way, Aimeric appears to counter the lover's submission to the erotic gaze by enjoining him to assume love as a moral calling:

> Qu'amors no fai mal ni desconoichensa,
> per que lunhs hom s'en deia rancurar,
> ni ges amors no pot apoderar
> neguna re, ses grat d'autra valensa.
> (Breviari, 29440–44, #77)

For love does nothing wrong or undiscerning that could give anyone grounds for complaint, nor indeed can love overpower any creature without benefiting from some other force.

By making Aimeric's starting point his own conclusion, Matfre has repeated his text while transforming its meaning. Or rather, from his own perspective, he has recuperated its lost meaning as a celebration of the love by which we all ought to be (to have been) inspired. Temporarily suspending the subject as courtly lover, he repositions it as lover of God.

The plags are a ground-clearing operation in which Matfre defends fin' amor against its critics by disclosing its occluded connection to divine love and sidelining anything that might weaken that connection. Aimeric de Peguilhan assists Matfre's cause, but even Aimeric needs Matfre's assistance in order to enter into the circle of language, desire, and knowledge that Aimeric himself knew to exist.

Diabolical Circularity in the Conselhs

After the adversarial structure of the plags, the perilhos tractat enters a phase in which Matfre volunteers advice to ladies and lovers and so engages more openly with their desire. No longer primarily in defensive mode, the text advances onto perilous terrain that the poet struggles to control. A large variety of troubadours are quoted, and an important role is assigned to two anonymous verses as the the defensive cycle threatens to turn into a diabolical one.[22]

The first *conselh*, aimed at women, is longer but the second, addressed to men, is riskier—or so it seems, from the appearance of devils at various points in the margins of *Breviari* manuscripts *G*, *M*, and *N*.[23] The struggle for men's souls is harder to fight, or maybe is given greater priority, than that for the souls of women (which features just one demon, in *G*). The location of these marginal demons is as follows:

Line	Position in text	Preceding rubric	Manuscript, folio
ca. 30262	Matfre advises women, fourteen lines after rubric and fifteen lines before quotation #116 (Garin lo Brun, *ensenhamen*)	Matfre replies, giving advice to the ladies	*G*, 214v
ca. 31140	Matfre advises men, twelve lines after rubric and twenty-two lines before quotation #144 (Monge de Montaudo, 305.14, "Mos sens e ma conoissensa," stanza 3)	Matfre replies, giving advice to the lovers	*G*, 220r *M*, 241r
31266 ff.	Immediately beside quotation #149 (Anon., 461.134, unknown elsewhere)	As above	*G*, 221r *M*, 242r *N*, 230v
ca. 31449	Immediately after quotation #155 (Anon., 461.149, "Luocs es qu'om chan")	As above	*G*, 222r *M*, 243r

That these diabolical figures are an early feature of the tradition is suggested by the manuscripts' agreement on where to place them, and the fact that all the copies concerned belong in what scholars agree is the "better transmission" of the *Breviari*.[24] The demons graphically represent the perils of the *perilhos tractat* forewarned of by Matfre in his introduction (27425–30), when he evokes them as "counseling" (*coselhar*) both men and women to succumb to sexual temptation and so replay the originary drama of the Fall. They also hark back to the paintings of devils haunting courtly scenarios found in these and other illuminated manuscripts at the start of the introductory section

(27385) (see Figure 3).[25] No longer confined within the frame of such a picture, the demons' presence in the margins of the text is menacing and rather disgusting, particularly in *G*, where they are most numerous, depicted with the most grotesque and bestial features, and also appear oversized in comparison with the other images in the manuscript.[26]

The two initial devils, positioned shortly after an introductory rubric, cast a premonitory shadow over the whole of each *conselh* that follows. The first, in *G* only, is a half-erased figure in the bottom margin of folio 214v, its outstretched paw gesturing at the lines

> Quar mout hai avut gran dezir
> tostems de las donas servir.
> A donas, doncs, en general
> do per cosseilh bon e lial . . .
>   (*Breviari*, 30260–63)

> For I have had a very great desire always to serve ladies. I therefore
> give ladies in general this good and honorable advice . . .

The next ensuing recommendation is to women to dress and behave decorously; it is supported by extracts from Garin lo Brun's *ensenhamen* recommending women to exercise, in their hospitality, discernment and restraint in their favor to guests. The second demon, found in both *M* (fo. 241r) and *G* (fo. 220r), is placed beside a very similar passage to the first one, but in the second *conselh*:

> A totz los verais aimadors
> que volon amar per amors
> domnas, do per lial cosseilh
> que quascus d'amar s'apareilh . . .
>   (*Breviari*, 31140–43)

> To all true lovers who wish to love ladies with love, I give this honorable advice that each should prepare himself for loving . . .

In *M*, the diabolical figure has wings and a tail and points to line 31140. In *G*, where it is also gesturing to line 31140, it is an upright, lionlike grotesque with great paws, head, and tail, and two additional emergent heads, one on its shoulder, the other on its behind (Figure 4). Lovers, Matfre continues,

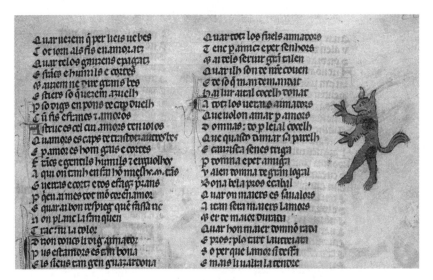

Figure 4. Vienna, Österreichische Nationalbibliothek, Hs 2583 (*Breviari* manuscript *G*), folio 220r. Demon with bestial features and three faces, placed opposite line 31140, where Matfre offers advice "a totz los verais aimadors" (to all true lovers).

should choose ladies of character who will inspire lasting regard and who will be slow to grant "that through which love is destroyed" (31153; sso per que l'amors si desfa), since to love such women is better than to find pleasure quickly with others. This advice is quickly supported by an extract from the Monge (monk) of Montaudo (305.14, #144) recommending honorable dedication to a noble lady over the disappointments (!) of satisfaction elsewhere.

The gross intrusion of these demons in the margins of both *conselhs* in *G* and the second *conselh* in *M* suggests that the very attempt to rein in sexual passion exposes its strength. Matfre urges decorum and control, but the topic alone excites our inner demons. The devil is the counselor's inevitable sinister twin.

The situation is only made worse by troubadours who bat for the other side, fanning the flames of desire when they ought to subdue them. Such is the case with #149 (anonymous, 461.134), an explicit declaration of sexual desire. Matfre has accumulated advice to lovers to choose a worthy lady and love her honorably; but times are perverted, he warns:

        E pessa quex cum puesc'aver
31255   sa dona et ab lieis *jazer*;
        et als fan pietz, al meu semblan,
        que quascus se vai avantan
        e dizen per gran nescies
        que *gran dezieg ha* cum pogues
31260   esser ab sidons en logual
        per far aquell fag deslial;
        d'aquells nescis baratadors
        que *desiron* aitals folors,
        fon us, lo qual no·us nomnarai
31265   per sso quar ges so nom no sai,
        ques digs mostran so foll voler:
            Gran dezir hai de ben jazer   [#149]
            en lieg de cossera d'amor,
            que fezes de me cobertor
31270   la bela que·m ten en poder,
            e dels pels saurs fos le coichis
            e·il lensol de gaug e de ris,
            e l'aurelhers fos de blanc bratz
            e·l matalatz vergiers o pratz.
31275   Ai! quans d'aitals trichadors son . . .
                    (*Breviari*, 31254–75)

and everyone is thinking about how to have his lady and *sleep* with her; and in other respects I think they behave worse, since everyone, in his great ignorance, goes vaunting and claiming that he has a *great desire* to contrive to be with his lady in a place where they can commit this unrighteous act. Among such ignorant schemers *desiring* such folly was one I shall not name to you, because I do not know his name, who declared, revealing his foolish intent: "*I have a great desire to sleep* in the featherbed of love and that the lovely one who has me in her power should make me her blanket, and that the cushion should be of golden hair and the sheets of joy and laughter and the pillow of white arms and the mattress a garden or meadow." Ah! How many such deceivers there are . . .

Matfre's elaborate disclaimers to knowing the author's identity (31264–65) are extraordinary in a text otherwise so keen to exhibit knowledge of the troubadours. This stanza is one of very few in the *Breviari* to be unattested elsewhere; one cannot fault Matfre's resourcefulness in unearthing a *cobla* so fit for condemnation; it is tempting to suspect him of having composed it himself in order to pillory it. In his preamble he whips up a storm of disapproval ("worse," 31256; "unrighteous," 31261; "ignorant schemers," 31262; "folly," 31263). But at the same time as castigating the *cobla*'s saucy opening line, he also reiterates and amplifies its phraseology (see italics): the circular relation between desire, language, and knowledge is here a vicious one in which Matfre too appears to be caught.

The stanza's inflammatory nature is signaled in three manuscripts. In *N* (fo. 230v) its initial G is borne in a flag by a devil with wings and horns, as if the very forces of hell fought under the banner of such wicked desire. Placed in the bottom left-hand corner of the folio, the devil's left foot rests against the paraph marking the end of the quotation, demarcating the whole of the offending passage. In *M* (fo. 242r), a demon in the left-hand margin points to the same initial; lacking wings, horns or tail, this is a simpler figure than the one in *N*, but like it his body extends alongside the *cobla* to the closing paraph. In *G* (fo. 221r) the extract is again identified as alarming by a demon painted exactly alongside it, this time in the space between the two columns (Figure 5). This grotesque and bestial figure has a fully formed face on its backside, as if to suggest that the *cobla* is not merely diabolical but fit to issue from a devil's anus. All these marginalia graphically remind readers that lyric poetry and the sentiments it expresses expose us more to mortal sin than to redemption.

A consequence of the demon in *G* being drawn between the two columns is that, while its upper mouth is turned toward quotation #149 in column *a*, the one on its backside is actually pointing toward the material in the facing column *b*. The impression is thereby given, perhaps involuntarily, that there is also a demonic menace lurking within the lines in question:

Enquaras es majers l'errors
d'aquestz deslials trichadors
que quascus ditz qu'ell es lials,
quan que sia trichaire e fals.
         (*Breviari*, 31311–14)

Figure 5a. Vienna, Österreichische Nationalbibliothek, Hs 2583 (*Breviari* manu-script *G*), folio 221r.

Figure 5. Vienna, Österreichische Nationalbibliothek, Hs 2583 (*Breviari* manuscript *G*), folio 221r. In the middle of this folio, a demon points to the inflammatory quotation (#149) that starts "Gran dezir hai de ben jazer" (I have a great desire to lie at ease; 461.134) at line 31267 in column *a*. Since its backside is a face, too, it also seems to address the "unprincipled deceivers" (or heretics?) stigmatized in lines 31311–12, immediately after quotation #150, in column *b*. Figure 5a (overleaf) shows the scale and position of the demon on the page; Figure 5b (above) shows the demon and texts close up.

The error of those unprincipled deceivers is greater still, each one of whom says he is upright, however deceiving and false he is.

Is the devil also implicated in the "error of the unprincipled deceivers"? Should *error* be understood here to include heresy? The lines in question are Matfre's conclusion to quotation 150 (225.10) in which Guillem de Montanhagol berates dishonorable lovers, and his introduction to 151 (167.15) in which Gaucelm Faidit likewise stigmatizes deceivers, so that in *G* no fewer than three quotations become corrupted by this particular demon's hellish taint.

The last marginal devil occurs in *G* and *M* immediately after quotation 155, another anonymous piece (461.149, also found in the *florilegium* in *chansonnier J*):

31440   Quar en totas res *deu guardar*
        luoc e sazo, qui be·u vol far,
        autramen pot hom leu falhir;

d'aquest bon cosseilh, ses mentir,
us trobaires enaichi·ns pais:
31445   *Luocs* es qu'om chan e que s'en lais   [#155]
    e *luocs* de rir' e de plorar,
    e de tot *deu hom luoc guardar*
    qui es savis, cortes ni guais.
    Doncs quan ve ira l'aimans verais
31450   sa dona en bon estamen . . .
                      (*Breviari*, 31440–50)

For if one wants to behave well one *should have regard for place* and season in all matters; otherwise one easily goes astray. A troubadour sus-
tained us quite truthfully with this advice in this way: "There is a *place*
to sing and a *place* to desist, a *place* to laugh and a place to weep, and a
man who is wise, courtly, or lighthearted *ought always to have regard for
place*." Thus, when a true lover is to see his lady in a good situation . . .

In a desperate bid to get the genie of desire back into the bottle of human
restraint, the passage continues with recommendations for self-control. In *M*
(fo. 243r) there is a devil in the right-hand margin immediately below the
quotation, pointing to line 31449 as if to underline the mortal peril in which
the exemplary lover finds himself with his lady. In *G* (fo. 222r), a demon is
stretching out to the same line, which, as in *M*, is further highlighted by a
paraph; but now the infernal figure is located in such a way that it could be
interpreted as speaking the *cobla* (Figure 6). Is this because its emphasis on
propriety of place, which reads like an attempt to erase the impropriety of
quotation 149, backfires, exciting the reader with thoughts of bedroom pleasures? Even its bland recommendations seem to pose a threat to the lover.
Devilish contamination predominates over regeneration.

    A final point to note about this demon in *G* is that its position in the inner
corner of a recto places it next to the foot of the facing verso (fo. 221v). Indeed a
grim black face growing out of its shoulder is actually directed to the text at the
bottom of that folio, which ends at line 31412. The passage thus falling within
the demon's purview includes Matfre's account of his brother's courtly ways:

Aichi dreg fai sos afaires
Raimons Ermengau mos fraires,

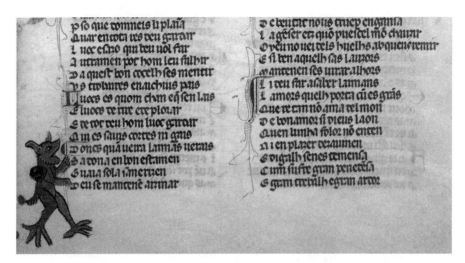

Figure 6. Vienna, Österreichische Nationalbibliothek, Hs 2583 (*Breviari* manuscript *G*), folio 222r. A demon in the bottom left-hand corner of the page points to the paraph on line 31449, which concludes quotation #155 (461.149; "Luocs es qu'om chan e que s'en lais") and draws the attention of lovers to the advice to draw from it: "So when a true lover is to see / his lady in a good situation . . ." (31449–50; Doncs quan veira l'aimans verais / sa dona en bon estamen). A grim black face growing out of its shoulder is directed to the foot of column *b* on folio 221v where Matfre's brother Raimon is described as being like a nightingale and a parrot.

> q'us rocinhols non es plus guais
> ni plus coenhdes us papaguais
> de lui, quar ja non sera las
> ni de cantar ni de solas,
> e plazo·lh sobre totas res
> belas raubas e bels arnes.
>   (*Breviari*, 31403–10)

My brother Raimon Ermengau lives just like this [viz., as recommended by Ovid, 31400], for a nightingale is not merrier nor a parrot smarter than he, for he will never be weary of singing and enjoyment, and more than anything he loves fine clothes and equipment.

The demon casts an ironic shadow on Matfre's praise, and perhaps even beyond it. Raimon is both nightingale and parrot; but a paraph cupping line 31406 in *G* separates the parrot from the nightingale and draws attention to it, provoking the reflection that Raimon is really much more like the parrot. Reference to his addiction to finery in 31409–10 recalls the courtly scenes with lurking devils from just before the *perilhos tractat*, one of which in *N* is inscribed "lo diables li fay desirer trop belas raubas *e* arnes" (the devil makes him desire fine clothes and equipment). The demon's fortuitous proximity to the two birds is made especially intriguing by the fact that it is depicted with huge bird's feet. The *mise en page* of *G* folios 221v–222r reminds readers that demons lurk not just in the *conselhs* but in all courtly activities, including singing and repeating other people's songs—the parrots' way of Raimon and of Matfre himself.

Tautologies in the Treatise of the Tree

Quotations in the *albre de saber* are embedded in a simpler framework than in the *perilhos tractat*, since they illustrate lists of virtues and their opposing vices; Matfre's commentaries primarily reiterate the words within each extract that relate to the quality in question. For example, between quotations 180 and 181[27] in the section on generosity he repeats the words *larc, donar,* and *dar* (generous, give); instances of *cortes* (courtly) and *cortezia* proliferate around quotations 189–194, which illustrate the virtue of courtliness;[28] and there is particularly dense repetition of *umilitat* and related forms around quotations 197–98 in the section on humility.[29]

Despite its simpler format, this section of the *Breviari* requires ingenuity in order to achieve such mutual reinforcement between quotation and commentary. Some virtues are hard to illustrate from the troubadour corpus. Even more than in the *conselhs* Matfre has recourse to anonymous stanzas; two-thirds of the *Breviari*'s anonymous or otherwise unknown examples occur in this section.[30] In discussing discernment, Matfre modifies the last line of Guiraut Riquier's song (248.18, #222), substituting *conoichensa* (discernment, knowledge) for *gran temensa* (great fear) in 33197 to make it conform better to his topic.[31] He quotes only a single line promoting the virtue of matrimony, Peire Cardenal's proverbial "You can recognize a tree by its fruit" (335.5, #219, line 32685; Qu'al frug conois hom lo fruchier), which accords strikingly with Matfre's structuring metaphor of a grafted tree. For children, the all-important fruit of the *albre de saber*, he cannot adduce a single quotation.

Some of the poets chosen here are unexpected. First, it is strange that more songs by Peire Vidal should appear illustrating the moral properties of

the tree than are found in any other section of the *Breviari*, and particularly
that four stanzas of a single, satirical, boasting song, "Quant hom es en autrui poder" (364.39), should be quoted to model three different virtues: patience (##220, 221), discernment (# 223), and courage (*bon coratge*, #239).[32]
Could Matfre have known Bertolome Zorzi's recuperation of this piece for
his own purposes (see Chapter 7)? When Matfre, in the same words as Bertolome, attributes to Peire "great natural judgment" (33166; gran sen natural),
could he be hailing Peire as a "holy fool," his apparent worldly folly an expression of divine wisdom and thus of the capacity for many virtues?

Second, it is noteworthy that Arnaut Daniel appears in the *Breviari* solely
to represent virtues of the tree: humility (#196, 29.6) and worth (*proeza*; #214,
29.9). I have commented elsewhere on the second instance, where Arnaut's
text has been modified from that of the *chansonniers* apparently in order to
celebrate *proeza* as a part of a grafted tree that is reminiscent of the *Breviari*
as a whole.[33] Matfre's recognition of Arnaut Daniel's aid in helping regenerate fallen humanity oddly anticipates Dante's placing him on the pilgrim's
pathway immediately before Paradise in the *Commedia* (see Chapter 9).

Despite its seemingly recursive format, then, quotations in this section of
the *Breviari* provoke strikingly revisionist interpretations of certain troubadours, interpretations that resonate with developments in troubadour quotation in Italy. Add to these the overlap with *florilegia* (*JG*) and the strategic
similarities with *H*, and quotations in the *Breviari* appear much more enmeshed in northern Mediterranean practice than is implied by Matfre's apparently local audience and the purely Occitan manuscript tradition of this
part of the *Breviari*.[34] Perhaps Matfre's transformation of quotation belongs
in a broader cultural context than previously thought.

Remedies for Love's Folly and the Regeneration of Occitania

Matfre has sketched out several circular discourses of love: defensive, potentially hellish, but also salvific. And so, where many medieval authors seek
remedies for love, at the end of his treatise Matfre need only quash its more
foolish aspects: enslavement to pleasure, blindness to women's deceits, and so
forth. (Praise of love does not mitigate antifeminism; if anything it increases
it, since love is too important to men to risk its being spoiled by women!) To
assist him, Matfre calls on Peire Cardenal for his last sequence of quotations

(##262–66). This well-known satirist of northern French oppression during the Albigensian Crusade becomes, in this section of the *Breviari*, the spokesman of responsible *fin' amor* as part of a virtuous life, occupying in the *remedis* the equivalent position to Aimeric in the *plags*.[35] Matfre's final quotation from Peire (335.48, #266) warns readers that the final judgment will overtake them when least expected (34528–32):

> Don digs En Peires Cardenal,
> mostran la via de salut:
>   Que Dieus te son arc tendut
>   e trai aqui on vol traire
>   e fai lo colp que deu faire
>   a quec si quo ha mergut,
>   segon vizi e vertut.
>   (*Breviari*, 34533–39, #267)

As Sir Peire Cardenal said, pointing the way to salvation: "For God holds his bow drawn and fires where he wishes to fire and shoots whom he has to shoot, each as he has deserved, according to his vice or virtue."

Cupid's bow is affirmed in the very image that displaces it with that of the true and only God of Love, who fires with the same terrifying unpredictability and far more devastating results.

Perhaps this quotation also advances a defense of specifically Occitan culture. According to Cardenal's editor, René Lavaud, the image here of God striking down the wicked recalls the description in the *Canso de la Crotzada* (Song of the Albigensian Crusade) of how a stone thrown by one of the town's defenders felled Simon de Montfort during the siege of Toulouse in 1218.[36] Peire's denunciation of treachery and wrongdoing in earlier stanzas may also allude to events in the Albigensian campaign.[37] Concluding his discussion of sexual love, Matfre seems to remind fellow poets in Béziers, the site of the Crusade's worst atrocity, that troubadour poetry is *their* poetry. Others may suspect it of heresy. Devils can make it as perilous as heresy. But by means of quotation, Matfre shows how it is also a uniquely privileged source of spiritual regeneration. In so doing, he transforms the meaning of troubadour poetry. He innovates even more, perhaps, in expanding theological discourse, which no one before him had found in secular love songs.[38] And, in the face of a mounting tradition of Occitan quotation elsewhere, he seeks to regenerate Occitan culture *in* Occitania.

This chapter has argued that quotation in the *Breviari* operates regeneratively according to a Lacanian view of knowledge as split. Quotation can serve to retrieve knowledge that was lost in the Fall of our essential connection with divine love and to identify the moral knowledge we thereby gained, and so help us arrest our precipitous descent into damnation. Defensive in the *plags*, exposing menace in the *conselhs*, tautological in the *albre*, the work of quotation is surprisingly historical in the *remedis*. By identifying different forms of circularity between desire and language, Matfre solicits different supposed subjects and the knowledge they may be supposed to possess. The intelligibility of his difficult poem depends on maintaining the value of the knowledge it purports to contain by imputing it—somewhere, somehow—to a series of subjects supposed to know. Readers are invited to acknowledge various troubadours as *auctoritates*; to recognize themselves as knowing the poems and troubadours that are quoted; to accept Matfre's own authority; and in the last resort to posit God's knowledge as the condition of all sound knowledge.

Such suppositions entangle readers in transferential play. They also expose the gaps between supposed *savoirs*, pointing the possibility for the subject to occupy a new, different position in the circle of language, desire, and knowledge. By thus addressing its transferential role, the *Breviari* both assimilates and transforms the preexisting culture of quotation. Matfre proposes quotations from the troubadours as offering an opportunity for salvation, but who knows what transformation his readers actually embraced.

Dante's Ex-Appropriation of the Troubadours in *De vulgari eloquentia* and the *Divina commedia*

The tradition of troubadour quotation sheds new light on the old topic of Dante and the troubadours.[1] Take the recurrent questions of how well and in what form Dante knew the troubadours. At different extremes, Marianne Shapiro quotes with approval Santangelo's *Dante e i trovatori provenzali* for suggesting that Dante's knowledge is heavily mediated by the Occitan treatises and biographical texts, whereas Maurizio Perugi thinks that Dante's phraseology is everywhere permeated by reminiscences of Arnaut Daniel's songs.[2] The debate is framed in such a way as to make it seem demeaning to Dante to suggest that he drew on the tradition of quotation described in this book—as though such a debt could only diminish his authority in relation to the poets themselves. But what if, in addition to having familiarity with the troubadours, Dante is seen as also intervening in the (by his time) long-standing practice of excerpting and commenting on them? How might Dante's texts be affected by the play between knowledge and subjectivity that it involves?

Of the eleven Occitan incipits quoted in *De vulgari eloquentia* (Of vernacular eloquence), seven are of songs featuring in a shortened form in *florilegia* and two of the rest (three in all) are included in *razos* (details are provided in Appendix 12).[3] Of the two remaining incipits, one (242.17) is quoted in another grammar, the *Mirall de trobar* (Mirror of composition) by Berenguer d'Anoia, and only one, Arnaut Daniel's "L'aur'amara" (29.13), is otherwise absent from both Appendix 1 and 2. This does not imply that Dante knew the others only from the sources covered by these appendices,[4] or that he did not also know copies of whole versions of these songs in *chansonniers*, but it certainly justifies exploring *De vulgari eloquentia* in light of the tradition of Occitan quotation which these appendices reflect.[5]

Reviewing the troubadours whom Dante quotes in this treatise, rather than the actual lines he selects, further reveals that all except Aimeric de Belenoi have previously been quoted in works that grammaticalize Occitan, whether by relating it to (Latin) grammar or by explaining the troubadours on the model of the (Latin) *accessus*. This observation, in turn, sheds light on differences between the troubadours represented in *De vulgari eloquentia* and in the *Divina commedia* (Divine comedy). Scholars have wondered why Giraut de Bornelh is celebrated in the first, but, in the second, he is subordinated poetically to Arnaut Daniel and morally to Folquet de Marselha.[6] An answer informed by the prior practice of quotation would explain that Dante's treatise develops from the tradition of Occitan grammatico-poetic writing in which Giraut is a central if contested model, whereas his generally biographical presentation of the troubadours in the *Comedy* owes more to Occitan's other grammaticalizing mode, that of the *vidas* and *razos*. In particular, the famous "Ieu sui Arnaut" of *Purgatorio* 26.142, though not a quotation in the sense I have defined for this study since it is under a line long, does nevertheless reprise one: that of three lines from 29.10 quoted in Arnaut Daniel's *vida*, a rare example of troubadour quotation in these biographical texts and the only one to be retained in the course of their adaptation in the *Comedy*.

Commentators have puzzled over Folquet de Marselha's awkwardly periphrastic account, in *Paradiso* 9.82–93, of his place of origin. In fully eleven lines, Provence is identified as part of a northern Mediterranean region that encompasses Catalonia and northern Italy rather than being demarcated from them. Has the *clus* style, purportedly abandoned by Arnaut Daniel in *Purgatorio* 26, been displaced onto Folquet?[7] The answer, in my view, is that Folquet's is no figurative utterance but a literal presentation of the Occitan-Catalan-Italian territory that is host to the parrots' way: a region united by its shared use of Occitan as a language possessing vernacular grammar, and as the medium of poetry, subjectivity and vernacular authority. That Dante acknowledges the unity of this cultural space should guide us to see him as reacting—like Jean Renart (see Chapter 5)—to its practices.[8] Similarly to the author of *Guillaume de Dole*, Dante polemicizes in favor of poetry in his native language: Occitan is to be displaced by the maternal idiom, even if, in Dante's case, most of the mothers turn out to be fathers. But whereas Jean Renart turned troubadour lyrics into blots of song, Dante responds to the parrots' way on its own terms, devising ways of divesting the Occitans of their ownership of poetry in the very act of seeming to acknowledge it.

I have argued throughout this book that the repetition involved in quotation is never simply repetition: it changes the meaning of that which is repeated and the subject position(s) that it implies. Since the passages Dante quotes from the troubadours preserve the original Occitan in their new linguistic environments—Latin in *De vulgari* and Italian in the *Commedia*—they are palpably transformed from native (or apparently native) utterances to fragments of an alien idiom; such linguistic divergence sharpens awareness that quotation implies relations between different subjects. This chapter analyzes troubadour quotations in the earlier and the later text to show how their play with knowledge and subjectivity is bound up in increasingly complex ways with notions of the alien and the proper, and how these notions concern Dante as a subject of poetry in the emergent language of Italian.

The term "ex-appropriation" in this chapter's title is adopted from *Le monolinguisme de l'autre*, where Derrida undermines the illusion on the part of the colonizers that they are masters of their own language, that as their property it is in some sense proper to them. To this fantasy of appropriation the philosopher opposes the concept of ex-appropriation, the contradictory prefixes "ex-" and "a-" indicating that the dream of owning one's own language is never realized, and that imagined proprietorship always leaves a trace of its failure, which Derrida here calls a "mark."[9] The term "mark," in turn, draws its significance from Derrida's earlier work on iteration, which underlines "the possibility of citational excerpting and grafting that characterizes the structure of every mark, spoken or written," so that the mark inherent in language is always being re-marked.[10] In the very act of quoting the troubadours, I shall argue, Dante re-marks them in such a way as both to recognize their preeminence and to eject them from it. In so doing, he ex-appropriates not only the troubadours themselves but also the grammaticalizing practices that, over the preceding century, constructed and cemented their seeming ownership of the language of poetry. Although in *De vulgari eloquentia* Dante presents himself and Italian as the beneficiaries of this process, by the *Commedia* he also acknowledges the extent that we are all inevitably alien to our own language; the troubadours can be ex-appropriated without his falling victim to a compensatory myth of appropriation.

"Since No One, Before Myself, Has Dealt with Eloquence in the Vernacular . . ."

All the Occitan treatises prior to or roughly contemporary with *De vulgari eloquentia* (1303–5) contain troubadour quotations except the *Donatz proensals* (Appendix 3). Texts of the Vidal tradition, which circulate freely between Catalonia and Italy, combine Occitan with Latin grammar and metaphysics and are peppered with examples from the lyric (see Chapter 1). The two short late thirteenth-century poetic treatises preserved in Ripoll also illustrate their points with incipits of troubadour songs.[11] The *Mirall de trobar*, which takes its direction from Isidore of Seville, includes a profusion of lyric excerpts (see Appendix 13). It has not been dated more precisely than to the first decade of the fourteenth century and so may be a contemporary or immediate successor rather than a forebear of *De vulgari eloquentia*, but in any case the texts invite comparison. The Catalan grammarian illustrates his points copiously with extracts from songs by four of the six troubadours quoted by Dante: Giraut de Bornelh (seven songs), Aimeric de Peguilhan (four songs), Folquet de Marselha (two songs, one of them quoted on two separate occasions), and Arnaut Daniel (two songs, one unknown elsewhere). Berenguer also regularly prefaces discussion of a particular point in a song by quoting its incipit (Appendix 13, ##2–25) or uses the incipit to stand for the entire song (##26–32). The prominence he accords to Giraut de Bornelh is not merely quantitative: the Limousin troubadour dominates the *Mirall*'s coverage of metaplasm (poetic license) and is cited for a linguistic failing only in his use of clitic forms. Dante's praise, in *De vulgari*, of Giraut's poetic substance and construction concords with his high standing for this contemporary grammarian and may even be intended to rebut the implied reservations of Raimon and Terramagnino discussed in Chapter 1.

As we saw in that chapter, the Vidalian treatises focus on nominal inflexion in order to demonstrate Occitan's kinship with Latin and as the means to poetic success, both in rhyming correctly and in elaborating a courtly *razo*. *De vulgari eloquentia* is of course about Italian not Occitan, and is written in Latin not the vernacular, but its approach nevertheless resembles that of its predecessors. Like Raimon, Terramagnino, and Jofre, Dante starts his treatise with reflections on the status relative to Latin of the spoken tongue, identified as a language of poetry that is coming into being, and which it is the author's purpose to promote and refine; like them, he seeks to strip this emergent literary language of incorrect or regional forms, while admitting that variation in usage constitutes the living quality of vernacular speech; his ambitions, like theirs, are not solely descriptive but have a metaphysical dimension; and like them, he marshals poetic extracts with a view to future poetic production. Dante cannot claim flexion as grounds for rapprochement with Latin, since medieval Italian by this stage did not inflect nominal forms for case, but he is if anything keener than the Vidal grammarians for Italian to be recognized both as the rightful heir of Latin, and as replacing it (1.10.1). He resembles Jofre de Foixà in affirming the autonomy of the vernacular, surpassing his Catalan predecessor in his enthusiasm for the spoken tongue. All these similarities point to Dante's familiarity with this grammatical tradition.

A major difference between *De vulgari eloquentia* and the Occitan grammars arises from the very fact of these treatises' existence, which challenges the Italian poet to acknowledge but also displace Occitan poetry as privileged site of vernacular poetic knowledge. Given his seeming knowledge of his predecessors, Dante's opening words, "Since I find that no one, before myself, has dealt in any way with the theory of eloquence in the vernacular . . ." (Cum neminem ante nos de vulgaris eloquentie doctrina quicquam inveniamus tractasse), appear to be intended humorously, alerting the reader to the ludic, draglike strain that runs throughout *De vulgari*; but their effect is also swiftly and unobtrusively to excise the entire Occitan grammatical tradition, and thereby discard the apparatus of learning with which it had surrounded the troubadours.[12] More positively, Dante innovates vis-à-vis the Occitan grammarians by explicitly admitting the dimension of time into his treatment of language, a move that has major repercussions for the status of literary Occitan and the earlier scholarship invested in it.

Raimon Vidal and his successors treat the diversity of Romance idioms in purely regional terms, but Dante distinguishes between linguistic variation in space and over time. The poetic weaknesses combated by the Occitan grammarians arise from alleged faults of conjugation or construction, but for *De vulgari*, as for the *Breviari*, poetry is more profoundly framed by a hermeneutic of Fall and redemption. All human speech, Dante says, is a flawed compromise between the wordless communication of the angels and the mindless empathy of the beasts (1.2.3–5); it has fallen away from the single original vernacular in which Adam saluted God in paradise (1.4–5); it demands reflection on "the process of change by which one and the same language became many" (1.9.1). Consequently, the difference between spatial and temporal difference is spiritually freighted. When documenting linguistic divergence in space, Dante's tone is that of farce or fabliau. On his panther hunt round Italy in quest of the true breath of the vernacular, examples of regional variation are quoted for laughs (1.9–14). The decline of language over time from its origin in paradise is presented with contrasting gravity. Of Babel, Dante writes that its "great confusion . . . brought nothing else than oblivion to whatever language has existed before" (1.9.6; confusionem illam que nil aliud fuit quam prioris oblivio). Language changes constantly and the past is made up of irrecoverable forms. Dante's project, in hunting down the true form of the illustrious vernacular among the comic distortions that proliferate, is to create a language for the future that will offer the best hope of recovering the glorious vernacular of paradise, long since irremediably lost.[13] This bid to regenerate linguistic loss follows the same theologically inspired trajectory as Matfre's quest for lost knowledge in his Breviari d'amor (see Chapter 8); in De vulgari it is additionally intended to give voice to the future, secular institutions, which Italy does not yet possess but which it will need if it is to become Italy (1.18). (Like Occitania, Italy is not unified politically, but, unlike it, Italy still lacks a single, recognized literary idiom. Dante wants, through his treatise, to contribute to a national identity, an aim different from the Vidal grammarians' leap into universality.)

In order to undergo linguistic regeneration, the forerunners of this future language must also be seen to be "lost." Daniel Heller-Roazen's comments on the passage about Babel (1.9.6), though their emphasis is different, support this interpretation: "Defined as the oblivion of its predecessor, each language, then, would repair the 'loss' of the one in whose wake it followed, and at the same time acknowledge its irreparable absence; each would constitute not only the reconstitution of the one before it, but also, paradoxically, its constitution."[14] The logic of regeneration is at the same time one of suppression. Occitan is peculiarly vulnerable to this logic. According to De vulgari (1.8.5–9.5), it is just one idiom of a single language of which Italian is also a form (and the langue d'oïl a third). As such it is contemporary with Italian; but such a status would risk exposing it to the vulgar triviality of spatial variation. If the language of the troubadours can be ejected from the present into the past, their poetry can be recuperated as a stepping-stone from the confusion of Babel to the true speech restored. Occitan must therefore be presented in such a way as to mark it as already sliding into the past. It is in this spirit, I believe, that Dante re-marks the troubadours.

Quotations from other poets in *De vulgari* are often read as inscribing a canonical lineage with Dante as its culmination. However, the notion of lineage and with it those of descent and chronology are ambiguous in this treatise. While, broadly speaking, four of the troubadours whom Dante quotes are twelfth century (Arnaut, Bertran, Folquet, and Giraut) and two had careers that fell in the thirteenth (the two Aimerics), in terms of the practice of quotation, they divide differently. Both Giraut and Folquet are quoted from the very earliest times, and Bertran de Born, too. Indeed Bertran is seldom quoted by later authors; his presence in *De vulgari* confirms Dante's debt to the grammaticalizing tradition, since the troubadour is very visible in the *razos* and appears regularly in works by, or influenced by, Raimon Vidal. The three other troubadours share a more recent quotation history. Arnaut Daniel is not referred to by the Vidal grammarians, makes few if significant appearances in the biographies, but comes gradually into vogue in the later thirteenth century.[15] Aimeric de Peguilhan has become a predictable reference point only in the decades immediately preceding *De vulgari*. And Aimeric de Belenoi is still somewhat marginal, since he is not quoted prior to (or beyond) the *Breviari*, though he is widely anthologized.

These different historicities illumine the divergent ordering of troubadours in the lists in *De vulgari*. The first (2.2.8), Bertran-Arnaut-Giraut, groups three poets of the golden age of Occitania; the second (2.6.6), Giraut-Folquet-Arnaut-Aimeric de Belenoi-Aimeric de Peguilhan, begins with those with the most venerable quotation history before progressing to the relative newcomers.[16] Arnaut's mobility between the two groups enables him to be both close to Dante and distant from him. His presence in the second group highlights the capacity of the practice of quotation to re-mark an older author in a new, more contemporary form. Thanks to this ambiguity, the troubadours can be thought of as both present and past; or rather, they can be just present enough to be consigned to the past.

As is well known, Dante exploits Arnaut's "presentness" in *De vulgari* to position his own poetry in a closer relation to Arnaut than to any other poet in any language.[17] But his distance is also useful in re-marking Occitan poetry as belonging to the past. In Dante's treatise, Italian poets (2.2.8, 2.5.4, 2.6.6) are interposed between Dante and the troubadours; whenever he lists examples in several languages, troubadours always comes first.[18] Arnaut's ambiguous historicity belongs in tandem, then, with Dante's efforts to recast a linguistic difference that, in reality, is spatial (hence discreditable) as one that is temporal (and thereby regenerative). Dante, in other words, has his own uniquely intellectual version of the stance adopted by authors who quote the troubadours toward the poets whom they quote. Like Matfre, he imputes knowledge to *antics troubadors* (the troubadours of old) to whom he is nevertheless linked as a kind of late contemporary; as with Raimon Vidal and others, this linkage takes the form of a particular bridge troubadour, here Arnaut Daniel. But *De vulgari eloquentia* is the only poetic treatise to elevate to a theological scheme this paradoxical coincidence of contemporaneousness with temporal separation.

The form of quotation practiced here by Dante also favors this scheme insofar as it serves as a concrete means of making a song present while at the same time causing most of it to recede into absence. *De vulgari* quotes only incipits, making it more laconic that any other treatise except those from Ripoll. In rare cases the repeated line is sufficient for the reader to understand the point (for example, the opening of Giraut de Bornelh 242.17 is quoted in the form "Ara ausirez encabalitz cantarz" in 2.5.4 to illustrate the syllable count of the line). Most require much more information than is provided: at least a stanza to appreciate the rhyme scheme indicated by the incipit "Se·m fos Amor de ioi donar tan larga" (29.17; 2.13.2), and an entire song to see that an incipit represents an exemplary treatment of a certain theme (2.2.8) or an illustrious composition (2.6.6). Admittedly French and Italian songs (including some by Dante himself) are accorded this same drastic abbreviation; the most brutal instance, in 2.6.6, is a salvo of eleven incipits in three languages; but the troubadours are always first on the slippery slope. Following this particular list Dante states that his readers need to be able to recall all these authorities, since with their help his concept of "supreme construction" will become clear (2.6.7). It is as if, instead of providing an anthology of earlier vernacular poems, he has archived them and provided an index to the archive. The next sentence, however, veers off unexpectedly, commending the study of "Virgil, the Ovid of the *Metamorphoses*, Statius and Lucan" to those who wish to become familiar with the rules of good construction. It seems there is no need to consult the vernacular archive after all, since Virgil and others will serve the purpose better. Poems that are hovering on the edge of being forgotten are here adroitly elbowed into oblivion.

When Dante begins *De vulgari eloquentia* by excising the earlier, Occitan treatises he occludes the very form in which he himself is writing. It is as though he wanted to compose something more like a poetic autobiography that would present him as the guardian of an archive of past poets, not as participating in an ongoing tradition of grammarians. In the case of the Occitan troubadours, quotation captures the moment of their ex-appropriation: the moment when they are just sufficiently present to be relegated to the past, so that they can form a worthy stepping-stone in the regeneration—theological and political—of poetic language. But in the case of the Occitan treatises that pioneered their appropriation, and which he surely knew, Dante's aim is to concede them no presence whatever, but forget them absolutely, so as to be able himself to inaugurate the new poetic language of the future.

In the *Commedia* the commitment to oblivion is still ongoing since, as part of an even more ambitious regenerative scheme, Dante contrives almost to forget even Arnaut Daniel. But while in some respects the move to ex-appropriate Arnaut is more complete than it was in *De vulgari*, it is also nuanced by the recognition of something profoundly alien (or inhuman) in language itself, while the connection between quotation and subjectivity is thrust to the fore by the choice, of all the possible phrases he could have chosen to repeat, of the words "I am Arnaut who . . ."

"I Am Arnaut Who . . ."

Unlike in *De vulgari eloquentia*, the presentation of troubadours in the *Comedy* is broadly biographical. Dante has Bertran de Born repeat phrases from his *vida* in *Inferno* 28.136,[19] and Folquet's self-presentation in *Paradiso* 9.97–108 as a reformed lover who has now embraced the perspective of providence just as clearly does not come from his songs—it replicates and amplifies his *vida*.[20] In the case of Arnaut Daniel, however, the *vida* already contained some of the poet's own words, the *tornada* of "En cest sonet coind' e leri" (29.10):

> Eu son Arnautz qu'amas l'aura
> e chatz la lebre ab lo bou
> e nadi contra suberna.
> > (*Biographies*, IX, 59)

I am Arnaut who gather up the breeze and hunt the hare with the ox and swim against the rising tide.

When the pilgrim meets the troubadour's shade on the last ledge of purgatory where lust is purged, included in Arnaut's eight-line speech is a declaration that similarly begins "I am Arnaut who": "I am Arnaut who weep yet am singing" (*Purgatorio* 26.142; Ieu sui Arnaut que plor e vau cantan).[21] The syntax "I am such and such" is by now formulaic in the *Comedy* since many figures have introduced themselves thus.[22] But the relative pronoun "who" with which Arnaut's self-naming continues is a departure from the pattern— only exceptionally does Dante use a similar construction in Italian.[23]

Prior to its quotation in the *vida*, the *tornada* of Arnaut's song had been alluded to several times by other troubadours. Indeed, all the earliest medieval references to Arnaut's poetry are to "En cest sonet" and almost all center on these three lines, identifying, as its most memorable core, the expression "Ieu sui Arnaut qu[e] . . . chatz la lebre ab lo bou." It is odd, to say the least, that the passage of Arnaut Daniel's corpus that other people most wanted to reiterate was one that identified them as someone other than who they were, only to confuse the identification further by relating it to nonhuman animals. I will argue that the *tornada*'s very problematization of identity makes it a potent vehicle of ex-appropriation, and that crucial to Dante's re-marking of Arnaut's words is his changing the qualification of this "who" from "who hunt the hare with the ox" (qu[e] . . . chatz la lebre ab lo bou) to "who weep yet am singing" (que plor e vau cantan).

In its original context in "En cest sonet," the first test of this "who" is to find a rhyme word for each of the difficult rhymes in *-aura*, *-ou*, and *-erna*, which have already been filled six times in the preceding stanzas. The words Arnaut decides to include, *aura* (breeze), *bou* (ox), and *suberna* (tide), surely among the nouns one least expects to find in a love poem, seem choices of last resort. Hence the phrase "gathering up the breeze" takes on the meaning "finding a means to include the rhyme word *aura*," "chasing with the ox" assumes the value "pursuing a line of verse such that it will end in *bou*," and "swimming against the tide" refers to the difficulty of concluding with such a recalcitrant word as *suberna*. Each rhyme word, that is, has a double function, both integrated into the song's syntax and detached from it as a citation form. In this respect, although they do not quote phrases from earlier in the text (as some *tornadas* do), the closing lines of "En cest sonet" nevertheless adopt a citational mode.[24] In Derrida's terms, the *tornada* re-marks the formal features of Arnaut's own text in such a way that the self-identification "I am Arnaut who" humorously recognizes the challenge posed by the formal demands of his song, putting his mastery in question. Such re-marking may have lent the *tornada* to being quoted and re-marked by others.

Each line of the *tornada* is an example of adynaton, the trope par excellence of dislocation, and thus an apt expression of the contortions to which the rhymes give rise. As well as the difficulty of form, these adynata convey in their contradictory nature the poet's self-deprecation in the face of unmasterable substance. While the "I am" voices the claim to be in the sense of "to be human" and "Arnaut" supplies that being with a human identity, what follows is at once a conundrum and an inhuman universe of wind, water, and beasts. Human subjectivity is framed by subjection to language, but the language of these lines exposes its potentially alien, inhuman dimension.

Arnaut's adynata have been traced back to Ecclesiasticus 34:1–2, which compares the man who chases empty dreams to a one who "catcheth at a shadow and followeth after the wind."[25] But Leslie Topsfield finds a more plausible model in *Ars amatoria*,[26] where Ovid recommends pretending compliance with a girlfriend's whims:

> Obsequio tranantur aquae: nec vincere possis
>   flumina, si contra, quam rapit unda, nates.
> obsequium tigresque domat Numidasque leones;
>   rustica paulatim taurus aratra subit.
> *Ars amatoria*, 2:181–84

> Waters can be crossed if you go with the flow, but you'll never be able to master rivers if you swim against the tide. Accommodating behavior will tame tigers and Numidian lions; and gradually the bull submits to the peasant's plow.[27]

True, Ovid's advice is to win one's girl through hypocrisy, whereas Arnaut's *tornada* enumerates fruitless strivings. But Ovid's trio of wry adynata overlaps with Arnaut's in the difficulty of swimming against the current and in the project of subduing wild animals. And while the animals are different in the two authors, Arnaut's ox responds to the adynaton of Ovid's bull, given that only an *ox* (a castrated bull) can be yoked to a plow. In replacing the improbable pairing of bull and plow with the impossible one of ox and hare, Arnaut seems to acknowledge the sexual impulse of the Ovidian passage while recasting it as inevitable failure. Both poets humorously represent human desire at cross-purposes with the nonhuman world, masterfully overcoming it in Ovid's case, helpless before it in the *canso*.

Among the troubadours who allude to "En cest sonet," Aimeric de Peguilhan in "Ses mon apleich" (10.6) is most concerned with its achievements in rhyme and is the only poet not to refer to the *tornada*.[28] In his gallery of portraits, the Monk of Montaudon mocks Arnaut's opacity in a stanza that retains the *tornada*'s introductory "Arnaut who . . ." and the two adynata closest to Ovid's—those of the tide and the ox/bull.[29] Others interpret the *tornada*—in particular in "I am Arnaut . . . / who hunt the hare with the ox"—as expressing erotic frustration. Arnaut himself refers, in 29.1, to his misadventures "last year, / when I hunted the hare with the ox" (Song 14, 3–4; l'autr'an / can cassava·l lebr' ab lo bou), deciding to put failure behind him and find satisfaction with a different lady. Reworking a similar scenario, Guiraut de Salaignac colors the image with disgust for the lady he has left (249.1):

> Aissi cum selh qu'a la lebre cassada
> e pueys la pert e autre la rete,
> tot atressi es avengut a me
> d'una falsa qu'ai lonjamen amada
> e servida de bon cor humilmen,
> e quan cugei penre mon iauzimen,
> pres sordeyor e mi mes en soan.
> Aisi o fetz cum las lobas o fan.
>
> (Song 1, 1–8)

> Like the man who hunted the hare and then loses her, and another lady engages him in her service, just the same thing happened to me with a false lady whom I have long loved and served sincerely and humbly and when I imagined I could take my enjoyment she disdained me and took up with someone inferior. She acted like she-wolves do.

Arnaut's sexy little female hare, the starting point of Guiraut's stanza, has ballooned by the end of it into the indiscriminate she-wolf of the bestiaries.

The *vida* combines both the stylistic and the sexual readings found in these poems. Arnaut, says the biographer, delighted in composing in *caras rimas* (rare and consequently precious rhymes), which make his songs hard to listen to and learn. An amorous anecdote then frames quotation of the *tornada*. In an effort to account for the ox, the biographer amusingly decides to read it not as a literal animal, but as the bovine husband of a lady whom Arnaut hunted—the inept and lumbering creature is no longer Arnaut himself, but his rival:

> Et amet une auta dompna de Gascoigna, moiller d'En Guillem de Bouvila, mas no fo crezut que anc la dompna li fezes plazer en dreich d'amor; per que el ditz:
> Eu sui Arnautz qu[e] . . . (*Biographies*, IX, 59)

> And he loved a lady of Gascony, the wife of Sir William Oxborough [or maybe "William Ox-peasant"], but it is not believed that the lady ever gave him any gratification in respect to love; and this is why he said: "I am Arnaut who . . ."

As we know from Chapter 3, *vidas* containing quotations are rare and seemingly modeled specifically on *accessus* to Ovid. If by quoting the *tornada* the biographer places Arnaut among Ovid's successors, this may reflect awareness of the parallel between it and *Ars amatoria*, book 2. In any event, identifying the troubadour as neo-Ovidian signals the impending ex-appropriation of Latin at the hands of Occitan, the newly grammatical vernacular. The *vida* was almost certainly composed in Italy for an Italian-speaking audience who would find themselves ex-appropriated from their native tongue by its assumption of Occitan as the medium of culture. The *vida*, in other words, performs a kind of linguistic musical chairs in which Occitan, the language with no home to go to, nevertheless commands a place, while Italian and Latin fail to find a seat.

By the time of the *vida* (ca. 1230), then, the core of the *tornada* of "En cest sonet" has been recognized as "I am Arnaut who . . . hunt the hare with the ox"; and the "who" in question has been further identified as a master of difficult and complex rhyme, a producer of opaque mumbo jumbo, the voice of frustrated desire, the discoverer of bestial urges, and a vernacular poet who challenges both Italian and the hegemony of Latin. In repeating the phrase "I am Arnaut who," Dante may have been drawn to various of these complements of "who I am."

Before teasing out these identifications in the *Commedia*, there is one quotation to note, which postdates Arnaut's *vida*. Matfre includes the opening stanza of Guiraut de Salaignac's "Aissi cum selh qu'a la lebre cassada" in his *Breviari d'amor*, thereby giving "En cest sonet" an indirect role in his program of spiritual regeneration. This quotation (#42; *Breviari*, 28745–52), figures in the second lawsuit of the *perilhos tractat* in which Matfre is rebutting the complaints made by troubadours against love (see Appendices 10 and 11). Matfre argues the need to distinguish, as wise poets do, between criticism of love (which he vigorously reproves) and criticism of women (which is just fine). Bernart de Ventadorn (70.23) is quoted approvingly for denouncing his treacherous lady (#41; *Breviari*, 28720–34). The same approval is accorded immediately afterward to Guiraut's stanza, attributed (as it is in *chansonnier C*) to Aimeric de Peguilhan, the troubadour on whom Matfre most relies in this part of the *perilhos tractat*. Concluding the quotation, Matfre reiterates that "it is therefore right to complain of unrighteous women but not of love" (*Breviari*, 28753–54; Dregz es donc qu'om fassa clamor / de las deslials, non d'amor). He then quotes himself (#43) and Aimeric again (#44) to the effect that accusing love is folly, a sequence of quotations discussed in Chapter 8. By quoting Guiraut de Salignac alluding to Arnaut, Matfre adds to existing responses to the famous *tornada*. This part of his *Breviari d'amor* seeks human spiritual regeneration through quotations from love poetry, in which different troubadours define different possible ways of returning to union with God or festering in sinful separation from him, all of which gives it similarities with Dante's masterpiece.

One of the main differences between them, however, is that Matfre quotes the troubadours meticulously, while in the *Comedy*, unlike in *De vulgari*, Dante no longer exactly quotes them—or at least, he no longer quotes them exactly. In view of the weighty tradition of quotation, Dante's apparent insouciance about accuracy in the *Comedy* is another element to be accounted for in interpreting what "I am" might have to say about "who" he thinks he is.

What Happened to the Ox?

We have seen that when Dante was working on his *Comedy* around 1308 to 1320, only a few decades after Matfre wrote the *Breviari d'amor*, there was a tradition of reflecting on the *tornada* of "En cest sonet" that extended back for over a century and that identified, as its most memorable core, the expression "Ieu sui Arnaut qu[e] . . . chatz la lebre ab lo bou." Several elements of this tradition resurface in *Purgatorio 26*.

First, when Arnaut Daniel is pointed out by Guido Guinizelli at the beginning of the canto, the gamut of meanings that might be covered by his famous phrase "the better wordsmith in the vernacular" (miglior fabbro del parlar materno) range from Aimeric de Peguilhan's tribute to the Monk of Montaudon's derision, but they could well all stem from the biographer's salute to Arnaut's mastery of *caras rimas* (*miglior fabbro*) and his implied ex-appropriation of Ovid in favor of the vernacular (*parlar materno*).[30]

Next, the fact that the opening words spoken by Arnaut Daniel in his greeting to the Dante figure are not from his own works but may be a quotation from Folquet de Marselha is an indication that Arnaut himself is to be ex-appropriated from mastery over his own corpus.[31] Dante's seeming forgetting of the unforgettable phrase "I am Arnaut who hunt the hare with the ox" confirms this. All that remain of the striking adynata are troubadour truisms: that the singer is singing at the same time as he weeps, and sorrowful at the same time as he rejoices.[32]

Yet the original adynata—unnatural, bestial, and elemental—which decenter subjectivity by yoking human language to inhuman impulse, each incommensurate with the other, are not absent from the canto as a whole. Instead they are displaced to its beginning. Canto 26 opens with groups of nameless shades coursing through flames. Some energetically exclaim at "sodomy," others rehearse the obscenity of Pasiphaë's seduction of the bull. Their sexual chorus is exuberantly frenetic, as expressive of fascination as of remorse:[33]

> Tosto che parton l'accoglienza amica,
> prima che 'l primo passo lì trascorra,
> sopragridar ciascuna s'affatica:
>   la nova gente: "Soddoma e Gomorra!"
> e l'altra: "Ne la vacca entra Pasife
> perché 'l torello a sua lussuria corra."
>   (26.37–42)

As soon as they break off their friendly greetings, before they take the first step to depart, each labors to outshout the other. The newcomers: "Sodom and Gomorrah!" and the others: "Into the cow goes Pasiphaë, so that the young bull will run to her lust."

The cries continue with admissions of hermaphroditism and of bestial appetite defying human law (26.82–84, "Nostro peccato fu ermafrodito . . . non servammo umana legge, / seguendo come bestie l'appetito"). The fundamental perversity of these shades' sexual sins finds expression in a series of dramatic adynata, in which they plunge in fire, wheel out of control, couple unnaturally, conflate male with female, and become beast.

It is noteworthy that the story of how Pasiphaë posed as a cow in order to seduce a bull, thereby giving birth to the Minotaur, is mentioned in *Ars amatoria* 2.23–24, not far from the line about the bull that Ovid's wily lover implausibly yokes to his plow, and reprising a much longer exposition of the same story in *Ars amatoria* 1.289–326. Is there a connection between one lover's desires yoking a bull to the plow (Ovid), those of another (Pasiphaë) securing her impregnation by a bull, and those of a third (Arnaut) hunting a hare with an ox? I wondered earlier if the ox in the *tornada* might be a response to Ovid's implausible harnessing of bull to plow. Perhaps another reason for the ox in Arnaut's *tornada* was Pasiphaë's own obscene adynaton, which prompted the troubadour to invent the comically unrealizable miscegenation of ox and hare. Or perhaps it was Dante who, seeing the potential link between Arnaut and Ovid, made the connection from the troubadour's ox to Ovid's bulls.[34] In any case, Dante has joined the tradition of seeing Arnaut's *tornada* as evoking desires that veer into animality, even though he displaces those desires to the other end of the canto.

The split he thereby introduces between "I am . . . who" and the subject's elemental passions affects the process of what, following Derrida, I am calling Dante's ex-appropriation of the troubadours: his challenge to their ownership of, and authority over, vernacular poetry. As Derrida reminds us, such ownership and authority are illusory: we cannot own or master language. What most differentiates troubadour quotation in the *Commedia* from in *De vulgari* is that in the later text Dante clearly avoids the error of believing that, by ex-appropriating the troubadours, he can claim another language— emergent Italian—as "proper" to himself. Instead, the standoff between language and desire staged in Arnaut's *tornada*, as a result of which the articulation of identity is always haunted by what is irreducibly alien to it, is transposed to the level of the entire canto.

In *De vulgari* the process of ex-appropriation is explored in relation to what language one speaks. In the *Commedia*, by comparison, it is extended to the question of human identification by or within language. The words "I am Arnaut who . . ." precisely raise this question of identification and, in so doing, realize the potential of quotation as a transferential act. The fact of repeating "I am Arnaut who . . ." while at the same time discarding the lines that once made up "Arnaut's" identity shows that it is possible to detach one's "I" from its previous identifications, enabling it to begin again and so to change.

As in *De vulgari eloquentia*, the practice of quotation is theologized in the *Comedy*. But in the later text, Dante is not concerned so much to cast the troubadours into the past as to regenerate their desire, a project analogous to Matfre's in the *Breviari*. Where Matfre uses commentary to interpret existing troubadour songs, Dante substitutes penitential verses for Arnaut's original adynata—but only after having recast these adynata as the wild, lustful landscape of purgatory. The moral distance between Arnaut's new "I am" and his earlier "who" is identified by Guido Guinizelli when he detaches himself from the bands of sinners and points to Arnaut further away again. The troubadour stands on the very threshold of paradise, having literally left his impossible, animal desires behind him.

By retaining Arnaut's original language but recasting his words, Dante has replaced the expected quotation with one he himself has composed. If the *tornada* imposed itself on people's memories and forced its way into their works, Dante's own version of "I am Arnaut who" has been just as frequently quoted and pored over. The next chapter will show how Guilhem Molinier will similarly attempt to author his own quotations in the *Leys d'amors*, though with conspicuously less success.

## CHAPTER 10

The *Leys d'amors*

Phasing Out the *antics troubadors* and Ushering in the New Toulousain Poetics

So far this book has shown quotation from the troubadours to be an engine of cultural change that works in two interconnected ways. It can draw Occitan poetry into the orbit of the school teaching of *grammatica*, which in the Middle Ages denotes both a discipline (grammar) and the language (Latin) to which it was addressed; and it can privilege this poetry as a source of social, moral, and even redemptive insight, and as a test of those of its readers. Many of the works that quote the troubadours have analogues in the Latin schoolroom, and this is particularly true of the most tenacious and prolific genre to contain troubadour quotations, those treatises of Occitan language and poetics that illustrate linguistic and poetic practice with examples from the classical troubadours (see Chapters 1 and 9). Successive redactions of the *Leys d'amors* (Laws of love), an ensemble of texts that are relative latecomers to this genre, reorient quotation away from this grammatical model and explore new ways of envisaging the substantive value of poetry. In so doing, they phase out reference to the classical troubadours in favor of more contemporary lyric production. This chapter, then, registers one way of drawing the culture of troubadour quotation to a close and marking the beginning of another; the poetry of Petrarch considered in the final chapter marks another, ultimately more successful bid to achieve the same two goals.

The *Leys d'amors* were compiled on behalf of the Consistori de gai saber at Toulouse, an institution founded in the first third of the fourteenth century, which continues in existence into the present day.[1] Their author is known as

Guilhem Molinier, although he probably headed a team of collaborators rather than writing solo. The love that this treatise aspires to regulate will ultimately be revealed as philosophy, the love of wisdom. The laws concerned are the Consistori's poetics and the guidelines for its annual poetry competitions, which are rather like those of the northern French poetic confraternities, or *puys,* except that the Consistori modeled itself on a university and awarded, in addition to poetry prizes, bachelor's and doctoral degrees for which the *Leys* define the syllabus.[2] Longer, fuller, and much more learned than any of the preceding handbooks, the *Leys* were recast at least three times. This chapter is about the first and second prose redactions; the first, probably composed 1328–37, was certainly in existence by 1341 while the second, which introduces important innovations, dates from 1355–56.[3] The so-called Toulouse school of poetry whose aims are formulated in these manuals had links with Catalonia, and a fellow consistory was founded in Barcelona in the late fourteenth century. Their impressive level of poetic activity has been documented by François Zufferey.[4]

The First Prose Redaction

Like earlier treatises, the first redaction places the study of Occitan in the domain of *grammatica.* After an introduction it devotes a book to phonetics and thence versification, one to grammar, the next to tropes, and the final unfinished one to composition. Its treatment of the tropes anchors them in the grammatical tradition since it situates them alongside linguistic vices and licenses, drawing on Donatus's discussions of barbarism and solecism in his *Ars grammatica.*[5] And the practice of earlier vernacular grammars of using quotations to illustrate poetic and linguistic forms and figures of speech continues in this redaction too (see Appendix 14). Molinier quotes old standbys like Raimbaut de Vaqueiras and Peire Vidal; some less familiar poets like Rigaut de Berbezilh and the more recently in vogue Arnaut Daniel; and a few unfamiliar references like the anonymous "Flor de paradis" (461.123) and the otherwise unknown P[eire] Arquier.[6] The way examples are introduced is fairly standard, for instance:

> E per que entendatz que vol dire quaysh engaltatz de sillabas. am bela cazensa podetz ayssi penre per ysshemple la canso que fo Arnaud Daniel can dish.

> Le ferms volers quel cor mintra
> Nom pot ges quey, escoysshendre ni ongla.
>
> Et aytals rimas apelam comunalmen estrampas. (Gatien-Arnoult ed., 3:330)
>
> And in order that you should understand what is meant by an approximate equality of syllables with a fine cadence you may take as example that song which Arnaut Daniel made when he said: "The firm desire that enters my heart . . ." And such rhymes are commonly called *estrampas*.

Alongside these quotations are examples originating within the Consistori or made up by Molinier himself;[7] this too is consistent with earlier practice, except that confected illustrations are far more dominant in the *Leys* than in any of the earlier treatises. The presence of a preferred poet who connects the author to the earlier troubadours, thus holding them together in a single tradition, is another traditional feature that Guilhem both adopts and amplifies in the fondness he shows for At de Mons. At (or Nath, that is, N'At, "Sir At," as Molinier consistently calls him, the honorific underlining his respect) is a late thirteenth-century troubadour from Mons, near Toulouse; he is the author of five long didactic poems in rhyming, mainly hexasyllabic couplets, which are all transmitted in the same section of *chansonnier R* as the *novas* discussed in Chapters 2 and 6.[8] At is elsewhere quoted only in the *Breviari*, which, like the *Leys*, preserves some passages by him that are not known elsewhere.[9] Thanks to At, in the 1341 redaction of the *Leys* Molinier appears as a late contemporary of the classical troubadours, much as do Matfre Ermengau in the *Breviari* and Dante in *De vulgari eloquentia*.[10]

The sense that there is a general community of approach between earlier treatises and those of the Consistori up to this first recension is confirmed by the fact that several texts closely associated with the *Leys*—Molinier's own verse abridgment the *Flors de gai saber* and two prose works by fellow Consistori member Joan de Castellnou, his *Glosari* and his *Compendi*—are found in the same Catalan manuscript *H* (Barcelona 239) as earlier grammars: the *Razos de trobar*, the *Regles de trobar*, the *Doctrina de compondre dictats*, and the *Mirall de trobar* (see Appendix 3).

The Second Prose Redaction

In the second prose redaction the *Leys* are completely overhauled. Whereas the first was in five books, the second is in three. It dispenses with the entire book on the tropes, which was book 4 of the earlier redaction, and it also discards the unfinished book 5, on composition. It creates a completely new first book. Books 1 and 2 of the 1341 version are then shortened and fused together to become the new book 2. Book 3 of the earlier redaction is retained, but is now the concluding book. In addition to reordering and reframing his materials, Molinier also extensively revises his earlier text, adding, deleting, and altering.

The use of troubadour quotations is transformed in the process (see Appendix 14). All the excerpts from twelfth and early thirteenth-century poets are either dropped (due to the suppression of the earlier book 4) or rendered anonymous by eliminating their attributions (in the revision of book 2). Consequently the only troubadours referred to by name in this new redaction are At de Mons and Molinier himself, since the compiler of the *Leys* finds various means of inscribing his own name. As a result of the addition of the new book 1, the number and length of the extracts quoted from At de Mons is increased and so is the amount of verse that can be attributed to Molinier. Unlike all the earlier treatises, including its own earlier incarnation, this new version of the *Leys* is not about continuing the troubadour tradition. Instead, it erases their names and begins again, in Toulouse, in the late thirteenth century.

Even more strikingly, the role played by quotation shifts. Although the excerpts that are retained from the earlier version continue to serve as illustrations of points of language and verse form, all the newly introduced ones are quoted for their content. In the new book 1 the opinions of At de Mons are quoted frequently and at length.[11] The middle book of the second redaction, which contains the examples of poetic forms of various kinds, almost all by Molinier, is further ornamented by a long religious poem, which is likewise by him and which is also included for its substantive content (*Leys*, ed. Anglade, 2:72–91). Thus, if there is to be an Occitan canon, its seminal elements are now At de Mons and Molinier. More than just linguistically sound, these seeds promise to bear fruit in an Occitan poetry endowed with wisdom, learning, and exemplary piety.

The approach of the new first book explains this new privilege attaching to poetic content. Turning its back on a century and a half of associating the troubadours with the teaching of grammar, book 1 of the 1356 redaction firmly inscribes poetry within the overall framework of philosophy, in the discipline of rhetoric, which in turn is based on ethics.

> Aras es a vezer sobre qual partida de philozophia es fondada la nostra prezens sciensa de las Leys d'Amors. E dizem que aquesta sciensa, en quant que toca bel ornat e bo de parlar, se fonda sobre rethorica. E quar en aytal parlar, coma en verses, chansos et en autres dictatz hom pauza e ditz bos essenhamens e doctrinas bonas e vertuozas per esquivar vicis e peccatz e per essenhar bos costums e vertutz, per so la prezens sciensa se pot fondar sobre ethica de laqual havem lassus parlat assatz, mas non ges de rethorica, per que d'aquela parlam per esta maniera. (*Leys*, ed. Anglade, 1:82)

> Now it must be seen on what branch of philosophy our discipline in the Laws of Love is based. And we say that our discipline, insofar as it involves fair ornament and good speaking, is based on rhetoric. And since in such speech—verses, songs, and other compositions— good teachings and sound and virtuous doctrines are placed and articulated, for this reason our present discipline is based on ethics, of which we have spoken sufficiently above; but we have not yet spoken at all of rhetoric, which is why we speak of it in this manner.

"Philosophy" here is to be understood as in those medieval encyclopedias that ultimately refer all knowledge to God.[12] Like Matfre Ermengau and Dante, Molinier situates his "law of love" within the overall framework of salvation; but unlike them, he shows little interest in poetry as a vehicle of individual spiritual change, concentrating instead on its furtherance of moral and civic values, and on the continuum between judging poetry (as the officers of the Consistori were bound to do) and the Last Judgment.[13] Poetry's value is as crucial for Molinier as for these other authors, but it is directed more toward the public domain.

Molinier's main guides as to the meaning of rhetoric and its place among the sciences are Brunetto Latini, whose encyclopedia *Le livre dou tresor* was composed in Montpellier in the 1260s, and another Italian, Albertano da Brescia, who wrote a number of educational and polemical tracts in Latin in the 1240s and 1250s. For both Brunetto and Albertano, rhetoric is seen not as an extension of grammar but as a tool of government. In Brunetto's mapping of fields of knowledge in the *Tresor*, rhetoric is placed under politics; Albertano looks to rhetoric to subdue the factionalism of the Italian city-states and create a society based on recognition of the general good; a jurist and politician, he is especially mindful of the public responsibilities of lawyers.[14] This civic conception of rhetoric is ultimately Aristotelian, but the principal sources on which both Brunetto and Albertano draw are Roman, especially Cicero and Seneca; and their address to medieval politics is pertinent to their own circumstances, since both Brunetto and Albertano underwent exile from their respective cities.

Such a conception must have appealed to the Consistori, which was a city institution made up of lay civic dignitaries, most of them professional men (including lawyers),[15] and which seems to have seen itself as mounting the defense of Occitan poetry against the University of Toulouse, center of the Inquisition, thus entering into contention with the church in a way similar to the factions that ripped apart the Italian city-states.[16] Toulouse was the city most strongly identified with resistance to the Albigensian Crusade, and the difficulties of life there in the mid-thirteenth century seem to have been responsible for driving away some of its poets, perhaps including At de Mons, another reason why reflections of the Italian experience will have seemed relevant to the Consistori.[17] Molinier's turn to Italian sources to reinvent Occitan poetry also parallels the gradual eclipse of the troubadours in fourteenth-century Italy (see Chapters 9 and 11), while his deafening silence as regards anything French suggests refusal to concede the obvious similarities between the Consistori and the northern *puys*.[18]

The new book 1 of the *Leys* introduces a series of alternatives to the traditional practice of quoting the classical troubadours, a practice that, as we have seen, this redaction is phasing out. A full half of the book is adapted and translated from works by Albertano, his *Liber de doctrina dicendi et tacendi* (Instruction in when to speak and when to be silent), *Liber consolationis et consilii* (Book of consolation and counsel), and his sermons.[19] In order to illustrate the wholesale character of these borrowings, Appendix 15 juxtaposes examples from each of the two Latin treatises to the corresponding section of the *Leys*; the sentences in both texts are numbered to facilitate comparison between them. An educator and compiler, Albertano proceeds by means of a skeleton framework of points (in bold typeface in Appendix 15): Should one address a foolish or a wise person? (A[1]); Should one address the scornful? (A[6]); Eradicate anger from yourself and from the one with whom you wish to take counsel (B[1]); Angry speakers risk being put outside the law (B[4]);

and between these points he accumulates *auctoritates* to provide them with weight and substance, quoting from Seneca, Tully (Cicero), Solomon, Jesus ben Sira (Ecclesiasticus), and the Gospels. Albertano highlights the rational and civic obligations of language, very different from the courtly concerns of the troubadours; the supporting authorities model a prestigious speech community regulated by an exalted combination of Roman wisdom and Christian revelation. It is easy to see how such a community, subject to such a transcendent law, would appeal to the regulatory ambitions of the *Leys*.

In what sense is Molinier quoting Albertano? Comparison between Albertano's text and that of the *Leys* shows that Molinier is content mainly to copy, add the occasional gloss, and of course translate his model (translation being a dimension of quotation we have not met with previously). Discursively, Molinier appears rather to be quoting the authorities whom Albertano had quoted—indeed, some of whom Albertano had already found quoted in *his* source (e.g., Alcuin).[20] These indefinitely reiterable sayings of Seneca, Cicero, and the like, surrounded as they are by the apparatus of citation in both Albertano and the *Leys*, are the regular stock-in-trade of medieval compilers.[21] Although for the most part Molinier merely copies them in translation, he does sometimes re-mark them in light of the poetic concerns of the Consistori, a process mediated by At de Mons (see below).

Quotations from At constitute copying of a different kind again. Whereas Molinier integrates Albertano, he promotes his fellow Toulousain. Since there is virtually no precedent for quoting At, Molinier's reliance on him is a personal, indeed idiosyncratic, decision. By copying verbatim several hundred lines of At's poetry, he makes the *Leys* (especially the second redaction) almost an At de Mons *chansonnier*. This spirit of quotation is markedly unlike the practice that obtained earlier, in which a premium was placed on the range and variety of sources. Nor are there any lyrics among the passages selected, which are all from didactic, nonstrophic verse. Earlier writers who quote the troubadours try to absorb them into a scholastic framework, but this is unnecessary in At's case; he is already thoroughly Aristotelian in inspiration and scholastic in his thought processes. Concomitantly, the question of sacrificing music to textual quotation no longer presents itself, since At's nonstrophic works were never intended to be sung. Molinier's selections from At are also a great deal longer than traditional troubadour quotations and than the authorities lifted from Albertano, running in one case to nearly eighty lines, though admittedly this passage is broken up into three sections by interpositions from Molinier.[22] Although Molinier appropriates close to sixty pages from Albertano, At's textual presence is much more apparent, partly because his authorship is standardly cited and also because his verse stands out in the predominantly prose environment of the *Leys* (though in the manuscript only the first verse quotation from At is set out line by line, the others being run on to blend with the prose; see Figure 7).

As both poet and fellow citizen, At lends himself to Molinier's construction of a poetic community; his role in its ideology is vital. He is first quoted in the course of a passage where Molinier invokes the rational powers of the soul, thereby opening an eschatalogical frame around book I, which concludes with the soul going before the Last Judgment. The lines in question show how *razo*, a term with a long history in Occitan poetics referring to the "subject matter" or "substance" of a song, is linked both to rationality and to all the virtues, theological and courtly. The passage helps to formulate the poetic and substantive ambitions of the Consistori:

> Don N'Ath de Mons, que fo garnitz
> de gran saber, enayssi ditz:
>   razos d'arma adutz
>   en home bona fe,
>   esperansa merce
>   pietat caritat
>   vergonha honestat,
>   mezura abstenensa,
>   patiensa suffrensa,
>   cortezia largueza,
>   leyaltat savieza.
>   (*Leys*, ed. Anglade, 1:68; 309.I, 471–79)

> Of which At de Mons, a man equipped with great knowledge, said in this manner "The rational soul [literally: the soul's reason/substance/subject matter] conduces, in man, to sound faith, hope to mercy, piety to charity, shame to decorum, moderation to abstinence, patience to endurance, courtliness to generosity, and uprightness to wisdom."

A subsequent cluster of quotations (the eighty-line series) serves to resolve a problem raised by Plato and Cicero over the extent to which rhetoric, as use of speech, is natural or also requires art. At's pronouncement in favor of art is used to set up the discussion of the bases of rhetoric into which the extracts from Albertano are then slotted (*Leys*, ed. Anglade, 1:84–87; At 309.V, 488–563). At is more intellectually dominant in book 1 of this version of the *Leys* than any other troubadour quoted in any of the other works I have studied. Gone is the play with recognizing and knowing that was the hallmark of troubadour quotation up to this point. Not so much a litmus of Molinier's knowledge as his guru, At is quoted in the sense that he is compiled and enshrined for posterity.

He is also the means whereby Brunetto, Albertano, and then also Seneca, Cato, Cicero, and the like, can be turned into Christian, civic, Occitan poetry. For at times Molinier varies his usual method of simply translating Albertano's quotations as though they were his own. In B[3] of Appendix 15, Molinier first repeats the Latin lines together with their attribution to Seneca, and then recasts them in Occitan verse:

Qui de far mays a cura
que no ha per natura
per cug son poder passa
don cove que mens fassa.
    (*Leys*, ed. Anglade, 1:147–48)

He who strives to do more than lies in his nature outstrips his capacities in imagination and therefore is bound to do less.

The hexasyllabic rhyming couplets and the learned content are altogether typical of At;[23] thanks to the model provided by the troubadour from Mons, Seneca has become a late thirteenth-century Toulousain poet. In Appendix 15 B[5], Cato is similarly quoted twice, the second time in verse:[24]

La tersa razo pauza Cato enayssi: "Can seras iratz, no cotendaz de cauza no certa, quar ira enpacha lo coratge d'ome et tant qu'l tot a vezer la vertat." L'Actors:

Iratz que de no cert conten
la vertat no ve claramen
quar ira fa la pessa trista

> e al coratge tol la vista
> (*Leys*, ed. Anglade, 1:148)

Cato expressed the third reason thus: "If you are angry, do not argue about a matter that is not certain, for anger impedes a man's mind and prevents him from seeing the truth." The Author: "An angry man who argues about what is not certain does not see the truth clearly because anger makes thought sad and deprives the mind of vision."

I take *l'Actors* to refer to Molinier as author of the *Leys*. These verses implement recommendations Molinier himself had drafted in book 5 of the 1341 redaction on how to incorporate Latin by translating it into Occitan couplets.[25] The term *actor* is commonly used to denote the author figure of late medieval didactic or narrative works, carrying the meanings of both witness to their contents and creator of their exposition,[26] and its first occurrence in the *Leys* infers as much, when *l'Actors* announces that he will compose mainly in prose, except when verse will redound more to the glory of God (*Leys*, ed. Anglade, 1:69). This rubric comes immediately after the initial quotation from At (1:68), thereby forging a connection between At and Molinier much as Matfre creates a bond with Aimeric de Peguilhan in the *Breviari* by juxtaposing his own words to the troubadour's.[27]

The exalted mission of versifying in God's honor is fulfilled when the author of the *Leys* transforms learning of all kinds into Occitan poetry for the benefit of the Consistori's future students. In some cases, the rubric *l'Actors* is used to preface verses that draw an argument together rather than translating it; for example:

> No solamen deu gardar am cuy parla, ans ho fa en prezencia de cuy parla. Sobre ausso ditz enayssi l'Actors:

> Qui secret vol parlar
> entorn se deu gardar
> per que cel que s'amaga
> so qu'om ditz no retraga.
> (*Leys*, ed. Anglade, 1:93)

Not only should he take care with whom he speaks, but also in whose presence he speaks. On which point the Author says: "Who-

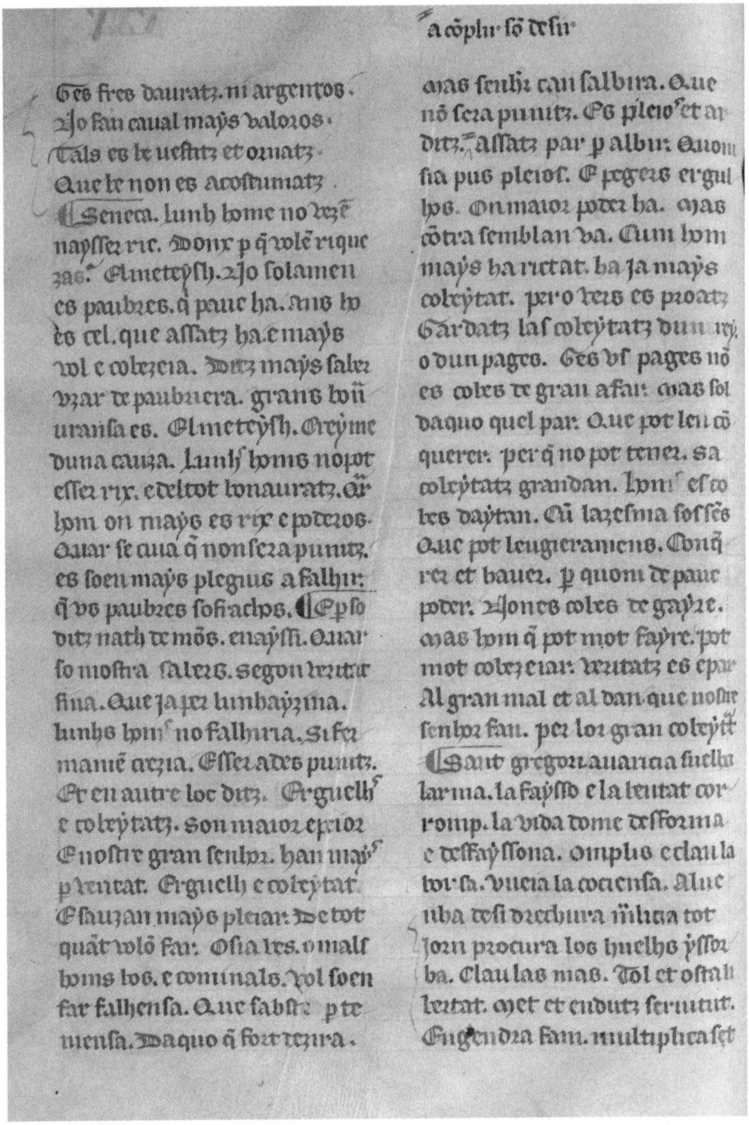

Figure 7. Toulouse, Bibliothèque Municipale, MS 2883 (*Leys d'amors*), folio 31v. Book 1 of the second (1356) redaction. In the first four lines of the first column on the left, verse by the "Author" is set out line by line. It is followed by a cluster of prose quotations translated from Seneca, and then by fifty lines of hexasyllables by At de Mons that continue down the second column, followed by further prose sayings attributed to Saint Gregory. The three paraphs visible on this page mark the point where each of these three is introduced. At's verses are run on so as to be difficult to distinguish from the surrounding prose; although each ends with a punctus, the excerpts from Seneca are similarly punctuated; only the "Author's" lines are set out as verse. This passage corresponds with Anglade's edition of the *Leys*, 1:105–6. Reproduced by permission of the Bibliothèque Municipale de Toulouse.

ever wishes to talk in secret should look around him so that anyone
who might come along should not repeat what is being said."

In other cases, *l'Actors* recasts the opinion of an authority who is cited but not
quoted, the Author's own verse taking the place of the expected quotation:[28]

> E jaciaysso que totas las sciensas e las auctoritatz no solamen dels sans
> mas dels anticz et aproatz philozophes hajan en mespretz riqueza et
> essenho cobezessa et avaricia esquivar, pero aysso non contrastan a
> penas pot hom trobar home que en riqueza no trobe plazer e no la
> vuelha am si; per so ditz l'Actors segon lo dig del Versifiayre:[29]

> > O bona paubriera, dura
> > foras a tota natura
> > si dieus no t'agues volguda
> > e per amor sostenguda.
> >   (*Leys*, ed. Anglade, 1:99)

And although all learned writings and authorities, not only those of
the saints but also those of antiquity and the confirmed philoso-
phers hold wealth in contempt and teach the avoidance of cupidity
and avarice, nevertheless and notwithstanding, it is difficult to find
anyone who does not take pleasure in wealth or desire to have it with
him; for which reason the Author says, according to the Versifier's
words: "O goodly poverty, you would have been harsh to every nature if God had not wanted you and supported you with love."

By these means, Molinier re-marks others' teaching with his own pedagogy,
helping his students to become lovers of wisdom and steering them toward
success in their poetry degrees. Deploying the same form as At de Mons, but
in snappier, more memorable gobbets, he becomes the author of future
quotations—verses short and pithy enough to be remembered and quoted by
students of poetry, whose value *as poetry* is underlined by the fact that they
are the only verse passages to be copied line by line in the main body of book
1 of the treatise (see Figure 7). Similarly, in book 2, almost the only verse passages to be set out as such are Molinier's own verse examples; quotations from
others are merged with his prose. More even than an At de Mons *chansonnier*, then, the *Leys* are a compilation of works by its Author.

Whereas previous authors of Occitan treatises see themselves as grammar teachers who quote the earlier troubadours and continue their compositions, Molinier presents himself as an encyclopedist and philosopher-poet who will be quoted by posterity, now that the days of the *antics troubadors* are finally over. His investment in the position of a subject supposed to know left little room for maneuver for his readers, but it did mark an important new beginning, even if the change did not ultimately last.

## CHAPTER 11

Petrarch's "Lasso me"

Changing the Subject

At the foot of the first folio of Occitan *chansonnier H* someone has written: "Dreitz e raizon quieu chant em demori" (It is rightful and reasonable that I should sing and take my ease), and immediately below it the Italian translation: "Dritto e ragion chio canti e mi soggiorno." Maria Careri has identified the hand as that of Giovanni Maria Barbieri (1519–74), a noted scholar of the medieval lyric.[1] She thinks he jotted down the line as a reminder to himself to look for it in the *chansonnier*. His search will have been unsuccessful: the not especially distinguished song of which it is the incipit is not copied there, but only in *CK*. Anonymous in *K*, where it is transcribed in a later hand on the last folio following an anonymous song, in *C* it is attributed to Guillem de Saint Gregori, an ascription accepted by Pillet-Carstens and reflected in its PC number of 233.4. According to Maurizio Perugi, the song's real author is probably Guilhem de Murs (PC 226), a late thirteenth-century poet who exchanged verses with Guiraut Riquier and belonged in the same patronage circle as Rostanh Berenguier de Marseilla (PC 427).[2] However, it is likely that Barbieri thought the incipit and its song belonged to Arnaut Daniel, a view with which Carl Appel concurred.[3] Barbieri probably also believed, as do scholars today, that Petrarch was convinced he was quoting Arnaut Daniel when he used this line in his canzone "Lasso me" (*Canzoniere*, no. 70): a song remarkable for incorporating, like the *Purgatorio*, a line of Arnaldian Occitan into an otherwise Italian text. Barbieri probably went looking for this song in *H*, a *chansonnier* containing an unusually large number of Arnaut's songs, many of them with extensive Latin glosses,[4] since he also believed that this manuscript was for a period in Petrarch's hands.[5] The line "Drez et rayson es qu'ieu ciant em demori" (as it appears in Rosanna Bettarini's edition of Petrarch's text; see Appendix 16) subtends a web of beliefs and suppositions about the authorship of the song from which it comes.[6]

The functioning of this web and its implications for subjectivity are the topic of this final chapter. I see line 10 of Petrarch's "Lasso me" as marking a terminal point in the practice of quoting the troubadours. Perhaps dating from 1337–40,[7] this canzone is contemporary with the Consistori's promotion of new directions for poetry in Toulouse. But whereas the *Leys d'amors* were successful regionally, in Occitania and Catalonia, the way Petrarch inflects the lyric was to prove irresistible across Europe.

Unlike the Occitan verses quoted by Dante, there is no previous history of quoting "Razo e dreyt." On the other hand, since Petrarch's song quotes an incipit at the end of each of its five stanzas, his obvious formal model is Jofre de Foixà's "Be m'a lonc temps menat a guiza d'aura" (Chapter 7 and Appendix 9). Jofre's song may also enter into the web of supposition surrounding "Razo e dreyt" given that, it has been suggested, Petrarch may also have associated it with Arnaut Daniel:[8] the *–aura* rhymes of Jofre's first stanza (*aura* = breeze, *daura* = gilds, *saura* = golden-haired), rhymes dear to Petrarch, recapitulate some of those in Arnaut's "En cest sonet" (29.10), the *tornada* of which I identify as the model for Dante's famous "I am Arnaut who . . ." Petrarch's choice of a line asserting the right to sing joyfully can be seen, thanks to this hypothetical detour, as a reversal of Dante's Arnaut who continues to weep even as he sings. What makes the web of assumptions about Petrarch's quotation more intricate still is that the Occitan incipit in "Lasso me," despite its confidence in the rightness of its song, is just as palinodic as Arnaut's words in *Purgatorio* 26. The difference lies in the technique of quotation: whereas Dante adjusts the Occitan text to suit his purpose, Petrarch quotes verbatim in such a way as to erode the meaning of the quoted line and transform it.

That Arnaut Daniel's authorship should be surrounded by conjecture and supposition is not surprising. From the second third of the thirteenth century, when he becomes fashionable both for imitators and for those who quote, cases of uncertain attribution arise involving him as with all the prominent troubadours. A stanza thought to be by Uc Brunenc (450.1), "Ab plazer receup et acuoill," is misattributed to Arnaut in the *r* fragment of Raimon Vidal's *So fo*.[9] An otherwise unknown song is attributed to Arnaut by Berenguer d'Anoia in the *Mirall*.[10] Although the wordplay of the latter example, which presumably provides the grounds for this attribution, may not seem especially Arnaldian, the lines could conceivably be from a lost song by Arnaut.

Many troubadours are recipients of optimistic attributions that extend their existence virtually, but Arnaut was always somewhat more spectral than other classical troubadours. Placed by his *vida* in the same territory as Arnaut de Maruelh, Daniel seems to some extent to be in the other Arnaut's shadow.[11] The absence of concrete information about his life leads the biographer visibly to fabricate its events on the basis of the *tornada* of 29.10. More disturbingly, the *razo* to 29.2, "Anc ieu non l'aic," frankly casts doubt on Arnaut's authorship. It narrates how the troubadour cheated in a song competition by stealing his competitor's composition and, when the theft was revealed, was nonetheless rewarded by being "given" the song by the judge, Richard Lionheart.[12] The story is atypical in a genre that usually works to identify songs as rooted in the experience of their composers. It is also unusually clear-sighted about the way *chansonniers* prefer to assign a name to a song rather than leave its authorship anonymous or in doubt, even if this means generating wrong or contradictory attributions.[13] Despite the authenticating, psychologizing moves of the biographies, authorship in the *chansonniers* is often understood as being ascribed *to*, not as emanating *from*, a named individual (as also in *florilegia*; see Chapter 4). Where quotation is concerned, the desire to cite a troubadour by name is similarly evident even if the name in question is the wrong one. Despite the seeming accuracy of the majority of citations, what is at stake is often less that a given opinion originated in the mind of an earlier author than that it could be ascribed to one; again, we are dealing with a direction *to*, not a movement *from*, the author in question.

The Arnaut inherited by the thirteenth and fourteenth centuries was a poet of whom it had been conceded in the *accessus* that a song could be given to him, whether or not he had composed it, and this status would surely give greater license to imitating, citing, and quoting him than was the case with other troubadours. If Guillem de Saint Gregori existed and was active in the 1220s, he may well have belonged in an early group of such imitators, since he is also credited by *D* with the authorship of "Ben gran avoleza intra" (233.2), a *contrafactum* of Arnaut's *sestina* "Lo ferm voler" (29.14) that uses the same rhyme words as its model in a political *sirventes* of praise and blame.[14] Even earlier, Raimon Vidal, father of troubadour quotation, is entangled with Arnaut Daniel since the song "Entre·l taur e·l doble signe," attributed to him by Pillet-Carstens with the number 411.3, is accorded by others to Arnaut Daniel.[15]

However, if Perugi is right and the poet responsible for "Razo e dreyt" is Guillem de Murs, then its date of composition moves forward to the 1280s and is the product of another circle of Arnaut groupies, this time based in Vaucluse. The poets who make up this group may have been connected to the Consistori at Toulouse since, as Perugi points out, there are significant overlaps between the rhymes of "Razo e dreyt" and the exemplary rhyme scheme that Molinier works through as a demonstration of how to construct a song in book 5 of the first prose redaction of the *Leys*, and also between it and songs furnished by Molinier himself.[16] The connections of "Razo e dreyt" extend to Catalonia, since a song by Cerveri de Girona has a similar meter;[17] Jofre de Foixà too may have formed part of this Arnaut appreciation society; this Catalan enthusiasm for Arnaut may be responsible for the dubious ascriptions to Arnaut Daniel in the *Mirall*; the text of *So fo* in the Italian fragment *r* may attest the spread of enthusiasm in the other direction, in northern Italy.

While on the one hand Perugi locates "Razo e dreyt" close in both region and date to Avignon, implying this proximity as the reason for Petrarch's encountering it, the Italian scholar also asserts that the poet "without doubt knew it as the work of Arnaut Daniel."[18] I want to explore the suppositions involved in this "knowledge." Does "knowing [the song] as the work of Arnaut" mean believing it to have *originated* in the mind of the twelfth-century troubadour? Or does it merely mean ascribing it to a network of writing *associated* with an *auctor* whose fame was nourished by having songs assigned him that he may not have composed?

Although there are no citations in "Lasso me," the question of attribution is central to the poem's development. Of the five incipits quoted, all but "Razo e dreyt" are rather recognizable. We can hardly suppose that Petrarch did not know that he himself was the author of the final quotation, since it is the first line of one of his own songs;[19] he probably supposed his readers would know it as such; the way the incipit is inserted into the text slyly underlines his connection to it. It also seems safe to infer that he would have expected readers to recognize the other three quotations from Tuscan poets: Guido Cavalcanti, Dante, and Cino da Pistoia. These are his immediate forebears, all are also quoted by Dante,[20] and by adding himself to the list Petrarch is doing what almost all writers do who quote the troubadours: he identifies himself as their late contemporary.

The very first song is different. It really can be doubted if many of Petrarch's readers would know it, or could reasonably have been expected to recognize it, whatever Petrarch may have known or not known about it. On first reading, the Occitan verse reveals itself as a foreign body in Petrarch's text by virtue of its linguistic strangeness, which contrasts with the manifold familiarity of the other incipits. The only clue to its being a line from a song lies in the way it is introduced, the preceding *dir* (line 9) setting up exactly the equivocation we found in Gilles de Viés-Maisons in Chapter 7 between quoting someone else's words and concluding a construction of one's own. The same means of drawing attention to the presence of a quotation is found at the end of stanza II as well; only with the more recent and better known quotations in stanzas III to V is the extraneousness of the incipits dissimulated, much as it was by Jofre de Foixà, by their integration to Petrarch's text. The inference that "Drez et rayson es qu'ieu ciant em demori" is the incipit of a song by a poet who should be known and admired is created *après coup*, as an aftereffect of the recognizability of the songs that are quoted later. In what follows I want to explore what happens when Petrarch's readers are lured into this intersubjective, transferential maze.

While the focus of my analysis remains the lone troubadour quotation, the workings of the whole canzone need to be addressed for these exchanges to be appreciated. Petrarch's song has remarkably lush versification. The *a* rhyme of each stanza, repeated four times, provides a frame into which are slotted three different pairs of rhyming couplets. The rhyme word of each incipit provides the second rhyme of the last of these couplets, binding each quotation eloquently into its stanza.[21] It is then woven into the song as a whole by the way earlier material from the quoted line is repeated at the start of the stanza following. This structure of repetition, known in the Occitan treatises as *coblas capfinidas*, fixes the stanza order—thereby confirming (or implying) a chronology among the quotations—and instigates retrospective reflection on each of the quoted songs. Whereas in the earlier goliardic Latin *versus cum auctoritate*, or "glossed song," the gloss (such as it was) operated proleptically in the lines preceding the quotation, now it begins in the stanza following. The resulting interplay of quotation and reaction impels the song forward via a process of self-reappraisal, in which the impulse to break with past guilt and progress toward a new future has to contend with wistfulness, reluctance, and inertia. As a consequence, whereas Jofre inserts quotations in such a way as to ensure the continuing of the troubadour *canso* as such, Petrarch constantly alters his perspective toward lyric composition: what starts as a love song inspired by the beauty of the beloved ends with aspirations to understand the beauty of creation. In this respect, the Arnaldian quotation in line 10 of "Lasso me" sets up Petrarch's own version of Dante's Arnaut when he says, "regretfully I see past folly, yet rejoicing I see ahead the joy I hope for" (*Purgatorio* 26.143–44; consiros vei la passada folor, /e vei jausen lo joi qu'esper denan).[22] Knowledge of desire transforms that desire into the desire to desire differently, and to desire new forms of knowledge; in its small compass, "Lasso me" veers away from the erotic lyric and its scholastic deployment at the hands of those who quote it, toward unmediated communion with the cosmos.

A key element in this transformation is the Occitan phrase ("drez et rayson," line 10), reprised in the line following as "ragion è ben." There is a self-justificatory cast to the song quoted and to the argument drawn from it that evokes the legislative framework with which troubadour lyric has been surrounded over the preceding century and a half, and which is epitomized in such titles as *Razos de trobar*, *Regles de trobar*, and *Leys d'amors*. The Occitan song adheres to its duty; its rationale (*razo*) is its theme (*razo*); it clings to the inertia of a certain expression of desire in which it is right and reasonable to linger in enjoyment (*demori* literally means "stay, remain").[23] Through stanzas I and II of "Lasso me" the first-person subject also appears frozen in this adherence. But step by step (21), the lofty impassivity of his lady induces Petrarch to begin reasoning differently (22). The exacting rationale of love is reinterpreted as delusion (31–32). Although still indulgent toward the self he was when he composed "nel dolce tempo de la prima etade," he is ready for change.

The change concerned is symbolic insofar as it involves reason, law, and language. The quotations play a vital role in showing how subjectivity is expressed in song. Nostalgia for a certain kind of love and renunciation of it are inseparably bound up with nostalgia for and renunciation of a certain kind of song: the spring opening in stanza I and the "I sing because I am asked to" of stanza II rehearse earlier modes of composition as well as more youthful emotions associated with spring and reciprocal desire. The Dante quotation in stanza III acts as a turning point: Petrarch's heart, when it grows harsh (*aspro*) behaves like Dante's speech" (*mio parlar . . . aspro*) and of course when he repeats Dante's words, Dante's language (*mio parlar*) becomes *his*.[24] After this, there is no longer a gap between singer and song, but that is because it is Petrarch's whole self that has to be relegated to the past; he is not yet quite free of such poetic convictions as the oppression of the look (stanza IV), or the guilt of youthful desire (stanza V). Still repeating quotations, he becomes poised to move forward to we know not what.

The poet's future is uncertain at the end of "Lasso me," but we can be sure that it will be one that does not quote the troubadours. To this extent, Petrarch and Molinier agree: the days of the *antics troubadors* are gone. Molinier's future, however, remains within a framework of scholastic pedagogy; his own poetry and that of the Consistori displace the century-old classics on his students' syllabus. Petrarch's forward movement—while it may in the end be just as masterful—relies on hesitation and supposition to achieve change.

The problematic attribution of the first quotation is crucial in inaugurating this subjective transformation. The author of "Razo e dreyt" is construed retroactively on the basis of the prestige of the quotations that follow. The line is supposed to emanate from a subject supposed to know, who has to be supposed only in order to be the support of the *razo* concerned; conversely, knowledge of this subject is supposed only in order to postulate a point of origin for the tradition in which Petrarch stands. The point about the genealogy inscribed in "Lasso me" is not that it starts with someone celebrated whom it is time to displace but with a figure so spectral and uncertain as to provide no firm anchorage. This is what enables the song to disengage from the subject position that the Occitan line implies, and then reengage differently with the poetic order, and so progress toward a different light. With its transferential structure, the song acts by positing but then dismantling subjects of knowledge in order to be free from the inertia of their desire and in order to desire afresh. The form of the poem is the exact formal corollary of this: by using incipits as explicits, it makes an end of earlier inaugurations, so as to be able to begin again.

Conclusion

This book turns the spotlight on the medieval practice of quoting the troubadours. Passages from a line to almost eighty lines in length are quoted verbatim in a wide range of vernacular (mostly Occitan) texts dating from the turn of the twelfth to thirteenth century to at least the middle of the fourteenth. Although the Latin Middle Ages is known for what Antoine Compagnon has called its *monographie*—the weaving together of textual authorities to form a single self-confirming discourse promoting the oneness of truth—this careful quoting of troubadour poetry is without precedent or parallel in other vernacular literatures. Yet it has by and large escaped comment until now. While the quotations concerned have mostly been identified and some (notably Dante's) have been analyzed in their own context, they have never been studied together as a cultural phenomenon.

I situate this practice in the wider context of troubadour transmission, and this has led me to propose the distinction, captured in this book's title, between the parrots' and the nightingales' modes of reception. What I call the nightingales' way is already familiar to historians of medieval poetry. It involves the gradual take-up of troubadour-inspired poetry among neighboring cultures by poets such as the trouvères, *Minnesänger*, and writers of the Sicilian school. The aspect of this transmission that is closest to the parrots' way but also points to the differences between them is the practice of inserting lyrics into romances, to which I devote Chapter 5. Instead of being carefully quoted, the Occitan lyrics in *Guillaume de Dole* are likened by Jean Renart to blots or stains, performed at the same time as other songs, linguistically mangled, bereft of precise or accurate attribution, and subordinated to French women's song.

What I call the parrots' way is typical of the cultures contiguous with Occitania along the northern Mediterranean. It differs from the well-known nightingales' trajectory in a number of ways. Primary among these are fidelity to the original language of the troubadours (instead of its adaptation to the local vernacular); commitment to accurately preserving and repeating troubadour texts (rather than recreating or reworking them); and privileging them as sources and objects of knowledge. For whereas the nightingales' way foregrounds the capacity of the lyric to voice sentiment (even though it may frame that sentiment with irony), the parrots' way underlines the knowledge that troubadour songs convey and their value as themselves constituting a field of knowledge. By inducing the troubadours to speak less about desire and more about their knowledge of desire, the parrots' way sustains a desire for knowledge through poetry. This lends it a scholastic quality, and indeed the kinds of texts that contain quotation are similar to Latin pedagogical or didactic works, particularly those concerned with the teaching of Latin grammar and poetry. The scholastic focus of the parrots' way also results in a relative disinterest in music as compared with text, though there are exceptions where, with a nod to the nightingales, music reasserts its importance (Chapter 7). Given that quotation grafts one speaker's discourse into another's, it is not only intertextual but also intersubjective; as a result, it foregrounds the intersubjectivity constitutive of what is recognizable *as* knowledge.

The distinction between parrots and nightingales may appear to be loaded against parrots. It is true that the early troubadours were pretty uniformly pro-nightingale, and this prejudice is perpetuated along the nightingales' way—even if it is so, paradoxically, by poets' unthinkingly reiterating the importance of spontaneous song! However, this book is committed to exploring and appreciating the significance of the alternate path. In line with medieval thinking about parrots, I have argued in favor of the potential creativity of the repetition with which they are associated. The avian protagonist of the *Novas del papagai* (Chapter 6) may seem to reiterate what the characters say to it, but equally it contrives the models that are subsequently imitated by *them*. Imitation and repetition lie at the heart of what we think of as "human" nature and are nowhere instantiated better than by resourceful parrots.

In line with this account of the creativity of repetition, this book elaborates a theory of quotation as a mechanism of change. By this is meant both that the repeated words take on new meaning and that the subject position they construct or suppose also changes. The first person in question might be that of the original quotation, of the one who quotes it, or of its eventual reader. The notion of change with which I am working is primarily psycho-analytic, as befits an account situated at the psychic level. Thus I identify a change as a new beginning: a new engagement of the subject with the symbolic order, and thus a renewed and potentially different relation to desire. I have theorized this process in light of Jacques Lacan's account of the thera-peutic concept of the transference. Dialogue between the analyst and analy-sand leads to exposing the extent to which the patient's stance is contingently bound up with knowledge that, in reality, is only supposed and with a sub-jectivity that is similarly hypothetical. This insight can free the patient from his inertia and enable him to redefine himself as a desiring subject. A more accessible version of these ideas is found in Jean-Bertrand Pontalis's autobiog-raphy, *L'amour des commencements*, where the author speaks of the gaps and hesitations that enable a person, in their aftermath, to comprehend his situa-tion differently or, as Pontalis puts it, to "touch a different earth."

In order to orient the views of these psychoanalysts more toward quota-tion as a literary phenomenon, I articulate them together with writings on verbal repetition by Jacques Derrida. His early work on the mark that is in-evitably re-marked when an utterance is repeated in a different context (as it must, by definition, be capable of being if it *is* an utterance) provides a way of thinking about how iteration generates symbolic instability around such con-cepts as "identity" and "subjectivity"; it also, as I noted, makes it difficult to distinguish quoting from other forms of copying. Derrida's more recent con-tribution to postcolonial thinking again returns to the mark as tracing the illusion of the subject's presence in, or ownership of, any particular language; the possible implications of this for Occitan are explored in Chapter 6 and for Dante in Chapter 9. Edward Saïd also situates beginnings in the literary field when he describes them as creating a parallel, essentially secular model of authority, as opposed to a hierarchical, descent-based one (such as that of Compagnon's *monographie*).

The insight that quotation introduces an authority *alongside* that of the one who quotes chimes with the broadly parodic streak in the texts I have written about in this book, since they all situate themselves intriguingly *be-side* rather than *in* the lineage of Latin. Perhaps nowhere is this more piquant than in Dante's *De vulgari eloquentia*, which specifically promotes the ver-nacular, using the language and conceptual apparatus of Latin. It is most widespread, however, in the practice of quotation by incipit: a practice that goes back to the very earliest grammars, is enshrined in the *ordinatio* of *chansonnier* manuscripts, and extends as far forward as Petrarch. Incipital quotation, I have argued, is a particularly telling instance of the way quotation involves the potential for change, since quoting a text's incipit can enable a moment of freedom in which its symbolic world can be inaugurated afresh and our relation to it can be redrawn. Even the fact of recognizing a troubadour song as *having* an incipit forges a connection between it and written texts in Latin, endowing what was formerly an oral courtly performance with new authority.

This constantly insinuated, oblique parallel to Latin is one of the kinds of work that troubadour quotation most consistently performs. By its means, Occitan and its poetry are "grammaticalized," or treated as though they were a kind of neo-Latin. The tendency to grammaticalize lies behind the compilation of vernacular grammars (a contradiction in terms for the early Middle Ages) and all the various strategies that elevate the troubadours to the status of *auctores*, such as the production of biographies and anthologies—including, of course, the patterns of quotation and citation themselves. This construction of Occitan as an international literary standard is an instance of what Derrida calls the *monolangue*: the language of a prestige culture that offers the lure of a uniquely meaningful identification for the speaking subject, and thus of a *formal* authorization of his knowledge, independent of the value of the *content* of what is said.

Content is at the core of the other main form of work performed by quotation, which is, broadly speaking, justificatory: that is, the quoted words are alleged as sustaining something supposed to be known (such as a moral insight) in the supposed speaking subject, whether that is the original troubadour, the one who quotes, or the prospective reader of their words, which justifies a particular belief or behavior. This aspect of quotation is manifested in the preference for quoting sententious excerpts, with the ostensible aim, from the time of Raimon Vidal's *novas* on, of bolstering the positions of those who quote them. Passages with potentially justificatory uses are assembled in *florilegia*; their interpretation reaches unexpected heights in the *Breviari d'amor* where *fin' amors* becomes identified as a means by which to understand God's essence as love; in different ways, Dante and Guilhem Molinier also integrate the work of quotation into an eschatological scheme. I have shown how these authors (except perhaps Molinier) present quotation in such a way as to expose the supposed nature of the knowledge concerned: for example, by insinuating the ineptitude of some of those who quote (Raimon

Vidal), or by showing that quotations rely on any number of competing hermeneutics that are inevitably circular (Matfre Ermengau).

Such techniques provoke an interplay of recognition and misrecognition between supposed subjects and the kinds of knowledge—including knowledge of desire—that can be imputed to quotation. Quotation does not simply require a modicum of scholarly expertise, it plays with our whole relationship to knowledge, exhibiting at every turn the duplicity that Derrida identifies in iteration and that Lacan attributes to the unconscious. Thus, while quoting relies on remembering or preserving, it also depends on forgetting or suppressing. It appears to repeat the words of another but overwrites them with the views of the one who quotes. While seeming to inform, it can withhold, challenge, or confuse. Different modulations of our supposed relation to supposed knowledge are presented in each of the chapters in this book, from the challenge to see troubadour poetry as constituting the very substance of thought (Chapter 1) to the provocation to accept that the prestige of the troubadours is an arbitrary legacy of a past that is now over (Chapter 11).

The span of a century and a half that separates my first from my last chapter is marked by shifts in the kinds of knowledge associated with the troubadours, though these are not sudden or abrupt. The earliest instances of quotation by Raimon Vidal imply the existence of social groups actively interested in performing or appreciating troubadour poems, especially in Catalan courts and hence at a significant geographical remove from the songs' birthplace in northern Occitania. Here knowledge of the troubadours involves speakers and oral memory; the sense of being still broadly contemporary with them is strong. The conviction that knowledge of the troubadours plays a vital part in a speech community persists as late as the *Breviari d'amor*, almost at the end of the thirteenth century. Musical performance, seemingly divorced from quotation from its earliest occurrences of quotation, is brought back later in the century when Jofre de Foixà's imitation of northern French trouvères incorporates aspects of the nightingales' way with that of the parrots. Considering performance in a different light, for native Italians like Bertolome Zorzi, and perhaps again for Dante, the accumulated tradition of quotation can make the whole process of quoting something of a drag act, my conception of "drag" here being guided by Judith Butler's application to gender theory of Derrida's work on iteration.

But the early grammatical treatises also insinuate that knowledge relies on the existence of written texts, and the various modes of quotation that follow tend to center more and more on writing and the archive (Chapters 3 and 4).

The practice of commentary contributes to the masterful overreading of seemingly unremarkable troubadour passages, banally misogynist in the compiler of the anthology in *H*, unexpectedly theological in the *Breviari d'amor*. In the fourteenth-century texts analyzed from Chapter 9 onward, techniques of copying the troubadours pioneered in the early songbooks take precedence over speech, and eventually the role of memory in quotation tips in favor of forgetting. The token acts of remembering, or misremembering, performed in these later texts have the effect of consigning the troubadours to oblivion.

The net effect of these negotiations over supposed knowledge and its supposed subjects, I have contended, is to bring about changes in poetic subjectivity in which the stance of courtly *fin' amors* and its postures of knowing desire give way to what is generally recognized as the rather different desiring postures of Petrarchanism and beyond. In outline, the process of change that I have proposed is that described by Lacan in the transference: a subject's relation to desire can only be given up in favor of another via a passage through supposed knowledge. Clearly the outcome of such transformation is itself never static, so I would certainly not affirm that the result of the changes described here is a stable, individual "self" defined by its own interior space, as some views of the Renaissance would have it. Indeed, to repeat what Adrian Armstrong and I wrote in our conclusion to *Knowing Poetry*, "It is important to avoid reifying precisely those distinctions between 'Middle Ages' and 'Renaissance' that recent reflection has shown to be difficult to sustain; nor should we hypostatize a cultural movement, the early modern Renaissance, as a historical epoch."[1]

Nevertheless, as that conclusion also argues, the way verse situates itself with respect to time does shift. While I certainly would not want to claim that the practice of quotation is solely responsible for this movement, it plays a part in it and may help to capture it. When, in "Lasso me," Petrarch both relies on troubadour quotation and seeks to end it as a practice, he provides a telling if small-scale instance of a mutation in historical consciousness. Medieval commitment to the continuous mediation of a still accessible past is in the process of being relinquished; it will be overtaken by what Thomas M. Greene calls "humanist pride and humanist despair" at the chasm that separates the scholar-poet from the remote culture of antiquity.[2] The double impulse of poetry in the Petrarchan manner, imitation and quasi-divine inspiration, are responses to this perceived temporal gap that the end of the tradition of troubadour quotation has helped to create.[3] Thus its Petrarchan obliteration is also the most significant moment of renewal that this tradition has enabled; in the end, the parrots' way of transmitting the troubadours proves more productive than the nightingales'.

Thus although the practice of troubadour quotation is certainly not the only mechanism of cultural change in the period described in this book, it is a driver, beside others, of a new beginning that is to prove enduringly important. It is ironic, in the circumstances, that this practice, one of the most concerted efforts to remember the troubadours, should itself have been forgotten until now.

Appendices

Electronic versions of Appendices 1 and 2 can also be consulted on https://wikis.nyu.edu/display/PNAppendices/home.

Quotations from the Troubadours

This appendix lists all passages from troubadour songs of a line or longer that are quoted in subsequent Occitan texts and in a small selection of related non-Occitan ones (*Guillaume de Dole, Roman de la violette, De vulgari eloquentia*, Petrarch's "Lasso me"). The appendix is organized by the troubadours quoted (column I), listed in the order they appear in Pillet-Carstens's bibliography (PC). The next column gives the PC number of each quoted song, as updated in the *Bibliografia elettronica dei trovatori*; the song's opening line follows in the third column. The entries in the next following columns indicate which lines of the song are quoted and in what context(s). Each entry gives, in order, the line(s) of the song quoted (as they appear in the modern edition); the text in which the quotation appears (though not for *Breviari d'amor*, since this column is dedicated to just this one text); the number assigned to that quotation (in cases where quotations have been previously inventoried); the location (e.g., line numbers) in the quoting text where the quotation is found; and any additional information about the quotation in question: if it is mis- or unattributed and if, in the case of the prose biographies, it appears in a text about a different troubadour (indicated by giving the name of the troubadour concerned). The final column cross-refers to Appendix 2, which lists the excerpted stanzas anthologized in six *chansonnier* manuscripts. In cases where the quoted material coincides at least partly with excerpted material, the final column indicates in which *chansonnier(s)* the anthologized extract appears. In cases where the same song is both quoted and excerpted, but not the same passage(s), the cross-reference is in parentheses. *Chansonnier sigla* are given in Appendix 17; abbreviations are explained on page vii; editions are listed in the "Primary Texts" section of the Bibliography.

Troubadour	Song	Incipit	Treatises of Occitan grammar and poetics	Novas	Biographies	Breviari d'amor	Other (lyrics, French romance, Dante, etc.)	Appendix 2
Ademar lo Negre	3.1	Era·m don Dieus qe repaire	5–8 DA (#2, 180–83) (attrib. "En Giraudos le Ros")					(Fa)
Ademar de Rocaficha	5.1	Ges per freg ni per calor				33–44 (#104, 29977–87)		
						45–55 (#53, 28942–52)		
	5.3	Si amors fos conoyssens				25–36 (#34, 28571–82)		
Aimeric de Belenoi	9.3	Aissi co·l pres que s'en cuia fugir				25–32 (#46, 28827–34)		Fa
	9.14	Nulls hom non pot complir adreizamen					1 DVE (2.6.6; 2.12.3)	DcFaG
	9.15	Per Crist, s'ieu crezes Amor				28–36 (#103, 29965–73)		
	9.18	Pos le gais temps de pascor				25–36 (#7, 27976–87)		Fa
						37–48 (#1, 27821–32)		Fa

Troubadour	Song	Incipit	Treatises of Occitan grammar and poetics	Novas	Biographies	Breviari d'amor	Other (lyrics, French romance; Dante, etc.)	Appendix 2
Aimeric de Peguilhan	10.2	Ades vol de l'aondansa				9–16 (#120, 30425–32)		
						17–24 (#39, 28661–68)		Dc
	10.7	Amors, a vos meteussa·m clam de vos	1 Mi (#19, 484–85; #21, 505–6)			1–8 (#63, 29162–9)		DcFa
			9–14 Mi (#21, 506–11)					DcFa
						33–40 (#52, 28925–32)		
	10.8	Anc mais de joy ni de chan				10–18 (#77, 29435–43)		
						19–27 (#74, 29377–85)		
						28–36 (#75, 29394–402)		
	10.12	Atressi·m pren quom fai al joguador				1–8 (#257, 33947–54)		Fa
						17–24 (#56, 28993–29000)		

10.15	Cel qui s'irais ni guerreia ab Amor		1–8 (#44, 28786–93)		Dc
			9–16 (#71, 29317–24)		
			17–24 (#173, 31977–84)		
			33–40 (#227, 33276–83)		
10.16	Chantar voill—per que?—ja·m platz	1 Mi (#25, 551–52)			
		17–21 Mi (#25, 552–55)			
10.17	De so dont hom a longuamen		5–8 (#15, 28139–42)		Dc
10.18	D'avinen sap enganar e trahir	1–4 Mi (#30, 639–42)			Dc
10.23	Domna, per vos estauc en greu turmen		1–24 (#129, 30696–719) (unattrib.)		
10.24	Yssamen cum l'aÿmans		1–8 (#57, 29010–17)		Dc
10.25	En Amor trob alques en qe·m refraing	25–27 ReT (#11, H 562–64, R 450–52)			(Fa)

Troubadour	Song	Incipit	Treatises of Occitan grammar and poetics	Novas	Biographies	Breviari d'amor	Other (lyrics, French romance, Dante, etc.)	Appendix 2
	10.27	En greu pantais m'a tengut longamen				15–21 (#38, 28645–51)		Fa
	10.33	Lonjamen m'a trebalhat e malmes				9–16 (#99, 29899–906)		Fa
						33–40 (#253, 33770–77)		
	10.34	Mangtas vetz sui enqueritz	17–24 ReT (#1, H 19–26)					
	10.40	Per razo natural				1–10 (#26, 28393–402)		DcFa
						35–40 (#10, 28034–39)		DcFa
	10.41	Per solatz d'autrui chant soven	1 Mi (#13, 339–40)					DcFa
						25–32 (#127, 30627–34)		
			33–40 Mi (#13, 340–46)					Fa
	10.43	Pus ma belha mal'amia				1–8 (#47, 28840–47)		

	10.50	Si cum l'arbres que, per sobrecargar			25–32 (#81, 29528–35)		
Aimeric de Sarlat	11.2	Fins e leials e senes tot engan				1 DVE (2.6.6)	Fa
Albertet de Sestaro	16.9	Destreytz d'amor, venc denant vos			33–40 (#133, 30782–89)		Fa
					1–24, 33–40 (#158, 31508–39) (attrib. Raimbaut de Vaqueiras)		
Andrian del Palais	22a.1—see unidentified quotations, DA						
Arnaut Daniel	29—see unidentified quotations, Mi						
	29.2	Anc ieu non l'aic, mas ella m'a		1 (IX.B, 13)			
	29.6	Chansson do·ill mot son plan e prim			19–20 (#196, 32289–90)		

Troubadour	Song	Incipit	Treatises of Occitan grammar and poetics	Novas	Biographies	Breviari d'amor	Other (lyrics, French romance, Dante, etc.)	Appendix 2
	29.9	En breu brisara·l temps braus				9–16 (#214, 32573–80)		
	29.10	En cest sonet coind' e leri			43–45 (IX.A, 4)			
	29.13	L'aur'amara					1–3 DVE (2.2.8)	
	29.14	Lo ferm voler q'el cor m'intra	1 Ri (#12, 98); 1 Mi (#27, 610); 1–2 Leys 1341 (3:330)					
	29.17	Si·m fos Amors de ioi donar tant larga					1 DVE (2.13.2)	Fa
	29.18	Sols sui che sai lo sobrafan qe·m sortz					1 DVE (2.6.6)	Fa
Arnaut de Maruelh	30.1	A gran honor viu cui jois es cobitz				1–7 (#203, 32409–15)		Dc
	30.3	Aissi cum cel c'am' e non es amaz				22–28 (#136, 30856–62)		Fa
	30.4	Aissi cum cel que anc non ac cossire				15–21 (#51, 28912–18)		

30.5	Aissi cum selh que tem qu'Amors l'aucia			29–35 (#229, 33304–10)		*DcFaCm*
30.8	Anc vas Amor no·m poc res contradire			15–21 (#98, 29885–91)		*DcFaCm*
30.15	La franca captenensa		1 (VII.A, 8)			*DcCm*
				31–40 (#135, 30837–46)		*DcCmH*
30.16	La grans beutatz e·l fis ensenhamens				1 Jofre de Foixà 304.1 (7)	*Fa*
30.18	Lo gens temps m'abelis e·m platz			28–36 (#122, 30510–18)		
				37–45 (#114, 30187–95)		
30.19	Mout eron doutz miei cossir		1 (VII.B, 6)			*DcFaCm*
30.22	Si cum li peis an en l'aiga lor vida	1–2 *DA* (#21, 351–52)				*DcFaCm*

Troubadour	Song	Incipit	Treatises of Occitan grammar and poetics	Novas	Biographies	Breviari d'amor	Other (lyrics, French romance, Dante, etc.)	Appendix 2
	30.23	Si·m destreig-netz, dompna, vos et Amors	1 RaT (#13, B 231, CL 217)				1 Jofre de Foixà 304.1 (14)	DcFaCm
						9–16 (#249, 33699–706)		Cm H
				38–40 So (LNR 239–41)	39–40 (VI.B, 4) (Bernart de Ventadorn)			DcFaCm
	30.VI (ensenhamen)	Razos es e mezura		64–74 Ab (1231–41)				
						77–84, 107–8, 101–4 (#224, 33218–31)		
				155–58 Ab (1022–25)				Dc
				209–12 Ab (603–6)				
Arnaut Plagues	32.1	Ben volgra midons saubes				1–45 (#162, 31643–86) (attrib. Uc Brunenc)		

Author		Incipit					
Arnaut de Tintinhac	34.2	Lo jois comens en un bel mes			22–28 (#113, 30160–66) (attrib. Guiraut de Quentinhac)		
Berenguer de Palazol	47.6	Dona, la genser qu'om veya			9–16 (#119, 30403–11)		
Bernart Arnaut d'Armagnac	54.1	Lombards volgr'eu eser per Na Lombarda		1–20 (LX, 5) (Na Lombarda)			
Bernart de la Fon	62.1	Leu chansonet' ad entendre			19–27 (#91, 29737–45)		
Bernart Marti	63.6	D'entier vers far ieu non pes			67–72, + 1 unknown v., 64–66 (#139, 30969–79)		
Bernart de Prades	65.1	Ab cor lial, fin e certa			21–30 (#36, 28613–22)		
Bernart de Rovenac	66.2	D'un sirventes m'es grans volontatz preza				1 Luquet Gatelus 290.1a (1)	
Bernart de Ventadorn	70.1	Ab joi mou lo vers e·l comens	1 Mi (#23, 530–31)				DcFa
			17–21 Mi (#23, 532–35)	17–24 (XCIV.D, 57) (Guillem de Cabestaing)	17–24 (#235, 33506–13)		

Troubadour	Song	Incipit	Treatises of Occitan grammar and poetics	Novas	Biographies	Breviari d'amor	Other (lyrics, French romance, Dante, etc.)	Appendix 2
						25–32 (#247, 33666–73)	25–32 Violette (fr. 1553, fo. 289, other MSS have 461.103a)	Fa
			33 RaT (#2, B 185); 33–34 (CL 165–66)	33–36 So (LNR 520–23)		33–36 (#130, 30727–30)		
			49 RaT (#3, B 187; CL 168)			49–56 (#157, 31473–80)		
	70.6	Era·m cosselhatz, senhor	1 RaT (#11, B 210); 1–2 (CL 191–92); 1 ReT (#8, H 386, R 288)		1 (VI.D, 7)			
			41 RaT (#8, B [203], CL 184)					
	70.7	Ara no vei luzir solelh	1 RaT (#16, B 190–91, CL 333)					Fa
			41–43 RaT (#17, B 368–70, H 196–98, CL 338–40)					
	70.10	Bel m'es qu'eu chan en aquel mes		35 So (LNR 47)				

						DcFa
70.12	Be m'an perdut lai enves Ventadorn	1 RaT (#26, B 456, CL 423–44) (omitted in H)				
		29–30 RaT (#27, B 459–60, H 285–86, CL 426–27)				Dc
70.15	Chantars no pot gaire valer			8–14 (#228, 33290–96)		
70.19	Estat ai com om esperdutz	1 Mi (#22, 520) (attrib. Peirol)				Dc
		33–36 Mi (#22, 521–23)				
70.21	Ges de chantar no·m pren talans			25–32 (#199, 32334–41)		
70.23	La dousa votz ai auzida			25–32 (#41, 28727–34)		
70.25	Lancan vei la folha	1–2 RaT (#14, B 361, H 189–90, CL 332–33)		61–72 (#248, 33681–92)		
		73–74 RaT (#15, B 364–65, H 192–93, CL 335–36)				
70.26	Lancan vei per mei la landa			29–35 (#168, 31800–31806)		

Troubadour	Song	Incipit	Treatises of Occitan grammar and poetics	Novas	Biographies	Breviari d'amor	Other (lyrics, French romance, Dante, etc.)	Appendix 2
	70.27	Lonc tems a qu'eu no chantei mai		10–11 So (LNR 171–72)				(Fa)
	70.28	Lo gens tems de pascor				9–16 (#16, 28149–56) (attrib. Peire Vidal)		
	70.29	Lo rossinhols s'esbaudeya				9–16 (#29, 28461–68)		Fa
	70.31	Non es meravelha s'eu chan	1 Mi (#17, 454–55)					Fa
			9–10 DA (#16, 291–92)			9–16 (#68, 29252–59)		
			49–51 Mi (#17, 456–58)			49–56 (#167, 31780–87)		
	70.41	Can par la flors josta·l vert folh				17–24 (#49, 28873–80)		DcFa
			28 RaT (#22, B 404, H 231, CL 373)					
	70.43	Can vei la lauzeta mover	1 DA (#27, 547)		1 (VI.C, 3)		1–8 Violette (4187–94), 1–16 GDole (#16, 5212–27)	Fa

			25 DA (#13, 263); 30–31 DA (#29, 560–61); 31 RaT (#21, B 402, H 229, CL 371)			25–32, (#88, 29675–82)	
			33–34, DA (#28, 548–49)				Fa
	70.45	Tuich cil que·m preyon qu'eu chan		49–56 So (LNrR 433–40)		22–28 (#59, 29057–63)	(Dc)
Bernart de Venzac	71.3	Pus vey lo temps fer frevoluc				49–53 (#240, 33565–69)	
Bertolome Zorzi	74.10	Mout fort me sui d'un chant meravilhatz			1 (C.B, 6)		
Bertran de Born	80.1	Ai, Lemozis, francha terra cortesa			1–14 (XI.D, 4)		
	80.2	Al nou doutz termini blanc			1–2 (XI.Q, 10)		Dc
	80.8	Be·m platz car trega ni fis			25 (XI.S, 5)		
	80.12	Dompna, puois de mi no·us cal			1 (XI.C, 6)		

Troubadour	Song	Incipit	Treatises of Occitan grammar and poetics	Novas	Biographies	Breviari d'amor	Other (lyrics, French romance, Dante, etc.)	Appendix 2
	80.13	D'un sirventes no·m cal far loignor ganda			1 (XI.M, 4)			
	80.15	Eu m'escondisc, dompna, que mal non mier			1 (XI.D, 6)			
	80.19	Ges de disnar non for'oimais maitis			1 (XI.F, 7)			J
	80.20	Ges de far sirventes no·m tartz			1 (XI.I, 3)			
					1–2 (XI.H, 24)			
	80.21	Ges no me desconort			1–2 (XI.K, 8)			Dc
					46–47 (XI.K, 9)			
	80.25	Miez sirventes vueilh far dels reis amdos	8 ReT (#7, H 302, R 211) (attrib. Bertran d'Alamanon)					
	80.26	Mon chan fenis ab dol et ab maltraire			1 (XI.N, 2)			

80.29	Non puosc mudar mon chantar non esparga		1 (XI.R, 2)	1 *DVE* (2.2.8)
80.31	Pois als baros enoia en lur pesa		1 (XI.P, 17)	
			1 (XI.Q, 1)	
80.32	Pois lo gens terminis floritz		1 (XI.H, 11)	
			1 (XI.L, 31)	
80.33	Pois Ventedorns e Comborns ab Segur		1 (XI.J, 3)	
			1–2 (XI.J, 6)	
80.34	Qan la novella flors par el vergan		1 (XI.T, 9)	
		41 *RaT* (#9, *B* 205, *CL* 186)		
80.35	Qan vei pels vergiers despleiar		1–2 (XI.O, 15)	
80.37	Rassa, tant creis e mont' e poia		1–2 (XI.B, 8)	*Dc*

Troubadour	Song	Incipit	Treatises of Occitan grammar and poetics	Novas	Biographies	Breviari d'amor	Other (lyrics, French romance, Dante, etc.)	Appendix 2
	80.38	S'abrils e fuoillas e flors			12–17 (XI.B, 5)			
					1 (XI.E, 17)			
				So 19–22 (a²R, 1407–10)				
				Ab 86–88 (468–71)				
	80.44	Un sirventes on motz non faill			1–2 (XI.G, 9)			
Bertran de Born lo filhs	81.1	Quan vei lo temps renovelar			1 (XII, 19)			
Bertran de la Tor	92.1	Mauret, al Dalfin agrada			1–8 (XLII.C, 2)			
Lo Vesques de Clarmon	95.3	Per Crist, si·l servens fos meus			1–9 (XLII.B, 3) (Dalfi d'Alvernha)			
Bonifaci Calvo	101.7	Ges no m'es greu, s'eu non sui ren prezatz			1 (C.B, 5) (Bertolome Zorzi)			
Cadenet	106.2	A! cu·m dona ric coratge				12–22 (#187, 32173–83)		DcFa

					23–25 (#188, 32189–91)		*Fa*
	106.10	*Be volgra, s'esser pogues*				1 Guiraut d'Espanha 244.1a (1)	*Fa*
	106.16	*Meravilh me de tot fin amador*			11–20 (#69, 29276–85)		*(Dc)*
	106.18	*Oimais m'auretz avinen*			12–22 (#170, 31836–46)		*Dc*
					23–33 (#126, 30600–30610)		
	106.22	*S'ieu pogues ma voluntat*			1–12 (#8, 27995–8006)		*DcFa*
					21–24 (#261, 34169–72)		*Dc*
			25–36 *So* (a^2 1568–79)				*DcFa*
Dalfi d'Alvernha	119.1a	*Al Dalfin man qu'estei dinz son hostal*		9–16 (XLII.D, 7)			
	119.4	*Li evesque troban en sos breus*		1–10 + 3 unknown vv. (XLII.B, 5)			
	119.5	*Mauret, Bertrans, a laisada*		1–8 (XLII.C, 1)			

Troubadour	Song	Incipit	Treatises of Occitan grammar and poetics	Novas	Biographies	Breviari d'amor	Other (lyrics, French romance, Dante, etc.)	Appendix 2
	119.8	Reis, pus vos de mi chantatz			1–2 (XLII.E, 20)			
Daude de Pradas	124.2	Amors m'envida e·m somo				31–40 (#200, 32368–77)		
	124.5	Belha m'es la votz autana					1–7 GDole (#15, 4653–59)	
	124.6	Ben ay' Amors, quar anc me fes chauzir				1–8 (#33, 28549–56)		DcFa
	124.10	En un sonet guay e leugier				11–20 (#182, 32116–25)		Dc
	124.14	Puois amors vol e comanda				25–32 (#97, 29870–77)		
	124.16	Si per amar ni per servir				17–24 (#50, 28889–96)		
						33–40 (#245, 33631–38)		
Elias de Barjols	132.3	Amors, que vos ai forfag	1 Mi (#6, 209–10) (attrib. Gaucelm Faidit)					
			9–18 Mi (#6, 210–17) (attrib. Gaucelm Faidit)					

	132.4	Ben deu hom son bon senhor				1–8 (#255, 33911–18) (attrib. Peire Bremon Ricas Novas)		
						9–16 (#256, 33921–28) (attrib. Peire Bremon Ricas Novas)		
Elias Cairel	133.8	Per mantener joi e can e solatz				9–16 (#40, 28680–7) (attrib. the Monk of Montaudon)		J
Elias d'Ussel	136.2	Gauselms, eu mezeis garantis			1–8 (XVIII.F, 8) (Gaucelm Faidit)			
	136.3	Manenz fora·l francs pelegris			1–10 (XVIII.F, 4) (Gaucelm Faidit)			
Folquet de Marselha	155.1	Amors, merce: non mueira tan soven					1 Jofre de Foixà 304.1 (35)	DcFa
			10–11 DA (#10, 225–26)	8–14 So (LNR 248–54)				Dc
						34–35 (#236, 33514.2–3)		DcFaHj

Troubadour	Song	Incipit	Treatises of Occitan grammar and poetics	Novas	Biographies	Breviari d'amor	Other (lyrics, French romance, Dante, etc.)	Appendix 2
	155.3	Ai! quan gen vens et ab quan pauc d'afan	1 RaT (#23, B 412, H 238–39, CL 380–81)					DcFa
				9–12 So (R 958–61)				Dc
				23–24 So (R 906–7)				DcFa
			25–26 RaT (#24, B 413–14, H 240–41, CL 382–83); 25–27 DA (#43, 648–50)					Dc
	155.5	Ben an mort mi e lor				1–10 (#78, 29453–62)		Dc
	155.6	Chantan volgra mon fin cor descobrir	1 Mi (#9, 272; # 20, 493–94)					Dc
			19–20, 22–24 Mi (#20, 494–99)					
			28–31 Mi (#9, 273–76)					
	155.10	Greu feira nuills hom faillenssa	1 Mi (#7, 236–37)					Dc
			28–34 Mi (#7, 238–42)					

155.11	Ja no·s cuig hom qu'ieu camje mas chansos				39–40 (#142, 31081–82)	*DcFa*
155.14	Molt i fetz gran pechat Amors	9–10 *ReT* (#6, H 290–91, R 200–201)				*Fa*
					11–20 (#61, 29103–12)	*Fa*
155.15	Oimais no·i conosc razo			1 (LXXI.E, 5)		
155.16	Per Dieu, Amors, ben sabetz veramen				1–8 (#198, 32316–23)	*DcFa*
					10–11 (#171, 31888–89)	*DcFaH*
			15–16 *So* (a^2 1492–93)		9–16 (#20, 28217–24)	*DcFaH*
			41–44 *So* (*LNrR* 407–10)			
155.18	S'al cor plagues, ben fora oimais sazos	1*RaT* (#12, CL 215)				*Dc*
					11–20 (#58, 29027–36)	*Dc*

Troubadour	Song	Incipit	Treatises of Occitan grammar and poetics	Novas	Biographies	Breviari d'amor	Other (lyrics, French romance, Dante, etc.)	Appendix 2
	155.20	Si com sel qu'es tan greujatz			1–3 (LXXI.D, 2)			
	155.21	Sitot me soi a tart aperceubuz				9–16 (#19, 28195–202)		
						25–32 (#60, 29087–94)		DcFa
						33–40 (#18, 28181–88)		
	155.22	Tan m'abellis l'amoros pessamens					1 DVE (2.6.6)	Fa
	155.23	Tan mou de cortesa razo	1–3 DA (#18, 297–99)		1–2 (LXXI.B, 10)			DcFa
			13 DA (#19, 302)					
			25–28 DA (#20, 303–6)					Dc
	155.27	Us volers outracuidatz			1–2 (LXXI.C, 3)			
					56–60 (LXXI.C, 6)			

				1–2 (LIII, 3)			
Garin d'Apchier	162.6	Quan foill' e flors reverdezis				157–60 (#213, 32564–67)	
Garin lo Brun	163.1 *ensenhamen*	El termini d'estiu				257–60, 271–72, 285–90, 295–98, 243–52, 391–94 (#116, 30278–307)	
						301–2, 595–604, 593–94, 607–10, 613–14, 352, 351, 353–54, 2 unknown vv., 359–60, 309–11, 361–66, 1 unknown v., 290? (#121, 30461–500)	
						427–40, 445–46, 457–60 (#191, 32222–41)	

Troubadour	Song	Incipit	Treatises of Occitan grammar and poetics	Novas	Biographies	Breviari d'amor	Other (lyrics, French romance, Dante, etc.)	Appendix 2
						515–22, 559–68, 587–92, 615–24, 627–30 (#128, 30641–78)		
Gaucelm Estaca	166.1	Qor q'ieu chantes desamatz				1–10 (#28, 28438–47)		
Gaucelm Faidit	167.12	Be·m platz e m'es gen	1–2 DA (#32, 573–74) (attrib. Folquet de Marselha)					
			47–48 DA (#33, 577–58) (attrib. Folquet de Marselha)					
	167.13	Ben auria obs pas e vis			9–16 (XVIII.F, 7)			
	167.15	Chant e deport, joi, dompnei e solatz			1–10 (XVIII.E, 13)	1–10 (#152, 31343–52)		DcFa
						11–20 (#151, 31324–33)		

167.18	De faire chansso	1 RaT (#31, CL 445)	25–36 So (a² 1550–61)				Dc
		37–38 DA (#34, 581–82) (attrib. Folquet de Marselha); 37–8 RaT (#32, CL 446–47)					Dc
167.22	Fortz chausa es que tot lo major dan	1 DA (#22, 354)					
167.33	L'onratz, jauzens sers sers			1–3 (XVIII.D, 10)			
167.35	Maintas sazos es hom plus voluntos				9–16 (#80, 29507–14)		
					25–32 (#66, 29214–21)		Dc
167.37	Mon cor et mi e mas bonas chansos					1 Jofre de Foixà 304.1 (42)	
167.40	Mout m'enojet ogan lo coindetz mes			1, 6–10 (XVIII.E, 4)			

Troubadour	Song	Incipit	Treatises of Occitan grammar and poetics	Novas	Biographies	Breviari d'amor	Other (lyrics, French romance, Dante, etc.)	Appendix 2
	167.43	No m'alegra chans ni critz			1–2 (XVIII.B, 32)			
				30–33 So (a²R 1328–31)				
	167.45	Pel joi del temps qu'es floritz	1 Mi (#5, 196–97)					
			10–11 Mi (#5, 197–98)					
	167.51	Razon e mandamen	27–28 DA (#35, 585–86) (attrib. Folquet de Marselha)					DcFa
	167.52	Si anc nuills hom, per aver fin coratge			1 (XVIII.C, 17)			(H)
	167.53	Si tot m'ai tarzat mon chan				19–27 (#67, 29235–43)		
						37–45 (#48, 28856–64)		
	167.56	S'om pogues partir son voler				1–11 (#258, 33962–71)		DcFa
			17 ReT (#4, H 251, R 162)					Fa

							DcFa
	167.59	Tant ai sofert longamen grand afan	50 ReT (#5, H 265, R 174)		1 (XVIII.B, 21)		
	167.60	Tot mi cuidei de chanssos far sofrir				46–54 (#2, 27865–73)	Fa
	167.62	Tuich cil que amon Valor				1–9 (#195, 32274–82)	Dc
			53–54 DA (#7, 212–13)				Dc
Gausbert de Poicibot	173.3	Car no m'abellis solatz	37–40 DA (#15, 284–87)			37–40 (#174, 31989–92) (attrib. Alberet de Sestaro)	
	173.7	Hueimais de vos non aten		25–36 So (a^2 1594–605)			
	173.11	S'ieu anc jorn dis clamans				13–24 (#12, 28074–86)	
	173.14	Una grans amors corals				45–55 (#11, 28053–63)	
Guilhem de Peitieu	183.11	Pos vezem de novel florir				31–36 (#205, 32435–40)	
Lo coms de Rodez	185.3 (=457.33)	Seign'en coms, no·us cal esmaiar			9–16 (XXXIV, 3)		

Troubadour	Song	Incipit	Treatises of Occitan grammar and poetics	Novas	Biographies	Breviari d'amor	Other (lyrics, French romance, Dante, etc.)	Appendix 2
Gui de Cavaillo	192.2	Doas coblas farai en aqest son			1–18 (LXXXII, 4)			
Gui d'Ussel	194.2	Ara·m digatz vostre semblan			1–8 (XXII.B, 8)			
	194.3	Ben feira chanzos plus soven			35–36 (VI.B, 4) (Bernart de Ventadorn)			Dc
	194.19	Si be·m partetz, mala dompna, de vos			1–8 (XXII.B, 13); 1 (XXIII, 4) (Maria de Ventadorn)			DcFa
				33–40 So (LNrR 455–62)		33–40 (#216, 32608–15)		DcFa
Guilhem Ademar	202.1	Ben for' oimais sazos e locs		8–14 So (LNR 282–88)		14 (#231, 33330)		Dc
	202.4	Comensamen comensarai	1–3 Mi (#29, 629–31)					
	202.11	Quan la bruna biza branda				9–16 (#96, 29855–62)		
Guillem de Balaun	208.1	Lo vers mou merceyan ves vos			1 (XLVIII, 37)			

Guillem de Berguedà	210.10a	E fetz una mespreison		1–8 (XI.O, 12) (Bertran de Born)			
	210.14	Mais volgra chantar a plazer			25–32 (#35, 28592–99)		
Guillem de Cabestanh	213—see unidentified quotations, Ri						
	213.3	Ar vei qu'em vengut als jorns loncs	1 Ri (#1, 5); 1–2 Ri (#17, 134–35)				
					36–42 (#54, 28962–68)		
					43–49 (#112, 30127–33)		
	213.5	Lo doutz cossire	1 Ri (#2, 7); 1–4 Ri (#13, 106–9)	1–2 (XCIV.C [HR], 9)		Fa	
				1–15 (XCIV.D, 93)			
				28–30 (XCIV.C [H])		Fa	
Guillem Magret	223.2	Atrestan be·m tenc per mortal			27–30 (#45, 28814–17)		

Troubadour	Song	Incipit	Treatises of Occitan grammar and poetics	Novas	Biographies	Breviari d'amor	Other (lyrics, French romance, Dante, etc.)	Appendix 2
Guillem de Montanhagol	225.7	Non an tan dig li primier trobador				21–30 (#109, 30055–63)		
						41–50 (#117, 30331–38)		
	225.10	Nulhs hom no val ni deu esser prezatz				1–9 (#238, 33538–46)		*Fa*
						10–18 (#147, 31223–31)		*Fa*
						19–27 (#148, 31243–51)		*Fa*
				37–45 So (*a*² 1519–27)		37–45 (#150, 31302–10)		*Fa*
	225.11	On mais a hom de valensa				1–9 (#226, 33262–70) (attrib. Peire Rogier)		
						19–27 (#180, 32073–81) (attrib. Peire Rogier)		

	225.13	Qui vol esser agradans e plazens			25–32 (#181, 32097–104)		*DcFa*
					25–27 (#254, 33853–55)		*DcFa*
Guillem de Saint Gregori	233.4	Razo e dreyt ai mi chant e·m demori				1, Petrarch "Lasso me," (10)	
Guillem de Sant Leidier	234—see unidentified quotations, *So*						
	234.4	Ben chantera si m'estes ben d'Amor			25–32 (#95, 29841–48)		*(H)*
	234.6	Compaignon, ab joi mou mon chan	57–58 *DA* (#4, 192–93) (attrib. Pons de Capdoill)				
	234.7	Dompna, ieu vos sui messatgiers	1 *RaT* (#4, *B* 189, *CL* 170)	1–2 (XLI.C, 8); 1 (XLI.C, 16)			
			50 *RaT* (#5, *B* 191, *CL* 172)				

Troubadour	Song	Incipit	Treatises of Occitan grammar and poetics	Novas	Biographies	Breviari d'amor	Other (lyrics, French romance, Dante, etc.)	Appendix 2
	234.16	Pois tant mi forss' Amors que m'a faich entremetre	1 Mi (#26, 602–3)		1–2 (XLI.B, 17)			
					43–44 (XLI.B, 18)			
Guiraudo lo Ros	240.4	Era sabrai s'à ges de cortezia		41–44 So (LNR 590–93)				(DcFa)
Giraut de Bornelh	242.5	Alegrar mi volgr'en chantan	74–76 DA (#9, 220–22)					(Dc)
	242.16	Era si·m fos en grat tengut	1 Mi (#3, 154)					
			77–93 Mi (#3, 155–61)					
	242.17	Ar auziretz	1–2 Mi (#4, 169–70)				1–2 DVE (2.5.4)	
			37–44 Mi (#4, 170–74)					
	242.31	De chantar	1–2 Mi (#2, 132–33)					Dc
			65–66 Mi (#2, 134)					
	242.34	Gen m'aten	1 DA (#30, 566); 1–3 RaT (#18, B 386–87, H 213, CL 355)					

		49–57 RaT (#19, B 388–96, H 215–23, CL 356–64); 54–57 DA (#31, 568–69)	69–72 Ab (1549–52)			
242.36	Ges aissi del tot non lais			1 (VIII.C, 4)		Dc
242.39	Ia·m vai revenen		85–106 So (LNrR, 322–43)			(Dc)
242.40	Iois e chanz				1461.142a (1)	Dc
242.45	Leu chansonet' e vil	41 RaT (#10, B 207, CL 188)				Dc
242.46	Lo dous chantz d'un auzel			1 (Sg 1–3) (VIII.F, 3)		
242.48	M'amiga·m men'estra lei	1 Mi (#24, 543–44)				
		45–47 Mi (#24, 544–46)				
242.51	Non puesc sofrir c'à la dolor			1 (Sg 1–2) (VIII.D, 4)		Dc
242.55	Per solatz reveillar			1 (Sg 1–5) (VIII.G, 1)	1–2 DVE (2.2.8)	

Troubadour	Song	Incipit	Treatises of Occitan grammar and poetics	Novas	Biographies	Breviari d'amor	Other (lyrics, French romance, Dante, etc.)	Appendix 2
				41–44 Ab (96–99)				
	242.58	Can creis la fresca fueil'els rams		23–33 So (LNR 291–301)				Dc
			45–46 RaT (#6, B 193–94, CL 174–75)					Dc
				48–50 So (LNR 261–63)				Dc
	242.59	Quant la brun'aura s'eslucha	1 Mi (#11, 313–14)					
			25–26 Mi (#11, 315–16)					
	242.66	S'era non poia mos chans	1–4 Mi (#1, 123–26)					
	242.69	Si·us qier cosseill, bell'ami' Alamanda			1 (VIII.B, 6), 1–8 (Sg)			
	242.71	Si·m plagues tant chans				41–50 (#234, 33489–98)		Dc
	242.72	Si·m sentis fizels amics	1–2 Mi (#12, 323–24)				1–2 DVE (1.9.3)	Dc

							1 *DVE* (2.6.6)	*Dc*
	242.73	Si per mon Sobre–Totz non fos			1 (VIII.E, 2), 1–2 (*Sg*)		1 *DVE* (2.6.6)	
Guiraut d'Espanha	244.9	Pus era suy ab senhor				34–40 (#31, 28511–17)		
Guiraut Riquier	248.18	Be·m meravelh, co non es enveyos				8–14 (#222, 33191–97)		
Guiraut de Salaignac	249.1	Aissi cum selh qu'a la lebre cassada				1–8 (#42, 28745–52) (attrib. Aimeric de Peguilhan)		
Izarn Rizol	257.1	Ailas! tan suy pessius e cossiros	1 *Mi* (#16, 445–46) (attrib. Peirol)					
			33–34 *Mi* (#16, 447–48) (attrib. Peirol)					
Jaufre Rudel	262.2						1–7 *GDole* (#14, 1301–7)	
	262.3	Non sap chantar qui so non di				7–12 (#76, 29417–22)		
Lanfranc Cigala	282.14 (= 200.1)	Na Guillelma, maint cavalier arratge			1–8 (XCIX.B, 21)			

Troubadour	Song	Incipit	Treatises of Occitan grammar and poetics	Novas	Biographies	Breviari d'amor	Other (lyrics, French romance, Dante, etc.)	Appendix 2
Lombarda	288.1	Nom volgr'aver per Bernart Na Bernarda			21–36 (LX, 6)			
Marcabru	293.15	Cortesamen vuoill comensar				13–18 (#192, 32244–49) (attrib. Uc de la Bacalaria)		
						19–24 (#193, 32251–56) (attrib. Uc de la Bacalaria)		
	293.18	Dire vos vuoill ses doptanssa				13–18 (MS C) (#21, 28231–36)		
					91–6 (III.A, 1)	91–96 (MS C) (#22, 28246–51)		
						115–20 (MS C) (#84, 29607–12)		
	293.31	L'iverns vai e·l temps s'aizina				46–54 (#140, 30995–1001)		
	293.32	Lo vers comenssa				(55–63, #190, 32206–14)		

				1–8 (XXII.C, 4) (Gui d'Ussel)					
Maria de Ventadorn	295.1 (=194.9)	Gui d'Ussel, be·m pesa de vos							
Matfre Ermengau				1 (XXIII, 9)					
	297.1	Cell que ditz qu'ell leialmen				(#138, 30909–15)			
	297.2	Cumpair', en aitan quo·l soleilh				(#164, 31714–23)			
	297.3	De midons puesc hieu dir en tota plassa				(#110, 30090–7)			
	297.4	Dregz de natura comanda				1–11 (#225, 33239–49, also quoted 300–301)			
	297.5	Lunhs homs no fai savieza				(#43, 28766–74)			
	297.5a	Greu er lunhs homs tan complitz				(#9, 28020–27)			
	297.6	Mens la pres que volp en estieu				(#259, 34083–90) (unattrib.)			
	297.7	Retenemens es mot nobla vertutz				(#206, 32447–54)			

Troubadour	Song	Incipit	Treatises of Occitan grammar and poetics	Novas	Biographies	Breviari d'amor	Other (lyrics, French romance, Dante, etc.)	Appendix 2
Monge de Montaudo	305.14	Mos sens e ma conoissensa				19–27 (#144, 31163–71)		
	305.16	Pos Peire d'Alvernh' a cantat				85–90 (#17, 28167–72)		
At de Mons	309—see unidentified quotations, Breviari and Leys							
	309.02	Reys romieus mas man milhors	1, Leys 1341 (1:250); 1–16, Leys 1341 (1:248–50)					
	309.I	Al bon rey de Castela	471–79 Leys 1356 (1:68)					
	309.II	Al bon rey, senhor d'Arago	134–57 Leys 1356 (1:118–19)					
	309.IV	Si N'At de Mons agues	111–54 Leys 1356 (1:106–7)					
			186–200 Leys 1356 (1:118)					
			319–20 Leys 1341 (2:236, 388); 319–20 Leys 1356 (3:163)					

309.V	Si tot non es enquistz	58–59 Leys 1341 (2:390); 58–76 Leys 1356 (3:109); 58–59 (3:128)				
		87–88 Leys 1341 (2:370); 77–94 Leys 1356 (1:70)				
		130–31 Leys 1341 (2:392)				
		210–11 Leys 1341 (3:62)				
		445–50 Leys 1356 (1:106)				
		488–502 Leys 1356 (1:84–85)				
		503–32 Leys 1356 (1:85–86)				
		541–42 Leys 1341 (2:78); 534–63 Leys 1356 (1:87); 541–42 (3:42)				
		564–72 Leys 1356 (1:127)				
		578–81, Leys 1341 (2:256); 578–79, Leys 1341 (2:390); 578–79 Leys 1356 (3:164)				

Troubadour	Song	Incipit	Treatises of Occitan grammar and poetics	Novas	Biographies	Breviari d'amor	Other (lyrics, French romance, Dante, etc.)	Appendix 2
			600–604 Leys 1356 (3:65–66)					
			966, 965, 967–70 Leys 1341 (2:78); 966, 965, 967–70 Leys 1356 (3:41)					
Peire d'Alvernha	323.11	Chantarai d'aquestz trobadors			19–24 (VI.B, 1) (Bernart de Ventadorn)			
					79–84 (XXXIX, 7)			
	323.15	Dejosta·ls breus jorns e·ls loncs sers			1 (XXXIX, 7)			
Pierre Bremon (Ricas Novas?)	330—see unidentified quotations, So and ReT							
Peire de Bussignac	332.1	Quand lo dous temps d'abril				41–50 (#86, 29649–57.1)		
						51–60 (#85, 29625–33.1)		
Peire Cardenal	335.5	Anc non vi Breton ni Baivier				12 (#219, 32685)		

	335.6	Aquesta gens, cant son en lur gaieza	1 Mi (#32, 662)	1–8 (#146, 3199–206)
			9–16 Mi (#32, 663–69)	
	335.7	Ar me puesc ieu lauzar d'Amor		31–40 (#263, 34277–86)
	335.11	Ben teinh per fol e per muzart		1–10, 21–30 (#265, 34326–45) (unattrib.)
				5 (#266, 34509) (unattrib.)
	335.38	Non cre que mos ditz		46–60 (#264, 34298–312)
	335.48	Razos es qu'ieu m'esbaudei		46–50 (#267, 34535–39)
	335.50	S'ieu fos amatz o ames		19–27 (#153, 31370–78)
	335.53	Senh En Ebles, vostre vezi		13–18 (#87, 29661–66)
Peire de Cols	337.1	Si co·l soleilhs per sa nobla clardat		32–36 (#72, 29338–42)
Peire Ermengau	341.1	Messier Matfre, pus de cosseilh		#163, 31693–712

Troubadour	Song	Incipit	Treatises of Occitan grammar and poetics	Novas	Biographies	Breviari d'amor	Other (lyrics, French romance, Dante, etc.)	Appendix 2
Peire Guillem de Luzerna	341.1a	En aquest gai sonet leuger				#6, 27948–56		
	344.3						1 anon. descort 461.104 (1)	Fa
Peire Guilhem de Toloza	345.2	Eu chantera de gauz e voluntos	28–30 DA (#12, 255–57) (attrib. Pons Fabre d'Uzes)					
Peire Pelisiers	353.1 (=119.1a)	Al Dalfin man q'estei dins son hostal			1–8 (XLII.D, 6) (Dalfi d'Alvernha)			
Peire Raimon de Toloza	355.3	Ar ai ben d'amor après				1–24 (#159, 31564–87)		
	355.6	De fin'amor son tuit mei pessamen	1 RaT (#28, CL 435–36)					
			15–16 RaT (#29, CL 437–38)					
			46 RaT (#30, CL 442)					
	355.7	Anqera·m vai recalivan				43–49 (#55, 28976–82)		
	355.13	Pus vey parer la flor el glay				28–36 (#118, 30369–77)		

	355.18	Tostemps aug dir q'us ioys autre n'adutz			1–9 (#202, 33393–400)		
	355.20	Us noels pessamens m'estai			10–18 (#208, 32473–81)	Dc	
Peire Rogier	356.4	Ges non puesc en bon vers fallir			17–24 (#94, 29825–32)		
					41–56 (#161, 31619–34)		
	356.7	Seign'en Raymbaut, per vezer		1–14 (XL, 10)		Dc	
					15–21 (#217, 32617–23)	Dc	
					22–8 (#218, 32634–40)	Dc	
			36–42 Ab (1155–61)				
Peire d'Ussel	361.1	En Gui d'Uisel, be·m plai vostra cançs		1–12 (XXII.D, 2) (Gui d'Ussel)			
Peire Vidal	364.2	Ajostar e lassar		16–19 (LVII.B, 14)			

Troubadour	Song	Incipit	Treatises of Occitan grammar and poetics	Novas	Biographies	Breviari d'amor	Other (lyrics, French romance, Dante, etc.)	Appendix 2
			74–75 DA (#36, 591–92)		21–28 (LVII.B, 17); 24–28 (LVII.B.b, 20)			
	364.4	Anc no mori per amor ni per al				1–8 (#251, 33736–43)		*DcFa*
						25–32 (#65, 29195–202)		*Dc*
	364.11	Be·m pac d'ivern e d'estiu				21–30 (#131, 30739–48)		*Dc*
						31–40 (#106, 30003–12)		
	364.13	Ben viu a gran dolor	45–48 *RaT* (#25, B 419–22, CL 387–90); 45 *RaT* (H 246)					*Dc*
	364.15	Car'amiga dols'e franca	1–3 DA (#11, 251–53)					
	364.16	De chantar m'era laissatz			1–2 (LVII.C, 19)			
	364.17	Dieus en sia grazitz				23–24 (#185, 32148–49)		

364.18	Drogoman senher, s'ieu agues bon destrier			13–18 (#186, 32153–58)	
364.21	Estat ai gran sazo		41–50 (LVIII.C, 8) (Raimon de Miraval)		
364.22	Ges quar estius	1–2 DA (#25, 536)			
		32–33 DA (#26, 537–38)			
364.27	Mos cors s'alegr'e s'esjau			8–14 (#90, 29716–22)	
364.29	Molt m'es bon e bell	1–3 RaT (#1, CL 148–50)			
364.30	Neus ni gels ni plueja ni fanh			41–48 (#169, 31821–28)	J
364.36	Plus que·l paubres, quan jai el ric ostal	1 Leys 1341 (3:286) (unattrib.)	13–15 (LVII.B, 16); 13–16 (LVII.B, 22)		Dc
364.36a	Pus que d'amor non pusch defendre	1 Mi (#14, 352–53)			
		4 lines from fourth stanza Mi (#14, 354–57)			
364.37	Pus tornatz sui em Proensa	1 (LVII.B.b, 28)			

Troubadour	Song	Incipit	Treatises of Occitan grammar and poetics	Novas	Biographies	Breviari d'amor	Other (lyrics, French romance, Dante, etc.)	Appendix 2
	364.38	Pus ubert ai mon ric thesaur	8–9 DA (#5, 196–97)		14–18 (LVII.B, 21)			(Dc)
	364.39	Quant hom es en autrui poder				1–8 (#220, 33159–66)	1–4 Bertolome Zorzi 74.9 (5–9)	DcFa
						9–16 (#221, 33176–83)	9–12 Bertolome Zorzi 74.9 (15–18)	DcFa
			17–19 DA (#24, 362–64)			17–24 (#223, 33206–13)	17–20 Bertolome Zorzi 74.9 (24–27)	Fa
							25–28 Bertolome Zorzi 74.9 (42–45)	
						33–40 (#239, 33550–57)	33–36 Bertolome Zorzi 74.9 (33–36)	

	364.42	S'ieu fos en cort on hom tengues dreitura	1 Mi (#10, 283–84)			41–48 (#105, 29992–99)	41–44 Bertolome Zorzi 74.9 (50–54) 49–52 Bertolome Zorzi 74.9 (60–63)	DcFa
	364.43	Si·m laissava de chantar	19–24 Mi (#10, 285–89)			21–30 (#194, 32260–69)		
	364.47	Tant an ben dig del marques			1 (LXX.C, 12) (Raimbaut de Vaqueiras)			Dc
	364.48	Tant me platz jois e solatz			25–27 (LVII.B, 15; LVII.B 21)			Dc
Peirol	366.1	Ab gran joi mou maintas vetz e comenssa		26–28 So (a^2 1506–8)				(Dc)
	366.9	Coras que·m fezes dolor				33–40 (#246, 33648–55)		(DcFa)

Troubadour	Song	Incipit	Treatises of Occitan grammar and poetics	Novas	Biographies	Breviari d'amor	Other (lyrics, French romance, Dante, etc.)	Appendix 2
	366.13	D'un bon vers vau pensan com lo fezes				15–21 (#165, 31733–39)		DcFa
	366.19	Mainta gens mi malrazona				33–40 (#73, 29351–58)		Fa
	366.21	Mout m'entremis de chantar voluntiers	27–28 RaT (#20, B 399–400, H 226–27, CL 367–68)					Fa
	366.33	Tot mon engeing e mon saber				33–40 (#160, 31604–11)		
	366.34	Tug miei cossir son d'amor e de chan		29–33 So (LNr 368–72) (attrib. Guillem de Sant Leidier)				(G)
Perdigon	370.3	Ben aio·l mal e·l afan e·l consir				1–9 (#64, 29179–87)	1 Jofre de Foixà 304.1 (21)	DcFa
				35–36 So (LNR 77–78)		28–36 (#132, 30764–72)		DcH
	370.8	Ir' e pezars e dona ses merce					1 Jofre de Foixà 304.1 (28)	

Author		Incipit					Dc
	370.9	Los mals d'Amor ai eu ben totz apres		19–27 So (*a²* 1473–81) (attrib. Folquet de Marselha)	28–36 (#92, 29776–84) (attrib. Folquet de Marselha)		
	370.13	Tot l'an mi ten Amors de tal faisso	8–9 DA (#42, 627–28) (attrib. Folquet de Marselha)				(*DcFa*)
	370.14	Trop ai estat mon Bon Esper no vi			9–16 (#252, 33757–64)		(*DcFa*)
Pistoleta	372.3	Ar agues eu mil marcs de fin argen			1–8 (#232, 33341–48)		
					33–40 (#107, 30018–25)		
Pons de Capdoill	375.3	Astrucs es cel cui amors ten jojos			1–9 (#143, 31104–12)		
	375.10	Humils e francs e fis soplei ves vos				1 Jofre de Foixà 304.1 (45)	*DcFa*

Troubadour	Song	Incipit	Treatises of Occitan grammar and poetics	Novas	Biographies	Breviari d'amor	Other (lyrics, French romance, Dante, etc.)	Appendix 2
	375.14 (?)	Lials amics, cui amors ten jojos			4 lines (match rhyme scheme but not extant elsewhere) (XLVII.B, 7)			Fa
	375.18	Qui per nesi cuidar			1–3 (XLII.B, 15)			
	375.20	Si com sellui c'a pro de valledors			1 (XLVII.B, 14)			DcH
	375.21	Se totz los gaugs els bes				1–9 (#101, 29932–40)		
	375.23	Tant m'a donat fin cor e ferm voler				28–29 (#25, 28383–84)		(Fa)
	375.27	Us guays conortz me fai guayamen far				19–27 (#197, 32298–306)		
Pons Fabre d'Uzes	376.1	Locx es c'om se deu alegrar	1 Ri (#8, 42) (attrib. Folquet de Marselha)					Dc
						17–24 (#176, 32018–25)		Dc
						33–40 (#209, 32488–95)		Dc

Pons Santolh	380.2	Per oblidar cela que pus m'agensa				#260, 34143–49	
Prebost de Valensa	384.1 (=432.3)	Savaric, ie us deman			1–2 (XXVIII.B, 14) (Savaric de Malleo)		
Raimbaut d'Aurenga	389—see unidentified quotations, *Biographies*						
	389.1	Ab nou cor et ab nou talen	1–3 *Mi* (#31, 645–66) (attrib. Raimbaut de Vaqueiras)				*Dc*
	389.17	Assaz m'es belh	1–2 *DA* (#1, 141)				
	389.18	Assatz sai d'amor ben parlar	1 *Mi* (#15, 366–67) (attrib. Guillem de Sant Leidier)				
			9–16 *Mi* (#15, 368–73) (attrib. Guillem de Sant Leidier)				
			17–25 *Mi* (#15, 374–80) (attrib. Guillem de Sant Leidier)				
	389.20	Ben s'eschai qu'en bona cort		29–35 *So* (LNR 92–98)			

Troubadour	Song	Incipit	Treaties of Occitan grammar and poetics	Novas	Biographies	Breviari d'amor	Other (lyrics, French romance, Dante, etc.)	Appendix 2
Raimbaut de Vaqueiras	392.2	Era·m requier sa costum'e son us			1 (LXX.B, 17)			Dc
	392.3	Ara pot hom conoisser e proar	1 Ri (#4, 24)			9–16 (#145, 31177–84)		
	392.4	Eras quan vey verdeyar	41–50 Leys 1341 (1:334); 41–50 Leys 1356 (2:72–3) (unattrib.)					
	392.9	Kalenda maia			1–14 (LXX.D, 21)			
	392.13	Eissamen ai gerreiat ab amor	1 DA (#37, 596) (attrib. Raimbaut d'Aurenga)					Dc
				So 23–24 (R, 815–16)				Dc
			25 DA (#38, 598) (attrib. Raimbaut d'Aurenga)					Dc

PC	Incipit						
							Dc
392.19	Ja hom pres ni dezeretatz	28–29 DA (#39, 599–600) (attrib. Raimbaut d'Aurenga)			1–11 (#178, 32040–50)		G
					12–22 (#141, 31068–78)		
					23–33 (#134, 30807–17)		
					34–44 (#250, 33714–24)		
392.20	Ja non cujei vezer			1–16 (LXX.B, 17)			Dc
392.23	Leu pot hom gauch e pretz aver		1–4 So (R 840–43)				
					11–20 (#14, 28121–30)		
					21–30 (#13, 28098–107)		
392.24	No m'agrad' iverns ni pascors			1 (LXX.B, 27)			Dc
				37–48 (LXX.B.b, 27)			

Troubadour	Song	Incipit	Treatises of Occitan grammar and poetics	Novas	Biographies	Breviari d'amor	Other (lyrics, French romance, Dante, etc.)	Appendix 2
	392.26	Nulhs hom en re no falh	1 DA (#40, 603) (attrib. Raimbaut d'Aurenga)					Dc
			37–39 DA (#41, 604–6)					
	392.27	Can lo dous temps comensa				33–36 (#242, 33596–99) (attrib. Guiraut de Quentinhac)		
	392.28	Savis e fols, humils et orgoillos				25–26 (#24, 28319–20)		(Dc)
						33–40 (#102, 29951–58)		
	392.30	Si ja amors autre pro non tengues				1–8 (#201, 32381–87) (unattrib.)		Dc/G
	392.31	Tuich me pregon, Engles, qe vos don saut			1–8 (LXXII, 14) (Guillem del Baus)			

Author	PC	Incipit					
Raimon Ermengau	397a.1	Qui vol jauzir de domnas et d'amor					
Raimon Jordan	404.5	No·m posc mudar no diga mon veiaire			#154, 31426–33 1–10 (#115, 30210–19)		
					11–20 (#23, 28280–89)		
	404.7	Per solatz e per deport				1 Guillem de Salaignac 235.2 (1)	
	404.9	Raimonz Jordan, de vos eis vuelh aprendre		1–7 (XVII.B, 20)			
	404.12	Vas vos soplei, e cui ai mes m'entensa		1 (XVII.B, 19)			
Raimon de Miraval	406—see also unidentified quotations, So						
	406.2	Aissi cum es genser pascors	28–36 So (LNd^1R 606–14)				DcFaHJ

Troubadour	Song	Incipit	Treatises of Occitan grammar and poetics	Novas	Biographies	Breviari d'amor	Other (lyrics, French romance, Dante, etc.)	Appendix 2
	406.5	Anc non attendiei de chantar		25–32 So (LNR 111–18)				HJ
	406.7	A penas sai don m'apreing				41–50 (#108, 30037–46)		Cm
				45–47 Ab (1730–32)		45–57 (#137, 30882–84)		Cm
	406.8	Er ab la forsa dels freys		9–13, 15–16 So (a²R 1358–64)				DcCmH
					41–48 (LVIII.D, 6)			
	406.12	Bel m'es q'ieu chant e coindei			1–2 (LVIII.E, 3)			FaCm
						28–36 (#125, 30574–82)		Cm
					46–51 (LVIII.B, 1)			H
	406.15	Ben aia·l messagiers			1 (LVIII.D, 52)			Dc
					23–24 (LVIII.B 2)			

			31–32 So (d^1R 770–71)			Dc
406.18	Selh, cui joys tanh ni chantar sap		1–8 So (LNR 490–97); 1–7 So (r 490–96)			
406.20	Cel que no vol auzir chanssos	1–2 Mi (#18, 471–72)				DcCm
				17–20 (#183, 32129–32)		DcCm
				22–24 (#189, 32197–99)		DcCm
				25–32 (#37, 28630–37)		DcCm
		33–38 Mi (#18, 473–76)				DcCm
406.23	Contr' amor vau durs et enbroncs		36–42 So (LNd^1R 641–47)			DcFaCm
406.24	D'Amor es totz mos cossiriers			1–8 (#4, 27908–15)		Cm
				9–16 (#111, 30115–22)		
406.25	Dels quatre mestiers valens		8–9 Ab (1147–48)			

Troubadour	Song	Incipit	Treatises of Occitan grammar and poetics	Novas	Biographies	Breviari d'amor	Other (lyrics, French romance, Dante, etc.)	Appendix 2
	406.27	Enquer non a guaire			49–50 (LVIII.C, 13)			
	406.28	Entre dos volers sui pensius			1 (LVIII.D, 15)			Dc
					21–24 (LVIII.B, 4)			
	406.31	Lonc temps ai agutz cossiriers	1 Mi (#8, 247–48)					(H)
			9–16 Mi (#8, 249–54)					
	406.38	S'ieu en chantar soven			1–4 (LVIII.C, 19)			
					18–20 (LVIII.B 3)			
	406.42	Tals vai mon chan enqueren		25–32 So (LNdlR 712–19)				(Dc)
				33–40 So (LNdlR 694–701)				
Raimon Vidal	411—see unidentified quotations, So							

	411.III. (= *Abril issia*)	Abril issi' e mays intrava				Ab 1162–70 (#230, 33319–27)	
Richard I	420.1	Daufin, je·us voill deraisnier			1–3 (XLII.E, 18)		
Rigaut de Berbezilh	421.1	Atressi com lo leos				28–36 (#70, 29299–307)	(Dc)
						37–45 (#100, 29914–22)	
	421.2	Atressi con l'orifanz	1 *Leys* 1341 (3:286) (unattrib.)		1–11 (XVI.B, 18)		Dc
			45 *DA* (#17, 295)				
					50 (XVI.B, 14)		
	421.5	Ben volria saber d'Amor				17–24 (#244, 33616–23)	Dc
	421.10	Tuit demandon qu'es devengu d'Amors	1–2 *DA* (#23, 357–58)				Dc
						17–24 (#233, 33360–67)	
						25–32 (#243, 33606–13)	Dc
Savaric de Malleo	432.2 (=167.26)	Gaucelm, tres jocs enamoratz			1 (XXVIII.C, 7)		
	432.3 (=384.1)	Savaric, je us deman			1–2 (XXVIII.B, 14)		

Troubadour	Song	Incipit	Treatises of Occitan grammar and poetics	Novas	Biographies	Breviari d'amor	Other (lyrics, French romance, Dante, etc.)	Appendix 2
Tibors	440.1	Bels dous amics, ben vos puosc en ver dir			1–9 (LXXIX, 4)			
Uc de la Bacalaria	449.5	Ses totz enjans e ses fals'entendensa				19–27 (#93, 29805–13)		
Uc Brunenc	450.1	Ab plazer receup et acuoill		17–24 So (r 348–55) (attrib. Arnaut)				DcFa
	450.2	Ara·m nafron li sospir		37–40 So (R 860–63)				(DcFa])
	450.3	Coindas razos e novellas plazens				7–12 (#210, 32516–21)		DcFa
						13–18 (#215, 32591–96)		DcFa
						25–30 (#204, 32425–30)		
	450.6	Lanquan son li rozier vermeil				17–24 (#82, 29562–69)		(G)
	450.7	Puois l'adrechs temps ven chantan e rizen				33–40 (#83, 29586–93)		Fa

Author	No.	Incipit			Siglum
Uc de Mataplana	454.1	D'un sirventes m'es pres talens	1 (LVIII.B, 18) (Raimon de Miraval)	41–48 (#32, 28527–34)	
			1 (XCV, 2)		
Uc de Saint Circ	457.3	Anc enemics q'ieu agues		1–10 (#79, 29476–85) (attrib. Uc Brunenc)	*Dc*
				21–30 (#30, 28482–91)	
	457.4	Anc mais non vi temps ni sazo	1–9 (XXXIII.B, 22)		
	457.18	Longamen ai atenduda			*DcFa*
	457.33	Seign'en coms, no·us cal esmaiar	1–8 (XXXIV, 2) (Lo coms de Rodez)		
Anonymous	461.21	Amors vol drut cavalcador		1–11 (#184, 32135–45)	*G*
	461.32	Atretan leu pot hom ab cortesia		1–7 (#211, 32533–38.1)	*GJ*
	461.48	Ben es nescis e desaventuros		1–8 (#241, 33579–86)	

Troubadour	Song	Incipit	Treatises of Occitan grammar and poetics	Novas	Biographies	Breviari d'amor	Other (lyrics, French romance, Dante, etc.)	Appendix 2
	461.86	D'ome fol ni desconoissen				1–8 (#123, 30538–45)		JG
						9–16 (#124, 30557–64)		J
	461.87	Dona, dieus sal vos e vostra valor				1–6 (#156, 31460–65)		JG
	461.91	Domna, no·i havetz dezonor				(# 237, 33522–28)		
	461.98	Dos gratz conquer hom ab un do				1–8 (#175, 32000–32006)		JG
	461.101	E doncz que val aquest amars				(#166, 31768–75)		
	461.123	Flors de paradis	1 Leys 1341 (1:250); 1 Leys 1356 (2:131)					
	461.123b	Fraire, tuit li sen e·l saber				1–10 (#179, 32052–61)		J
	461.132	Ges per frachura de saber				(#207, 32458–65)		
	461.134	Gran dezir hai de ben iazer				1–8 (#149, 31267–74)		

					Lines	
461.149	Locs es c'om chan e c'om s'en lais				1–4 (#155, 31445–48)	J
461.155	Ma donna am de bona guisa				1–8 (#262, 34210–17)	G
461.210	Qui enten en amar				(#172, 31970–71)	
461.227	Tals conois busq'en autrui huell				1–10 (#212, 32553–62)	
Unidentified quotations						
RaT		*RaT #7, B 197, CL 178 (Raimon Vidal?)*				
		RaT #7a, B 199–200, CL 180–81 (Raimon Vidal?)				
ReT		*ReT #2, H 144–55, R 60–71 (Jofre de Foixà?)*				
		ReT #3, H 158–59, R 74–75 (Jofre de Foixà?)				
		ReT #9, H 503–6, R 393–96 (attrib. Peire Bremon)	also quoted in So 469–79			
		ReT #10, H 556–59, R 445–47 (attrib. us trobadors)				

Troubadour	Song	Incipit	Treatises of Occitan grammar and poetics	Novas	Biographies	Breviari d'amor	Other (lyrics, French romance, Dante, etc.)	Appendix 2
DA			DA #3, 187–89 (attrib. "cell qui fes l'Acort")					
			DA #6, 202–9 (attrib. Andrianz del Palais = 22a), #14, 266–67 (attrib. Andrianz)					
			DA #8, 216–17 (attrib. "N'Ucs")					
Ri			Ri #3, 17 (attrib. Guilhem de Cabestanh)					
			Ri #5, 26 (unattrib.)					
			Ri #6, 33 (attrib. Peire de Vilademayn)					
			Ri #7, 40; #18, 144 (attrib. Capela de Bolquera)					
			Ri #9, 53–57, 59–62 (attrib. Capela de Bolquera)					
			Ri #10, 73 (unattrib.)					

	Ri #11, 79–80 (unattrib.)		
	Ri #14, 115–18 (unattrib.)		
	Ri #16, 128–30 (attrib. Dalmau de Castellnou)		
	Ri #18, 144 (attrib. Capela de Bolquera)		
Miralh de trobar	*Mi* 617–18 (unattrib., no # in edition)		
	Mi #28, 619–20 (attrib. Arnaut Daniel)		
	Mi 653 (unattrib., no # in edition)		
	Mi 675–81 (unattrib., no # in edition)		
Leys	*Leys* 1341 (3:286)		
	Leys 1341 (1:316) (in later hand, attrib. Peire Arquier); *Leys* 1356 (2:160), (unattrib.)		
	Leys 1341 (2:86); *Leys* 1356 (3:44) (attrib. At de Mons)		

Troubadour	Song	Incipit	Treatises of Occitan grammar and poetics	Novas	Biographies	Breviari d'amor	Other (lyrics, French romance, Dante, etc.)	Appendix 2
			Leys 1341 (2:236, attrib. At de Mons); Leys 1356 (3:128, attrib. At de Mons)					
			Leys 1341 (3:286) (or is this French?)					
Ab				Ab 1184–89				
So				So 270–73 (LNR) (attrib. Guillem de Sant Leidier)				
				So 469–79 (LNrR) (attrib. Raimon Vidal)				
			also quoted in ReT, H 503–6, R 393–96	So 512–15 (LNR) (attrib. Peire Bremon [Ricas Novas?])				
				So 625–32 (LNdʲR)				

					#3, 27878–99 (attrib. At de Mons)	
					#177, 32029–30	
So 786–94 (d'R) (attrib. Raimon Vidal)						
So 829–31 (R) (attrib. Raimon de Miraval)						
So 1008–9 (R)						
So 1271–81 (R) (attrib. Raimon Vidal)						
	1–7 (LXVIII, 10) (attrib. Raimbaut d'Aurenga)					
Biographies						
Breviari						

Excerpted Stanzas Anthologized in Selected Troubadour
Chansonnier Manuscripts

Like Appendix 1, this appendix is organized alphabetically by troubadour (first column), then by song using the PC number of each song (column 2) and its opening line (column 3). The next six columns detail all of the excerpted passages featuring in the anthology section, or *florilegium*, of each of six *chansonnier* manuscripts, each identified by its alphabetical *siglum*. (Note that Appendix 2 is selective; several manuscripts containing excerpted or isolated stanzas are not included; for discussion, see Chapter 4). Each entry in these six columns gives line references identifying which passages from the song in question appear in that manuscript, together with the item number it has been assigned within that manuscript. These numbers are those listed in the *BEdT*, except in the case of *H* where they are those of Maria Careri, *Il canzoniere provenzale H*. The last column indicates whether (part of) the passage excerpted also features as (part of) a quotation and hence is also included in Appendix 1; the abbreviated title(s) in this final column indicate in which text(s) the quotation appears. In cases where the same song appears in both appendices, but not the same passage(s), the cross-reference to Appendix 1 is placed in parentheses. Expansions of *chansonnier sigla* are given in Appendix 17; abbreviations are explained on p. vii; editions cited are listed in the Bibliography.

Troubadour	Song	Incipit	Dc	Fa	Cm	H	J	G	Appendix 1
Ademar lo Negre	3.1	Era·m don Dieus qe repaire		Incipit, #125					(DA)
				9–16 (st. II)					
Aimeric de Belenoi	9.3	Aissi co·l pres que s'en cuia fugir		Incipit, #84					
				25–32 (st. IV)					Breviari
	9.7	Ara·m destrenh Amors	Incipit, #194	Incipit, #83					
				11–20 (st. II)					
			41–50 (st. V)	41–50 (st. V)					
	9.8	Cel que promet a son coral amic	1–7 (st. I), #193						
	9.14	Nulls hom non pot complir adreizamen	1–8 (st. I), #192	1–8 (st. I), #85				1–8 (st. I), #270	DVE
				9–16 (st. II)					
			17–24 (st. III)	17–24 (st. III)					
			25–32 (st. IV)	25–32 (st. IV)					
			33–40 (st. V)	33–40 (st. V)					

Troubadour	Song	Incipit	Dc	Fa	Cm	H	J	G	Appendix 1
	9.18	Pos le gais temps de pascor		Incipit, #65, attrib. Uc Brunenc					
				37–48 (st. IV)					Breviari
				25–36 (st. III)					Breviari
Aimeric de Peguilhan	10.2	Ades vol de l'aondansa	Incipit, #35						
			17–24 (st. III)						Breviari
			25–32 (st. IV)						
	10.3	N'Albertz, chauzetz al votre sen	Incipit, #44, repeated, #157, attrib. Albertet.						
			23–24 (from st. III), #44						
			31–32 (from st. IV), #157, attrib. Albertet						
	10.7	Amors, a vos meteussa·m clam de vos	Incipit, #33	1–8 (st. I), #75					Mi, Breviari
			9–16 (st. II)	9–16 (st. II)					Mi

10.12	Atressi·m pren quom fai al joguador	Incipit, #70	17–24 (st. III)				*Breviari*
			25–32 (st. IV)				
			33–40 (st. V)				
10.14	Car fui de dura acoindansa	Incipit, #42					
		15–21 (st. III)					
		22–28 (st. IV)					
10.15	Cel qui s'irais ni guerreia ab Amor	1–8 (st. I), #39					*Breviari*
10.17	De so dont hom a longuamen	1–8 (st. I), #41					*Breviari*
10.18	D'avinen sap enganar e trahir	1–8 (st. I) (copied just after, as if part of #42, 10.14)					*Mi*
		25–32 (st IV)					
10.24	Yssamen cum l'aÿmans	1–8 (st. I), #37					*Breviari*
		9–16 (st. II)					

Troubadour	Song	Incipit	Dc	Fa	Cm	H	J	G	Appendix 1
	10.25	En Amor trob alques en qe·m refraing		1–8 (st. I), #74					(ReT)
				9–16 (st. II)					
				33–40 (st. V)					
	10.27	En greu pantais m'a tengut longamen	Incipit, #31	Incipit, #68					
			7–14 (st. II)	7–14 (st. II)					
				15–21 (st. III)					Breviari
				22–28 (st. IV)					
			29–35 (st. V)						
	10.28	Gaucelms Faiditz, de dos amic leials	Incipit, #43						
			21–24 (from st. III)						
			37–40 (from st. V)						
	10.33	Lonjamen m'a trebalhat e malmes		Incipit, #69					
				9–16 (st. II)					Breviari

10.38	Nulhs hom non es tan fizels vas senhor		Incipit, #71				
			29–34 (st. V)				Breviari
10.40	Per razo natural	Incipit, #38	Incipit, #76				
		11–20 (st. II)	11–20 (st. II)				Breviari
		31–40 (st. IV)	31–40 (st. IV)				Mi
10.41	Per solatz d'autrui chant soven	Incipit, #36	Incipit, #66				
		17–24 (st. III)					
			33–40 (st. V)				Mi
10.46	Qui sofrir s'en pogues	1–14 (st. I), #32	1–14 (st. I), #67				
10.49	S'ieu tan ben non ames	Incipit, #34					
		13–24 (st. II)					
10.50	Si cum l'arbres que, per sobrecargar	Incipit, #72	Incipit, #72				DVE
			16–24 (st. III),				
			25–32 (st. IV)				

Troubadour	Song	Incipit	Dc	Fa	Cm	H	J	G	Appendix 1
	10.52	Totz hom qui so blasma que deu lauzar	Incipit, #40	Incipit, #73					
			9–16 (st. II)	9–16 (st. II)					
Aimeric de Sarlat	11.2	Fins e leials e senes tot engan		1–8 (st. I), #122					
				9–16 (st. II)					
				17–24 (st. III)					
				25–32 (st. IV)					
				33–40 (st. V)					Breviari
Albertet de Sestaro	16.1	Ab joi comensi ma chanson		Incipit, #135					
				10–18 (st. II)					
	16.2	Ab son gai e leugier	11–20 (st. II), #156 (copied just after, and as if part of, #155 = 16.12)						
	16.12	En Amor ai tan petit de fiansa	Incipit, #155						
			16–21 (st. III)						
			22–8 (st. IV)				22–28 (st. IV), #13		

	16.18	Mout es greus mals de qu'om no s'auza planher	36–42 (st. VI)	1–8 (st. I), #123, attrib. Aimeric de Sarlat				
Arman	25.1a = 58.1	Bernart de la Barta, ·l chausit	67–68 (from 2nd *tornada*), #212 *bis* (copied just after, and as if part of, #212= 227.7)					
Arnaut Daniel	29.17	Si·m fos Amors de ioi donar tant larga		1–8 (st. I), #99				*DVE*
				9–16 (st. II)				
				33–40 (st. V)				
				41–48 (st. VI)				
	29.18	Sols sui che sai lo sobrafan qe·m sortz		1–7 (st. I), #100				*DVE*
				8–14 (st. II)				

Troubadour	Song	Incipit	Dc	Fa	Cm	H	J	G	Appendix 1
Arnaut de Maruelh	30.1	A gran honor viu cui jois es cobitz	Incipit, #125						Breviari
			7–14 (st. II)						
			29–35 (st. III)						
	30.3	Aissi cum cel c'am' e non es amaz	Incipit, #126	Incipit, #20					
			8–14 (st II)	8–14 (st. II)					
				15–21 (st III)					
				22–28(st. IV)					Breviari
	30.8	Anc vas Amor no·m poc res contradire	Incipit, #124	Incipit, #21	Incipit, #13				
			15–21 (st III)	15–21 (st. III)	15–21 (st. III)				Breviari
			22–28 (st. IV)		22–28 (st. IV)				
			36–42 (st. VI)	36–42 (st. VI)	36–42 (st. VI)				
	30.15	La franca captenensa	Incipit, #122		Incipit, #11				Biographies VII.A

	Incipit				31 (for stanza IV), 167 #28 <21>		Breviari
		31–40 (st. IV)		31–40 (st. IV)			
		41–50 (st. V)		41–50 (st. V)			
30.16	La grans beutatz e·l fis ensenhamens	41–50 (st. V)	Incipit, #22				Jofre de Foixà 304.1
			16–24 (st. III)				
30.17	L'ensenhamens e·l pretz e la valors		Incipit, #19				
			7–14 (st. II)				
			29–35 (st. V)				
30.19	Mout eron doutz miei cossir	Incipit, #123	Incipit, #18	Incipit, #12			Biographies VII.B
		11–20 (st. II)	11–20 (st. II)	11–20 (st. II)			
		21–30 (st. III)		21–30 (st. III)			
		31–40 (st. IV)		31–40 (st. IV)			

Troubadour	Song	Incipit	Dc	Fa	Cm	H	J	G	Appendix I
	30.22	Si cum li peis an en l'aiga lor vida	Incipit, #120	Incipit, #16	1–8 (st. I), #9				DA
				9–16 (st. II)					
			17–24 (st. III)	17–24 (st. III)	17–24 (st. III), #9				
	30.23	Si·m destreignetz, dompna, vos et Amors	1–8 (st. I), #121	Incipit, #17	1–8 (st. I), #10				RaT, Jofre de Foixà 304.1
					9–16 (st. II)	9 (for st. II), 167 #26 <20>			Breviari
						17 (for st. III), 167 #27 <20>			
				25–32 (st. IV)					
			33–40 (st. V)	33–40 (st. V)	33–40 (st. V)				So, Biographies VI.B
									Ab
	30.VI		155–58, #127						
Azar	44.1	Dompna plaz vos el vers auzir		3 stanzas, unicum, #138					

Bernart de la Barta	58.1, *see* 25.1a				
	58.2, *see* 227.7				
	58.3	Eu non cugei a trestot mon viven	Incipit, #210	Incipit, #177	
			10 lines (non-initial st., unattested apart from here and *Fa*)	10 lines (non-initial st., unattested apart from here and *Dc*)	
	58.4	Foilla ni flors, ni chautz temps ni freidura	Incipit, #211		
			8–14 (st. II)		
Bernart de Ventadorn	70.1	Ab joi mou lo vers e·l comens	1–8 (st. I), #55	Incipit, #45	*Mi*
				25–32 (st. IV)	*Breviari, Violette*
	70.7	Ara no vei luzir solelh	Incipit, #42		*RaT*
			17–24 (st. III)		

Troubadour	Song	Incipit	Dc	Fa	Cm	H	J	G	Appendix 1
	70.8	A! tantas bonas chansos		Incipit, #41					
				17–24 (st. III)					
				41–48 (st. VI)					
	70.12	Be m'an perdut lai enves Ventadorn	Incipit, #60	Incipit, #44					RaT
				15–21 (st. III)					
			22–8 (st. IV)	22–8 (st. IV)					RaT
			29–36 (st. V)						
	70.16	Conortz, era sai eu be	Incipit, #59						
			34–40 (st. V)						
	70.19	Estat ai com om esperdutz	Incipit, #56						Mi
			25–32 (st. IV)						
	70.27	Lonc tems a qu'eu no chantei mai		Incipit, #40					(So)
				19–27 (st. III)					
				55–63 (st. VII)					

70.29	Lo rossinhols s'esbaudeya	Incipit, #61	Incipit, #47				*Breviari*
			9–16 (st. II)				
			25–32 (st. IV)				
		33–40 (st. V)	33–40 (st. V)				
		41–4, 29–32 (1st half of st. VI + 2nd half of st. IV)					
70.31	Non es meravelha s'eu chan		Incipit, #46				*Mi*
			17–24, (st. III)				
			25–32 (st. IV)				
			33–40 (st. V)				
70.36	Pos preyatz me, senhor		Incipit, #49				
			19–27 (st. III)				
			37–45 (st. V)				
70.41	Can par la flors josta·l vert folh	Incipit, #57	Incipit, #39				
		17–24 (st. III)	17–24 (st. III)				*Breviari*
		33–40 (st. V)	33–40 (st. V)				

Troubadour	Song	Incipit	Dc	Fa	Cm	H	J	G	Appendix I
	70.42	Can vei la flor, l'erba vert et la fuolha	Incipit, #58	Incipit, #43					
			29–35 (st. V)	29–35 (st. V)					
	70.43	Can vei la lauzeta mover		Incipit, #48					DA, Biographies VI.C, GDole, Violette
				49–56 (st. VII)					So
	70.45	Tuich cil que·m preyon qu'eu chan	Incipit, #54						(Breviari)
			15–21 (st. III)						
Bertran d'Alamanon	76.19	S'ieu agues virat l'escut		2 10-line stanzas and tornada, unicum in Fa, #155; no rubric or attribution but follows immediately from #153 = 76.20					

ID	Incipit					Biographies
76.20		Lacunary stanzas, unicum in Fa, #154				
Bertran de Born						
80.2	Al nou doutz termini blanc	Incipit, #169	8–14 (st. II)	22–28 (st. IV)	29–35 (st. V)	Biographies XI.Q
80.4	Ara sai eu de pretz quals l'a plus gran	1–7 (st. I), #173	8–14 (st. II)			
80.19	Ges de disnar non fo roimais maitis	1–8 (st. I), #66				Biographies XI.F
80.21	Ges no me desconort	Incipit, #170	31–45 (st. III)			Biographies XI.K
80.30	Nostre seingner somonis el mezeis	1–9 (st. I), #172	10–18 (st. II)			

Troubadour	Song	Incipit	Dc	Fa	Cm	H	J	G	Appendix 1
	80.37	Rassa, tant creis e mont' e poia	Incipit, #171						Biographies XI.B
			34–44 (st. IV)						
Bertran de Gordo	84.1	Totz sos affars es niens	16–18, 52–54, #188 bis, follows on from 188 = 355.20						
Bertran del Poget	87.2	De sirventes aurai granren perdutz		Incipit, #152					
				9–16 (st. II)					
				17–24 (st. III)					
Blacasset	96.1	Amics Guillems, lauzan etz maldizens		2 stanzas, unicum in Fa, #167					
	96.11	Si·m fai amors ab fizel cor amar		1–8 (st. I), #168					
				9–16 (st. II)					
Blacatz	97.3 = 353.2	En Pelizier, cauzetz de tres lairos						1–8 (st I), #241	

	Incipit			Source
Cadenet				
97.7 = 364.32	Peire Vidals, puois far m'aven tenson	#72: see 364.32 attrib. Peire Vidal		
106.2	A! cu.m dona ric coratge	1–11 (st. I), #75	1–11 (st I), #129	
		12–22 (st. II)	12–22 (st. II)	Breviari
			23–33 (st. III)	Breviari
			34–44 (st. IV)	
			45–55 (st. V)	
106.3	A home meilz non vai	Incipit, #82		
		51–60 (st. VI)		
106.7	Amors, e com er de me		Incipit, #128	
			13–24 (st. II)	
			37–48 (st. IV)	
			25–36 (st. III)	
			65–68 (2nd tornada)	
106.8	Ans que·m jauzis d'amor	1–10 (st. I), #81		

Troubadour	Song	Incipit	Dc	Fa	Cm	H	J	G	Appendix 1
	106.10	Be volgra, s'esser pogues		1–10 (st. I), #126, no attribution or rubric, follows on from 3.1					Guiraut d'Espanha 244.1a
				11–20 (st. II)					
				21–30 (st. III)					
				31–40 (st. IV)					
				41–50 (st. V)					
				51–60 (st. VI)					
	106.13	De nuilla ren non es tant grans cartatz	1–10 (st. I), #84	1–10 (st. I), #131					
			11–20 (st. II)	11–20 (st. II)					
			21–30 (st. III)	21–30 (st. III)					
			31–32 (tornada)	31–2 (tornada)					
	106.16	Meravilh me de tot fin amador	Incipit, #78						(Breviari)

		21–30 (st. III)			
106.17	No sai qual cosselh mi prenda	Incipit, #79			
106.18	Oimais m'auretz avinen	11–20 (st. II)			
		Incipit, #80 & #83			
		12–22 (st. II), #80			*Breviari*
		45–55 (st. V), #83			
106.20	S'ieu ar endevenia	Incipit, #77			
		13–24 (st. II)			
		49–60 (st. V)			
106.22	S'ieu pogues ma voluntat	Incipit, #76	Incipit, #130		*Breviari*
		13–24 (st. II)			*Breviari*
		25–36 (st. III)	25–36 (st. III)		*So*
		36–48 (st. IV)			

Troubadour	Song	Incipit	Dc	Fa	Cm	H	J	G	Appendix 1
	106.24	S'ieu trobava mon compare'en Blacatz	1–10 (st. I), #85	1–10 (st. I), #127					
			11–20 (st. II)	11–20 (st. II)					
Daude de Pradas	124.6	Ben ay' amors, quar anc me fes chauzir	1–8 (st. I), #151	1–8 (st. I), #150					*Breviari*
			9–16 (st. II)						
	124.10	En un sonet guay e leugier	Incipit, #153						
			11–20 (st. II)						*Breviari*
			31–40 (st. IV)						
	124.11	No cugiey mais ses comjat far chanso	Incipit, #152						
			10–18 (st. II)						
	124.17	Tan sen al cor un amoros desir	Incipit, #154						
			41–4 (*tornada*)						
Elias de Barjols	132.7	Car compri vostras beutatz		1–8 (st. I), #178					
				9–16 (st. II)					

Author	PC	Incipit					Source
Elias Cairel	133.6	Mout mi platz lo doutz temps d'abril		Incipit, #50			
				28–36 (st. IV)			
	133.8	Per mantener joi e can e solatz		37–45 (st. V)		9–16 (st. II), #20	*Breviari*
Folquet de Marselha	155.1	Amors, merce: non mueira tan soven	Incipit, #24	Incipit, #52			*Jofre de Foixà 304.1*
			8–14 (st. II)				*DA, So*
			29–35 (st. V)	29–35 (st. V)	29 (for st. V), 167 #29 <22>	29–35 (st. V), #49	*Breviari*
	155.3	Ai! quan gen vens et ab quan pauc d'afan	1–8 (st I), #26	1–8 (st. I), #57			*RaT*
			9–16 (st. II)				*So*
			17–24 (st. III)	17–24 (st. III)			*RaT, DA*
			25–32 (st. IV)				
	155.5	Ben an mort mi e lor	Incipit, #21				*Breviari*

Troubadour	Song	Incipit	Dc	Fa	Cm	H	J	G	Appendix 1
	155.6	Chantan volgra mon fin cor descobrir	11–20 (st. II)						
			Incipit, #28						Mi
			10–18 (st. II)						
			37–45 (st. V)						
	155.8	En chantan m'aven a membrar	Incipit, #22						
			41–50 (st. V)						
	155.10	Greu feira nuills hom faillenssa	1–9, (st. I), #27						Mi
			37–45 (st. V)						
			19–27 (st. III)						
	155.11	Ja no·s cuig hom qu'ieu camje mas chansos	Incipit, #23	Incipit, #56					
			25–32 (st. IV)						
			33–40 (st. V)	33–40 (st. V)					
	155.14	Molt i fetz gran pechat Amors		1–7 (st. I), #58					Breviari

			8–14 (st. II)			*ReT, Breviari*
155.16	Per Dieu, Amors, ben sabetz veramen	1–8 (st. I), #29	Incipit, #53			*Breviari*
		9–16 (st. II)	9–16 (st. II)	9 (for st. II), 167 #30 <23>		*So, Breviari*
			17–24 (st. III)	17 (for st. III), 167 #31 <23>		
		33–40 (st. V)				
155.18	S'al cor plagues, ben fora oimais sazos	1–10 (st. I), #20	Incipit, #51			*RaT*
		11–20 (st. II)				
		21–30 (st. III)				*Breviari*
			31–40 (st. IV)			
		55–57 (2nd tornada)				
155.21	Sitot me soi a tart aperceubuz	Incipit, #30	Incipit, #55			

Troubadour	Song	Incipit	Dc	Fa	Cm	H	J	G	Appendix 1
			25–32 (st. IV)	25–32 (st. IV)					*Breviari*
	155.22	Tan m'abellis l'amoros pessamens		Incipit, #54					*DVE*
				17–24 (st. III)					
	155.23	Tan mou de cortesa razo	Incipit, #25	Incipit, #59					*DA*, *Biographies* LXXI.B
			25–36 (st. III)						*DA*
				49–60 (st. V)					
Gaucelm Faidit	167.7	Ara cove		Incipit, 66–78 (st. VI), #27					
	167.14	Chascus hom deu conoisser et entendre					1–5 (#70)		
	167.15	Chante deport, joi, dompnei e solatz	Incipit, #45	Incipit, #32					*Biographies* XVIII.E, *Breviari*
			21–30 (st. III)	21–30 (st. III)					
			51–60 (st. VI)						

167.18	De faire chansso	Incipit, #52						RaT
		25–36 (st. III)						So
		61–72 (st. VI)						
167.30	Ja mais nuill temps no·m pot ren far amors	Incipit, #47	Incipit, #26					
		37–45 (st. V)	28–36 (st. IV)					
167.35	Maintas sazos es hom plus voluntos	Incipit, #49						
		25–32 (st. IV)						Breviari
		33–40 (st. V)						
167.39	Mout a poignat Amors en mi delir	1–10, #51						
167.51	Razon e mandamen	Incipit, #53	Incipit, #31					
		16–30 (st. II)	16–30 (st. II)					DA

Troubadour	Song	Incipit	Dc	Fa	Cm	H	J	G	Appendix I
	167.52	Si anc nuills hom, per aver fin coratge				61–70 (st. VI), 167, #34 <25> [attrib. Uc de Saint Circ?]			(Biographies XVIII.C)
	167.56	S'om pogues partir son voler	1–11 (st. I), #46	1–11 (st. I), #28					Breviari
				12–22 (st. II)					ReT
			34–44 (st. IV)	34–44 (st. IV)					
			56–66 (st. VI)	56–66 (st. VI)					
	167.59	Tant ai sofert longamen grand afan	Incipit, #50	Incipit, #30					Biographies XVIII.B
			10–18 (st. II)	10–18 (st. II)					
			19–26 (st. III)	19–26 (st. III)					
				27–36 (st. IV)					
	167.60	Tot mi cuidei de chanssos far sofrir		Incipit, #29					
				19–27 (st. III)					
				46–54 (st. VI)					Breviari

								Breviari
167.62	Tuich cil que amon Valor	Incipit, #48	46–54 (st. VI)					
173.6 Gausbert de Poicibot	Merces es et chauzimens			Incipit, #115	14–26 (st. II)			DA
187.1 Comtessa de Proensa	Vos que·m semblatz desl corals amadors			1–9 (st. I) #146				
192.6 Gui de Cavaillo	Bona dompna, vostr' onrada valors			10–18 (st. II), #147				
194.3 Gui d'Ussel	Ben feira chanzos plus soven	Incipit of 198.4, #129	10–18 (st. II)	Incipit, #23	10–18 (st. II) (follows st. III)			
		28–36 (st. IV)	37–45 (st. V)	19–27 (st. III)		36–45 (st. V), #9		*Biographies* VI.B

Troubadour	Song	Incipit	Dc	Fa	Cm	H	J	G	Appendix 1
	194.6	En tanta guisa·m men amors	Incipit, #131						
			31–40 (st. III)						
			41–50 (st. IV)						
	194.8	Ges de chanter no·m faill cors ni razos	Incipit, #128	Incipit, #25					
			119–27 (st. III)	119–27 (st. III)					
	194.19	Si be·m partetz, mala dompna, de vos	Incipit, #130	Incipit, #24					Biographies XXII.B, XXIII
			33–40 (st. V)	33–40 (st. V)					So, Breviari
			41–48 (st. VI)						
Guilhem Ademar	202.1	Ben for' oimais sazos e locs	Incipit, #147						
			8–14 (st. II)						
	202.2	Be m'agr'ops q'ieu saubes faire	Incipit, #148						So, Breviari
			9–18 (st. II)						
			19–24 (st. III)						

	202.9	Non pot esser sofert ni atendut	Incipit, #146					
			9–16 (st. II)					
			25–32 (st. IV)					
Guilhem Augier Novella	205.4a	Per vos bella dolz amia		1–9 (st. I), #137				
				10–18 (st. II)				
				19–27 (st. III)				
				28–36 (st. IV)				
				37–45 (st. V)				
Guillem de Berguedà	210.3	Ara voill un sirventes far	Two 12-line stanzas, *unicum* in Dc, #214					
	210.16	Qan vei lo temps camjar e refrezir		Incipit, #124				
	210.20	Un sirventes ai en cor de bastir	Incipit, #213	25–32 (st. IV)				

Troubadour	Song	Incipit	Dc	Fa	Cm	H	J	G	Appendix 1
			32–40 (st. V)						
			44–46 (2nd tornada)						
Guillem de Cabestanh	213.5	Lo doutz cossire		Incipit, #117					Ri, *Biographies* XCIV.C, XCIV.D
				16–30 (st. II)					*Biographies* XCIV.C
				31–45 (st. III)					
Guillem Figueira	217.6	Pel joi del belh comensamen	Incipit, #215						
			9–16 (st. II)						
			17–24 (st. III)						
Guillem Magret	223.6	No valon coblas ni arrazos		9-line stanza, #139			9-line stanza, #65		
Guillem de Montan-hagol	225.1	A Lunel lutz una luna luzens		1–8 (st. I), #166					
				9–16 (st. II)					
				17–20 (tornada)					

Number	Incipit			Notes
225.2	Ar ab lo coinde pascor	Incipit, #218	Incipit, #164	
		11–20 (st. II)	11–20 (st. II)	
225.4	Del tot vey remaner valor		10–19 (st. II), #165	
			30–39 (st. IV)	
225.10	Nulhs hom no val ni deu esser prezatz		1–9 (st. I), #162	Breviari
			10–18 (st. II)	Breviari
			28–36 (st. IV)	
			37–45 (st. V)	So, Breviari
			19–27 (st. III)	Breviari
			46–54 (st. VI)	
			55–9 (tornada)	
225.13	Qui vol esser agradans e plazens	1–8 (st. I), #217	1–8 (st. I), #163	
		9–16 (st. II)	9–16 (st. II)	
		17–24 (st. III)	17–24 (st. III)	
		25–32 (st. IV)	25–32 (st. IV)	
		33–40 (st. V)	33–40 (st. V)	Breviari

Troubadour	Song	Incipit	Dc	Fa	Cm	H	J	G	Appendix 1
Guillem Peire de Cazals	227.7 (= 58.2)	Bernart de la Bart', ancse·m platz	17–18 (from st. II), #212, attrib. Bernartz						
Guillem Rainol d'At	231.1a	A tornar m'er enquer al premier us	Incipit, #220						
			17–24 (st. III)						
Guillem de Sant Leidier	234.3	Aissi cum es bella cill de cui ehan	Incipit, #149						
			25–32 (st. IV)						
			33–40 (st. V)						
	234.4	Ben chantera si m'estes ben d'Amor				33 (for st. V), 167 #36 <26>			(Breviari)
						41 (for st. VI), 167 #37 <26>			
	234.14	Malvaza m'es la moguda	Incipit, #150						
			8–14 (st. II)						
Guillem de Salaignac	235.1	A vos cuy tenc per dompn'e per senhor				Incipit (for st. I), 167 #8 <6>	1–8 (st. I), #59		

Guillem de la Tor	236.6	Quant hom regna vas cellui falsamen	1–9 (st. I), #205	1–9 (st. I), #134				
			10–18 (st. II)					
	236.9	Si mos fis cors fos de fer	Incipit, #204	1–10 (st. I), #133				
			11–20 (st. II)	11–20 (st. II)				
				21–30 (st. III)				
				31–40 (st. IV)				
				41–50 (st. V)				
				51–55 (tornada)				
	236.12	Uns amic et un' amia	29–30 (from st. III), #206					
Guiraudo lo Ros	240.1	A la mia fe, Amors	1–9 (st. I) #158	Incipit, #120				
			19–27 (st. III)	19–27 (st. III)				
	240.4	Era sabrai s'a ges de cortezia	Incipit, #159	Incipit, #121	(So)			
			17–24 (st. III)					
			25–32 (st. IV)	25–32 (st. IV)				
	240.5	Auiatz la derreira chanso	1–7 (st. I), #160					

Troubadour	Song	Incipit	Dc	Fa	Cm	H	J	G	Appendix 1
	240.6	Be·m te en son poder Amors					25–32 (st. IV), #23		
							33–40 (st. V), #24		
Giraut de Bornelh	242.5	Alegrar mi volgr'en chantan	Incipit, #7						
			49–60 (st. V)						(DA)
	242.15	Era, quan vei reverdezitz	Incipit, #19						
			29–42 (st. III)						
			71–84 (st. VI)						
	242.18	Ben deu en bona cort dir	Incipit, #12						
			19–27(st. III)						
	242.20	Be m'era bels chantars	Incipit, #16						
			27–39 (st. III)						
			40–52 (st. IV)						
	242.23	Mout era dous e plazens					1–12 (st. I), #28		
							13–24 (st. II), #29		
							25–36 (st. III), #30		

242.31	De chantar	1–2, #2				Mi
		17–32 (st. II)				
		33–48 (st. IV)				
242.36	Ges aissi del tot non lais	Incipit, #11				Biographies VIII.C
		31–40 (st. III)				
242.39	Ia·m vai revenen	Incipit, #5				(So)
		61–72 (st. VI)				
		73–84 (st. VII)				
242.40	Iois e chanz	1–2, #1				461.142a
		20–38 (st. II)				
242.42	La flors el vergan	Incipit, #9				
		76–90 (st. VI)				
		91–105 (st. VII)				
		106–9 (1st tornada)				
242.45	Leu chansonet' e vil	Incipit, #8				
		41–50 (st. V)				RaT
		51–60 (st. VI)				

Troubadour	Song	Incipit	Dc	Fa	Cm	H	J	G	Appendix I
	242.47	Los apleiz	1–2, #10						
			18–34 (st. II)						
			35–51 (st. III)						
			52–68 (st. IV)						
			69–85 (st. V)						
	242.51	Non puesc sofrir c'a la dolor	Incipit, #14						*Biographies* VIII.D
			41–50 (st. V)						
			51–60 (st. VI)						
	242.53	Nuilla res	1–2, #3						
			14–39 (st. II)						
			53–65 (st. V)						
	242.54	Ops m'agra, si m'o cossentis	1–2, #13						
			9–16 (st. II)						
			25–32 (st. IV)						
			33–40 (st. V)						
			41–48 (st. VI)						
			49–56 (st. VII)						
	242.57	Can brancha·l brondels e rama	Incipit, #17						

			41–50 (st. V)			
	242.58	Can cries la fresca fueil'els rams	Incipit, #6			
			12–22 (st. II)			So
			23–33 (st. III)			
			34–44 (st. IV)			
			45–55 (st. V)			RaT, So
	242.71	Si·m plagues tant chans	Incipit, #18			
			11–20 (st. II)			
			41–50 (st. V)			Breviari
	242.72	Si·m sentis fizels amics	Incipit, #4			Mi, DVE
			12–22 (st. II)			
	242.73	Si per mon Sobre–Totz non fos	Incipit, #15			Biographies VIII.E, DVE
			33–48 (st. III)			
Jordan Bonel de Cofolen	273.1	S'ira d'amor tengues amic jauzen		1–9 (st I), #156		
				10–18 (st. II)		
				28–32 (st. IV)		

Troubadour	Song	Incipit	Dc	Fa	Cm	H	J	G	Appendix 1
Jordan de L'Isla de Venessi	276.1	Longa sazon ai estat vas amor	Incipit, #216, attrib. Rostaing de Merguas	17–24 (st. III)					
Lanfranc Cigala	282.6	Estier mon grat mi fan dir vilanatge	1–8 (st. I), #189	1–8 (st. I), #157					
	282.8	Ges eu non vei com hom guidar si deia	Incipit, #190	1–10 (st I), #161					
				11–20 (st II)					
				21–30 (st. III)					
				31–40 (st. IV)					
			41–50 (st. V)	41–50 (st. V)					
				51–54 (tornada)					
	282.11	Hom que de domna se feigna		8-line stanza, unicum in Fa, #159					

Author	Number	Incipit				
	282.24	Tan franc cor de domn'ai trobat	1–8 (st. I), #191	1–8 (st. I), #158		
				9–16 (st. II)		
			17–20 (tornada)	17–20 (tornada)		
	282.26	Un sirventes m'adutz tant vils razos		9 lines of ?-line stanza, unicum in Fa, #160		
Marcabru	293.17	Dirai vos e mon latin			1–6 (st. I), #36	
					7–10 and 17–18 (from sts. II and III), #63	
					25–30 (st. V), #64	
					18–24 (st. IV), #65	
Monge de Montaudo	305.3	Aissi cum selh qu'es en mal senhoratge		Incipit, #116		
	305.6	Era pot ma domna saber		41–50 (st. V)	10–18 (st. II), #19	10–18 (st. II), #245

Appendix 1

Troubadour	Song	Incipit	Dc	Fa	Cm	H	J	G	Appendix 1
Palais	315.3	Mout m'enoja d'una gen pautoneira					8-line stanza, #7		
Peire d'Alvernha	323.1	Abans que·l blanc puoi sion vert	Incipit, #143, attrib. Peire Rogier						
			22–28 (st. IV)						
Peire Bremon Ricas Novas	330.2	Ben dey istar ses gran joi totztemps mais	1–10 (st. I), #201	1–10 (st. I), #148					
			11–20 (st. II)	11–20 (st. II)					
	330.5	Be volgra de totz chantadors	Incipit, #202						
			11–20 (st. II)						
			21–30 (st. III)						
	330.15	Pus que tug volon saber		1–8 (st. I), #153, attrib. Bertran d'Alamanon					
				9–16 (st. II)					
				17–24 (st. III)					
				25–28 (tornada)					
	330.16	Si·m ten Amors	1–2, #203						

Peire Cardenal	335.4	Anc mais tan gen no vi venir pascor		25–36 (st. III)	1–8 (st. I) #175, attrib. Bernart Arnaut de Moncuc					
					9–18 (st. II)					
Peire Guillem de Luzerna	344.3	En aquest gai sonet leuger			Incipit, #171	461.104.				
					10–18 (st. II)					
					19–27 (st. III)					
	344.4	No·m fai chantar amors ni drudaria		Incipit, #207	Incipit, #172					
				8–14 (st. II)						
				22–28 (st. IV)	22–28 (st. IV)					
Peire Guillem de Toloza	345.2	Eu chantera de gauz e volontos		Incipit, #209, attrib. Guillem Peire						
				10–18 (st. II)						
				28–36 (st IV)						
				37–45 (st. V)						

Troubadour	Song	Incipit	Dc	Fa	Cm	H	J	G	Appendix 1
Peire Raimon de Toloza	355.5	Atressi cum la candela	1–11 (st. I), #184	Incipit, #119					
			23–33 (st. III)	23–33 (st. III)					
				12–22 (st. II)					
	355.9	No·m puosc sufrir d'una leu chanso faire	Incipit, #187	Incipit, #118					
				15–28 (st. II)					
				29–42 (st. III)					
			57–70 (st. V)						
	355.15	S'ieu foz aventuratz	Incipit, #186						
			31–40 (st. IV)						
			41–50 (st. V)						
	355.16	Si cum seluy qu'a servit son senhor	1–8 (st. I), #185						
			25–32 (st. V)						
	355.20	Us noels pessamens m'estai	Incipit, #188						
			10–18 (st. II)						
									Breviari

Author	Number	Incipit			Source
Peire Rogier	356.5	No sai don chant, e chantars plagra·m fort	19–27 (st. III)		
			1–7 (st. I), #141		
			36–42 (st. VI)		
	356.7	Seign'en Raymbaut, per vezer	Incipit, #144		*Biographies* XL
			15–21 (st. III)		*Breviari*
			22–28 (st. IV)		*Breviari*
			36–42 (st. VI)		
	356.9	Tan t'ai mon cor en joy assis	Incipit, #142		
			8–14 (st. II)		
			21–28 (st. IV)		
Peire de Valeira	362.1; in fact stanza II of 262.2	Ja hom qes vol recrezer	11-line stanza, #145	11-line stanza, #169	
	362.2	So q'az autre vei plazer	1–11 (st I), *unicum* in Dc, #145; same rhyme scheme as 362.1		
Peire Vidal	364.4	Anc no mori per amor ni per el	Incipit, #66	Incipit, #34	*Breviari*

Troubadour	Song	Incipit	Dc	Fa	Cm	H	J	G	Appendix 1
			25–32 (st. IV)	9–16 (st. II)					Breviari
			17–24 (st. III)						
	364.8	Baron, Jhesus, qu'en crotz fon mes	Incipit, #71						
			25–32 (st. IV)						
	364.10	Be m'agrada la covinens sazos	41–48 (st. VI)				41–48 (st. VI), #57		
	364.13	Ben viu a gran dolor	Incipit, #62						
			36–48 (st. IV)						
	364.24	Ges pel temps fer e brau				41–2 (for st. V), 167 #9 <7>			RaT
	364.25	La lauzet' e·l rossinhol					1–8 (st. I), #25		
							9–16 (st. II), #26		
							17–24 (st. III), #27		
	364.30	Neus ni gels ni plueja ni fanh					41–48 (st. VI), #58		Breviari

364.31	Nulhs hom non pot d'amor gandir	Incipit, #63	Incipit, #38					
		9–16 (st. II)						
		17–24 (st. III)	17–24 (st. III), #38					
		25–32 (st. IV)						
364.32=97.7	Peire Vidals, puois far m'aven tenson	15–16 (from st. II), 25–32 (st. IV), #72						Biographies LVII.B
364.36	Plus que·l paubres, quan jai el ric ostal	Incipit, #68	1–8 (st. I), #35					
		9–16 (st. II)						
		25–32 (st. IV)	25–32 (st. IV)					
364.38	Pus ubert ai mon ric thesaur	Incipit, #73						(DA)
		13–24 (st. II)						
		49–60 (st. V)						
364.39	Quant hom es en autrui poder	1–8 (st. I), #70	1–8 (st. I), #37					Breviari, Bertolome Zorzi 74.9

Troubadour	Song	Incipit	Dc	Fa	Cm	H	J	G	Appendix 1
			9–16 (st. II)	9–16 (st. II)					*Breviari*, Bertolome Zorzi 74.9
				25–32 (st. IV)					Bertolome Zorzi 74.9
				17–24 (st. III)					*DA, Breviari*, Bertolome Zorzi 74.9
	364.40	Quant hom honratz torna en gran paubreira	1–7 (st. I), #67						
			43–49 (st. VII)						
	364.42	S'ieu fos en cort on hom tengues dreitura	1–6 (st. I), #69	1–6 (st. I), #33					*Mi*
	364.44	Si saupesson mei oil parlar						1–11 (st. I), #266	
	364.46	Tant ai lonjamen sercat	1–14 (st. I), #64						
			42–56 (st. IV)						

Troubadour	Song	Incipit	Dc	Fa	Cm	H	J	G	Appendix 1
	366.6	Camjat ai mon consirier		7–12 (st. II)					
			1–9 (st. I), #93 *bis*, (follows after, as if part of, #93 = 366.22)	19–24 (st. IV)					
			19–27 (st. III)						
			37–45 (st. V)						
	366.9	Coras que·m fezes dolor	1–8 (st. I), #96	Incipit, #111					(*Breviari*)
			17–24 (st. III)	17–24 (st. III)					
				41–8 (st. VI)					
	366.11	D'eissa la razo qu'ieu suoill		Incipit, #109					
	366.12	Del seu tort farai esmenda	Incipit, #97	9–16 (st. II)					
			15–21 (st. III)						
	366.13	D'un bon vers vau pensan com lo fezes	Incipit, #92	Incipit, #112					
				8–14 (st. II)					
			15–21 (st. III)	15–21 (st. III)					*Breviari*

						Breviari
366.14	D'un sonet vau pensan	Incipit, #106	9–16 (st. II)	17–24 (st. III)	25–32 (st. IV)	33–40 (st. V)
		22–28 (st. IV)	29–35 (st. V)			
366.19	Mainta gens mi malrazona	Incipit, #110	25–32 (st. IV)	33–40 (st. V)	41–48 (st. VI)	
366.20	M'entencion ai tot' en un vers mesa	Incipit, #95	Incipit, #108	25–32 (st. IV)	33–40 (st. V)	
		33–40 (st. V)				
366.21	Mout m'entremis de chantar voluntiers	Incipit, #91				
		15–21 (st. III)	15–21 (st. III), #102			

Troubadour	Song	Incipit	Dc	Fa	Cm	H	J	G	Appendix 1
				21–28 (st. IV)					RaT
			36–42 (st. VI)	36–42 (st. VI)					
	366.22	Nuills hom no s'auci tan gen	Incipit, #93	Incipit, #103					
			25–32 (st. IV)	25–32 (st. IV)					
				41–48 (st. VI)					
				49–92 (tornada)					
	366.26	Per dan que d'amor mi veigna		Incipit, #107					
				33–40 (st. V)					
	366.31	Si be·m sui loing et entre gent estraigna		Incipit, #36, attrib. Peire Vidal					
				36–42 (st. VI)					
	366.34	Tug miei cossir son d'amor et de chan						22–28 (st. IV), #264	(So)
Perdigon	370.3	Ben aio·l mal e·l afan e·l consir	1–9 (st. I), #138	Incipit, #86					Jofre de Foixà 304.1
				10–18 (st. II)					

				19–27 (st. III)	19 (for st. III), 167 #24 <19>		So, Breviari
	370.9	Los mals d'Amor ai eu ben totz apres	28–36 (st. IV), #138		28 (for st. IV), 167 #25 <19>		
			1–9 (st. I), #137	Incipit, #88			
			10–18 (st. II),	10–18 (st. II)			So
			19–27 (st. III)				
	370.13	Tot l'an mi ten Amors de tal faisso	Incipit, #139	Incipit, #87			(DA)
			28–36 (st. IV)	28–36 (st. IV)			
	370.14	Trop ai estat mon Bon Esper no vi	Incipit, #140	Incipit, #89			(Breviari)
			25–32 (st. IV)				
				33–40 (st. V)			
			41–44 (1st tornada)				
Pistoleta	372.2	Anc mais nulhs hom non fon apoderatz	Incipit, #96, attrib. Pons de Capdoill				

Troubadour	Song	Incipit	Dc	Fa	Cm	H	J	G	Appendix 1
				9–16 (st. II)					
Pons Barba	374.1	Non ha tan poder en se		25–32 (st. IV)					
			1–9 (st. I), #223	1–9 (st. I), #145					
			10–18 (st. II)	10–19 (st. II)					
			19–27 (st. III)						
	374.2	Sirventes non es leials	1–8 (st. I), #222						
			9–16 (st. II)						
			17–24 (st. III)						
Pons de Capdoill	375.1	Aissi m'es pres con sellui, que cerquan	Incipit, #102	Incipit, #95					
			9–16 (st. II)	9–16 (st. II)					
	375.10	Humils e francs e fis soplei vas vos	1–8 (st. I), #101	1–8 (st. I), #94					Jofre de Foixà 304.1
			9–16 (st. II)	9–16 (st. II)					
				17–24 (st. III)					
						33 (for st. V), 167 #23 <18>			

375.11	Ja non er hom tan pros			40 (for st. IV), 167 #21 <17>		(*Biographies* XLVII.B?)
				53 (for st. V), 167 #22 <17>		
375.14	Lials amics, cui amors ten jojos	Incipit, #97				
		25–32 (st. IV)				
375.19	S'ieu fis ni dis nuilla saisso	1–8 (st. I), #99				
		9–16 (st. II)				
		33–40 (st. V)				
375.20	Si com sellui c'a pro de valledors	1–8 (st. I), #100		1 (for st. I), 167 #18 <16>		*Biographies* XLVII.B
				9 (for st. II), 167 #19 <16>		
				17 (for st. III), 167 #20; belongs to <16>, though copied after <17> (=375.11)		

Appendix I

Troubadour	Song	Incipit	Dc	Fa	Cm	H	J	G	Appendix I
	375.23	Tant m'a donat fin cor e ferm voler	34–40 (st. V)	Incipit, #98					(Breviari)
				10–18 (st. II)					
Pons Fabre d'Uzes	376.1	Locx es c'om se deu alegrar	1–8 (st. I), #219						Ri
			9–16 (st. II)						
			17–24 (st. III)						Breviari
			25–32 (st. IV)						
			33–40 (st. V)						Breviari
Pons de la Guardia	377.5	Sitot no m'ai al cor gran alegransa					1–6 (st. I), #31		
							7–12 (st. II), #32		
Raimbaut d'Aurenga	389.1	Ab nou cor et ab nou talen	Incipit, #164						Mi
			36–42 (st. VI)						
	389.5	Als durs, crus, cozens, lauzengiers	Incipit, #165						
			43–49 (st. VII)						

	389.21	Brais, chans, quils, critz	Incipit, #166					
			43–48 (st. VIII)					
	389.27	Entre·l gel e·l vent e fanc	Incipit, #162					
			36–42 (st. VI)					
	389.34	Peire Rotgier, a trassaillir	Incipit, #167					
			15–21 (st. III)					
	389.36	Pois sals sabers mi sortz e·m creis	1–8 (st. I), #163 (attribution inserted after incipit)					
	389.41	Un vers farai de tal mena	Incipit, #168					
			22–28 (st. IV)					
Raimbaut de Vaqueiras	392.2	Era·m requier sa costum' e son us	Incipit, #108					*Biographies* LXX.B
			25–32 (st. IV), #108					
	392.13	Eissamen ai gerreiat ab amor	Incipit, #107					*DA*

Troubadour	Song	Incipit	Dc	Fa	Cm	H	J	G	Appendix 1
			25–32 (st. IV), #107						DA
			17–24 (st. III), #107						So
	392.18	Gerras ni plaich no·m son bo	1–12 (st. I), #105						
			37–48 (st. IV), #105						
	392.19	Ja hom pres ni dezeretatz						1–11 (st. I), #246	Breviari
	392.20	Ja non cujei vezer	1–16 (st. I), #103						Biographies LXX.B
			16–32 (st. II), #103						
			64–80 (st. V), #103						
			81–96 (st. VI), #103						
	392.24	No m'agrad' iverns ni pascors	Incipit, #110						
			49–52 (first 4 lines of stanza V), 110						Biographies LXX.B

									DA
392.26	Nulhs hom en re no falh	1–9 (st. I), #106							
		10–18 (st. II),							
		19–27 (st. III)							
		28–35 (st. IV)							
392.28	Savis e fols, humils e orgoillos	1–8 (st. I), #104							*(Breviari)*
		9–16 (st. II),							
		17–24 (st. III),							
392.30	Si ja amors autre pro non tengues	1–8 (st. I) #109				1–8 (st. I), #6		1–8 (st. I), #262	*Breviari*; NB this st. appears alone everywhere except *a*[1]
Raimon Jordan									
404.2	Ben es camjatz eras mospes-samens	Incipit, #113							
		10–18 (st. II)							
404.4	Lo clar temps vei brunezir	Incipit, #114							
		37–45 (st. V)							
		46–54 (st. VI)							

Troubadour	Song	Incipit	Dc	Fa	Cm	H	J	G	Appendix 1
Raimon de Miraval	406.2	Aissi cum es genser pascors	Incipit, #112	Incipit, #93					
			28–36 (st. IV)	28–36 (st. IV)		28 (for st. IV), 167 #14 <12>	28–36 (st. IV), #54		So
			37–45 (st. V)						
			55–59 (1st tornada)						
	406.4	Amors me fai chantar et esbaudir				8 (for st. II), 167 #5 <4>	8–14 (st. II), #50		
	406.5	Anc non attendiei de chantar				15 (for st. III), 167 #6 <4>	15–21 (st. III), #51		So
	406.6	Anc trobars clus ni braus				25 (for st. IV), 167 #10 <8>	25–32 (st. IV), #52		
						37 (for st. V), 167 #11 <9>	37–45 (st. V), #53		
	406.7	A penas sai don m'apreing			Incipit, #7				
					41–50 (st. V)				Ab, Breviari
	406.8	Er ab la forsa dels freys	Incipit, #119		Incipit, #3				

PC	Incipit						Source
406.9	Era m'agr'ops que m'aizis	9–16 (st. II)		9–16 (st. II)	9 (for st. II), 167 #12 <10>		So
				Incipit, #6			
406.12	Bel m'es q'ieu chant e coindei		Incipit, #90	33–40 (st. V)			Biographies LVIII.E
				Incipit, #8			Breviari
			37–45 (st. V)	28–36 (st. IV)	46 (for st. VI), 167 #13 <11>		Biographies LVIII.B
406.13	Be m'agrada·l bels tems d'estiu	Incipit, #116	Incipit, #91				
		41–48 (st. VI)	17–24 (st. III)				
406.15	Ben aia·l messagiers	1–8 (st. I), #113					Biographies LVIII.D
406.15a	Ben sai que per aventura	25–32 (st. IV)				17–24 (st. III), #56	So

Troubadour	Song	Incipit	Dc	Fa	Cm	H	J	G	Appendix I
	406.20	Cel que no vol auzir chanssos	Incipit, #118		Incipit, #2				Mi
						11 (for st. II), 167 #17 <15>			
			17–24 (st. III)		17–24 (st. III)				Breviari
			25–32 (st. IV)		25–32 (st. IV)				Breviari
			33–40 (st. V)		33–40 (st. V)				Mi
	406.23	Contr' amor vau durs e enbroncs	Incipit, #117	Incipit, #92					
			15–21 (st. III)			15 (for st. III), 167 #15 <13>	15–21 (st. III), #55		
			36–42 (st. st. VI)	36–42 (st VI)	40–42 (all that remain of st. VI), #1				So
	406.24	D'Amor es totz mos cossiriers			1–8 (st. I), #4				Breviari
	406.28	Entre dos volers sui pensius	Incipit, #111						Biographies LVIII.D

	406.31	Lonc temps ai agutz cossiriers	25–32 (st. IV) 41–8 (st. VI)		25 (for st. IV), 167 #16 <14>			(Mi)	
	406.33	Puois de mon chanter disetz			25 (for st. IV), 167 #7 <5>				
	406.34	Pueis onguan no·m valc estius	1–8 (st. I), #115						
	406.38	S'ieu en chanter soven	9–16 (st. II)	Incipit, #5					
	406.42	Tals vai mon chan enqueren	Incipit, #114 9–16 (st. II) 17–24 (st. III) 41–48 (st. VI)	11–20 (st. II)				(So)	
Raimon de las Salas	409.1	Ancse m'avetz tengut a nonchaler	1–8 (st. I), #151, attrib. Bernart del Poget 9–16 (st. II)						

Troubadour	Song	Incipit	Dc	Fa	Cm	H	J	G	Appendix I
Raimon Bistortz d'Arles	416.1	Aissi co·l fortz castels ben establitz		17–24 (st. III)					
				1–9 (st. I), #141					
				10–18 (st. II)					
				19–27 (st. III)					
				28–36 (st. IV)					
				37–45 (st. V)					
				46–51 (2 tornadas)					
	416.2	Aissi com arditz entendenz		1–32 (st. I), unicum in Fa, #140					
				33–64 (st. II)					
				65–96 (st. III)					
	416.3	Ar' agues eu, Dompna, vostra beutatz		10-line stanza, unicum in Fa, #143					
	416.4	A vos, meillz de meill, q'om ve		1–12 (st. I), #144					
				13–24 (st. II)					
				25–36 (st. III)					

416.5	Qui vol vezer bel cors e benestan		37–48 (st. IV)	
			49–60 (st. V)	
			61–64 (tornada)	
			1–7 (st. I), unicum in Fa, #142	
			8–14 (st. II)	
			15–17 (tornada)	
Rigaut de Berbezilh 421.1	Atressi com lo leos	Incipit, #133		(Breviari)
		10–18 (st II)		
421.2	Atressi con l'orifanz	Incipit, #132		Leys 1341, Biographies XVI.B; (DA)
		12–22 (st. II)		
		23–33 (st. III)		
421.5	Ben volria saber d'Amor	Incipit, #136		
		17–24 (st. III)		
421.6	Li nous mes d'abril comensa	Incipit, #134		Breviari
		28–36 (st. IV)		

Troubadour	Song	Incipit	Dc	Fa	Cm	H	J	G	Appendix 1
	421.10	Tuit demandon qu'es devengud' Amors	Incipit, #135						DA
			25–32 (st. IV)						Breviari
Sordello	437.2	Aitant ses plus viu hom quan viu jauzens	1–8 (st. I), #195						
	437.4	Ar ai proat q'el mon non a dolor	Incipit, unicum in Dc, #200						
			8-line stanza						
	437.5	Atretan deu ben chantar finamen	Incipit, #196						
			17–24 (st. III)						
			33–40 (st. V)						
	437.8	Meravelll me com negus honratz bars	1–8 (st. I), #199						
			9–16 (st. II)						
	437.13	Domna, tot eissamens	11-line stanza, #198						
	437.19	Lai a'n Peire Guillem man ses bistenza	1–7 (st. I) #197						

	PC	Title							
	437.24	Planher vuelh en Blacatz en aquest leugier so				8–10 (*tornada*)			
						31–2 (from st. IV), #200, follows on from 437.4.			
Uc Brunenc	450.1	Ab plazer receup et acuoill				Incipit, #89	Incipit, #63		*So*
	450.2	Ara·m nafron li sospir		Incipit, #90			Incipit, #64		(*So*)
					17–24 (st. III)		17–24 (st. III)		
			9–16 (st. II)		9–16 (st. II)		9–16 (st. II)		
					13–18 (st. III)		13–18 (st. III)	13–18 (st. III), #60	
	450.3	Coindas razos e novellas plazens	25–32 (st. IV)		1–6 (st. I), #86		Incipit, #62		
					13–18 (st. III)		13–18 (st. III)		
					7–12 (st. II)		7–12 (st. II)		
	450.4	Cortesamen mou en mon cor mesclanza	9–16 (st. II)	Incipit, #87			Incipit, #60		*Breviari*
								25–32 (st. IV), #61	*Breviari*

Troubadour	Song	Incipit	Dc	Fa	Cm	H	J	G	Appendix 1
	450.6	Lanquan son li rosier vermeil	33–40 (st. V)	33–40 (st. V)				33–40 (st. V), #265	(Breviari)
	450.7	Puois l'adrechs temps ven chantan e rizen	Incipit, #88	Incipit, #61					
			9–16 (st. II)	9–16 (st. II), copied after st. III					
			17–24 (st. III)	17–24 (st. III)					
			25–32 (st. IV)						
				33–40 (st. V)					Breviari
Uc de Pena	456.1	Cora qe·m desplagues Amors		Incipit, #136					
				25–32 (st. IV)					
Uc de Saint Circ	457.3	Anc enemics q'ieu agues	Incipit, #178						Breviari
			51–60 (st. VI)				51–60 (st. VI), #42		
	457.12	Enaissi cum son plus car	Incipit, #176						
			31–40 (st. IV)						

457.15	Estat ai fort langamen	Incipit, #177	1–9 (st. I), #80		51 (for st. VI), 167 #4 <3>	51–60 (st. VI), #46	51–60 (st. VI), #263	
		19–27 (st. IV)						
457.16	Gent ant saubut miei uoill		Incipit, #77					
			9–16 (st. II)					
			17–24 (st. III)					
			25–32 (st. IV)					
457.18	Longamen ai atenduda	Incipit, #175	Incipit, #81					Biographies XXXIII.C
			31–40 (st. IV)		31 (for st. IV), 167 #2 <2>	31–40 (st. IV), #44		
		41–50 (st. V)			41 (for st. V), 167 #3 <2>	41–50 (st. V) #45		
		51–60 (st. VI)	51–60 (st. VI)					
		61–7 (tornada)	61–7 (tornada)					

Troubadour	Song	Incipit	Dc	Fa	Cm	H	J	G	*Appendix 1*
	457.20	Mains greus durs pessamens	31–40 (st. IV), #183			31 (for st. IV), 167 #33 <25>	31–40 (st. IV), #39		
	457.25	Nuilla ren que mestier m'aia					1–10 (st. I), #33		
							11–20 (st. II), #34		
							31–40 (st. IV), #35		
	457.26	Nuills hom no sap d'amic, tro l'a perdut	1–8 (st. I), #174	1–8 (st. I), #78					
			41–44 (*tornada*), #181						
	457.26a	Passada es la sasos				11-line stanza, *unicum* in *H*, 167 #34 <25>			
	457.28	Qui Na Cuniça guerreia	25–27 (*tornada*), #182, follows on directly from #181 = 457.26						

	457.34	Servit aurai longamen		1–9 (st. I) #79					
	457.35	Ses dezir et ses razo			37 (for st. V), 167 #32<25>				
	457.39	Totz fis amicx ha gran deszaventura	1–7 (st. I), #179			1–7 (st. I), #40			
			8–14 (st. II)			8–14 (st. II), 41			
	457.40	Tres enemics e dos mals seignors ai		Incipit, #82					
				10–18 (st. II)					
				19–27 (st. III)	19 (for st. III), 167 #1 <1>	19–27 (st. III), #43			
	457.43	Valor ni prez ni honor non atrai	Unicum in Dc, #180						
Anonymous	461.21	Amors vol drut cavalcador						10-line stanza, #260	Breviari
	461.31a	A tot mon amic clam merce					9-line stanza, unicum in J, #73		

Troubadour	Song	Incipit	Dc	Fa	Cm	H	J	G	*Breviari*
	461.32	Atretan leu pot hom ab cortesia					7-line stanza, #15	7-line stanza, #243a, (follows on from 243 = 461.130)	
	461.35	A vos volgra metre lo veit qe·m pent						#255	
	461.54	Bona dona, a Deu vos coman					1–8 (st. I) #47		
							9–16 (st. II), #48		
	461.57	De bona domna vuoill						8-line stanza, #271	
	461.74	De ben aut pot om bas cazer					11-line stanza, #67		
	461.75	Del cap li trairai la lenda						7-line stanza, *unicum* in G, #254	
	461.76a	Dels plazers plazens					1–13 (st. I), #37		
							14–26 (st. II), #38		

ID	Incipit					
461.79	De tan tenc per nesci Andreu					7-line stanza, #261 *bis*, (follows on from #261= 461.155)
461.79a	De tot' autra pudor cre				12-line stanza, #72	
461.82	Deus vos sal, delz pez sobeirana					6-line stanza, *unicum in* G, #252
461.83	Deuz vos sal, de pretz sobeirana				6-line stanza, #11	6-line stanza, #251
461.86	D'ome fol ni deconoissen				1–8 (st. I), #17	1–8 (st. I), #247	*Breviari*
					9–18 (st. II), #18		*Breviari*
461.87	Dona, dieus sal vos e vostra valor				6-line stanza, #10	6-line stanza, #250	*Breviari*
461.95	Domna que de cognat fai drut				8-line stanza, #2	
461.98	Dos gratz conquer hom ab un do				8-line stanza, #5	8-line stanza, #268	*Breviari*

Troubadour	Song	Incipit	Dc	Fa	Cm	H	J	G	Appendix 1
	461.123b	Fraire, tuit li sen e·l saber					11-line stanza, #1		Breviari
	461.130	Ges li poder no·s parton per egal					8-line stanza, #14	8-line stanza, #243	
	461.135	Grans gaugz m'ave la noit, quans sui colgat						10-line stanza, #258	
	461.149	Locs es c'om chan e c'om s'en lais					10-line stanza, #12		Breviari
	461.154	Lo sen volgra de Salamo					8-line stanza, #4	8-line stanza, #256	
	461.155	Ma donna am de bona guisa						8-line stanza, #261	Breviari
	461.202	Quand lo pels del cull i venta					10-line stanza, #71	10-line stanza, #253	
	461.213a	Qui ves bon rei si prezenta					1–8 (st. I), *unicum* in J, #68		
							7–16 (st. II), *unicum* in J, #69		

	461.214	Qui vol conquerer pretz verais			1–15 (st. I), #16	1–15 (st. I), #244
	461.220a	Si be·m soi forfaitz ni mespres			8-line stanza, #22	
	461.225	Si ves home e no saps cui			14-line stanza or fragment, #74	
	461.232	Tota beutat e tota cortesia				8-line stanza, #249
	461.237	Tot lo mon vei reverdejar			10-line stanza, #8	
	461.241	U fotaires qe no fo amoros				1–9 (st. I), *unicum* in G, #242
						10–18 (st. II), *unicum* in G
	461.250	Vilans dic qu'es de sen eissitz			8-line stanza, #3	8-line stanza, #267

Occitan Treatises of Grammar and Poetics from the Beginning
to the Mid-Fourteenth Century

(For manuscript *sigla*, see the relevant section of Appendix 17; for editions, see Bibliography.)

Author and text	Date and place of composition	MSS	Form	Grammar	Poetics
Raimon Vidal de Besalú, *Las Razos de trobar*	Catalonia, ca. 1200 or earlier	BHCL	About fifteen printed pages of prose; contains up to thirty-two quotations (number varies by manuscript) from troubadour songs.	*Trobar* requires knowledge of Lemosi and *grammatica*, "art" and usage. Word classes categorized as inflecting or noninflecting. In the former, "substantive" distinguished from "adjective" usage. Systematic review of declension of adjectives, nouns, and pronouns; errors of conjugation in songs by famous troubadours reproved.	Aim is to promote discernment of troubadour poetry among audiences and future poets. Teaching of grammar motivated by need for correct rhymes. Recommends consistency of diction and criticizes self-contradiction in Bernart de Ventadorn 70.12.

Uc Faidit, *Donatz proensals*	Veneto, ca. 1240	ABCDL	Prose with accompanying Latin prose translation/interlinear gloss, varying by manuscript. Long word lists; total in longest version about 180 pages. No quotations.	Modeled on Donatus's *Ars minor*. Reviews morphology of the parts of speech. Includes long verb lists, organized by conjugation.	Distinguishes open and closed vowels. Followed in *ALB* by a rhyme list or rhyming dictionary (incomplete in *LB*).
Terramagnino da Pisa, *Doctrina d'acort*	Sardinia, second half of thirteenth century, perhaps between 1282 and 1296	H	Eight hundred lines of rhyming couplets, mostly octosyllabic but also many heptasyllables and some lines of other lengths; grammatical paradigms in prose inserts; forty-three troubadour quotations.	Recasts Raimon Vidal in simpler terms. Morphology of nouns, pronouns, and verbs described; grammatical errors corrected in famous songs; readers told to avoid linguistic vices.	Inspired by author's beloved and addressed to lovers; brief remarks on consistency, including of rhyme.
Jofre de Foixà, *Las Regles de trobar*	Catalan court of Sicily, between 1289 and 1291	HR	About eighteen printed pages of prose, contains eleven troubadour quotations.	Recasts Raimon Vidal for laymen. Avoids reliance on *grammatica* and devises a vernacular framework and terminology; morphology treated initially in the context of agreement, then again in the framework of the parts of speech with emphasis on case.	The nine *causas*, or prerequisites, of *trobar* start with *razo* and *maniera* (consistent theme and regular versification) and include rhyme (analyzed in terms both of stress and the identification of syllables).
Anon., *Doctrina de compondre dictats*, possibly by Jofre de Foixà	Catalonia, second half of thirteenth century?	H; copied as continuation of the *Razos*	About four printed pages of prose, no quotations; possibly continuation of the *Razos*.	Does not deal with grammar.	Brief description of lyric genres, mainly in terms of content, very little on form; intended to complement and complete the *Regles*?

Author and text	Date and place of composition	MSS	Form	Grammar	Poetics
Anon., two Ripoll treatises	Catalonia, late thirteenth century?	R	Prose, totaling about five printed pages; eighteen troubadour quotations.	Nothing apart from a passing observation on the position of adjectives.	The first is about generic forms and the second about rhyme.
Dante Alighieri, *De vulgari eloquentia*	Italy, between 1303 and 1305	3 MSS [not connected to any of the Occitan treatises]	Latin prose, two quotations from one trouvère and twelve quotations from six troubadours, as well as others from Italian poets.	Not primarily a grammar but reflects on the place of language(s) in universal history and Italian in Romance; weaves a path between vernacular variation in time and place and the need for a standard.	Themes, genres, and versification.
Berenguer d'Anoia, *Mirall de trobar*	Mallorca, 1300–1310	H	Prose, about thirty printed pages, with long inset verse prologue/epitome, and thirty-four or thirty-five troubadour quotations, usually a full stanza in length	Based on Isidore, *Etymologies*. The alphabet, forms of metaplasm, vices to be avoided.	Self-titled "mirall de trobar o de versificar o de rimar"; a third is on ornament; many figures are described in terms of their impact on line length and rhyme.
Raimon Cornet de Saint-Antonin, *Doctrinal de trobar*	1324, written for the future Peter IV of Aragon	H	543 hexasyllabic lines, illustrations from troubadours. Apparently a crib for the Consistori competition in the first year it was held. Survives only in a damning commentary by Joan de Castellnou.	Overview of parts of speech; verbs; rhetorical figures.	Rhyme and genre; discussion of the *antics trobadors*, especially Peire Cardenal.

Guilhem Molinier, *Las flors del gai saber, estier dichas Las leys d'amors*	Toulouse, earliest version composed ca. 1327–38, text ed. Gatien-Arnoult dated 1341	Toulouse, B.M., MS 2884	Occitan prose with prolific use of inset verse, mainly examples (by the author?), but also mnemonic verses, many featuring At de Mons but including several other troubadours. Conceived as five books. Nearly six hundred printed pages.	Very detailed treatment of grammar; incorporates discussion of rhetoric within framework of faults and licenses, as well as classification of the tropes; encyclopedic use of sources including Priscian, Donatus, Cicero, and Bede.	Detailed exposition of phonetics harnessed to study of rhyme scheme and stanza form, and extensive study of genre. The final, unfinished book is about how to compose, beginning with a rhyme scheme and establishing one's rhyme words.
Guilhem Molinier, *Las leys d'amors*	Toulouse, 1356	Toulouse, B.M., MS 2883	Occitan prose. Entirely rewritten version of the earlier *Leys*, full of inset verse, including examples, many long quotations from At de Mons, and texts promulgating the activities of the Consistori. About 580 printed pages.	Detaches poetry from grammar and subordinates it to rhetoric conceived in relation to politics and ethics, in the tradition of Brunetto's *Tresor*. Recapitulates in revised form the grammar of the earlier redaction but omits the entire book on tropes.	Recapitulates in revised form the phonetics and versification of the earlier redaction but omits the final book on composition.

Troubadour Quotations in Grammars of the Vidal Tradition

This appendix compares the organization of the *Razos de trobar*, the *Doctrina d'acort*, and the *Regles de trobar*, and their use of quotations relative to that organization in manuscripts *B* and *CL* of the *Razos* and *H* of the *Regles*. The first column indicates in which section of the treatise each quotation appears. Next, within each treatise, quotations are numbered using the numbering assigned by J. H. Marshall in his edition of the treatises. The next following column identifies the source of each quotation by PC and line numbers (for full names of troubadours and incipits of the quoted songs, see Appendix 1; for editions, see Bibliography). In quotations that serve as grammatical examples, the forms that are the focus of the example are in italics; where these forms appear at the rhyme they are additionally in bold; I also indicate which quotations are incipits that serve to identify the song under discussion. For incipits and attributions of the quoted songs, see Appendix 1.

		Razos de trobar				Doctrina d'acort			Regles de trobar	
	#	Passage quoted (PC and line numbers) in B and/or CL texts	Line reference in B text and word on which the example bears (rhyme words in bold)	Line reference in CL text and word on which the example bears (rhyme words in bold)	#	Passage quoted (PC and line numbers)	Line reference and word on which the example bears (rhyme words in bold)	#	Passage quoted (PC and line numbers) in H text	Line reference in H and word on which the example bears (rhyme words in bold)
Preamble								1	10.34, 17–24	19–26, defense of the author
								2	Unattrib.	144–55, equivocal rhyme
								3	Unattrib.	158–59, equivocal rhyme
Nouns and other nominal forms	1	364.29, 1–3		148–50, *bon e bel*	1	389.17, 1–2	141, *bell*	4	167.56, 17	251, *bell*, *avinen*
	2	70.1, 33 (B), 33–34 (CL)	185, *ardimenz*	165–66, *ardimenz*	2	3.1, 5–8	180–83, *amichs*	5	167.59, 50	265, *douçors*
	3	70.1, 49	187, *genz*	168, *gentz*	3	"cell qui fes l'Acort"	187–89, *amics*	6	155.14, 9–10	290–91, *merces*
	4	234.7, 1	189, *messagiers*	170, *mesagiers*	4	234.6, 57–58	192–93, *amichs*	7	80.25, 8	302, *espervers*
	5	234.7, 50	191, *cavaliers*	172, *cavaliers*	5	364.38, 8–9	196–97, *enemics*	8	70.6, 1	386, *senyor*
	6	242.58, 45–46	193–94, *bes*	174–75, *bes*	6	22a.1	202–9, *amich*			
	7	Unattrib.	197, *pros*	178, *pros*	7	167.62, 53–54	212–13, *amic*			

	Razos de trobar				Doctrina d'acort				Regles de trobar	
#	Passage quoted (PC and line numbers) in B and/or CL texts	Line reference in B text and word on which the example bears (rhyme words in bold)	Line reference in CL text and word on which the example bears (rhyme words in bold)	#	Passage quoted (PC and line numbers)	Line reference and word on which the example bears (rhyme words in bold)	#	Passage quoted (PC and line numbers) in H text	Line reference in H and word on which the example bears (rhyme words in bold)	
7a	Unattrib.	199–200, **presanz**	180–81, **prezanz**	8	Unidentified	216–17, amic			
8	70.6, 41	[203– emended, Li sei bel ueill **trahidor**]	184, li sei bell oil **trahidor**	9	242.5, 74–76	220–22, amic			
9	80.34, 41	205, Peitavin et **Norman**	186, Pitavin e **Norman**	10	155.1, 10–11	225–26, amic			
10	242.45, 41	207, **gentil**	188, **gentil**	11	364.15, 1–3	251–53, amia			
11	70.6, 1 (B) 1–2 (CL)	210, **senhor**	191–92, **segnor**	12	345.2, 28–30	255–57, domna			
12	155.18, 1		215, **sazos**	13	70.43, 25	263, domnas			
13	30.23, 1	231, **Amors**	217, **Amors**	14	22a.1	266–67, domnas			
				15	173.3, 37–40	284–87, **valors**			
				16	70.31, 9–10	291–92, **sabor**			
				17	421.2, 45	295, chansos			
				18	155.23, 1-3	297–99, **razon**			
				19	155.23, 13	302, **canson**			
				20	155.23, 25–28	303-6, **sazon**			

Category	No.	Reference	Form 1	Form 2
Adverb				
Verbs	14	70.25, 1-2	361, incipit	332-33, incipit
	16	70.7, 1	362, incipit	333, incipit
	15	70.25, 73-74	364-65, *trai* for *trac*	335-36, *trai* for *trac*
	17	70.7, 41-43	368-70, *retrai* for *retrac*	338-40, *retrai* for *retrac*
	18	242.34, 1-3	386-87, incipit	355, incipit
	19	242.34, 49-57	388-96, *cre* for *crei*	356-64, *cre* for *crei*
	20	366.21, 27-28	399-400, *cre* for *crei*	367-68, *cre* for *crei*
	21	70.43, 31	402, *mescre* for *mescrei*	371, *mescre* for *mescrei*
	22	70.41, 28	404, *recre* for *recrei*	373, *recre* for *recrei*
	23	155.3, 1	412, incipit	380, incipit

No.	Reference	Form
21	30.22, 1-2	351-52, *totz*
22	167.22, 1	354, *tot*
23	421.10, 1-2	357-58, *tuit*
24	364.39, 17-19	362-64, *tot*
25	364.22, 1-2	536, incipit
26	364.22, 32-33	537-38, *tray* for *trac*
27	70.43, 1	547, incipit
28	70.43, 33-34	548-49, *retrai* for *retrac*
29	70.43, 30-31	560-61, *mescre* for *mescrey*
30	242.34, 1	566, incipit
31	242.34, 54-57	568-69, *cre* for *crey*
32	167.12, 1-2	573-74, incipit
33	167.12, 47-48	577-78, *cre* for *crey*
34	167.18, 37-38	581-82, *cre* for *crey*

No.	Reference	Form
9	Unidentified	503-6, *volonter*
10	Unidentified	556-59, *t[r]ar*
11	10.25, 25-27	562-64, *retray, estray, tray*

	Razos de trobar				Doctrina d'acort			Regles de trobar	
#	Passage quoted (PC and line numbers) in B and/or CL texts	Line reference in B text and word on which the example bears (rhyme words in bold)	Line reference in CL text and word on which the example bears (rhyme words in bold)	#	Passage quoted (PC and line numbers)	Line reference and word on which the example bears (rhyme words in bold)	#	Passage quoted (PC and line numbers) in H text	Line reference in H and word on which the example bears (rhyme words in bold)
24	155.3, 25–26	413–14, **traï** for **traïc**	382–83, **traï** for **traïc**	35	167.51, 27–28	585–86, **cre** for **crey**			
25	364.13, 45–48	419–22, **moric, enriquic, ferric, noiric**	387–90, **moric, enriquic, ferric, noiric**	36	364.2, 74–75	591–92, **cre** for **crey**			
				38	392.13, 25	598, incipit of stanza			
				39	392.13, 28–29	599–600 **recre** for **recrey**			
				40	392.26, 1	603, incipit			
				41	392.26, 37–39	604–6, **recre** for **recrey**			
				42	370.13, 8–9	627–28, **son** for **sui**			
				43	155.3, 25–27	648–50, **traï** for **trahic**			
Construction 26	70.12, 1	456, incipit	423–24, incipit						
27	70.12, 29–30	459–60, self-contradiction	426–27, self-contradiction						

Miscellaneous other errors						435–36, incipit				
	28	355.6, 1				435–36, incipit				
	29	355.6, 15–16				437–38, *cels* for *celui*				
	30	355.6, 46				442, *mantenir* for *mantener*				
	31	167.18, 1				445, incipit				
	32	167.18, 37–38				446–47, **ve** for **vei**				

Troubadour Quotations in the *Novas* of Raimon Vidal

This appendix includes troubadour quotations (numbered) and references to named troubadours (bulleted) in the order in which they appear in the text of *R* (Raimon Vidal, *Obra poètica*, ed. Hugh Field). Quotations are identified by author (and PC number), incipit, and line range in the editions listed in the Bibliography (followed by line references in Raimon Vidal's *novas* and an indication of who quotes to whom).

ABRIL ISSIA

- Reference to Giraut de Bornelh's *vers* and *chansos* and those of Arnaut de Maruelh (44–45, *joglar* to narrator)
1. Giraut de Bornelh (242.55), "Per solatz reveillar," 41–44 (96–99, narrator, remembering to himself)
- Episode at the court of Dalfi d'Alvernha, troubadour and patron (140–620, recounted by *joglar* to narrator)
- Dalfi named by the *joglar* as the poet whose songs his father first taught him to sing (201, *joglar* to Dalfi, reported to narrator)
2. Bertran de Born (80.38), "S'abrils e fuoillas e flors," 86–88 (468–71, Dalfi to *joglar*, as recounted by *joglar* to narrator)
3. Arnaut de Maruelh (30.VI), "Razos es e mezura," 209–12 (603–6, Dalfi to *joglar*, as recounted by *joglar* to narrator)
- Reference to Uc de Mataplana (troubadour and patron) (639–44, *joglar* to narrator)
- References to other patrons, some of whom were also troubadours, including Frederick II, Richard I, Bernart Arnaut d'Armagnac, Arnaut Guillem de Marsan, possibly Bertran de Saissac (856–89, narrator to *joglar*)

4. Arnaut de Maruelh (30.VI), "Razos es e mezura," 155–58 (1022–25, narrator to *joglar*)

5. Raimon de Miraval (406.25), "Dels quatre mestiers valens," 8–9 (1147–48, narrator to *joglar*)

6. Peire Rogier (356.7), "Seign'en Raymbaut, per vezer," 36–42 (1155–61, narrator to *joglar*)

7. Anonymous (unidentified) (1184–89, narrator to *joglar*)

8. Arnaut de Maruelh (30.VI), "Razos es e mezura," 64–74, (1231–41, narrator to *joglar*)

9. Giraut de Bornelh (242.34), "Gen m'aten," 69–72 (1549–52, narrator to *joglar*)

10. Raimon de Miraval (406.7), "A penas sai don m'apreing," 45–47 (1730–32, narrator to *joglar*)

SO FO E·L TEMS

1. Bernart de Ventadorn (70.10), "Bel m'es qu'eu chan en aquel mes," 35 (47, narrator)

2. Perdigon (370.3), "Ben aio·l mal e·l afan e·l consir," 35–36 (77–78, narrator)

3. Raimbaut d'Aurenga (389.20), "Ben s'eschai qu'en bona cort," 29–35 (92–98, narrator)

4. Raimon de Miraval (406.5), "Anc non attendiei de chantar," 25–32 (111–18, narrator)

5. Bernart de Ventadorn (70.27), "Lonc tems a qu'eu no chantei mai," 10–11 (171–72, first lady to knight)

6. Arnaut de Maruelh (30.23), "Si·m destreignetz, dompna, vos et Amors," 38–40 (239–41, knight to *donzela*)

7. Folquet de Marselha (155.1), "Amors, merce: non mueira tan soven," 8–14 (248–54, knight to *donzela*)

8. Giraut de Bornelh (242.58), "Can creis la fresca fueil'els rams," 48–50 (261–63, *donzela* to knight)

9. Guillem de Sant Leidier (verses unknown elsewhere) (270–73, *donzela* to knight)

10. Guilhem Ademar (202.1), "Ben for' oimais sazos e locs," 8–14 (282–88, *donzela* to knight)

11. Giraut de Bornelh (242.58), "Can creis la fresca fueil'els rams," 23–33 (291–301, *donzela* to knight)

12. Giraut de Bornelh (242.39), "la·m vai revenen," 85–106 (322–43, *donzela* to knight)

13. Folquet de Marselha (quoted anonymously) (155.16), "Per Dieu, Amors, ben sabetz veramen," 41–44 (407–10, narrator)

14. Bernart de Ventadorn (70.43), "Can vei la lauzeta mover," 49–56 (433–40, knight to *donzela*)

15. Gui d'Ussel (194.19), "Si be·m partetz, mala domna, de vos," 33–40 (455–62, *donzela* to knight)

16. Raimon Vidal de Besalú (verses unknown elsewhere) (469–79, *donzela* to knight)

17. Raimon de Miraval (406.18), "Selh, cui joys tanh ni chantar sap," 1–8 (490–97, *donzela* to knight)

18. Peire Bremon (Ricas Novas?) (verses unknown elsewhere, though also quoted in the *Regles de trobar*) (512–15, narrator)

19. Bernart de Ventadorn (70.1), "Ab joi mou lo vers e·l comens," 33–36 (520–23 narrator)

20. Guiraudo lo Ros (240.4), "Era sabrai s'a ges de cortezia," 40–41 (590–93, first lady to knight)

21. Raimon de Miraval (406.2), "Aissi cum es genser pascors," 28–36 (606–14, knight to first lady)

22. Anonymous (unidentified, by "us castellas") (625–32, knight to first lady)

23. Raimon de Miraval (406.23), "Contr' amor vau durs et enbroncs," 36–42 (641–47, knight to first lady)

24. Anonymous ("us frances") (666–85, first lady to knight)

25. Raimon de Miraval (406.42), "Tal vai mon chan enqueren," 33–40 (694–701, first lady to knight)

26. Raimon de Miraval (406.42), "Tal vai mon chan enqueren," 25–32 (712–19, knight to first lady—this makes his rupture with her definitive)

27. Raimon de Miraval (406.15), "Ben aia·l messagiers," 31–32 (770–71, first lady to second lady)

28. Raimon Vidal de Besalú (verses unknown elsewhere) (786–94, first lady to second lady)

29. Raimbaut de Vaqueiras (392.13), "Eissamen ai gerreiat ab amor," 23–24 (815–16, first lady to second lady)

30. Raimon de Miraval (verses unknown elsewhere) (829–31, first lady to second lady)

31. Raimbaut de Vaqueiras (392.23), "Leu pot hom gauch e pretz aver," 1–4 (840–43, first lady to second lady)

32. Uc Brunenc (450.2), "Ara·m nafron li sospir," 37–40 (860–63, first lady to second lady)

33. Folquet de Marselha (155.3), "Ai! quan gen vens," 23–24 (906–7, second lady to first lady)

34. Folquet de Marselha (155.3), "Ai! quan gen vens," 9–12 (958–61, second lady to first lady)

35. Anonymous (unidentified, heard sung by "un joglaret") (1008–9, second lady to first lady)

- Uc de Mataplana is appealed to as arbitrator between the two women (1104–end)

36. Raimon Vidal de Besalú (verses unknown elsewhere) (1271–81, Uc de Mataplana)
37. Gaucelm Faidit (167.43), "No m'alegra chans ni critz," 30–33 (1328–31, Uc de Mataplana)
38. Raimon de Miraval (406.8), "Er ab la forsa dels freys," 9–13, 15–16 (1358–64, Uc de Mataplana)
39. Bertran de Born (80.38), "S'abrils e fuoillas e flors," 19–22 (1407–10, Uc de Mataplana)

Lyric Insertions in Jean Renart's *Guillaume de Dole*

The first column numbers the lyric insertions in the order they appear in Félix Lecoy's edition of *Guillaume de Dole*. The second provides the number assigned to each in Lecoy's inventory and the line numbers at which it occurs in his edition. The column headed "Reference #" indicates whether the quotation is from a source identified by Gennrich (G: for refrains), Raynaud and Spanke (RS: for Northern French trouvère lyrics), and Pillet-Carstens (PC: for troubadour lyrics); see Bibliography for details of these works.

# in text	# and lines in Lecoy	Reference #	Genre	Exordium	Attested elsewhere?	Attributed to?	Could be by Jean Renart?	Integrated to rhyme?	Sung by?
1	#43, 291–92	—	Refrain		no	—	yes	no	Conrad's knights
2	#35, 295–99	G 1	*Rondet de carole*	"la jus"	yes	—	conceivably	no	Another knight at Conrad's court
3	#44, 304–5	—	Refrain		no	—	yes	no	Pucele at Conrad's court
4	#27, 310–15	G 3	*Rondet de carole*	"Main se leva"	yes	—	conceivably	no	Sister of duke of Mainz

5	#26, 318–22	G 2	Rondet de carole	"Main se leva"	yes	—	conceivably	no	Count of Savoy
6	#36, 329–33	G 4	Rondet de carole	"la jus"	yes	—	conceivably	no	Count of Luxembourg
7	#32, 514–19	G 5	Rondet de carole	"la jus"	yes		conceivably	no	Lady in coat with *graine*
8	#37, 522–27	G 6	Rondet de carole	"la jus"	yes	—	conceivably	no	Page of the steward of Epire
9	#28, 532–37	G 7	Rondet de carole	"Main se leva"	yes	—	conceivably	no	Son of count of Aubours
10	#29, 542–47	G 8	Rondet de carole	"Main se leva"	yes	—	conceivably	no	Lady at Conrad's court
11	#1, 846–52	RS 1779	*Grand chant courtois*	Spring opening with birdsong	yes	Gascon	unlikely	no	Conrad and Jouglet
12	#2, 923–30	RS 985	*Grand chant courtois*	Spring opening with nightingale	yes	—	conceivably	no	Conrad
13	#17, 1159–66	RS 1834	*Chanson de toile*	". . . siet"	no	—	yes	no	Guillaume's mother
14	#18, 1183–92	RS 202	*Chanson de toile*	". . . siet"	no	—	yes	no	Lienor
15	#21, 1203–16	RS 744	*Chanson dramatique à refrain*	". . . siet"	no	—	yes	no	Lienor
16	#14, 1301–7	PC 262.2	*Occitan canso*	Spring opening with birdsong	yes	—	unlikely	yes	Guillaume and Nicole

# in text	# and lines in Lecoy	Reference #	Genre	Exordium	Attested elsewhere?	Attributed to?	Could be by Jean Renart?	Integrated to rhyme?	Sung by?
17	—,1335–67	—	Extract from chanson de geste		no	—	conceivably	no	Jongleur
18	#3, 1456–69	RS 1635	*Grand chant courtois*	"loial amour"	yes	Renaut de Beaujeu	no	yes	Conrad
19	#30, 1579–84	G 9	*Rondet de carole*	"Main se leva"	yes	—	conceivably	no	Jouglet
20	#4, 1769–76	RS 420	*Grand chant courtois*	Spring opening with birdsong	yes	—	conceivably	yes	Conrad
21	#34, 1846–51	G 10	*Rondet de carole*	"la jus"	yes	—	conceivably	yes	Jouglet and a lady
22	#5, 2027–35	RS 857	*Grand chant courtois*	Winter opening provokes song	yes	—	unlikely	yes	Jouglet to Conrad
23	#19, 2235–95	RS 1379	*Chanson de toile*	"Bele Aiglentine"	no	—	yes	no	Knight
24	#38, 2369–74	G 11	*Rondet de carole*	"la jus"	yes	—	conceivably	no	Galerans de Limbourg
25	#41, 2379–85	G 12	*Rondet de carole*	"la jus"	yes	—	conceivably	no	Conte de Tré (Maastricht)
26	#22, 2389–91	—	*?Chanson de toile*	"Renaus et s'amie chevauche"	no	—	yes	yes	Valet of the count of Loos
27	#25, 2398–2404	RS 1871a	Song of praise (genre unknown)	"de Renaut"	no	—	yes	no	Minstrel of the Empire

28 = 2	#35, 2514–18	G 1	Rondet de carole	"la jus"	yes	—	conceivably	yes	Jouglet
29	#39, 2523–27	G 14	Rondet de carole	"rive de mer"	yes	—	conceivably	yes	Nephews of Lord of Dinant
30	#6, 3107–14	RS 1132	Grand chant courtois	"moult es fouls"	no	—	yes	yes	Conrad
31	#7, 3180–95	RS 1319	Grand chant courtois	Spring opening with nightingale	no	—	yes	yes	Conrad
32	#23, 3403–6	RS 1877a	Pastourelle	"Quant je li donnai . . ."	no	—	yes	no	Jongleur
33	#46, 3419–30	—	Tournoi des dames	"Cele . . ."	no	—	yes	no	Jongleur, for Conrad
34	#8, 3625–31	RS 1232	Grand chant courtois	"c'est granz folie"	yes	Mon segnor Gasson	no	yes	Conrad
35	#9, 3751–59	RS 1872	Grand chant courtois	"por quel forfet?"	yes	—	conceivably	yes	Conrad
36	#10, 3883–98	RS 1229	Grand chant courtois	"ja de chanter"	yes	Renaut de Sablé	no	yes	Conrad
37	#11, 4127–40	RS 2086	Grand chant courtois	Spring opening, "chanter m'estuet"	yes	Vidame de Chartres	no	yes	Page, for Conrad
38	#40, 4164–69	G 15	Rondet de carole	"la jus"	yes	—	conceivably	no	Two young noblemen
39	#24, 4568–83	RS 1914b	Pastourelle	Spring opening	no	—	yes	yes	Minstrel
40	#12, 4587–93	RS 754	Grand chant courtois	"Amours"	no	—	yes	yes	Minstrel

# in text	# and lines in Lecoy	Reference #	Genre	Exordium	Attested elsewhere?	Attributed to?	Could be by Jean Renart?	Integrated to rhyme?	Sung by?
41	#15, 4653–59	PC 124.5	Occitan *canso*	Spring opening with nightingale	yes	"Auvrignace"	unlikely	no	Minstrel for Lienor
42	#42, 5106–11	G 16	Refrain	"Que demandez vous?"	not in this form	—	yes	no	Lienor
43	#45, 5113–15	—	Refrain	"Tendez tuit"	no	—	yes	yes	Onlookers, for Lienor
44	#20, 5188–5208	—	Romance	Spring opening with birdsong	no	—	yes	no	Nephew of the bishop of Liège
45	#16, 5212–27	PC 70.43	Occitan *canso*	Nature opening with lark	yes	"Son poitevin"	unlikely	no	Knight from the Danmartin family
46	#13, 5232–52	RS 1322a	*Grand chant courtois*	Spring opening with birds	yes	Gautier de Soignies	no	no	*Un bon baceler* (a brave young knight)
47	#31, 5427–34	G 17	*Rondet de carole*	"la jus"	yes	—	conceivably	yes	Lord of Huy-sur-Meuse
48	#33, 5440–45	G 18	*Rondet de carole*	"la jus"	yes	—	conceivably	no	Sung by the same lord as above?

Manuscript Versions of the *Novas del papagai*

This is a schematic representation of the contents of the five different manuscript versions of the *novas*. Three (*RJG*) recount the core of the narrative in which the parrot courts the lady, and a fragment of this also occurs in π. This core is developed differently in *R* and *J*. *J* ends with an oath of fidelity by the lover, which appears as a separate text, a little before the rest of the *novas*, in *G*, and completely independently in *D*. Although *G* does not contain the full narrative development of *J*, it ends with the parrot returning to Antiphanor and without the motif of the lady's gifts, suggesting greater proximity to *J* than *R*. The text of π is corrupt but closer to *JG* than to *R*. For the meaning of *sigla*, see Appendix 17.

R	Parrot courts lady	Lady's gifts; lovers meet (Greek fire) & separate
J	Parrot courts lady	Lady agrees; lovers meet / Lover's oath
G	Parrot courts lady	
D	Lover's oath	
π	Parrot courts lady	

Bertolome Zorzi 74.9 and Peire Vidal 364.39

This appendix gives the texts of Bertolome Zorzi 74.9 (ed. Levy) and Peire Vidal 364.39 (ed. Avalle). Italics are used to mark the material common to both. It is not translated twice over but the text as it appears in the two editions is provided. I follow the stanza order used by Bertolome, who interverts Avalle's stanzas IV and V; Avalle's line numbers appear in square brackets to the right of his text.

Translation	Bertolome Zorzi 74.9 (ed. Levy, 9)	Peire Vidal 364.39 (ed. Avalle, 43)	Translation
A man commits superlative folly if he says anything foolish about Peire Vidal, for no one could say what he does without great natural judgment; and this is my witness: "When a man . . ."	1 Mout fai sobrieira folia 2 qui ditz fol d'En Peire Vidal, 3 car senes gran sen natural 4 sos motz dir hom non sabria. 5 E d'aisso m'es garentia: 6 *quand hom es en autrui poder,* 7 *non pot totz sos talans complir,* 8 *anz l'aven sovens a giquir* 9 *per l'autrui grat lo sieu voler.*	1 *Quant hom es en autrui poder,* 2 *non pot totz sos talens complir,* 3 *ans l'ave soven a gequir* 4 *per l'autrui grat lo sieu voler.* 5 Doncs pos em poder mi sui mes 6 d'amor, segrai los mals e·ls bes 7 e·ls tortz e·ls dreitz e·ls dans e·ls pros, 8 c'aissi m'o comanda razos.	*When a man is in someone else's power he is unable to realize all his own wishes and is often obliged to sacrifice his desire to the pleasure of another.* Thus, since I have placed myself in Love's power, I shall follow the bad things and good, the rights and wrongs, the losses and the gains [which it imposes], for that is what reason commands me to do.

English translation	Occitan	Occitan (variant)	English translation
But for all that, I wouldn't say that I can't tell good from bad and that I wouldn't regard as corrupt anyone who believed another in this matter; but I should hold my tongue, *for if a person . . .*	10 Mas per o ges non diria 11 qu'ieu non conogues ben de mal 12 e qu'ieu non tengues per venal 13 tot home c'autr' en creiria; 14 ni no·is tanh qu'ieu plus en dia, 15 car qui vol al segle caber, 16 maintas vetz l'aven a sofrir 17 so que·lh desplatz ab gen cobrir 18 per semblansa de non-caler.	9 *Car qui vol al segle plazer,* 10 *mantas vetz l'aven a sufrir* 11 *so que·lh deplatz ab gen cubrir,* 12 *ab semblansa de nonchaler;* 13 *e pueis, quant ve que sos luecs es,* 14 *contra sel que l'aura mespres* 15 *no sia flacs ni nualhos,* 16 *qu'en gran dreg notz pauc d'uchaizos.*	*For if a person wants to please others in this world, he must often be patient and conceal agreeably what displeases him with a show of indifference; and then, when he sees his opportunity, let him not be cowardly or slack against the one who ill-treated him; for a small accusation can do a lot of harm when one has great right on one's side.*
And if it were appropriate for me to say more, I would dare to say what would harm me. For I was at once found to have behaved lawfully by the one who ought to have thought that I could say without deceit that *"I have so much sense and wisdom . . . "*	19 E si plus dire·m tanhia, 20 ben ausera dir que·m desval, 21 c'adreich m'a trobat lejal 22 tals qu'apensar si deuria 23 qu'eu pogra dir ses bausia: 24 tant ai de sen e de saber 25 que del tot sai mon mielh chauzir 26 e gen conoisser e grazir 27 qui·m sap honrar ni car tener.	17 *Tant ai de sen e de saber* 18 *que de tot sai mo mielhs chauzier,* 19 *e sai conoisser e grazir* 20 *qui·m sap honrar ni car tener,* 21 *e tenc m'a l'us dels Genoes,* 22 *qu'am bel semblan gai e cortes* 23 *son a lor amics amoros* 24 *et a·ls enemics orgulhos.*	*I have so much sense and wisdom that I know how to distinguish the best of everything and I know how to discern and befriend whoever is wise enough to honor me and hold me dear. And I observe the practice of the Genoese who, in a pleasant, cheerful and courtly fashion, are loving toward their friends and haughty to their enemies.*
And since he is so felonious that he does not use his valor to help those he should help and whom he would have the most occasion to, without any harm to himself, I would scarcely be willing to help him. *But a man [such as him] who is capable of valor . . .*	28 E car tant a de feunia 29 qu'a celz cui deu valer non val 30 on plus en auria·l logal 31 que pogues e no·lh nozia, 32 gaire valer non volria, 33 mas qui pot e non vol valer, 34 cum non s'esforsa de morir, 35 des que la mortz no·l denha aucir 36 per far enoi e desplazer?	25 *Cel qui pot e no vol valer,* [33] 26 *com no s'esforsa de murir,* 27 *Dieu, quar la mortz no·l denh' aucir,* [36] 28 *per fag enueg a desplaser?* 29 *et es trop lag, d'onrat pages* 30 *quan recuelh las rendas e·ls ces:* 31 *cor poirit ab cors vermenos,* 32 *viu ses grat de Dieu e de nos!* [40]	*If a man is capable of valor but doesn't wish to exercise it, since he doesn't rush to expose himself to death, God, why does Death not stoop to kill him for the tedium and displeasure that he causes? A man is too cowardly when he [merely] gathers up rents and taxes from an honored territory. Rotten heart with a worm-eaten body, he lives without the favor of either God or us!*

Translation	Peire Vidal 364.39 (ed. Avalle, 43)	Bertolome Zorzi 74.9 (ed. Levy, 9)	Translation
I intend to uphold Merit and Youth and be subject to good ladies and serve courtly people; and I don't care much for wealth. And yet, if I had the power, there is no count or duke or marquis who would be more delighted with spending or less willing to put up with base barons. Good lady, I imagine, when I gaze on your lovely person, that I am looking at God. And since I love and desire you so much, great good should come to me from it! For your love has so conquered me and vanquished and bound and imprisoned me that if I had all the world, and so was best of all, I would still think myself poor without you. Lady, when I saw you remain there and I had to leave you, my sighs caused me so much anguish I almost collapsed! Oh lovely lady, noble creature! May God and mercy avail me with you. Retain me and my songs in your service, however much it may annoy the courtly jealous one!	[25] 33 Pretz e Joven vuelh mantener 34 a bonas donas obezir 35 et a corteza gen servir; 36 e non ai gran cura d'aver. [28] 37 e pero, s'ieu poder agues, 38 non es coms ni ducs ni marques, 39 a cui meihs plagues messios, 40 Ni meins se pac d'avols baros. [32] 41 Bona dona, Dieu cug vezer, 42 quan lo vostre gen cors remir: 43 a quar tan vos am e·us dezir, 44 grans bes m'en deuri' eschazer. 45 qu'aissi m'a vostr' amors conques 46 e vencut e lassat e pres, 47 qu'ap tot lo segle, que mieus fos, 48 mi tenri'eu paubres ses vos. 49 Dona, quan vos vi remaner 50 e m'avenc de vos a partir, 51 tan m'angoisseron li sospir; 52 Qu'a pauc no m'avenc a cazer. 53 ai! bella dona, franca res! 54 valha·m ab vos Deus e Merces! 55 retenetz mi e mas chansos, 56 sitot pez' al cortes gilos.	37 Huoimais fastics mi seria 38 coblejars d'aisso que no·m cal, 39 qu'en lonc plaich avol deslejal 40 no·is tanh c'adreitz hom estia. 41 don volh segre autre via, 42 c'onor e pretz vuolh mantener 43 e bonas dompnas obedir 44 e a cortesa gen servir 45 e non ai gran cura d'aver. 46 Doussa res, dir no·us sabria 47 cum vos port fin' amor coral 48 ni cum sont faich trist miei jornal 49 pois nous vi cum far solia, 50 qu'ieu sai aisso, on qu'ieu sia, 51 bella dompna, dieu cuich vezer, 52 quand lo vostre gen cors remir; 53 e car tant vos am e desir. 54 grans bens m'en deuria escazer. 55 E non per tant sis faria, 56 s'acsetz chausit lo dol mortal 57 qu'el cor m'intret sobre·l portal 58 Qu'ieus dis: A dieu, doussa amia! 59 c'ab l'amor que·m destrenhia, 60 dompna, quand vos vi remaner 61 ni m'avenc de vos a partir, 62 tant m'angoisseron li sospir 63 c'a pauc no m'en venc a cazer.	From now on it would be distasteful to me to compose stanzas about something that I care for so little. For it's not seemly for an upright man [like me] to persist in a long complaint on a base, unlawful subject. And so I wish to follow another path, for I wish to uphold honor and merit . . . Sweet creature, I would not be able to express to you how true a heartfelt love I bear you, nor how sad my days are now that I don't see you as I used to. For I know this, that wherever I am, good lady, I imagine . . . However, if it were the case that you could perceive the mortal pain that entered my heart when I said to you at the gate, "Farewell, sweet lady"; for, on account of the love that constrains me, lady, when I saw you . . .

In my half song I let it be known that a man should indeed reveal his meaning, but it is a sign of great learning to conceal one's sense when nonsense is more use.	64 E mon dimei chant fatz saber 65 com deu ben son sen descobrir, 66 mas grans sciensa es sen cobrir, 67 lai on non-sens pot plus valer.
	[3 *tornadas*, not quoted]

APPENDIX 9

Text and Translation of Jofre de Foixà's
"Be m'a lonc temps menat a guiza d'aura" (304.1)

The text follows the edition by Martín de Riquer. The final line of each stanza is the incipit of the song identified below the translation in the facing column.

I	Be m'a lonc temps menat a guiza d'aura ma bon' amors, quo fai naus sobre vens; mas lo peril m'asuava e·m daura	As if it were a breeze, my good love has driven me like a ship in the path of the wind; but the great danger I am in is sweetened and gilded by the good hope I have firmly fixed on you, in loving whom my desire is altogether firm; for thus, the *great beauties and exquisite manners that are yours* have made a conquest of me, blonde lady with the golden hair.
4	lo bos espers qu'ay en vos fermamens, en cuy amar es ferms totz mos talens: qu'aissi m'an pres de vos, qu'es blond' e saura, *las grans beutatz e·ls fis ensenhamens.*	
		Arnaut de Maruelh 30.16
II 8	No m'agra ops que·m fos tan agradiva vostr'amistats, dona de bos aibs flors, pus deviatz envas mi tan autiva de cor esser, e lunhar mi·l secors	It would not be right that your friendliness toward me should be too welcoming, lady, flower of good qualities, since your feelings toward me should be haughty and keep at a distance the help that I have waited for such a long time: for my tears rise up so painfully in me that I don't think I can live long, *so much, lady, do you distress me, you and love between you.*
12	qu'ay atendut lonjamens: quar us plors m'en sors tan grieus que non cre guaire viva, *si me destrenhetz, dona, vos et amors.*	
		Arnaut de Maruelh 30.23

III	Et ja de vos no·m do so qu'ieu dezire jamais Ihezus, si per als a murir tem, mas per so quar sai ses contradire que pos mortz fos no·us poyria servir. Pero si·l mal vos plazen ni·l martir, ni·l grieu afan de que yeu suy suffrire, *ben aya·l mal e l'afan e·l cossir.*	And may Jesus never give me what I want of you if I were ever to fear dying for some other reason [than love for you]—except I know for certain that once I was dead I wouldn't be able to serve you. However, if the suffering and martyrdom and painful anguish I suffer please you, *may the suffering and anguish and longing be rewarded.* Perdigon 370.3
16 20		
IV	Qu'a mi non deu plazer mas so que·us playa, pus del tot suy vostres ab bona fe, sol no vulhatz que d'amar vos m'estraya, quar le poders non es ges mieus de re. Be suy conques, mas trop suy luenh de be, qu'en tal cossir m'an empench que m'esglaya *ir' e pezars e dona ses merce.*	For nothing should please me except what pleases you, since I am utterly yours, with good faith, provided you don't wish me to stray from loving you—the power to do so certainly doesn't lie with me. I am well conquered, but too far from well, for *distress and sorrow and a pitiless lady* have struck me with longing such as torments me. Perdigon 370.8
24 28		
V	E vos, Amors, pus ab tan ferm coratge vos am e·us ser, per que·us truep tan nozen? Qu'ades m'ausizetz tolhen alegrage et ades mi revivetz joys renden, per qu'ieu trac piegz d'ome del tot moren. Doncx pus avetz en mi·l plen poderatge *Amors, merce! no mueyra tan soven.*	And you, Love, since with such a firm heart I love and serve you, why do I find you so hurtful? One moment you kill me, taking away all my mirth, and then you bring me back to life again restoring my joys, so that I suffer worse than someone who was dying once and for all. So, since you have total power over me, *have have mercy, love! Let me not die so many times over.* Folquet de Marselha 155.1
32		
VI	Dona, per vos m'es Amors tan sobreira; et si m'auci, de vos mou l'ochaizos. Don volgra be que·us auzes esquerreira nomnar vas fe: mas en vos falhizos non dey pensar sia, pero de vos tenc er, que·m fatiz mal, dona plazentiera, *mon cor et mi e mas bonas chansos.*	Lady, it's because of you that Love has such sovereignty over me; if she kills me, you are the reason. I wish I dared to call you halting with regard to faith, but I ought not to think there is any shortcoming in you, because from you who are hurting me now, lovely lady, I hold *my heart and myself and my good songs.* Gaucelm Faidit 167.37
36 40		

VII	Vostres suy tan, don' agradiv' e pros,	I am so much yours, pleasing and worthy lady, that the more harm you do me, with a more
44	qu'on piegz mi faitz, ab amor pus enteyra	perfect love do I *beg you, humble, candid, and sincere.*
	humils e francs e fis sopley vas vos.	Pons de Capdoill 375.10

Structure of the "Branch of Sexual Love" in Matfre Ermengau's *Breviari d'amor*

This Appendix reproduces (from Ricketts' edition) and translates the rubrics, organizes them according to my understanding of the structure of Matfre's argument, and indicates the distribution of quotations (as numbered by Ricketts) among the sections thus defined. Italics are used for English translations and bold typeface for major subdivisions. The quotations are identified in Appendix 11.

D'AMOR DE MASCL' AB FEME *CONCERNING LOVE OF MALE WITH FEMALE*

Quez est'amors de mascle ab feme es bona de se ab qu'om n'uze be, et en qual manieira·n pot hom ben uzar *That this love of male with female is good in itself, provided one practices it well, and in what manner one may practice it well*

Quo es mout perilhos a las gens uzar d'est' amor de mascl' ab feme *How it is very perilous to humanity to practice this love of male with female*

Aisi comensa le perilhos tractatz d'amor de donas, seguon qu'en han tractat li antic trobador en lurs cansos

Here begins the perilous exposition of the love of women, according to what the troubadours of old said about it in their songs   #1

- Del plag quez an mogut li maldizen contra Matfre, reprenden lui quar enten en amor de donas *Concerning the suit brought by the detractors against Matfre, criticizing him for dedicating himself to the love of women*
  - Respon Matfres als maldizens *Matfre replies to the detractors*   ##2–10
  - Aras parlon li maldizen *Now the detractors speak*   #11
  - Respon Matfres als maldizens *Matfre replies to the detractors*   #12
  - Aisi parlon li maldizen *The detractors speak in this way*   #13
  - Respon Matfres als maldizens *Matfre replies to the detractors*   ##14–15
  - Aisi parlon li maldizen *The detractors speak in this way*   #16
  - Respon Matfres als maldizens *Matfre replies to the detractors*   #17
  - Aisi parlon li maldizen *The detractors speak in this way*   #18
  - Respon Matfres als maldizens *Matfre replies to the detractors*   ##19–20
  - Aisi parlon li maldizen *The detractors speak in this way*   #21
  - Respon Matfres als maldizens *Matfre replies to the detractors*   ##22–28
- Del plag quez an mogut contra aquest' amor li trobador, reprenden lieis *Concerning the suit brought by the troubadours against this love, criticizing it*
  - Respon Matfres als trobadors *Matfre replies to the troubadours*   ##29–30
  - Aisi parlon li trobador reprenden amor *The troubadours speak in this way, criticizing love*   ##31–33
  - Respon Matfres escuzan amor *Matfre replies, exculpating love*   #34
  - Aisi parlon li trobador reprenden amor *The troubadours speak in this way, criticizing love*   #35
  - Respon Matfres escuzan amor *Matfre replies, exculpating love*   #36
                                                                         ##37–44

- De cortezia et en qual maniera deu hom uzar de sa cortezia *Concerning courtliness and in what manner one should practice ones courtliness* ##189–94
- D'umilitat *Concerning humility* ##195–98
- De domnei *Concerning courtship of women* ##199–200
- D'alegranza *Concerning gaity* ##201–4
- De retenemen *Concerning restraint* ##205–9
- D'essenhamen *Concerning manners* ##210–13
- De proeza et en qual maniera deu hom proeza mantener *Concerning worth and in what manner one should maintain worth* ##214–18
- De matremoni *Concerning marriage*
  - Del frug de matremoni e de las diversas gracias que dieus a fachas al orde de matremoni *Concerning the fruit which is marriage and the various forms of grace God has bestowed on the order of marriage* #219
  - De la error de cels que blasmo matremoni *Concerning the heresy of those who decry marriage*
  - Ab qual entencio deu hom venir a matremoni *With what intent one should approach marriage*
  - Ab qual persona se deu hom ajustar de matremoni *With what person one should be joined in marriage*
  - Per quals razos et en qual maniera quascus deu amar sa molher *Why and how each man should love his wife*
  - En qual maniera quascus deu tener recglada sa molher *In what way each man should keep his wife in order*
- De pacientia *Concerning patience* ##220–21
- De conoichensa *Concerning discernment* ##222–26
- De sen e de saber *Concerning judgment and knowledge* #227
- De bon coratge e d'esforss *Concerning courage and commitment* ##228–33
- Del frug que nais del albre de saber be e mal, le quals es filhs e filhas *Concerning the fruit that is born of the tree of the knowledge of good and evil, namely sons and daughters*

- Del maldizen le quals en l'albre d'amor destrui ab so feramen l'albre de saber be e mal *Concerning the detractor who,*
  on the tree of love, destroys the tree of the knowledge of good and evil by striking it
  - De decelar *Concerning indiscretion* ##234–37
  - D'avareza *Concerning avarice* ##238–41
  - De cocha *Concerning lust* ##242–44
  - De lauzengiers *Concerning slanderers* ##245–47
  - D'erguelh *Concerning arrogance* ##248–50
  - De vilhitge *Concerning old age* #251
  - De fadeza *Concerning imbecility* ##252–53
- Del enamorat d'amor de mascle e de feme, le quals en l'albre d'amor cuelh fuelhas e flors del albre de
  saber ben e mal *Concerning the man in love with the love of male with female who plucks the leaves and*
  flowers of the tree of the knowledge of good and evil #254

Remedis per escantir folia d'amor *Remedies to cure love's madness* ##255–67

Quotations in Matfre Ermengau's *Breviari d'amor*

Quotations in the *Breviari* as numbered by Ricketts in the order they appear in the text, followed by their PC number, the first line of the passage quoted as it appears in the *Breviari*, and the lines occupied by the quotation. My thanks to Peter Ricketts for providing this material.

Ricketts #	PC	Opening line	Breviari lines
1	9.18	Qui vol apenre d'amor	27821–32
2	167.60	Lunhs hom no pot ses amor far que pros	27865–73
3	309, fragment	Sabchon li fin aiman	27878–99
4	406.24	D'amors mou totz mos cossiriers	27908–15
5	trouvère	Amor, que m'a sorpris	27933–37
6	341.la	Messier Matfre, no·us desplassa	27948–56
7	9.18	Mas qui vol d'entendedor	27976–87
8	106.22	S'ieu pogues ma voluntat	27995–28006
9	297.5a	Greu er lunhs homs tan complitz	28020–27
10	10.40	Ges no failh quan s'ave	28034–39
11	173.14	Vostr'uzatges es aitals	28053–63
12	173.11	Humils e mercejans	28074–86
13	392.23	Mas per sso m'en vueilh estener	28098–107

14	392.23	Pero be say, si·m dezesper	28121–30
15	10.17	Quar cell qui se mezeis desmen	28139–42
16	70.28	A vos mi clam, senhor	28149–56
17	305.16	Peire Vidals es le deriers	28167–72
18	155.21	Amors, per sso mi soi hieu recrezutz	28181–88
19	155.21	Ab bell semblan que fals'amors adutz	28195–202
20	155.16	Mas vos no·m par puscatz far failimen	28217–24
21	293.18	Fams ni mortaudatz ni guerra	28231–36
22	293.18	Brus Marcz, le filhs Marcabruna	28246–51
23	404.5	E tug aquist quez eron bon trobaire	28280–89
24	392.28	D'amor digs mal e mas autras cansos	28319–20
25	375.23	Anc pueis no fe·l segles mas decazer	28383–84
26	10.40	Per razo natural	28393–402
27	trouvère	Ge ne sui pass si cum sel'autra gant	28422–29
28	166.1	Quor qu'ieu chantess dezamatz	28438–47
29	70.29	Mais ha d'amor qui domneja	28461–68
30	457.3	Mas una tals sazos es	28482–91
31	244.9	Totz hom qu'ab fin cor leial	28511–17
32	450.7	Per que val mais d'amor sso qu'om n'aten	28527–34
33	124.6	Ben ai' amors quar anc me fetz chauzir	28549–56
34	5.3	Amors apoder' e vens	28571–82
35	210.14	Ar aujatz quant ha de poder	28592–99
36	65.1	Amors no garda pro ni dan	28613–22
37	406.20	Ben es nescis a lei de tos	28630–37
38	10.27	E s'ieu cum fols siec mon dan folamen	28645–51
39	10.2	Mas anc no vi fin'aimansa	28661–68
40	133.8	Mas cell que vol tot jorn esser senatz	28680–87
41	70.23	Una falsa deschauzida	28727–34
42	249.1	Aichi cum cell qu'a la lebre cassada	28745–52
43	297.5	Lunhs homs no fai savieza	28766–74

(Continued)

Ricketts #	PC	Opening line	Breviari lines
44	10.15	Cell qui s'irais ni guerej' ab amor	28786–93
45	223.2	Si·m faitz me mezeis oblidar	28814–17
46	9.3	Tan m'es al cor que, quan de lieis cossir	28827–34
47	10.43	Pos ma bela mal'amia	28840–47
48	167.53	Mantas sazos s'esdeve	28856–64
49	70.41	Be sai la nueg, quan mi despuelh	28873–80
50	124.16	Ai! quant badailh e quant sospir	28889–96
51	30.4	Ves qualque part qu'ieu an ni torn ni vire	28912–18
52	10.7	Hai! co m'an mort vostre bell hueilh e vos	28925–32
53	5.1	Si las lagremas qu'ieu plor	28942–52
54	213.3	Mas hieu, lass! que sueffre l'ardor	28962–68
55	355.7	Que·l febles corss vai sospiran	28976–82
56	10.12	Anc mais lunh tems no trobiei liador	28993–9000
57	10.24	Eisamen cum l'azimans	29010–17
58	155.18	E s'ieu anc jorn fui gais ni amoros	29027–36
59	70.45	Amors m'à mes en soan	29057–63
60	155.21	Fells for' ieu trop, mas so m'en retengutz	29087–94
61	155.14	S'er no·us vens, venqutz soi, amors	29103–12
62	trouvère	Rois de Navare, sire de vertus	29142–50
63	10.7	A vos, amors mezeicha, ·m clam de vos	29162–69
64	370.3	Ben aio·ilh mal e·ilh afan e·ilh cossir	29179–87
65	364.4	Estra mon grat am tot sols per egal	29195–202
66	167.35	Le mals qu'ieu trai mi fora bells e bos	29214–21
67	167.53	Amix, quan se vol partir	29235–43
68	70.31	Ben es mortz qui d'amor no sen	29252–59
69	106.16	Nuls hom no viu ni renha ab amor	29276–85
70	421.1	Irat me ten e joios	29299–307

71	10.15	Que·ilh plazer son plus que·ilh enueg d'amor	29317–24
72	337.1	Que·l fuocs que m'art es d'un'aital natura	29338–42
73	366.19	E vueilh be qu'amors m'assalha	29351–58
74	10.8	Ni fin'amors, sso vos man	29377–85
75	10.8	Quar li hueilh son drogoman	29394–402
76	262.3	Nulhs hom no·s meravilh de mi	29417–22
77	10.8	E seilh que si van claman	29435–43
78	155.5	Ben an mort me e lor	29453–62
79	457.3	Anc enemics qu'ieu hagues	29476–85
80	167.35	Be m'an trait siei bell hueilh amoros	29507–14
81	10.43	Peitz m'es que si m'ausizia	29528–35
82	450.6	Ges bona domna non quereilh	29562–69
83	450.7	Qu'ieu vi d'amor que·lh gaug e·ilh ris e·ilh sen	29586–93
84	293.18	Aitan quan l'avers li dura	29607–12
85	332.1	Qui en luoc femenil	29625–33.1
86	332.1	Si las tenetz ta vil	29649–57.1
87	335.53	En jurar de femna no·m fi	29661–66
88	70.43	De las donas mi dezesper	29675–82
89	trouvère	Un tans fu ja que ces dames amoient	29693–700
90	364.27	Non ai enemic tam brau	29716–22
91	62.1	L'escut e·l basto vueilh render	29737–45
92	370.9	Sa grans beutatz e·l ricz pretz qu'en lieis es	29776–84
93	449.5	Be·us dei amar sens neguna falhensa	29805–13
94	356.4	Be·m puesc los autres escarnir	29825–32
95	234.4	Ses tot dubtar hai chauzit la gensor	29841–48
96	202.11	Que tals mi tramet e·m manda	29855–62
97	124.14	En tan quom le cels garanda	29870–77
98	30.8	Si Dieus volgues lo seu ric pretz devire	29885–91
99	10.33	Mezur' e sen, qu'es razitz de totz bes	29899–906
100	421.1	Totas las belas faisos	29914–22

(Continued)

Ricketts #	PC	Opening line	Breviari lines
101	375.21	Si totz los gaugz e·ls bes	29932–40
102	392.28	Jois e jovens et avinens faisos	29951–58
103	9.15	Regardan la vei gensor	29965–73
104	5.1	Mielhs de dona, mielhs d'amor	29977–87
105	364.39	Bona dona, Dieu cug vezer	29992–99
106	364.11	D'onrat pretz nominatiu	30003–12
107	372.3	Domna, mon corss e mon castell vos ren	30018–25
108	406.7	Tug li trobador egual	30037–46
109	225.7	Be·m platz qu'ieu chan, quan pes la gran honor	30055–63
110	297.3	De midons puesc hieu dir en tota plassa	30090–97
111	406.24	Amors ha tans de bos mestiers	30115–22
112	213.3	Quar donas fan valer adess	30127–33
113	34.2	S'anc amors tornet en desses	30160–66
114	30.18	Domna vol qu'om sia privatz	30187–95
115	404.5	Non puesc mudar no·n digua mon vejaire	30210–19
116	163.1	Dins sa maizo s'eschai	30278–307
117	225.7	Trop fai son dan dona que·s don ricor	30331–38
118	355.13	Dona promet e don'estrai	30369–77
119	47.6	Ilh no promet ni autreja	30403–11
120	10.2	Quar no sab, a ma semblansa	30425–32
121	163.1	Donas, qui·us ve vezer	30461–500
122	30.18	A dona non eschai beutatz	30510–18
123	461.86	D'ome foll ni desconoichen	30538–45
124	461.86	Mas qui vol entieira lauzor	30557–64
125	406.12	Be vol qu'om gen la cortei	30574–82
126	106.18	En re, al meu escien	30600–30610
127	10.41	Per sso·m so·ilh mal qu'ieu n'ai plazen	30627–34

128	163.1	Seguon qu'ome veiretz	30641–78
129	10.23	Domna, per vos estauc en greu torment	30696–719
130	70.1	Ben s'eschai a domn' ardimens	30727–30
131	364.11	E fa·s temer plus de griu	30739–48
132	370.3	E fin' amors no manda ges cauzir	30764–72
133	11.2	Domna, be sai qu'à vostra valor gran	30782–89
134	392.19	Vilas es et otracujatz	30807–17
135	30.15	Domna, per gran temensa	30837–46
136	30.3	Vos valetz tan que cre que conoscatz	30856–62
137	406.7	Que qui trop mais que no val	30882–84
138	297.1	Cell que ditz qu'ell leialmen	30909–15
139	63.6	Pro sab e ben es apres	30969–79
140	293.31	Domna no sab d'amor fina	30995–1001
141	392.19	Be pot hom en autruis foudatz	31068–78
142	155.11	Qu'ells falhimens d'autrui tanh qu'om se mir	31081–82
143	375.3	Astrucs es cell cui amors ten joios	31104–12
144	305.14	E ja de lieis bes no·m venha	31163–71
145	392.2	Anc non amet tan aut quom hieu negus	31177–84
146	335.6	Aquestas gens, quan son en lur guaieza	31199–206
147	225.10	Mas hieu non dic sia enamoratz	31223–31
148	225.10	Pero a mi no sobret volontatz	31243–51
149	461.134	Gran dezir hai de ben jazer	31267–74
150	225.10	Quar ges li pro, el tems que n'es passatz	31302–10
151	167.15	Mans drutz i ha e domnas, si·n parlatz	31324–33
152	167.15	Chant e deport, joi, domnei e solatz	31343–52
153	335.50	Amors, qui la semeness	31370–78
154	397a.1	Qui vol jauzir de donas e d'amor	31426–33
155	461.149	Luocs es qu'om chan e que s'en lais	31445–48
156	461.87	Domna, Dieus mi sal vos e la vostra valor	31460–65
157	70.1	Bona domna, vostre cors gens	31473–80

(Continued)

Ricketts #	PC	Opening line	Breviari lines
158	16.9	Destreitz d'amors, venc denan vos	31508–39
159	355.3	Er ai ben d'amor apres	31564–87
160	366.33	La nueg quan sui anatz jazer	31604–11
161	356.4	Ailass!—Que·t planhs?—Ja tem morir	31619–34
162	32.1	Be volgra midons saubes	31643–86
163	341.1	Messier Matfre, pus de cosseilh	31693–712
164	297.2	Cumpair', en aitan quo·l soleilh	31714–23
165	366.13	Be vuelh s'amor, mas querre non l'aus ges	31733–39
166	461.101	E doncz que val aquest amars	31768–75
167	70.31	Bela domna, re no·us deman	31780–87
168	70.26	Mal o fara, si no·m manda	31800–31806
169	364.30	A drut de bona dona tanh	31821–28
170	106.18	Pero chantan e rizen	31836–46
171	155.16	Pero, quan failh cell qu'es pros ni prezatz	31888–89
172	461.210	Qui enten en amar	31970–72
173	10.15	Enquaras truep mais de bes en amor	31977–84
174	173.3	Quar dobla valors	31989–92
175	461.98	Dos gratz conquer hom ab .i. do	32000–32006
176	376.1	Qui gran cor ha de larguejar	32018–25
177	unidentified	Qui mai despen que no guazanha	32029–30
178	392.19	Ja homs pres ni desbaratatz	32040–50
179	461.123b	Fraire, tot lo sen e·l saber	32052–61
180	225.11	Dieus, quo pot haver sufrensa	32073–81
181	225.13	Homes trob' om larcs e mal conoichens	32097–104
182	124.10	Joios son hieu et hai mestier	32116–25
183	406.20	Pauc val qui non es emvejos	32129–32
184	461.21	Amors vol drut cavalguador	32135–45

185	364.17	Be·s tanh qu'ieu si' arditz	32148–49
186	364.18	D'ardimen valh Rotlan ez Olivier	32153–58
187	106.2	A faire gran vassalatge	32173–83
188	106.2	Temer deu om vilanatge	32189–91
189	406.20	E per amor es om cortes	32197–99
190	293.32	Qui ses bauzia	32206–14
191	163.1	Cortezia es tals	32222–41
192	293.15	De cortezia·s pot vanar	32244–49
193	293.15	Mezura es en gen parlar	32251–56
194	364.43	Qu'om no·s deuria tarzar	32260–69
195	167.62	Tug cilh quez amo valor	32274–82
196	29.6	Re no val ergueilh d'aimador	32289–90
197	375.27	S'umilitatz la·m fai humiliar	32298–306
198	155.16	Per Dieu, amors, be sabetz veramen	32316–23
199	70.21	Per re non es hom tan prezans	32334–41
200	124.2	No sab de domnei pauc ni pro	32368–77
201	392.30	Si ja amors autre pro no·m tengues	32381–87
202	355.18	Tostems aug dir q'us jois autre n'adutz	32393–400
203	30.1	A gran honor vieu cui jois es cobitz	32409–15
204	450.3	Mas d'una re sui en greus pessamens	32425–30
205	183.11	Obediensa deu portar	32435–40
206	297.7	Retenemens es mot nobla vertutz	32447–54
207	461.132	Ges, per frachura de saber	32458–65
208	355.20	Honramens grans cre que·l n'eschai	32473–81
209	376.1	Qui som bom pretz vol tener car	32488–95
210	450.3	Ab los joios deu hom esser jauzens	32516–21
211	461.32	Atretan leu pot hom ab cortezia	32533–38.1
212	461.227	Tals conois busqu' en l'autrui uelh	32553–62
213	163.1	Totz hom fora cortes	32564–67
214	29.9	Amors es de pretz la claus	32573–80

(Continued)

Ricketts #	PC	Opening line	Breviari lines
215	450.3	E qui·us cujatz que·us sia defendens	32591–96
216	194.19	Tan quant hom fai aquo que deu, es pros	32608–15
217	356.7	Guardatz que vos puscatz tener	32617–23
218	356.7	Qu'ab pro manjar ez ab jazer	32634–40
219	335.5	Qu'al frug conois hom lo fruchier	32685
220	364.39	Quant hom es en autrui poder	33159–66
221	364.39	E qui vol el segle caber	33176–83
222	248.18	Conoichensa ha tans de mestiers bos	33191–97
223	364.39	Tant hai de sen e de saber	33206–13
224	30.VI	Ja non aura proeza	33218–31
225	297.4	Dregz de natura comanda	33239–49
226	225.11	On mais ha hom de valensa	33262–70
227	10.15	Bona domna, de vos tenc e d'amor	33276–83
228	70.15	Ja Dieus no·m do aquel poder	33290–96
229	30.5	Julis Sezars conquis la senhoria	33304–10
230	411.III	Us homes i a nualhos	33319–27
231	202.1	Que bos esforss malastre vens	33330
232	372.3	Ar agues hieu mil marcz de fin argen	33341–48
233	421.10	Quar sens e pretz, largueza e valors	33360–67
234	242.71	Cel es drutz truans	33489–98
235	70.1	D'una re m'aonda mos sens	33506–13
236	155.1	Quar s'ieu no·m sai celar, non es razos	33514.2–3
237	461.91	Dona, no·i havetz dezonor	33522–28
238	225.10	Nulhs hom no val ni deu esser prezatz	33538–46
239	364.39	E qui pot e no vol voler	33550–57
240	71.3	Esquass no vol qu'om lo pessuc	33565–69
241	461.48	Ben es nessis e dezaventuros	33579–86

Appendix II   387

242	392.27	Mot fai gran vilanatge	33596–99
243	421.10	E per aisso vuelh sufrir las dolors	33606–13
244	421.5	Qu'aichi ve bes apress honor	33616–23
245	124.16	Anc no cugiei que per maldir	33631–38
246	366.9	Soven l'anera vezer	33648–55
247	70.1	Non es enuegz ni falhimens	33666–73
248	70.25	Ben es dretz qu'ieu planha	33681–92
249	30.23	Bona domna, paratges e ricors	33699–706
250	392.19	Hieu dic que ben es estraguatz	33714–24
251	364.4	Anc no mori per amor ni per al	33736–43
252	370.14	Si ma foudatz m'enguana ni m'ausi	33757–64
253	10.33	Qu'a mi eis dic lo plus bel prec qu'ieu pes	33770–77
254	225.13	Homes trob' om larcs e mal conoichens	33853–55
255	132.4	Ben deu hom son bo senhor	33911–18
256	132.4	Atressi·s deu hom d'amor	33921–28
257	10.12	Atressi·m pren quo fai al joguador	33947–54
258	167.56	S'om pogues partir so voler	33962–71
259	297.6	Mens la pres que volp en estieu	34083–90
260	380.2	Per oblidar cela que pus m'agensa	34143–49
261	106.22	E senhers qu'adess vol traire	34169–72
262	461.155	Hieu am midons de bona guiza	34210–17
263	335.7	Mas deu hom amar vencedor	34277–86
264	335.38	Homs, quar no·t sove	34298–312
265	335.11	Ben tenc per foll e per muzart	34326–45
266	335.11	Tals se cuja calfar que s'art	34509
267	335.48	Que Dieus te son arc tendut	34535–39

Troubadour Quotations in *De vulgari eloquentia* in Relation to the Preceding Tradition of Quotation

This appendix lists in PC order the incipits quoted by Dante as they appear in Botterill's edition and indicates their place and role in Dante's text. It then indicates other quotations of this same incipit, song, and troubadour. The order in which entries are listed in the last three columns is that of Appendix 1: (1) grammars (in chronological order), (2) *novas* of Raimon Vidal, (3) biographies, (4) the *Breviari d'amor*, (5) any other quotations, and (6) *florilegia* included in Appendix 2.

Troubadour	Incipit as quoted by Dante	PC	Where quoted in DVE	Reason quoted	Same incipit quoted elsewhere (including as rubric in florilegia)	Other passages of same song quoted elsewhere	Same troubadour quoted elsewhere
Aimeric de Belenoi	Nuls hom non pot complir adrecciamen	9.14	2.6.6	Illustrious *canso* because of its construction	(6) DcFaG	(6) DcFaG	(4) *Breviari*; (6) DcFaG
			2.12.3	Monometric hendecasyllabic stanza			

Aimeric de Peguilhan	Si con l'arbres che per sobrecarcar	10.50	2.6.6	Illustrious *canso* because of its construction	(6) *DcFa*	(6) *DcFa*	(1) *ReT, Mi*; (4) *Breviari*; (6) *DcFa*
Arnaut Daniel	L'aura amara fa·l bruol brancuz clarzir	29.13	2.2.8	Exemplifies subject matter of love			(1) *Ri, Mi, Leys* 1341; (2) misattributions in version *r* of *So*; (3) Arnaut's *vida* and one *razo*; (4) *Breviari*; (6) *Fa*
	Se·m fos Amor de ioi donar	29.17	2.13.2	*Rims estramps* (stanza containing no internal rhymes)	(6) *Fa*	(6) *Fa*. Note that 80.29 is a *contrafactum* of this song.	
	Sols sui che sai lo sobraffan che·m sorz	29.18	2.6.6	Illustrious *canso* because of its construction	(6) *Fa*		
Bertran de Born	Non posc mudar c'un cantar non exparia	80.29	2.2.8	Exemplifies subject matter of arms	(3) *Razo* XI.R to this song (in *FIK*)		(1) *RaT, ReT*; (2) *Ab, So*; (3) many *razos*; (6) *DcFaj*
Folquet de Marselha	Tan m'abellis l'amoros pensamen	155.22	2.6.6	Illustrious *canso* because of its construction	(6) *Fa*		(1) *RaT, DA, ReT, Mi*; (2) *Ab, So*; (3) many *razos*; (4) *Breviari*; (5) Jofre de Foixà 304.1; (6) *DcFaHJ*

Troubadour	Incipit as quoted by Dante	PC	Where quoted in DVE	Reason quoted	Same incipit quoted elsewhere (including as rubric in florilegia)	Other passages of same song quoted elsewhere	Same troubadour quoted elsewhere
Giraut de Borneil	Ara ausirez encabalitz cantarz	242.17	2.5.4	Use of the preferred line length, the hendecasyllable	(1) *Mi* (169-70)	(1) *Mi* (170–74)	(1) *RaT, DA, Mi*; (2) *Ab, So*; (3) several *razos*; (4) *Breviari*; (6) *DcJ*
	Per solaz reveilar che s'est trop endormitz	242.55	2.2.8	Exemplifies subject matter of "rectitude"	(3) *Razo* VIII.G (in *Sg*)	(2) *Ab*	
	Si·m sentis fezelz amics per ver encusera amor	242.72	1.9.3	Consistency of word *amor* across Romance	(1) *Mi* (323–24) (6) *Dc*	(6) *Dc*	
	Si per mos Sobretos non fos	242.73	2.6.6	Illustrious *canso* because of its construction	(3) *Razo* VIII.E (in *Sg*) (6) *Dc*	(6) *Dc*	

Troubadour Quotations in Berenguer d'Anoia's *Mirall de trobar*

Quotations in the order they appear in the *Mirall*. The numbers in the first column are those assigned by Alcover in his edition.

#	Troubadour	Song	Lines quoted	Reason for quotation	Lines in the Mirall
1	Giraut de Bornelh	242.66	1–4	Metaplasm: prosthesis (addition of a syllable at the beginning of a word)	123–26
2	Giraut de Bornelh	242.31	1–2	Incipit	132–33
			61–62, 132–34	2nd example of prosthesis	
3	Giraut de Bornelh	242.16	1	Incipit	154–61
			77–93	Metaplasm: aphaeresis (removal of a syllable from the beginning of a word)	
4	Giraut de Bornelh	242.17	1–2	Incipit	169–74
			37–44	2nd example of aphaeresis	
5	Gaucelm Faidit	167.45	1	Incipit	196–98
			197–98	Metaplasm: epenthesis (adding syllable in the middle of a word)	

#	Troubadour	Song	Lines quoted	Reason for quotation	Lines in the Mirall
6	Elias de Barjols (attrib. Gaucelm Faidit)	132.3	1	Incipit	209–17
			9–18	2nd example of epenthesis	
7	Folquet de Marselha	155.10	1	Incipit	236–42
			28–34	Metaplasm: syncope (removal of a syllable from the middle of a word)	
8	Raimon de Miraval	406.31	1	Incipit	247–54
			9–16	2nd example of syncope	
9	Folquet de Marselha	155.6	1	Incipit	272–76
			28–31	Metaplasm: paragoge (adding a final syllable)	
10	Peire Vidal	364.42	1	Incipit	283–89
			19–24	2nd example of paragoge	
11	Giraut de Bornelh	242.59	1	Incipit	313–16
			25–6	Metaplasm: apocope (taking away a final syllable)	
12	Giraut de Bornelh	242.72	1–2	2nd example of apocope	323–24
13	Aimeric de Peguilhan	10.41	1	Incipit	339–46
			33–40	Metaplasm: epizeuxis (repetition of a word), here *merce merce*	
14	Peire Vidal	364.36a (unknown elsewhere)	1	Incipit	352–57
				2nd example of epizeuxis	
15	Raimbaut d'Aurenga (attrib. Guillem de Sant Leidier)	389.18	1	Incipit	366–80
			9–16	Metaplasm: antiphrasis (saying the contrary of what is meant)	
			17–25	2nd example of antiphrasis	

16	Izarn Rizol (att. to Peirol)	257.1	1	Incipit	445–48
			33–4	Vices: *amphibola* (ambiguity)	
17	Bernart de Ventadorn	70.31	1	Incipit	454–58
			49–51	2nd example of *amphibola*	
18	Raimon de Miraval	406.20	1–2	Incipit	471–76
			33–38	Vices: tautology	
19	Aimeric de Peguilhan	10.7	1	Incipit, 2nd example of tautology	484–85
20	Folquet de Marselha	155.6	1	Incipit	493–94
			19–20, 22–24	Vices: *assirologia* (incorrect use of words)	
21	Aimeric de Peguilhan	10.7	1	Incipit	505–11
			9–14	2nd example of *assirologia*	
22	Bernart de Ventadorn (attrib. Peirol)	70.19	1	Incipit	520–23
			33–36	Vices: hiatus (juxtaposing a word ending in a vowel with one that starts with a vowel)	
23	Bernart de Ventadorn	70.1	1	Incipit	530–35
			17–21	2nd example of hiatus	
24	Giraut de Bornelh	242.48	1	Incipit	543–46
			45–47	Vices: *metatisme* (enclisis or proclisis—foreshortening a word and attaching it to another starting with a vowel)	
25	Aimeric de Peguilhan	10.16	1	Incipit	551–55
			17–21	2nd example of *metatisme*	

#	Troubadour	Song	Lines quoted	Reason for quotation	Lines in the Mirall
26	Guillem de Sant Leidier	234.16	1	Rhetorical ornament: anadiplosis (rotation of rhyme words to different positions in the song)	602–3
27	Arnaut Daniel	29.14	1	2nd example of anadiplosis	610
—	[Berenguer d'Anoia?]	unknown elsewhere		Rhetorical ornament: *agnominacio* (same form but with different meanings placed at the beginning or end of consecutive lines)	617–18
28	Attrib. Arnaut Daniel	unknown elsewhere		2nd example of *agnominacio*	619–20
29	Guilhem Ademar	202.4	1–3	Rhetorical ornament: *gradasia* (accumulation of forms derived from the same root)	629–31
30	Aimeric de Peguilhan	10.18	1–4	Rhetorical ornament: repetition (the same form repeated at the beginning of a series of phrases)	639–42
31	Raimbaut d'Aurenga (attrib. Raimbaut de Vaqueiras)	389.1	1–3	2nd example of repetition	645–46
—	[Berenguer d'Anoia?]	unknown elsewhere		Rhetorical ornament: *traductio* (the same expression used with different meanings)	653
32	Peire Cardenal	335.6	1	Incipit	662–69
			9–16	Rhetorical ornament: *sinatism* (repetition of a single word with the same meaning harnessed to praise or blame)	
—	[Berenguer d'Anoia?]	unknown elsewhere		Rhetorical ornament: *anapolensis* (the same rhyme or line begins and ends a stanza)	675–81

Troubadour Quotations in Guilhem Molinier's *Leys d'amors*

Comparison between the use of troubadour quotations, and mentions of the troubadours, in the 1341 and the 1356 prose redactions of the *Leys*. Reference is by volume and page number in the two editions. That by Gatien-Arnoult of the earlier redaction prints its five books in three volumes (books 1 and 2 in vol. 1, book 3 in vol. 2, and books 4 and 5 in vol. 3); Anglade's edition prints each of the three books of the later redaction in a separate volume.

Gatien-Arnoult, ed., Las flors del gay saber estier dichas (1341)	*Anglade, ed., Las leys d'amors (1356)*		
[no equivalent]	Book	1:68 At de Mons 309.I, 471–79 (the rational soul)	
	1	1:70 At de Mons 309.V, 77–94 (the value of transmitting one's learning according to one's capacities)	
		1:84–85 At de Mons 309.V, 488–502 (the basis of rhetoric)	
		1:85–86 At de Mons 309.V, 503–32 (the basis of rhetoric, cont.)	
		1:87 At de Mons 309.V, 534–63 (the basis of rhetoric, cont.)	
		1:106 At de Mons 309.V, 445–50 (discipline is essential to learning)	
		1:106–7 At de Mons 309.IV, 111–54 (on vices, especially the arrogance and covetousness of the powerful)	

Gatien-Arnoult, ed., Las flors del gay saber estier dichas (1341)		Anglade, ed., Las leys d'amors (1356)	
			1:118 At de Mons 309.IV, 186–200 (condemning flatterers)
			1:118–19 At de Mons 309.II, 134–57 (condemning flatterers, cont.)
			1:127 At de Mons 309.V, 564–72 (condemning lies)
Books 1 and 2	1:138 At de Mons cited but not quoted (ex. of verse form for *novas rimadas*)	2	2:118, as 1341
	1:248–50 At de Mons 309.2 (ex. of a stanza form)		2:129, as 1341
	1:250 incipits of two stanzas, one of them At de Mons, 309.2, quoted anonymously, the other the anonymous "Flors de paradis," 461.123 (exs. of stanza forms)		2:131, as 1341
	1:316 P[eire] Arquier (unknown troubadour) (ex. of acrostic verse)		2:160, as 1341, quoted but without attribution
	1:334 En Raimbaut [de Vaqueiras], 392.4, 41–50 (ex. of multilingual *descort*)		2:172–73, as 1341, quoted but without attribution
3	2:78 At de Mons, 309.V, 966, 965, 967–70 and 309.V, 541–42 (ex. of use of case with prepositions)	3	3:41–42, as 1341
	2:86 two unidentified lines attrib. At de Mons (ex. of singular verb after singular nouns joined by copula)		3:44, as 1341
	[no equivalent]		3:65–66 At de Mons 309.V, 600–604, quoted but without attribution (ex. of enclisis)
	[a shorter version of this quotation appears at 2:236, see below]		3:109 At de Mons 309.V, 58–76 (on language change and variation) (= expanded version of the quotation in 1341, book 3, 2:236)

	2:210 reference to the observance of the case system by the *antic troubador* [no actual quotations]	3:114, as 1341
	2:236 At de Mons 309.IV, 319–20; 309.V, 58–61; and an otherwise unknown line attrib. At de Mons "Gaugz se pren de plazer" (exs. of reflexive for passive)	3:128 two of the three quotations found in the 1341 text: At de Mons 309.V, 58–59; and "Gaugz se pren de plazer"
	2:256 At de Mons 309.V, 578–81 (*deura* for *deu*)	[no equivalent]
	2:370 At de Mons, 309.V, 87–88 (*cre* for *crey*)	[no equivalent]
	2:388 At de Mons, 309.IV, 319–20 (authorizing the usage of Toulouse)	3:163, as 1341
	2:390 At de Mons, 309.V, 578–79 (*deura* for *deu*), "Gaugz se pren de plazer" (*pren* for *pres*); 309.V, 58–59 (*cambia* for *cambiatz*)	3:164, as 1341 but exs. reduced to one, At de Mons 309.V, 578–79
	2:392 At de Mons (ex. of Toulouse dialectal usage), 309.V, 130–31	no equivalent]
4	3:62 At de Mons, 309.V, 210–11 (venial case of *paronomasia*)	[no equivalent]
	3:216 At de Mons named as author of a corpus (ex. of metonymy)	
	3:286 incipit of Peire Vidal 364.36, quoted anonymously (ex. of *icon*)	
	3:286 incipit of Rigaut de Berbezilh 421.2, quoted anonymously (ex. of *icon*)	
	3:286 incipit of anonymous song (Thibaut de Champagne? Or its Occitan model?) (ex. of *icon*)	
	3:330 incipit of Arnaut Daniel 29.14 (ex. of *compar* or harmonious near-equality of syllables, and of *rimas estrampas*)	

Comparison Between Passages from Albertano da Brescia and the 1356 Redaction of the *Leys d'amors*

Sentences are numbered for ease of comparison; bold typeface is used to pick out the skeleton of the argument, which is then fleshed out with quotations.

PASSAGE A

Albertano da Brescia, Liber de doctrina dicendi et tacendi, *ed. Paola Navone, pp. 24–26.*

[1] **Item requiras utrum inspienti an sapienti loquaris.**

[2] Ait enim Salomon: "In auribus insipientium ne loquaris, quia despicient doctrinam eloquii tui."

[3] Et iterum: "Vir sapiens si cum stulto contenderit, sive irascitur sive rideat, non inveniet requiem.

[4] Et iterum: Non recipit stultus verba prudentie, nisi ea dixeris que versantur corde suo."

[5] Et Jesus Sirac dixit: "Cum dormiente loquitur qui narrat stulto sapientiam et in fine narrationis dicet 'Quis est hic?'"

Guilhem Molinier's adaptation in Las leys d'amors, *ed. Anglade, 1:91–92.*

[1] **De parlar am fol se deu hom gardar,**

[2] quar Salamos ditz que hom no deu parlar am fol home, quar hom que es fols no troba plazers en bonas paraulas ni en bona doctrina.

[3] En autre loc ditz: "savis homs que conten o s'iraysh o ri o ganha am fol no trobara repaus."

[4] Encaras ditz enayssi: "le fols no recep paraulas de savieza, mas be pren e recep qui li ditz so que porta en son cor."

[5] Jesus Sirac ditz: "qui reconta paraulas de saviez a fol ayssi es cum parlar am cel que dorm."

[6] **Item requiras ne cum irrisore loquaris.**

[7] Scriptum est enim: "Cum irrisore consortium non habeas, loquele eius assiduitatem quasi toxica fugias. Societas eius cui laqueus est, alternaque affabilitas despectio."

[8] Et Salomon dixit: "Noli arguere irrisorem, ne te oderit. Argue sapientem et diliget te."

[9] Et Seneca dixit: "Qui corripit irrisorem ipse sibi iniuriam facit. Qui arguit impium ipse sibi maculam querit."

[10] **Item requiras ne cum linguoso vel loquaci colloquium habeas.**

[11] Ait enim propheta: "Vir linguosus non dirigetur in terra."

[12] Et Jesus Sirac dixit: "Terribilis est in civitate sua homo linguosus et temerarius in verbo suo odibilis erit."

[13] Et iterum: "Qui odit loquacitatem extinguit malitiam."

[14] Et alibi idem dixit: "Cum viro linguoso non loquaris nec in ignem illius struas ligna."

[15] Et alibi idem ait: "Ne cum fatuis consilium habeas: non enim poterunt diligere nisi que eis placent."

[16] **Item requires ne cum cinicis multum loquaris.**

[17] Ait enim Tullius: "Ratio cinicorum penitus abicienda est."

[18] "Cinos" grece, latine dicitur "canis"; inde "cinici" dicuntur latrantes ut canes.

[19] De quibus et similibus Dominus dixit: "Nolite proicere margaritas inter porcos."

[6] **Amb hom janglayre, estribotayre ni escarnidor no deu hom gayre parlar,**

[7] quar escriut es que am escarnidor ne deu hom aver companhia, ans enayssi co hom fug a tueyshec et a vere, deu hom fugir a sas paraulas;

[8] e per so ditz Salamos: "No vuelhas reprendre escarnidor per que no t'haja en odi ni t'escarnissca; repren lo savi et aquel te amera."

[9] E Seneca ditz: "qui repren escarnidor enjuria fa a si meteysh, quar qui repren fol serca quo sia sulhatz e vil tengutz."

[10] **Amb hom parlier e lengos no deu hom gayre parlar.**

[11] Le propheta David: "homs lengos no sera endressatz en terra."

[12] Jesus Sirac: "fols homs e lengos es cauza mot terribbla en ciutat," e d'aytal ditz que en sas paraulas sera mot odios.

[13] El meteysh "qui azira locacitat, so es parlaria, escantish maleza."

[14] En autre loc ditz: "Am home lengos no vuelhas parlar si·l sieu foc no vols alucar."

[15] Encaras ditz: "Amb homes nescis e fatz not·t vuelhas acosselhar, quar no aman mas so que lor platz, so es folia."

[16] **Amb homes entercz, natres e regancz no deu hom gayre parlar.**

[17] Aytals homes regancz apella Tullis *cinicis*,

[18] quar *cinos* en grec vol dire *ca*. Et per so ditz Tullis que de la razo ni del parlar d'aytals homes cinicis, entercz, natres e regancz e tot jorn layrans a maniera de ca no deu hom curar;

[19] e sembla que en aysso hajan loc las paraulas de Jhesu nostre Salvayre: "no vuelhatz semenar margaridas, so es peyras preciozas, entre porcz."

PASSAGE B

De ira vitanda in consiliis (*Albertano da Brescia*, Liber consolationis et consilii, *chap. 12*).

[1] **Primo itaque provideas, ne iratus vel ab irato consilium petas;**

[2] et hoc multis rationibus: **prima, quia iratus semper plus putat posse facere, quam possit, et ideo posse suum superat;**
[3] scriptum est enim:

Qui plus posse putat, sua quam natura ministrat,
Posse suum superans, se minus esse potest.

[4] **Secunda vero ratione, quia "iratus nil nisi criminis loquitur [loco],"** ut Seneca dixit; et ita te et alios ad iram cito provocares, nam "lex videt iratum, iratus non videt illam."

[5] **Tertia vero ratione, quia ira impedit animum;** quare Cato dixit:

Iratus de re incerta contendere noli:

Ira impedit animum, ne possit cernere verum.

De las cauzas qu'om deu esquivar en cosselh (*ed. Anglade, 1:147–48*).

[1] **Primieramen osta de te ira e d'aquel o d'aquels que volras per cosselhiers.** Quar hom que·s carga d'ira e vol cosselh d'ome irat aytals cosselhs a penas pot haver bona fi per motas bonas razos.

[2] **La primiera quar hom qu'es iratz mays cuja far que non pot.**

[3] Et enayssi passa e sobremonta son poder e per conseguen mes fa; per que ditz Seneca enayssi:

Qui plus posse putat sua quam natura ministrat
Posse suum superans se minus ipse potest.

Soes a dire:
Qui de far mays a cura
Que no ha per natura,
Per cug son poder passa,
Don cove que mens fassa.

[4] **La segonda razos: quar qui es iratz e corrossatz a penas parlara temprada-men, mas braydivamen e de cauza mala e criminoza blaspheman, maldizen e condempnan.**

[5] **La tersa razo pauza Cato enayssi:** "Can seras iratz, no cotendas de cauza no certa, quar ira enpacha lo coratge d'ome et tant que·l tol a vezer la vertat."
L'Actors:
Iratz que de no cert conten
la vertat no ve claramen
quar ira fa la pessa trista
e al coratge tol la vista.

Petrarch's "Lasso me"

The text follows the edition by Bettarini (*Canzoniere*, no. 70). As in Appendix 9, italics are used to mark the quoted incipits, and their authors are identified following the translation in the facing column.

Lasso me, ch' i' non so in qual parte pieghi la speme, ch' è tradita omai piú volte: che se non è chi con pietà m'ascolte, perché sparger al ciel sí spessi preghi? 5 Ma s'egli aven ch' ancor non mi si nieghi finir anzi 'l mio fine queste voci meschine, non gravi al mio signor perch' io il ripreghi di dir libero un dí tra l'erba e i fiori: 10 *"Drez et rayson es qu'ieu ciant em demori."*	Alas, weary me, for I do not know where to direct the hope that has now been betrayed so many times. For if there is no one to offer me an ear of pity, why cast so many prayers to heaven? But if it should come about that I am not refused an end, before my end, to these wretched words, may it not grieve my lord that I beg him once more to say one day, free in the grass and flowers, *"It's right and just that I should sing and feel pleasure."* [?]

Ragion è ben ch'alcuna volta io canti, però ch' ò sospirato sí gran tempo, che mai non incomincio assai per tempo per adequar col riso i dolor' tanti. 15 E s'io potesse far ch'agli occhi santi porgesse alcun dilecto qualche dolce mio detto, o me beato sopra gli altri amanti! Ma piú, quand' io dirò senza mentire: 20 "*Donna mi priegha, per ch' io voglio dire.*"	There is good reason that I should sing sometimes, since I have been sighing for so long that I could never start soon enough to compensate for my many woes with laughter. If I could only make those holy eyes take some delight from some sweet saying of mine, how blessed would I be above all lovers! But more so, were I to say truthfully: "*A lady asks me, and so I wish to compose.*" [Guido Cavalcanti]
Vaghi pensier' che cosí passo passo scorto m'avete a ragionar tant' alto, vedete che madonna à 'l cor di smalto, sí forte, ch'io per me dentro nol passo. 25 Ella non degna di mirar sí basso che de nostre parole curi, ché 'l ciel non vòle al qual pur contrastando i' son già lasso: onde, com nel cor m'induro e 'naspro 30 *cosí nel mio parlar voglio esser aspro.*	You wandering thoughts that, as though step by step, have led me to reason so loftily, you can see that my lady has a heart of enamel so hard that, on my own, I cannot penetrate within it. She does not deign to look down low enough to care about our words, for heaven does not wish it, and I am weary now from battling against it: and from all this, as my heart grows hard and harsh, *so likewise in my speech I wish to be harsh.* [Dante Alighieri]
Che parlo? O dove sono? E chi m'inganna altri ch'i' stesso e'l desïar soverchio? Già s' i' trascorro il ciel di cerchio in cerchio, nessun pianeta a pianger mi condanna; 35 se mortal velo il mio veder appanna, che colpa è de le stelle o de le cose belle? Meco si sta chi dí e notte m' affanna, poi che del suo piacer me fe' gir grave 40 *la dolce vista e 'l bel guardo soave.*	What am I saying? or where am I? and who deceives me more than I myself, and my excessive desire? Even if I scour the heaven from sphere to sphere, no planet condemns me to lament. If a mortal veil covers my sight, what fault is it of the stars or of the things of beauty? The force that torments me day and night dwells within me, since *the sweet sight of her and her soft and lovely glance* overburden me with pleasure. [Cino da Pistoia]

Tutte le cose di che 'l mondo è adorno
uscír buone de man del mastro eterno;
ma me, che cosí adentro non discerno
abbaglia il bel che mi si mostra intorno;
45 et s' al vero splendor già mai ritorno,
l'occhio non pò star fermo:
cosí l'à fatto infermo
pur la sua propria colpa, e non quel giorno
ch' i' volsi inver l'angelica beltade
50 *nel dolce tempo de la prima etade.*

All things adorning the world with their beauty came forth good from the Master's hand, but I who cannot see so deeply within am dazzled by the beauty showing itself all about; and if I ever again turn back to the true light my eyes will not be able to withstand it, so weak have they become by their own fault and not by that of the day when I turned them toward her angelic beauty *in the sweet season of my youthful age.*

[Francesco Petrarca]

Key to *Sigla* of the Principal Manuscripts Discussed in This Book

For transcriptions and facsimiles consulted, see the "Primary Texts" section of the Bibliography.

BREVIARI D'AMOR

G   Vienna, Österreichische Nationalbibliothek, Hs 2583. Ca. 1350. Languedoc.

M   Madrid, Escurial, Biblioteca de San Lorenzo, S.I.3. Ca. 1350, Languedoc.

N   St. Petersburg, National Library of Russia, Hisp. F. v. XIV. 1. Ca.1320, Lerida (scribe from Avignon).

NOVAS

D, G, J, L, N, R, r: see "Troubadour *chansonniers*," below.

a^1 Archives départementales, Perpignan. Occitan fragment, now lost, published by Alart, "Un fragment."

a^2 Fragment published by Moliné i Brasés, "Textes catalans-provençals."

π Florence, Biblioteca Riccardiana, 2756.

OCCITAN TREATISES OF GRAMMAR AND POETICS

A Florence, Biblioteca Laurenziana, Aedilium 187. Thirteenth century, Italian. Also contains medical texts in French and Italian.

B Florence, Biblioteca Laurenziana, XLI.42. Early fourteenth century, northern Italian. (=Occitan *chansonnier P*; also contains an Occitan-Italian word list).

C Florence, Biblioteca Riccardiana, 2814. Late sixteenth-century Italian copy of a lost thirteenth-century manuscript (=Occitan *chansonnier a*).

D Milan, Biblioteca Ambrosiana, D. 465. Late sixteenth-century Italian miscellany; the *Donatz* is followed by a different rhyme list from that in *ABL*; also contains two Italian translations of the *Donatz*.

H Barcelona, Biblioteca Central, 239. Late fourteenth century, Catalan. The largest and most important collection of Occitan treatises.

L New York, Pierpont Morgan Library, MS M 831. End thirteenth/beginning fourteenth century, Italian. Also contains a fragment of a different rhyme list from the *Donatz*.

R Barcelona, Archiva de la Corona de Aragón, Ripoll 129. Mid-fourteenth-century Catalan miscellany from the monastery of Santa Maria de Ripoll, which includes Augustine's *Palma*; the treatises are followed by nineteen Catalan poems.

TROUBADOUR *CHANSONNIERS*

(All *sigla* are explicated in Pillet-Carstens and in the *BEdT*.)

A Vatican, Biblioteca Vaticana, Lat. 5232. Late thirteenth century, northern Italian.

a Florence, Biblioteca Riccardiana, 2814. Sixteenth-century paper manuscript ("the *chansonnier* of Bernart Amoros"). = Grammar manuscript *C*.

B Paris, Bibliothèque nationale de France, fr. 1592. Late thirteenth century. Origin debated: probably Occitan, but copied by an Italian scribe from an Italian model; might be Italian.

C Paris, Bibliothèque nationale de France, fr. 856. Fourteenth century, Occitan, region of Toulouse.

Cm Castagnolo Minore, Archivio Parrocchiale. Fragment of a *florilegium*.

D Modena, Biblioteca Estense, alpha, R, 4, 4. Mid-thirteenth century in its oldest part, northern Italian. *D* comprises several elements including *D* proper (fos. 1–151), *Da* (fos. 152–216) and *Dc* (fos. 243–60). *Da* is the oldest part of the manuscript (1254), compiled for Alberico da Romano. *Dc* is the *florilegium* of Ferrarino da Ferrara.

E   Paris, Bibliothèque nationale de France, fr. 1749. Fourteenth century. Like *B*, disputed between Occitania and Italy.

e   Vatican, Biblioteca Vaticana, Barb. Lat. 3965. Eighteenth-century Italian paper manuscript.

F   Vatican, Biblioteca Vaticana, , Chigi L.IV.106. Fourteenth century, northern Italian. The section referred to as *Fa* is the *florilegium* that extends from 13r to 62r.

G   Milan, Biblioteca Ambrosiana, R. 71 Sup. Fourteenth century, northern Italian, contains music.

H   Vatican, Biblioteca Vaticana, Lat. 3207. Last third of thirteenth century, northern Italian.

I   Paris, Bibliothèque nationale de France, fr. 854. Thirteenth century, northern Italian.

J   Florence, Biblioteca Nazionale, Conventi Soppressi F.IV.776. Fourteenth century. Copied in eastern Languedoc (Nîmes?), but from Italian sources.

K   Paris, Bibliothèque nationale de France, fr. 12473. Thirteenth century, northern Italian.

L   Vatican, Biblioteca Vaticana, Lat. 3206. Fourteenth century, northern Italian.

N   New York, Pierpont Morgan Library, M. 819. Fourteenth century, northern Italian.

N²   Berlin, Staatsbibliotek, Phillipps 1910. Sixteenth century.

P   Florence, Biblioteca Laurenziana, XLI.42. = Grammar manuscript *B*.

Q   Florence, Biblioteca Riccardiana, 2909. Fourteenth century, northern Italian.

R   Paris, Bibliothèque nationale de France, fr. 22543. Copied in the region of Toulouse, first quarter of the fourteenth century, for the court of Rodez. The only Occitan manuscript to contain music.

r   Florence, Biblioteca Riccardiana, 294. Fragment. Italian.

Sg   Barcelona, Biblioteca de Catalunya, 146. Fourteenth century, Catalan.

TROUVÈRE *CHANSONNIERS*

As individual manuscripts are not discussed in this book I refer the reader to the conventional *sigla* listed in Raynaud-Spanke, 1–6.

NOTES

INTRODUCTION

1. Grafton, *Footnote*, 29, shows that footnotes originate partly in quotations because citing sources is one of their earliest functions.

2. Pfeffer, *Change of Philomel*, 4, and chap. 4.

3. Songs 25 and 26.

4. Ovid, *Amores* 2.6. Ovid's poem was in turn parodied by Statius; see Dietrich, "Dead Parrots' Society."

5. Meneghetti, *Pubblico*, 92–93, suggests that the Occitan allegorical narrative *Cort d'amor* is so saturated with troubadour poetry as to be virtually a cento. The same could be said of the *Roman de Flamenca*.

6. The expression "secondhand" is from Compagnon's brilliant *La seconde main; ou, Le travail de la citation*, as is that of the "work of quotation" (calqued on the "work of mourning").

7. See notably Boulton, *The Song in the Story*, which opens: "The practice of quoting songs or song fragments in narrative texts arose first in northern France in the early thirteenth century and remained popular there for another two hundred years." I use "Northern French" to refer to the language of northern France, a region qualified as "northern French."

8. Though see Washer, "Paraphrased and Parodied," for an exemplary case study of Folquet's "Amors, merce" (155.1).

9. Gruber, *Dialektik*.

10. Kay, "La seconde main."

11. Meneghetti, "Il florilegio" and "Les florilèges."

12. See Meneghetti, "Il florilegio," 865.

13. The term "solicitation" is used by Compagnon, *La seconde main*, 26, to refer to the way certain passages of texts call out to be quoted; see below.

14. For doubts on the date and origin of this *novas*, see Gaunt, "Linguistic Difference."

15. Francesco da Barberino's *I documenti d'amore*, composed in the early fourteenth century (but after Dante), contains ten quotations in original Occitan; see Pillet-Carstens, *Bibliographie*, xxxiii; and Albertazzi's edition of Barberino. William of Aragon's *De no-*

bilitate animi contains some seven quotations from six troubadours, paraphrased and adapted into Latin; see Guillelmus de Aragonia, *De nobilitate*, 35–45.

16. The troubadours are quoted by Jacme March in *Lo rauser de la vida gaya*, and by Francesc Ferrer in *Lo conhort*; see Raimon Vidal, *Obra poètica*, ed. Field, 1:50, for details.

17. Pillet and Carstens, *Bibliographie*. I use PC numbers as updated in the invaluable *Bibliografia elettronica dei trovatori,* http://w3.uniroma1.it/bedt/BEdT_03_20/index.aspx (henceforth *BEdT*).

18. Nineteen manuscript copies not counting excerpts such as those in *DcFa* (see Appendix 2) and three, perhaps four, formal imitations; see J. H. Marshall, "Pour l'étude."

19. See Tavani, *Raimon Vidal*, for an overview of the lyrics.

20. J. H. Marshall, *The "Razos de trobar" of Raimon Vidal*, 100–105.

21. See Corbellari, *La voix des clercs*; Bolduc, *Medieval Poetics of Contraries*; Butterfield, *Poetry and Music*; Beer, *Beasts of Love*. On the quotations in Richard de Fournival's *Bestiaire d'amours*, see Kay, "La seconde main."

22. See also Léglu, *Multilingalism and Mother Tongue*, on the Mediterranean diffusion of Occitan.

23. Derrida, *Monolinguisme*, 53: "On se *figure* toujours que celui ou celle qui écrit doit savoir dire *je*. En tout cas la *modalité identificatrice* doit être déjà ou désormais assurée: assurée de la langue et dans sa langue."

24. Ibid., 55: "Il se serait alors *formé*, ce *je*, dans le site d'une *situation* introuvable, renvoyant toujours ailleurs, à autre chose, à une autre langue, à l'autre en général. Il se serait *situé* dans une expérience insituable de la *langue*, de la langue au sens large, donc, de ce mot."

25. French examples have been inventoried by O'Sullivan, "Contrafacture." For German examples, see Sayce, *Medieval German Lyric*, 119; and Mertens, "Kontrafaktur," especially the diagram, 276; Catalan examples are identified by Billy, "Contrafactures."

26. On the progressive translation of Occitan songs into French in Northern French manuscripts, see Raupach and Raupach, *Französierte Trobadorlyrik*.

27. Roncaglia, "De quibusdam Provincialibus"; the troubadour most extensively relied on is Folquet de Marselha. However, according to Formisano, "Troubadours, trouvères, Siciliens," 112–24, evidence points to French influence being in some ways stronger than Occitan on Sicilian lyric.

28. Zingesser, "French Troubadours."

29. Beyond Catalonia and Aragon we find native courtly poetry springing up in the courts of Castile in the second half of the twelfth century, and in those of Galicia, Portugal, and Leon from the late twelfth to early thirteenth; the emergence of literary Catalan is dated to the fourteenth century; see Alvar, *Poesía trovadoresca*; Cabré, "Italian and Catalan Troubadours"; Massó Torrents, "La cançó provençal"; Resende de Oliveira, "Surgissement"; Snow, "Iberian Pensinsula."

30. Rieger, "Relations interculturelles," proposes that French, German and Occitan lyric poets were most likely to meet, if at all, on crusade.

31. Paterson, *World of the Troubadours*, 3, 95–96.

32. Paden, "The Troubadours and the Albigensian Crusade."

33. Among others, Boulton, *The Song in the Story*; Butterfield, *Poetry and Music*; Cerquiglini,*"Un engin si soutil"*; Huot, *From Song to Book*; Taylor, "Lyric Insertion"; Armstrong and Kay, *Knowing Poetry*, chap. 5.

34. Such as the ballade by Thomas Paien included by Machaut in the *Livre du voir dit* or Froissart's insertion of songs by his patron Wenceslas of Brabant in his Arthurian romance *Meliador*.

35. Compare Menocal, *Shards of Love*, in which the author argues that lyric poetry inevitably has its origins in exile.

36. Boulton, *The Song in the Story*, chaps. 2 and 3.

37. Ibid., p. 2.

38. There is no work of which all manuscripts contain music for all the lyric insertions, but manuscripts of eleven works contain at least some music while there are blank staves in those of thirteen others. In the copies of five other works the lyrics are indicated as different in one way or another: by a rubric; by being written in red; by being underlined in red. See Boulton, *The Song in the Story*, app. 2.

39. See Ramon Vidal, *Obra poètica*, ed. Field, 1:51, 63, 65, 66, 68; the copy of *So fo e·l tems* in fragment *r* alone stands out in setting out quotations as in the *chansonniers*, viz., occupying the whole column with no offset initial, and not line by line, the ends of lines of verse being marked by a full stop (ibid., p. 68); also Kay, "How Long Is a Quotation?"

40. Photographs illustrating this practice in *Breviari* manuscripts can be seen in Kay, "How Long Is a Quotation?"

41. See Lemaire, *Introduction à la codicologie*, 164; Parkes, *Pause and Effect*, 22, 27, and plates 7 and 11.

42. Boulton, *The Song in the Story*, 3, 5.

43. Dallenbach, *Le récit spéculaire*, 18: "toute enclave entretenant une relation de similitude avec l'oeuvre qui la contient. " Dallenbach later refines his definition in ways less appropriate to these texts.

44. Orr discusses quotation as an aspect of intertextuality in *Intertextuality*, chap. 4.

45. Grafton, *Footnote*, 9.

46. Meyer, *Poetics of Quotation*, 8.

47. Derrida, "Signature événement contexte," 381: "Tout signe . . . peut être *cité*, mis entre guillemets; par là il peut rompre avec tout contexte donné, engendrer à l'infini de nouveaux contextes. . . . Cette citationnalité, cette duplication ou duplicité, cette itérabilité de la marque n'est pas un accident ou une anomalie. . . . Que serait une marque que l'on ne pourrait pas citer? Et dont l'origine ne saurait être perdue en chemin?"

48. Derrida himself is uncharacteristically evasive as to whether there is a difference between quotation and other forms of iteration.

49. Compagnon, *La seconde main*, 26.

50. Garber, *Quotation Marks*, 2, drawing on Walter Benjamin.

51. Meneghetti, "Il florilegio," 865.

52. Marnette, "Ponctuation."

53. Kay, "How Long Is a Quotation?"

54. Kay, "Knowledge and Truth"; Lacan's ideas are developed in three successive years (1967–70) of his famous seminar, as recorded in *Le séminaire*, books 15, 16, and 17.

55. D. V. Smith, *Book of the Incipit*, 4.

56. Ibid., 6.

57. Ibid.

58. Saïd, *Beginnings*, 13.

59. Pontalis, *Love of Beginnings*, 86 (*L'amour des commencements*, 98: "Quant les mots manquent, c'est qu'à son insu on s'apprête à toucher un autre sol").

60. Kay, "Poésie."

61. Saïd, *Beginnings*, 34.

62. Dragonetti, *Mirage des sources*, 41: "reconnaître un auteur, en faire l'éloge, le prendre pour guide peut être donc une façon élégante de faire le vide sous le décor de la source."

63. Analogously the *coblas* quoted in many of the biographical texts in *H* are all that we have of the songs in question. In some cases—that of Tibors, for example—they are almost certainly abridgments of longer works, but in others—such as the exchanges with Dalfi—they are probably isolated *coblas*. Because of the impossibility of distinguishing between the two possibilities, all the verses in the *H* biographies published in *Biographies*, ed. Boutière and Schutz, are included in Appendix 1.

64. Eco, "Riflessioni."

65. Leach, *Sung Birds*.

66. Carter, *Parrot*, 8.

67. Boehrer, *Parrot Culture*, 33; Boehrer's chaps. 1 and 2 provide a wide-ranging study of the equivocal reception of the parrot in antiquity and the Middle Ages.

68. *Le bestiaire*, ed. Baker, §27.

69. Compare Caluwé, *Du chant*, 174–78, for a different valuation of parrots as narrative and nightingales as emblems of the lyric.

CHAPTER 1. RHYME AND REASON

1. Grammars are cited by manuscript version and line number from J. H. Marshall, ed., *The "Razos de trobar" of Raimon Vidal*. Marshall thinks the *Razos* is Raimon Vidal's earliest work (lxx), reflecting attitudes "around 1200" (lxxxvi). See Shapiro, *"De vulgari eloquentia,"* 113–26, for an English translation of the *Razos*. For critical readings, see Poe, *From Poetry to Prose*, chap. 4; and Stone, *Death of the Troubadour*, chap. 1.

2. Burgwinkle, *Love for Sale*, 149–59.

3. Stone, *Death of the Troubadour*, 17; Leach, *Sung Birds*, chap. 1.

4. J. H. Marshall, *The "Razos de trobar" of Raimon Vidal*, xcvi–xcviii.

5. Expansions of manuscript *sigla* for the grammars are given in Appendix 17.

6. Terramagnino's text is closest to the *CL* version of the *Razos*, which is probably a later, Italian reworking of the earlier *BH* redaction.

7. The *H* copy of the *Razos* and the *R* copy of the *Regles* both contain a number of omissions.

8. Unlike Uc Faidit's treatise, the transmission of which is uniquely Italian.

9. Kay, "Occitan Grammar."

10. Cf. the *vidas* and *razos* composed on the model of scholastic *accessus ad auctores* in the decades following (Chapter 3).

11. See J. H. Marshall's note for the translation of *galliardias*.

12. Poe, *From Poetry to Prose*, 77: "Perhaps the most distinctive feature of Vidal's book is its consolidation of poet and audience as coworkers in an endless process of language refinement."

13. Kay, "Occitan Grammar," 56–60.

14. J. H. Marshall, *The "Razos de trobar" of Raimon Vidal*, xxx–xxxiv, suggests that some of Terramagnino's misattributions could come from careless consultation of a *chansonnier*, perhaps *D-Da*, others from his quoting from memory.

15. Cf. J. H. Marshall, *The "Razos de trobar" of Raimon Vidal*, lxxx.

16. They are conflated by J. H. Marshall, whose main concern is with establishing the text of the *Razos* and its relation to the *chansonniers*; see *The "Razos de Trobar" of Raimon Vidal*, xxii–xxiii (table 5).

17. See Molinier, *Leys d'amors*, ed. Anglade, 3:91; cf. Anglade, *Etudes*, 77; also Swiggers, "La plus ancienne grammaire," 186.

18. J. H. Marshall amends *B* at line 203, thereby gaining a quotation; but he counts as one quotation the disjunct lines that I have counted as 7 and 7a so as not to disrupt his numbering. These unattributed lines may be by Raimon Vidal himself, but are not assigned to him by Tavani, ed., *Raimon Vidal*, whose survey of Raimon Vidal's lyrics is the most complete, nor by Field.

19. See Washer, "Paraphrased and Parodied."

20. He does not provide incipits for Bernart de Ventadorn's "Can vei la lauzeta mover" (70.43) or "Can par la flors" (70.41) or for Peirol's "Mout m'entremis de chantar voluntiers" (366.21) or Peire Vidal's "Ben viu a gran dolor" (364.13), although he quotes from each.

21. Compare *RaT* #21 with *DA* #27–#29, all from Bernart de Ventadorn's "Can vei la lauzeta mover" (70.43); *RaT* #23–#24 with *DA* #43, from Folquet de Marselha's "Ai! quan gen vens et ab quan pauc d'afan" (155.3); and *RaT* #18–#19 with *DA* #30–#31, from Giraut de Bornelh's "Gen m'aten" (242.34); Gaucelm Faidit's "De faire chansso" (167.18), quoted in *RaT* only in the *CL* redaction (#32), is also reprised in *DA* #34.

22. The only exception is the quotation from Peire Vidal, #25.

23. Jofre is an exception to a growing trend, since from the Ripoll treatises onward (see. J. H. Marshall, *The "Razos de trobar" of Raimon Vidal*, 100–105) quotation by incipit predominates. See also Chapters 3, 7 and 9.

24. See also Poe, "Cantairitz."

25. This strategy is brought to a fine art in Matfre Ermengau's *Breviari d'amor*, with which the *Regles de trobar* is roughly contemporary. The *Breviari* also quotes Aimeric de Peguilhan more than any other troubadour; see Chapter 8.

26. The six songs quoted are 30.23, 70.1, 70.43, 155.3, 242.34, 242.58; 167.18 is also quoted in both the *Razos* and the late manuscript fragment *a²* of *So fo*.

CHAPTER 2. QUOTATION, MEMORY, AND CONNOISSEURSHIP

1. On performance in *Abril issia*, see Page, *The Owl and the Nightingale*, 53–60.

2. On *Abril issia* as *ensenhamen*, see Monson, *Les "ensenhamens" occitans*, 90–94; cf. Tavani, *Raimon Vidal*, 26; on Raimon's self-promotion, see Francis, "The *Joglar* as Salesman."

3. On this section of *R*, see Zufferey, "La partie non-lyrique"; on a possible link between *Abril issia* and Guerau de Cabrera's *ensenhamen*, see Pirot, *Recherches*, 206–15. A longer version of *So fo* is copied alongside *Abril issia* in *R*; a shorter version is found in *chansonniers L* and *N*; and *r*, *a¹*, and *a²* are isolated fragments (see Appendix 17 for expansions of *sigla*). I refer to *So fo* by the incipit in *LN* adopted by Field, *Obra poètica*, the edition of reference for this chapter; the *novas* is also known by its incipit in *R*, *En aquel temps* (It was at that time) and as the *Judici d'amor* (Judgment of love). Arguments for dating rely on references to historical figures within the *novas* but the latest possible date for either is 1213 (death of Uc de Mataplana); cf. Huchet's introduction to his edition of Raimon Vidal's *novas* in *Nouvelles occitanes*, 16. Field, *Obra poètica*, 1:61, proposes "well before 1209" as the most likely for *Abril issia*; Tavani, *Raimon Vidal*, 31–45, puts it as early as 1196–1200.

4. *Obra poètica*, 1:77–115. Field is right, however, that the passages in *r* and *a²* are later additions. The ending in *a²* contains seven quotations not found in any of the other manuscripts, one of which is from a poem by Guillem de Montanhagol that probably postdates Raimon Vidal. The *r* fragment consists mainly of material not found in other versions and, given its two misattributions to Arnaut Daniel, is most likely not by the punctilious Raimon Vidal (*Obra poètica*, 1:117–18).

5. Lee, " 'Versi d'amore.' " Also, if *R* is a later redaction of the *LN* version, it is odd that the *R* redactor left the quotations in the first part unchanged (contrast the more pervasive divergences between the *BH* and *CL* redactions of the *Razos de trobar*; see Chapter 1).

6. Field's other main argument for dual authorship is based on his interpretation of the *novas'* relation to poems by Raimon de Miraval and Uc de Mataplana, with which I disagree (see below).

7. On attribution and anonymity in the *novas*, see Field, *Obra poètica*, 1:117–19 (tables 1 and 2).

8. Also true of the *Razos de trobar*; see J. H. Marshall, *The "Razos de trobar" of Raimon Vidal*, xxiii.

9. Both Field and Huchet translate *joglars* as a singular, whereas I take the plural *us* to designate a collective: "a troupe of *joglars*."

10. For a different account of memory in the *novas*, see Limentani, *L'eccezione*, 45–60.

11. Trans. Sharman in her edition of Giraut de Bornelh.

12. "D'aitan me puosc vanar / qu'anc mos hostals petitz / non fon d'elz envazitz; / que·l vei per totz doptar / ni non fes mais honrar / lo volpils ni l'arditz,/ don Mos Seingner chauzitz /si deuria pensar / que non l'es ges pretz ni laus ni bobanz / q'eu, que·m laus d'els, sia de lui clamanz!" (Song 74, 71–80). "I can at least boast that my small house was never invaded by them, for I see it respected by everyone; cowards and brave men alike have never ceased to honor it. And so My distinguished Lord should reflect that it would certainly not be to her credit, her reputation or splendor if I, who praise such men as these, were to complain about *her*" (Sharman trans., modified).

13. Cf. Poe, "The Meaning of *Saber*."

14. *R* reads *luy*, emendation from *LN*.

15. In *R* at least; the endings of *LN* and *a²* are kinder to the *donzela*.

16. Cf. Meneghetti's description, *Pubblico*, 46–47, of *Abril issia* as a "discursive mapping of Provençal patronage."

17. *Obra poètica*, 1:89ff.

18. I use Gouiran's edition in preference to Paden's in this chapter for reasons that become clear below. Gouiran identifies this as an early song and describes it (*L'amour et la guerre*, 1:cxlviii) as a kind of *ensenhamen*. Paden, Sankovitch, and Stäblein, in their edition of Bertran de Born, *Poems*, date it later, making it their Song 20.

19. Gouiran, 1:146. Cf. earlier in the same song, where Bertran fiercely criticizes noblemen who use tournaments as a means of self-enrichment. Nichols, "Urgent Voices," has argued that Bertran is not the gung-ho warlord he is often mistaken for, but a poet whose views on violence reflect church thinking. This would make it highly unlikely that he would favor flouting the Peace of God promulgated by the church.

20. However, in the Paden, Sankovitch, and Stäblein edition of Bertran these lines are interpreted, as they are in *Abril issia*, as expressing nostalgia for the days before the Peace of God forbade war during Lent and Advent; see also Paden, "Imaginer," for Bertran's promotion of violence in war.

21. The line missing in *R* reads "Sofraita par, e gran non-sens" in *a¹*.

22. For Meneghetti, *Pubblico*, 144–45, Uc's verdict here, and in the exchange of *sirventes* with Raimon de Miraval, affirms class difference between himself and knights like the protagonist, whose obligation is unending service.

CHAPTER 3. STARTING AFRESH

1. Meneghetti, *Pubblico*, 182.

2. Uc signs one version of Bernart de Ventadorn's *vida* and implies authorship of the *razos* for Savaric de Malleo. He features as a character in several other *razos* and is, of

course, the protagonist of his own *vida*. His most admiring reader is Burgwinkle, *Love for Sale*, chap. 2.

3. But see Burgwinkle, *Love for Sale*, 149–59, for the range of meaning of this term.

4. On Uc's anthology and the da Romano manuscript, see Avalle, *Letteratura medievale*, 102; and Meneghetti, "Uc de Saint Circ." On the *vidas* and *razos*, see Guida, "Ricerche"; Poe, especially *"L'autr' escrit"*; Burgwinkle, *Love for Sale,* 5 and chap. 3; Meneghetti, *Pubblico*, 138–40. On Uc's possible responsibility for *chansonnier H*, see Poe, *Compilatio*. On the date and authorship of the *Donatz proensals*, see Janzarik, "Uc de St. Circ"; and Burgwinkle, *Love for Sale*, 136–39. Although J. H. Marshall in his edition of the *Donatz* dismisses the possibility that its author was Uc de Saint Circ, his disagreement concerns the deciphering of the manuscript not the wider historical arguments.

5. Burgwinkle, "For Love or Money," 348–49: "As poet, biographer, literary historian, and mythographer, Uc must be accorded his rightful place as the inventor (*trobador*) of 'troubadour poetry' and the ideological trappings with which it came to be associated"; cf. *Love for Sale*, chap. 2. Guida comments on the ineluctable rise of Uc in "Ricerche," 92.

6. *B* might have been copied in the south of France, from an Auvergnac-Venetan source (Zufferey, *Recherches*, 63), others think it was copied in Italy; *E* is similarly disputed between Occitania and Italy; *R* was copied in Occitania; *Sg*, in which the only prose works relate to Giraut de Bornelh, is Catalan. Avalle (*Letteratura medievale*, 131–32) contends that all versions of the *vidas* and *razos* stem from Italian sources; see in more detail Burgwinkle, *Love for Sale*, 124–42.

7. Poe, *"L'autr' escrit,"* 131–32. There are eighteen *razos* accompanying Bertran de Born songs in *IK*, nineteen in *F*, and several more transmitted in fragments; references in the surviving texts reveal that other Bertran *razos* existed that have been lost.

8. Minnis and Scott, *Medieval Literary Theory*, 12; cf. Raban Maur's definition of the art of grammar as "the science of interpreting the poets" (Meneghetti, *Pubblico*, 216); see also Egan, "Commentary"; Meneghetti, *Pubblico*, 207–44; Hunt, "Introductions."

9. Poe, "Teaching Troubadours"; Kay, "Occitan Grammar," 48–50.

10. Poe identifies stylistic differences in *From Poetry to Prose*, 16; in "At the Boundary," 317, Poe contends that Uc used the term *razo* only; Burgwinkle, *Love for Sale*, 4–5, notes that in some manuscripts what are elsewhere distinct *vidas* and *razos* are run together.

11. Burgwinkle, *Razos*, xix: "Some of the texts that are considered *vidas* by virtue of their adherence to the rhetorical patterns outlined above could, however, be considered *razos* in that they cite lines from specific poetic compositions."

12. All references are to *Biographies*, ed. Boutière and Schutz, in the form *Biographies*, number and version, page. Only one *razo* contains no quotation at all (the *Sg* text of Giraut de Bornelh's 242.36, *Biographies*, VIII.C, 49–50), and only one contains only one quotation not from the beginning of any song (Bertran de Born, *razo* to 80.8, XI.S, 134–35), though several contain more than one quotation from within songs and only one incipit.

13. E.g., the *razo* to Peire Vidal 364.2, 364.36, 364.37 and 364.48, found in different versions in *H* and *EN²PRe* (*Biographies*, LVII.B, 356–67).

14. Maria de Ventadorn, Lombarda, Tibors.

15. See *Biographies*, IX, 58–61; VII, 32–35; VI.B, 26–28; III.A, 10–11; XXXIX, 263–66; XL, 267–70; LXVIII, 441–44. The others are the relatively unknown Garin d'Apchier, inventor (according to his *vida*) of the *descort*, *Biographies*, LIII, 343–44; and Bonifaci Calvo/Bertolome Zorzi, *Biographies*, C.B, 576–78.

16. Meneghetti, *Pubblico*, 226; for examples of Ovidian *accessus* containing quotations, see Minnis and Scott, *Medieval Literary Theory*, 21, 23, 24, 25, 26, 29.

17. *Biographies*, XVII.B, 161–66; cf. Poe, "At the Boundary."

18. *Biographies*, C.B, 576–78.

19. The *razos* in *P* are followed by the quotation of a stanza, not the whole poem or just the incipit, a trait that links them with *coblas triadas* (of which there is also a collection in *P*); cf. Chapter 4.

20. That of Ferrarino da Ferrara in *Dc*, *Biographies*, CI, 580, is too late to be by Uc.

21. Poe, "*L'Autre Escrit*," 124.

22. Cf. Boutière, "Quelques observations."

23. *I* is also examined by Poe in *From Poetry to Prose*, chap. 5. The makeup of *I* and *K* has been scrupulously documented by Meliga, *Bibliothèque nationale*, in the series "*Intavulare*."

24. Graphies of *I*, fo. 177v.

25. Cf. Poe's observation (*From Poetry to Prose*, 16) that *vidas* are written in the third person in historic tenses and take as their horizon the lyric corpus, whereas *razos* include traces of present tenses and the first person, and their horizon includes other compositions like themselves.

26. *D*, 6r: "Haec sunt inceptiones cantionum de libro qui fuit domini Alberici et nomina repertorum eorum cantionum" (Here are the beginnings of the songs from Lord Alberico's book and the names of their authors).

27. See Avalle, *Letteratura medievale*, 91, for a typology of how *chansonniers* are ordered; he classes *IK* as "cronologico-estetico," an order whereby the most important troubadours are presented in some kind of historical order.

28. The images of troubadours in *chansonniers I* and *K* (and consequently the presentation of their *vidas*) can be seen on the Mandragore website of the Bibliothèque Nationale de France; see also Meneghetti, *Pubblico*, chap. 7; Peters, *Das Ich im Bild*.

29. Did thirteenth-century poets exploit this new resonance, for instance in Aimeric de Peguilhan's exchange with Folquet de Marselha about good and bad beginnings (*comensamen*) and good and bad endings (*fenimen*)? See Mancini, "Aimeric de Peguilhan," 59–60.

30. Argument brilliantly explored by Galvez, *Songbook*.

31. Limentani, *L'eccezione*, 243, suggests that one reason why lyrics do not feature in the catalog of works performed at Flamenca's wedding in the eponymous romance is that they have neither titles nor the kind of episodic content that can be cited in a list.

32. Derrida, "Signature événement contexte," 381; cf. Introduction.

33. There are a few troubadours with no accompanying *vida* toward the end of the *canso* section.

34. Later on, *I* and *K* both include in their *canso* section the *vidas* containing quotations of incipits for Raimon Jordan and Bertolome Zorzi, and *K* has in addition the *vida* for Marcabru in which the quotation is not an incipit; Garin d'Apchier, a *vida* that quotes an incipit, is included among the *tensos* in *IK*.

35. See the commentary on this *vida* by Meneghetti, *Pubblico*, 237f.

36. Two lines are quoted rather than one in the *vida* in *ABER a*. In *P*, readers are helped by the inclusion of the entire first strophe.

37. The version in *A* is more explicit, saying that Peire "fetz los meillors sons de vers que anc fosson faich e·l vers que ditz 'Dejostal·s . . .'" (composed the best melodies that were ever made, and the *vers* that goes "Alongside . . ."). For text and discussion, see Gruber, *Dialektik*, 24–25.

38. "Al poco giorno e al gran cerchio d'ombra," Dante, *Rime*, 7; the editor's note to this line does no more than indicate the similarity between *poco giorno* and Peire d'Alvernha's *breus iorns*. See Bondanella, "Arnaut Daniel," 418–20, for reservations about Dante's debt to Arnaut in this song.

CHAPTER 4. SOLICITING QUOTATION IN *FLORILEGIA*

1. *Dc* has been consulted in Teulié and Rossi's transcription, "L'anthologie provençale"; and in *Il canzoniere provenzale estense,* introd. Avalle and Casamassima.

2. Meneghetti, "Il florilegio," 854, substitutes this number for Teulié and Rossi's 223, in which #42 conflates two different songs by Aimeric de Peguilhan, 10.14 and 10.18; #93 combines two texts by Peirol, 366.22 and 366.6; and #212 comprises two quotations from Bernart de la Barta, 58.2 and 58.1. These corrections are integrated in the *BEdT* (which, however, retains Teulié and Rossi's numbering) and in Appendix 2, where both are included in entries dealing with their respective interlocutors, Arman (25.1a) in the case of 58.1 and Guillem Peire de Cazals (227.7) in that of 58.2, since the interlocutor's words are the first to be quoted.

3. *Biographies*, CI, 581: "E fe[s] un estrat de tutas las canços des bos trobador[s] del mon; e de chadaunas canços o serventes tras .i. cobla o .ii. o .iii.. aqelas qe portan la[s] sentenças de las cansos e o son tu[i]t li mot triat."

4. Washer, "Paraphrased and Parodied," 568.

5. Meneghetti, "Les florilèges," 44.

6. Cf. Garber, *Quotation Marks*, 2.

7. Compagnon, *La seconde main*, 26.

8. *Fa* is consulted from Stengel, *Blumenlese*; and *Cm* from Allegri, "Frammento."

9. *H*, transcribed by Careri, *Il canzoniere*, chap. 6. I also consulted the edition and translation by Poe, *Compilatio*, chaps. 6 and 7. The part of *H* that contains this anthology is designated H^3.

10. Numerals in angle brackets < > identify the twenty-six sections set off by a rubric within *H* #167. Not included in this total is the exchange of *coblas* between the Count of Rodez and Uc de Sant Circ, which is not viewed as part of the anthology by Careri; see below.

11. A Northern French analogue, though not an exact equivalent, to this systematic abridgment of stanzas in *H* is the practice of abbreviating refrains in manuscript copies of *chansons avec des refrains* and *forme fixe* lyrics. Modern scholars are not always certain exactly how to reconstruct the full form of the texts from the "etcetera" to which they are abridged.

12. See transcriptions in Bertoni, *Il canzoniere* (for *G*); and Stengel, "Studi" (for *J*); the *G florilegium* is on fos. 128v–130v and contains thirty-three items; that of *J* is on fos. 12v–14v and contains seventy-four items.

13. Careri, *Il canzoniere*, 296–97.

14. Meneghetti, "Les florilèges," 48–52.

15. Ibid., 51–52.

16. Meneghetti, "Il florilegio," 864.

17. Ibid., 865.

18. Is it possible that Uc Brunenc, a relatively late troubadour whose career was contemporary with quotation as a widespread practice, composed with quotation and excerption in mind?

19. The lone example of a song by Peire d'Alvernha in Appendix 2 ("Abanz qe·il blan puoi sion vert," 323.1) is misattributed to Peire Rogier.

20. Meneghetti, "Il florilegio," 867.

21. Whereas Sordello is anthologized within *Dc*, a collection of songs by him immediately prefaces the anthology of stanzas in *F*.

22. Careri, *Il canzoniere*, 297, notes that the *coblas* in *H* <19>–<23> are all quoted at least in part by Matfre; and Poe, *Compilatio*, 231–33, demonstrates differences in content between the commentaries in the two cases.

23. Quoted from Poe, *Compilatio*, 209–10; my translation.

24. Such antifeminism is typical of *H*. In <5>, for instance, the prose says bullyingly, "This stanza is about a lover who says to his lady that if there is some reason why he is not a suitable lover for her, it will be an honor to her if she accepts his homage," while the stanza following, once restored in full, requires of the lover at least that he demonstrate good will to the lady and is far more circumspect in the burdens it places on her. The prose introduction to <7> states baldly, "This stanzas shows that a lady ought to love the knight who is in love with her," when the stanza in question recommends the social and personal benefits of *bon' amor*. See also Armstrong and Kay, *Knowing Poetry*, 117–18, with reference to Folquet de Marselha 155.16, *H* <23>.

25. Quotations in the *Breviari* are referred to by the numbers assigned to them by the text's editor, Peter. T. Ricketts, see in particular Appendix 11.

26. Washer, "Paraphrased and Parodied."

27. Ibid., 569.

28. "A vos volgra metre lo veit qe·m pent" (461.35), *G* #255; see Washer, "Paraphrased and Parodied," 579.

29. It stands next to stanza 2 of Raimon de Miraval's "Amors me fai chantar et esbaudir" (406.4), likewise also anthologized in *H*.

CHAPTER 5. THE NIGHTINGALES' WAY

1. *Guillaume de Dole* is imitated ca. 1230 by Gerbert de Montreuil in the *Roman de la violette*, the Occitan insertions in which are included in Appendix 1; an Occitanized insertion is also found in the later *La cour de paradis*. There are textual allusions to the troubadours, and even quotations from them, in at least two other Northern French romances that do not practice insertion: the *Bestiaire d'amours* of Richard de Fournival (see Kay, "La seconde main") and *Joufroi de Poitiers*. For a broader study of the treatment of Occitan lyric in Northern French romances and manuscripts, see Zingesser, "French Troubadours."

2. Lecoy's inventory is in his edition of *Guillaume de Dole*, xxiii–xxix; see Boulton, "Lyric Insertions," and Van der Werf, "Jean Renart," for qualifications.

3. Zink, "Suspension," questions whether *noter* in the prologue means that the text was ever intended to be transmitted with music; though see Butterfield's reservations about his conclusions, *Poetry and Music*, 19–22.

4. Aside from lyric insertion, this has been the most studied feature of the romance.

5. Baldwin, *Aristocratic Life*, chap. 2, concludes on the basis of historical reference in the text and the identity of the dedicatee that "the years immediately following 1209 appear to be the most likely time of the work's composition" (49). His " 'Once There Was an Emperor' " confirms this dating; Butterfield, *Poetry and Music*, 314–15 n. 8, also favors 1210. Many scholars favor the later date of 1228; see Paden, "Old Occitan," 36 n. 1. Supporting the later dating are the (in my view, convincing) arguments that place *Guillaume de Dole* after the *Lai de l'ombre*, and date the *Lai de l'ombre* to 1218–19.

6. Paden, "Old Occitan."

7. Baldwin, " 'Once There Was an Emperor.' "

8. See Toch, "Welfs, Hohenstaufen and Habsburgs," 375–92; Abulafia, "Kingdom of Sicily," 497–506; on troubadours and the Guelf-Ghibelline hostilities, see Bossy, "L'art belliqueux."

9. Boulton, "Lyric insertions," 87: "the verb *chanter* occurs twenty-eight times, while less explicit verbs such as *commencer, recomencer*, and *dire* are usually qualified by nouns such as *chant, chançon*, or *chançonete*." In addition, two of the Occitan songs are introduced simply as *sons*, "tunes" (##16, 45).

10. Appendix 6, ##11, 17, 19, 21, 22, 27, 28, 32, 33, 39, and 40.

11. Appendix 6, ##1–10, 23–26, 29, 37–38, 43–48.

12. Zink, "Suspension," 114–17.

13. Butterfield, *Poetry and Music*, 27, suggests that the romance is a kind of early *chansonnier*.

14. Nine exordia mention birds or birdsong, in three cases nightingales (Appendix 6, ## 11, 12, 16, 20, 22, 31, 41, 45, 46). Other sounds of nature—most often the noise of a running spring or the waves on a seashore—are implied in many of the more popular lyric pieces, especially those with a "la jus" type of beginning.

15. Jones, "Uses of Embroidery," 36; cf. Jewers, "Fabric and Fabrication," 908–9.

16. The red color may also evoke the practice of copying lyric insertions in red ink, as occurs in manuscripts of the *Violette*, though not, as it happens, in the surviving manuscript of *Guillaume de Dole*.

17. Jewers, "Fabric and Fabrication," 912. The disjunction, originally noted by Gaston Paris, has been interpreted in different ways by Baumgartner, "Citations"; Huot, *From Song to Book*, 111–13; Butterfield, *Poetry and Music*, 66–70. It has received widespread feminist and more recently queer interpretations; see, for example, Krueger, *Women Readers*, 128–55; Ramm, "A Rose."

18. Baumgartner, "Citations," 262, speaks of the sidelining of the Occitan songs and Renart's attempt to situate Conrad as the new Chastelain de Couci.

19. See Rosenstein, "Translation," 337–38.

20. Raupach and Raupach, *Französierte Trobadorlyrik*, 134–35, document the Gallicization of this stanza in various langue d'oïl contexts.

21. Also in *Dc*; see Appendix 2.

22. Only a third of the songs inserted into *Guillaume de Dole* are integrated metrically, most of them *grands chants*; see Appendix 6.

23. See Appendix 6, ##18, 36, 37, 41, 45, 46. Of these, #18, Renaut de Beaujeu (Rhône), is described by Jean Renart as being from the region of Reims.

24. For example, by means of an acrostic in the final lines of *Guillaume de Dole* and *L'Escoufle*; see Dragonetti, *Mirage des sources*, 156–8.

25. Faral, "Les chansons de toile." Zink, *Belle*, 1–12, accepts that the archaism of the *chansons de toile* is illusory but does believe them to preexist the text; Dragonetti, *Mirage*, 154, casts doubt on the authenticity of the epic fragment; however, Baumgartner, "Citations," 264, sees in Lienor the living spirit of historic French song, as opposed to the fantasy mode of the male-authored *canso*.

26. Appendix 6, ## 4, 7–10, 19, 21, 25, 26, 33, 41, 44, 47.

27. Appendix 6, ## 5, 13–15, 23.

28. Appendix 6, ## 1, 3, 42.

29. See Paden, "Old Occitan," 46–47.

CHAPTER 6. THE PARROTS' WAY

1. The suggestion that the bird is a jay is put forward by Gaunt, "Linguistic Difference." Other scholars see it as a parrot. Like other medieval parrots, the *jeai* comes from India and its plumage is that of a parrot not a European jay. Gaunt also suggests that the tale may be thirteenth century and Occitan (but transmitted in Catalan copies), rather than Catalan and fourteenth century as generally thought.

2. Thiolier-Méjean,"Le motif du perroquet"; Boehrer, *Parrot Culture*, 7, 26–33.

3. See Caluwé, *Du chant*, 178. For more on parrots in general, see Boehrer, *Parrot Culture*, especially chaps. 1 and 2; and Carter, *Parrot*.

4. Thiolier-Méjean, "Le motif du perroquet" and "Le langage du perroquet."

5. Derrida, *Monolinguisme*, 47: "Je n'ai qu'une langue et ce n'est pas la mienne, ma langue propre m'est une langue inassimilable. Ma langue, la seule que je m'entende parler et m'entende à parler, c'est la langue de l'autre."

6. Limentani, *L'eccezione*, 61.

7. Lee, "Versi d'amore."

8. Texts are quoted as follows: *R* from the edition by Huchet, *Nouvelles occitanes*; *DGJ* from the transcriptions/facsimiles generated (for *D*) by Avalle and Casamassima, eds., *Il canzoniere, D,* fo. 216r, cols. a–b; (for *G*) by Bertoni, *Il canzoniere*, especially 424–27, 391–93; and (for *J*) by Stengel, "Studi," 36–39; my source for π is Wesselofsky, "Un nouveau texte."

9. See Zufferey, "La partie non-lyrique."

10. Copied in the region of Toulouse in the first quarter of the fourteenth century.

11. Zufferey, "La partie non-lyrique," 22.

12. Lee, "Versi d'amore"; Zufferey thinks it may have been copied in Nîmes (*Recherches*, 189–97).

13. Commune of Laroque-de-Fa; see the introduction to their edition of the *novas* by Lavaud and Nelli, *Les troubadours*, 2:214; and for more detail, Nelli, "Arnaut de Carcassès."

14. Cf. Coulet, "Sur la nouvelle," which contends that the original form of the *novas* is that of *J* without this final *salut*; Zufferey, "La partie non-lyrique," 8, refers to the *R* version as reworked (*remaniée*) but declines to amplify.

15. This form of reference gives line numbers in *R* (Huchet's edition) and then indicates whether these lines are present in other manuscripts.

16. The equivalent lines are absent from *G*.

17. Only parts of this speech are found in π.

18. Variants for this passage imply that the parrot's slanders in *JG* will be confined to the facts, but in *R* only by what it is capable of inventing.

19. Huchet here reorders the lines in conformity with *JG*. This passage falls after the end of the π excerpt.

20. Carter, *Parrot*, 8.

21. I thank Elena Russo for this suggestion.

22. While many have noted the parrot's role as bird messenger familiar from lyric, perhaps with Oriental antecedents, the link has been overlooked with clerk-knight debates in which the knight is championed by a parrot and the clerk by a nightingale. In such debates, the clerk usually wins and the knight seems gaudy and shallow: a possible implication of the *novas*'s swaggering opening. There is more deflation of knighthood in *R*; in *J*, the protagonist appears predominantly as a courtier and suitor.

23. The view that the *salut* is an independent text is defended by Coulet, "Sur la nouvelle," 293.

24. Both are also in the nonlyric section of *R*.

25. Likewise in the nonlyric section of *R*.

26. Lee, "Versi d'amore."

27. Thiolier-Méjean, "Le langage du perroquet," 273–74.

CHAPTER 7. SONGS WITHIN SONGS

1. Gruber, *Dialektik*, 118–42; Meneghetti, *Pubblico*, 89.

2. Gruber, *Dialektik*, 104 n. 2.

3. Asperti in his edition of Raimon Jordan, note to line 1 of this song (Song 7) says we cannot be sure of the order of composition of these two songs.

4. Zemp, *Poésies du troubadour Cadenet*, 208, notes that the dance is anonymous in the sole manuscript, *W*, and was attributed to Guiraut d'Espanha by Suchier.

5. Aside from the quotations discussed here, Raimon Jordan's "Per solatz" does not figure in Appendix 1 or 2, and the same is true of Bernart de Rovenac's "D'un sirventes m'es grans volontatz preza" (and indeed of any other of this troubadour's songs).

6. The only two of these songs that do not elsewhere appear in Appendix 1 or 2 are Perdigon, "Ir' e pezars et dompna ses merce" (370.8), whose imagery overlaps with Jofre's, and which is elsewhere widely diffused; and Gaucelm Faidit, "Mon cor et mi e mas bonas chansos" (167.37).

7. The only pair among these five that might be *contrafacta* of one another, and thus share the same music, are Bernart de Rovenac and Luquet Gatelus, which number among twelve formally identical pieces modeled on Peirol's "M'entencion ai tot' en un vers mesa" (366.20), a piece anthologized in *DcFa*.

8. Armstrong, *Virtuoso Circle*: "The twin mechanisms of collaboration and competition foster ongoing development and innovation, so that the formal and rhetorical intricacy of French poetry steadily increases. Poets in this culture, then, are a circle of virtuosi: they implement these innovations, and thereby master their art, through interaction with each other" (14), thereby producing "a cycle whose iteration reinforces the positive momentum of events" (18).

9. Levy speculates that Bertolome was born between 1230 and 1240 (*Troubadour Bertolome Zorzi*, 6).

10. Songs 2, 4, 13, 14; 12 has numerous analogues but none with identical rhymes; 14 is a reply to and also a *contrafactum* of Bonifaci Calvo's "Ges no m'es greu" (101.7).

11. Levy, *Bertolome Zorzi*, 13: "mich will es dünken, als wäre ihm das 'sen cobrir' nur gar zu gut gelungen."

12. See Folena, *Culture*, 106–37 (although he does little more than mention this text).

13. Manuscripts of songs that quote verbatim from other songs do not mark the quotation in any way, unlike the practices observed in other genres.

14. I use "drag" here in the sense theorized by Butler, e.g., in "Imitation."

15. Van der Werf, *Extant Troubadour Melodies*, 248–50.

16. Details in Massó Torrents, "A propos."

17. See Riquer, *Los trovatores*, 3:1648. Massó Torrents, "A propos," adds a comic exchange on the subject of food of which the first *cobla* is rubricated "Hoc dicit monachus de Fuxano."

18. Quotation #8, also found as #11 in the *Razos de trobar* (see Appendix 4).

19. See the edition of Gace Brulé by Dyggve, 55–62; and Dyggve,"Trouvères et protecteurs," 66–74; see also the opposing argument by F. Marshall, "Blondel." The longer version is preserved in trouvère *chansonniers IKMNPTX.*

20. Gilles's song is quoted from F. Marshall, "Blondel," 10–16; and checked against Dyggve, "Trouvères et protecteurs," 70–72.

21. Frank, "La chanson 'Lasso me,'" 265–66.

22. *Analecta hymnica*, vol. 21, hymn 25; Perugi, *Trovatori*, 231–32 n. 7, identifies this hymn as a kind of *sirventes* composed for the expedition of Louis le Gros in 1127; see also Gruber, *Dialektik*, 108.

23. Gruber, *Dialektik*, 107; cf. Frank, "La chanson 'Lasso me,'" 267: "Ces hymnes à citations ambrosiennes, nous les retrouvons tout au long du xiiie siècle, de Thomas a Capua (d. 1243), à travers les Carmina Burana . . . et un grand nombre d'exemples anonymes, rassemblés surtout au t. XXII des inépuisables Analecta Hymnica, jusqu'au cardinal Jacopo Gaetani de' Stefani, contemporain de Pétrarque, et qui mourut en 1343 à Avignon."

24. "Mit sange wânde ich mîne sorge krenken"; see Sayce, *Medieval German Lyric*, 15, 119.

25. *Poèmes de Gaucelm Faidit*, ed. Mouzat, Song 29, p. 244; Frank, *Répertoire*, #301:2; Jofre's "Be m'a lonc temps menat a guisa d'aura" is Frank, *Répertoire*, #301:3.

26. Frank, *Répertoire*, #301:1.

27. Frank, "La chanson 'Lasso me,'" 264; Gruber, *Dialektik*, 111, also notes that Jofre's stanza V has the same rhyme as Gace Brulé's opening stanzas.

28. See Tischler, *Trouvère Lyrics*, vol. 1, #30; Van Os, "Structure mélodique," studies the text-melody relation with regard to the majority form of the music in trouvère *chansonniers KLMNOX.*

29. Frank, "La chanson 'Lasso me,'" 262: "Le troubadour catalan a fait preuve de beaucoup d'aisance et d'habilité techniques dans la façon très naturelle dont il a incorporé ses citations à la pensée. . . . Faire de ces mots le sujet de phrases nouvelles, qu'ils termineront au lieu de les commencer comme dans leur contexte primitif, ce jeu des renversements syntactiques devait ajouter son grain de sel littéraire à la réussite du moine de Foixà."

30. Kay, "Poésie."

31. Orr, *Intertextuality*, 133.

CHAPTER 8. PERILOUS QUOTATIONS

1. *Breviari*, 33319–27, quotation #230.

2. Most scholars identify the *perilhos tractat* with the entire discussion of sexual love. I do not, because of the passage 17611–21 in which Matfre indicates that the "peril" ex-

tends up to the "goodness" of the treatment of the tree. For more detail, see Kay, "L'arbre et la greffe."

3. If the *Breviari*'s quotations are thought of as composing a *florilegium*, then it is longer than the longest known one of 226 items in *Dc* (see Chapter 4). Ricketts's edition numbers quotations up to #267. The same line from Peire Cardenal 335.11 is quoted twice, once as part of #265 and again as #266. Similarly the lines from Raimon de Miraval 406.7 which are quoted as #137 are quoted again as part of #108. Richter, *Troubadourzitate*, identifies 266 quotations; she accords separate numbers to the duplicated passages from Peire Cardenal and Raimon de Miraval, but omits #177. Ricketts, "Une nouvelle citation," has since identified another possible quotation beginning at line 34262, which he suggests may be by Peire Cardenal. All manuscripts mark some quotations but not all the manuscripts mark all quotations, and certain quotations are not identified in any; see Kay, "How Long Is a Quotation?"

4. Lacan, *Le séminaire, livre XVI*, 39.

5. Armstrong and Kay, *Knowing Poetry*, 112–16.

6. See Fasseur, "Mort et salut" and "Une expérience"; I have also benefited from Bolduc, *Medieval Poetics of Contraries*, chap. 2, and "Naming Names"; and from Nicholson, "Branches of Knowledge."

7. Kay, "L'arbre et la greffe."

8. Fasseur, "Mort et salut," 431, speaks of "citer pour régénerer."

9. Kay, "How Long Is a Quotation?"

10. One of the Aimeric extracts, #129, is quoted anonymously, and one (#42) that is attributed to Aimeric by Matfre is in fact by Guiraut de Salaignac (249.1); we encounter this passage again in Chapter 9. The only Aimeric quotations to occur outside the *perilhos tractat* are ##173, 227, 253, and 257.

11. Nicholson, "Branches of Knowledge," 381–82. After Aimeric the next most frequently quoted poet in the whole of the *Breviari* is Bernart de Ventadorn, named as the author of fifteen quotations (and who is also responsible for two that are misattributed: one to Guiraut de Quentinhac, another to Peire Vidal). Bernart is followed by Peire Vidal with fifteen citations (though one belongs to Bernart de Ventadorn) and Folquet de Marselha with eleven (plus #92, ascribed erroneously to Perdigon).

12. Song 40, lines 35–40, in the edition by Shepard and Chambers.

13. Shepard and Chambers, *Poems of Aimeric de Peguilhan*, 3: "Aimeric's poems are consistently noble in thought, if sometimes pedestrian in expression."

14. See Nicholson, "Branches of Knowledge"; and, for the phenomenon of prequotation in the *Breviari* generally, Kay, "How Long Is a Quotation?" and "Knowledge and Truth."

15. The attribution to Aimeric is erroneous; see note 10 above.

16. Song 15, in Shepard and Chambers ed.

17. Song 8, in Shepard and Chambers ed.

18. 1 John 2:16: "For all that is in the world, the lust of the flesh, and the lust of the eyes, and the pride of life, is not of the Father, but is of the world."

19. Song 8, lines 28–29, according to Shepard and Chambers, *Poems of Aimeric de Peguilhan*, 77, "one of the best-known expositions of the medieval theory of the origin of 'courtly love.'"

20. The song is preserved in seventeen manuscripts and the editors do not signal any variation in stanza order.

21. Song 8, line 33; the editors read "Adoncas prend veray' Amors nasquensa," but *valensa* not *nasquensa* is found in *chansonniers CEGQR*.

22. It is also worth signaling that three of four quotations from Garin lo Brun's *ensenhamen* fall in the *conselhs*, and that here too Matfre favors songs by members of his own family.

23. For *sigla*, see Appendix 17; *N* can be consulted in facsimile; the illuminations in *M* are reproduced by Laske-Fix, *Bildzyklus*.

24. The "better" manuscripts are *G, I, M,* and *N*; see Richter, *Troubadourzitate*, 66–106, especially 106; also Ricketts, "Le problème du manuscrit *H*"; Ferrando, "El *Breviari d'amor.*"

25. Those in *N* are exceptionally developed, occupying most of 199v and all of 200r. Laske-Fix catalogs this scene in *M* as #137 and identifies the scenarios where the devil seduces courtly lovers as (a) pleasure, (b) clothes and weapons, (c) vanity, (d) falconry, (e) feasting, (f) tournaments, (g) battles, (h) dancing, (i) women's beckoning, concluding with (j) the devil wins the lover's soul.

26. Laske-Fix, *Bildzyklus*, does not mention the marginal devils in *M*.

27. 225.11 and 225.13.

28. 406.20, 293.32, 163.1 (Garin lo Brun's *ensenhamen*), 293.15 quoted twice, 364.43.

29. 375.27, 155.16.

30. See quotations 172 (461.210), 175 (461.98), 177 (unidentified; see Ricketts's edition, li), 179 (461.123b), 184 (461.21), 207 (461.132), 211 (461.32), 212 (461.227), 230 (461.245a, since identified as an excerpt of Raimon Vidal's *Abril issia*, quoted anonymously), 237 (461.91), 241 (461.48), 263 (unidentified; see Ricketts's edition, V: 32).

31. Richter, *Troubadourzitate*, 113.

32. Song 43 in Avalle ed.; it is also quoted as #105 in Matfre's response to lovers complaining about women, making it the *Breviari*'s most quoted song.

33. Kay, "L'arbre et la greffe"; Armstrong and Kay, *Knowing Poetry*, 118–20.

34. Did Jofre de Foixà know the *Breviari*? There is a resemblance between the grammarian's quotation of Aimeric de Peguilhan alongside Solomon to imply that he shares their wisdom, and Matfre's similar juxtaposition of himself, Aimeric, and Solomon, 28020–39, also underlining their common conviction that the virtuous should persevere in good works even when vilified.

35. Ricketts's identification of a quotation at 34262 ("Une nouvelle citation") interrupts the sequence, coming between #262 and #263, unless, as Ricketts suggests, it is also by Peire Cardenal; see also note 3.

36. *Poésies complètes de Peire Cardenal*, ed. Lavaud, Song 69, note to these lines.

37. Lavaud also mentions earlier conjectures linking the song to the death of Baudouin of Toulouse in 1214 (*Poésies complètes de Peire Cardenal*, 458, note).

38. Armstrong and Kay, *Knowing Poetry*, 166.

CHAPTER 9. DANTE'S EX-APPROPRIATION OF THE TROUBADOURS

1. Quotations from *De vulgari eloquentia* are from Botterill's edition, with minor modifications to his translation, notably as regards the Occitan, where all translations are my own. Quotations from the *Commedia* are from Durling's edition, with the same provisos.

2. Shapiro, *De vulgari eloquentia*, 99–100; Perugi, "Arnaut Daniel in Dante."

3. In *florilegia*, 9.14, 10.50, 29.17, 29.18, 155.22, 242.72, 242.73; in *vidas* or *razos*, 80.29, 242.55, 242.73.

4. Five of the incipits he quotes, for instance, are inserted into the biographical compilations in manuscript N^2: 155.22, 242.17, 242.55, 242.72, 242.73. N^2 dates from the sixteenth century, but may copy an earlier model; for reservations about its standing, see Poe, "A Re-evaluation."

5. Editions of "Dante's troubadours" containing the whole texts of the songs from which Dante quotes (like Monaci, *Poesie* and Chaytor, *Troubadours*) distort the range of his potential sources, both exaggerating and reducing them.

6. Bergin, "Dante's Provençal Gallery," 23–24; Barolini, *Dante's Poets*, 98–100, 108–19, 175–76.

7. Bergin, "Dante's Provençal Gallery," 22–23. Scholars of Dante usually claim Arnaut as a poet of *trobar clus*, but see Peirone's useful corrective ("Il 'trobar leu' di Arnaut Daniel"). Arnaut does not adhere to any stylistic school, but the terms that best qualify his compositions are *prim* and *car* rather than *clus*.

8. While the reference in *De vulgari* 1.2.7 to the magpies of Ovid, *Metamorphoses*, book 5, seems negative, Dante concedes the value of intelligent copying in *Purgatorio* 26.58–60, where the pilgrim is told that his pen follows dictation better than that of his predecessors.

9. Derrida, *Monolinguisme*, 46: "il n'y a jamais d'appropriation ou de réappropriation absolue. Parce qu'il n'y a pas de propriété naturelle de la langue, celle-ci ne donne lieu qu'à de la rage appropriatrice, à de la jalousie sans appropriation . . . rappelons d'un mot, en passant, que ce discours sur l'ex-appropriation de la langue, plus précisément de la 'marque,' ouvre à une politique, à un droit et à une éthique."

10. Derrida, "Signature événement contexte," 381: "possibilité de prélèvement et de greffe citationnelle qui appartient à la structure de toute marque, parlée ou écrite."

11. J. H. Marshall, *The "Razos de trobar" of Raimon Vidal*, 100–105.

12. Compare Grafton, *Footnote*, 13: "Jacob Thomasius offered a neat taxonomy of the wrong forms of citation as early as 1673. Some authors 'say nothing, at the most significant point, about one whom they then cite only on a point of no or little importance.' Wickeder ones 'take the most careful precautions never to mention [their source] at all.' And the wickedest 'mention him only when they disagree with or criticize him.'"

13. See also Marchesi, *Dante*, 38–40, for a thoughtful reading of Dante's project at this point.

14. Heller-Roazen, *Echolalias*, 225–26.

15. Mancini, "Aimeric de Peguilhan," documents the beginnings of Arnaldian imitation in northern Italy in the first half of the thirteenth century; Perugi, *Trovatori*, 240, suggests that the late thirteenth century in Rodez was a period of Arnaldian imitation; Di Girolamo and Siviero, "Da Orange," speak of an Arnaldian fashion extending into Catalonia; see also Chapter 11.

16. Though in the manuscripts they are not enumerated consecutively in 2.6.6 as they are in editions. See Pfeffer, "A Note On Dante."

17. E.g., in 2.10, where he claims to have imitated Arnaut's use of the *oda continua* form in "Al poco giorno e al gran cerchio d'ombra"; or 2.13, where he likewise cites Arnaut as his model for the use of *rims estramps*. See also Bondanella, "Arnaut Daniel."

18. In manuscript copies of 2.6.6, however, the first-named troubadour Giraut de Bornelh is followed by the French Thibaut de Champagne, who thereby interrupts the sequence of troubadours. See Pfeffer, "A Note On Dante."

19. See Dante's editors' notes to this line, *Divine Comedy*, 1:448; and Boutière and Schutz, eds., *Biographies*, IX, 65.

20. Boutière and Schutz, eds., *Biographies*, LXXI, 470. The way Folquet is used in the *Breviari* may also have prepared the way for Dante's reading. Matfre quotes him in the *plags*, the *conselhs*, and the tree of knowledge (illustrating humility), successfully transforming him from a somewhat peevish troubadour who was unhappy in love to a promoter of love's supreme value, regardless of the defects of individual lovers. See Chapter 4; Washer, "Paraphrased and Parodied," 253–55; Armstrong and Kay, *Knowing Poetry*, 117.

21. While it is true that Arnaut names himself in most of his songs, the formula "I am Arnaut" occurs in "En cest sonet" alone and is therefore not "typical of the troubadour" (pace N. B. Smith, "Arnaut Daniel," 101). Although for Hayes, "Arnaut Daniel," 128, it is obvious that Dante is referring to the *tornada*, this does not seem to be universally accepted; even for Hayes, Dante is guided more by the song itself than the quotation in the *vida*. My translation brings out the contrastive meaning of *e* (not "and" but "yet"); the analogues suggested by N. B. Smith, "Arnaut Daniel," 103–4, and Hayes, "Arnaut Daniel," 130, are helpful.

22. To list only instances from *Purgatorio*: 3.112–13, "Io son Manfredi, / nepote di Costanza imperadrice"; 5.88, "io fui di Montefeltro, io son Bonconte"; 6.74–75, "O Mantoano, io son Sordello / de la tua terra"; 7.7, "Io son Virgilio"; 9.55, "I' son Lucia"; 11.67, "Io sono Omberto"; 14.81, "io fui Guido del Duca." A variant form occurs in 5.133, "ricorditi di me, che son la Pia."

23. E.g., *Paradiso* 3.49–51, "i' son Piccarda / che . . . beata sono"; and cf. *Inferno* 23.118–20.

24. On this "turn of the voice" of the *tornadas* of twelfth-century troubadour songs in relation to their previous content, see Peraino, *Giving Voice*, chap. 1, especially 33–50,

25. See Perugi's note to these lines in his edition of Arnaut Daniel.

26. Topsfield, *Troubadours and Love*, 210–11.

27. Mozely's translation modified.

28. Song 47, in *Poems of Aimeric de Peguilhan*, ed. Shepard and Chambers.

29. 305.16, Song 18, ed. Routledge, 43–48: "Ab Arnaut Daniel son set, / Qu'a sa vida be no cantet, / Mas us folhs motz qu'om non enten; / Pus la lebr' ab lo bou casset / E contra suberna nadet, / No val ses chans un aguillen." ("That makes seven with Arnaut Daniel, who never sang well in his whole life, but only a bunch of foolish words no one can understand. His singing hasn't been worth a hip, ever since he hunted the hare with the ox and swam against the tide.")

30. Menocal, *Writing*, 102–4, is right to point out that the phrase "better word-smith" is hardly fulsome and may be depreciative; N. B. Smith, "Arnaut Daniel," 106–7, points out the universality of the Occitan speech given to Arnaut: it echoes many troubadours, maintains a rigorous simplicity, and abounds in Italian cognates.

31. Though this much discussed "Tan m'abellis" is found in the incipits of other songs as well as 155.22; see, among others, N. B. Smith, "Arnaut Daniel," 103; and Hayes, "Arnaut Daniel."

32. On the contrastive meaning of *e*, see note 21 above. One of the Press's readers pointed out to me that the phrase in Arnaut's mouth should be filtered through Dante's emphasis throughout *Inferno* on weeping in response to sin.

33. See the brilliant commentary by Burgwinkle, "The Form of Our Desire," 572–73.

34. Hiscoe, "Dante's Poetry," links Dante's Arnaut with Pasiphaë differently, seeing the poet as a master maker (like Daedalus) but also pointing to Christ (via the prophet Daniel); Hayes sees the third of Arnaut's adynata—that of swimming against the tide—as "un aveu de son homosexualité" ("Arnaut Daniel," 127).

CHAPTER 10. THE *LEYS D'AMORS*

1. See Anglade, *Etudes*, 15–51, for a history of the institution and its texts.

2. Léglu, "Languages in Conflict"; Dauvois, "Évolution."

3. Each of these two redactions survives in just one manuscript, formerly held by the Toulouse Académie des Jeux Floraux, now Toulouse Bibliothèque Municipale MS 2883 (the 1356 recension) and 2884 (that of 1341); see Anglade, *Etudes*, 129–35. The earlier redaction, ed. Gatien-Arnoult, is often called *Las flors del gay saber*; the later one, ed. Anglade. In addition to these prose versions there is one in verse and a number of related treatises also capitalizing on the Consistori's prestige; see Anglade, *Etudes*, 92–120.

4. See Zufferey, *Bibliographie*, for this later poetic production.

5. J. H. Marshall, "Observations."

6. The attribution to P. Arquier has been added in what looks like a later hand at the foot of the column.

7. Zufferey, *Bibliographie*, 27.

8. Bernhardt's edition of At de Mons, *Werke*, vii–xii; Cigni, "Il trovatore."

9. Bernhardt's ed., xii–xiii; Cigni, "Il trovatore."

10. Gonfroy, "Reflet."

11. Anglade, "Le troubadour."

12. Armstrong and Kay, *Knowing Poetry*, 102–3, 107–8.

13. See especially the end of book 1 (Last Judgment) and beginning of book 2 (judging standards). On the interconnection between divine and poetic judgment in the *Leys*, see Moreau, "Eschatological Subjects."

14. Powell, *Albertanus*.

15. Molinier (*Leys*, ed. Anglade, 1:13–14) lists the seven troubadours of Toulouse on the occasion of the first meeting: a young nobleman, a bourgeois, two bankers, two merchants, and a notary. Also present at this first meeting, civic dignitaries and other bourgeois (named), plus unnamed "doctors, licenciatz, borguezes, mercadiers, e motz autres ciutadas de Tholoza" (14).

16. Léglu, "Languages in Conflict." Within Toulouse there was an internal split similar to that between the Welfs (or Guelphs) and the Ghibellines in the Italian city states.

17. Cigni,"Il trovatore," 297.

18. Similar politics of the footnote were also observed in Dante; see Chapter 9.

19. Pasero,"Sulle fonti," reviews and corrects the notes to Anglade's edition and his *Etudes*, 52–70. For Molinier's treatment of Albertano, see especially Pasero, 140–47, 161–85.

20. Powell, *Albertanus*, 61.

21. Such self-generating *monographie* is reminiscent of Compagnon's account of quotation in *La seconde main*; see Introduction.

22. At, 309.V, 488–563; *Leys*, ed. Anglade, 1:84–87.

23. Only one of the nonstrophic poems, 309.V, is in octosyllables; all the rest are hexasyllabic.

24. The same treatment is meted to Aesop (*Leys*, ed. Anglade, 1:156), Ovid (1:185), and Seneca (1:189).

25. On fo. 150; ed. Gatien-Arnoult, 3:374–76; see also Kay, "La seconde main."

26. Chenu, "Auctor."

27. *Breviari* quotations ##9 and 10, lines 28020–39; see Chapter 8.

28. The Author also speaks "according to" Ignoscum (*Leys*, ed. Anglade, 1:102), and Anselm (1:129).

29. The *Versifiayre* may be Alexander of Villedieu, thirteenth-century author of the *Doctrinale*, a versified Latin grammar.

CHAPTER 11. PETRARCH'S "LASSO ME"

1. Careri, *Il canzoniere provenzale H* [*H*], 50–51 and plate 1.

2. Perugi, *Trovatori*.

3. Appel, the first scholar to study "Razo e dreyt," took "Saint Gregori" to be a *senhal* (code name) derived from line 46 of the song, where the speaker swears an oath by the saint; on the basis of stylistic analysis Appel, "Petrarka," confirmed the song as being by Arnaut Daniel.

4. Ten songs in an Arnaut section, plus the obscene *sirventes* in another part of the *chansonnier*; see also Careri, *Il canzoniere*, 135–58, transcription 463–84, and plates 3–7.

5. Bembo, owner of the manuscript in the mid-sixteenth century, believed it to have belonged to Petrarch; Careri, *Il canzoniere*, 51.

6. Petrarch's opening binomial "Drez et rayson" is closer to the copy in *K*, "Dreg e razos," than of *C*, which begins "Razo e dreyt."

7. Or later; see Bettarini's discussion in her edition of Petrarch's *Canzoniere*, 345–46.

8. Perugi, *Trovatori*, 239.

9. The stanza, *r*, lines 348–55, quoted from Ramon Vidal, *Obra poètica*, ed. Field, 2:50: "No·i a cor tan serrat d'erguelh / qu'amor, s'il plai, dedinz no reinh / [qu'il sap ab son cortés engeinh / traire joi de l'ausor] capdueilh / e qui no·n lei so q'ill escriu / pauc sap de l'amorosa lei; / c'amors non ha ges dig de rei, / que·l 'non' son 'oc' ses qu'il s'en triu?"

10. Berenguer d'Anoia, *Mirall de trobar*, ed. Alcover, #28, 619–23: "En ausi car eu no say cora jaz se cora deu a cor mausi cor eu no say cora jam se cora den quant dougens nom estant los mals si tot las bocas quanta nages non val quem nestança"; Alcover, 136, supplies this transcription by Anglade: "En ausi, car eu no say, / cora jazse cora / Deu a cor m'aus' cor / eu no sai cora, /ja·m secora / Deu quant don / Gens nom estant lo mals / sitot l'abocas / quanta·n hagues no val / Que·m rrescança."

11. Boutière and Schutz, eds., *Biographies*, IX.A.1, 59: "Arnaut Daniel was from the same region as Arnaut de Maruelh."

12. Boutière and Schutz, eds., *Biographies*, IX.B, 63.

13. Galvez, *Songbook*, chap. 3.

14. See Beltrami, "Remarques," for arguments to this effect; Paden, Sankovitch, and Stäblein, in their edition of Bertran de Born, *Poems*, award him this song, guided in part by the marginal note in *chansonnier H* that identified Bertran as the "desirat" to whom Arnaut's *sestina* is addressed.

15. This move was initiated by J. H. Marshall, "La chanson provençale."

16. Perugi, *Trovatori*, 56–59.

17. Ibid., 59–69.

18. Ibid., 236: "senza dubbio la conosceva come opera di Arnaut Daniel."

19. Canzone 23.

20. Dante actually quotes the same song by Cavalcanti in *De vulgari* 2.12.3 and 8.

21. Note the semantic value of the rhymes *fiori:demori*; *mentire:dire*; *aspro:aspro*; *grave:soave*; *beltade:etade*.

22. Menocal, *Writing*, 141–53, offers a fascinating reading of the canzone's response to Dante, marred only by her uncritical acceptance of the view that the quoted line is by Arnaut.

23. Most strikingly in line 37: "Dous m'es e bos s'ieu per dezir en mori" (Perugi, *Trovatori*, 16; it is a pleasure to me if I die of love).

24. Compare Dante's reference to "hirsute" speech in *De vulgari eloquentia* 2.7.6.

CONCLUSION

1. Armstrong and Kay, *Knowing Poetry*, 204–5; the reference is to Tucker, *Forms of the "Medieval."*

2. Greene, *Light in Troy*, 9; the "Conclusion" to Armstrong and Kay, *Knowing Poetry*, suggests some of the differences between lyric poetry prior to and after Petrarch, but its concern is with the French genres that replace troubadour lyric along the nightingales' way.

3. On imitation and its challenges, see Greene, *Light in Troy*. For fifteenth- and sixteenth-century ideas of inspiration as divine fury, see Castor, *Pléiade Poetics*, 24–36, 195–99. The importance I have attributed in this book to evolving patterns of misprision in relation to poetry and knowledge may also find an echo in new work by early modern scholars. In *Lying Mirror*, a study of the first person in sixteenth-century French literature, James Helgeson characterizes its stance as indirect, dissimulating, and dependent on social recognition—relayed, as I would put it, by the supposed knowledge of supposed other subjects. The knowledge economy uncovered in Neil Kenny's *Uses of Curiosity* operates in terms of curiosity and its repression, in a manner that also parallels, albeit more distantly, the equivocation between memory and suppression outlined here.

BIBLIOGRAPHY OF PRINTED
AND ELECTRONIC SOURCES

For manuscript sources, see Appendix 17.

PRIMARY TEXTS

In cases where more than one edition is listed, the one marked with an asterisk is the one referred to, unless otherwise indicated.

Editions of Troubadour Songs Included in Appendices 1 and 2

[Listed in PC order]

[3] Ademar lo Negre. Adolf Kolsen, "Altprovenzalisches Nr. 3: Zwei Gedichte des Ademar lo Negre." *Zeitschrift für Romanische Philologie* 39 (1919): 156–62.

[5.1] Ademar de Rocaficha. In *Provenzalische Inedita aus Pariser Handschriften*, 3. Ed. Carl Appel. Leipzig: O. R. Reisland, 1890.

[9] Aimeric de Belenoi. *Le poesie.* Ed. Maurizio Perugi. Florence: Positivamail, 1997.

[10] Aimeric de Peguilhan. *The Poems of Aimeric de Peguilhan.* Ed. William P. Shepard and Frank M. Chambers. Evanston, Ill.: Northwestern University Press, 1950.

[11] Aimeric de Sarlat. "Le canzoni di Aimeric de Sarlat." Ed. M. Fumagalli. *Travaux de linguistique et de littérature* 17 (1979): 121–69.

[16] Albertet de Sestaro. "Les poésies du troubadour Albertet." Ed. Jean Boutière. *Studi medievali* 10 (1937): 1–129.

[22.a.1] Andrian del Palais. In Terramagnino da Pisa, *Doctrina d'acort*, vv. 202–9, 266–67. In *The "Razos de trobar" of Raimon Vidal and Associated Texts.* Ed. J. H. Marshall. London: Oxford University Press, 1972.

[25.1a] Arman, with Bernart de la Barta. In *The Troubadour Tensos and Partimens: A Critical Edition.* Ed. Ruth Harvey, Linda Paterson, et al., 1:107. Woodbridge: D. S. Brewer, 2010.

[29] Arnaut Daniel. **Canzoni.* Ed. Gianluigi Toja. Florence: G. G. Sansoni, 1961.

———. *Canzoni di Arnaut Daniel.* Ed. Maurizio Perugi. 2 vols. Milan: Riccardo Ricciardi, 1978.

[30] Arnaut de Maruelh. *Les poésies lyriques du troubadour Arnaut de Mareuil.* Ed. R. C
   Johnston. Paris: E. Droz, 1935.

[30.VI] Arnaut de Maruelh. Mario Eusebi, "L'ensenhamen di Arnaut de Mareuil," *Romania* 90 (1969): 14–30.

[32.1] Arnaut Plagues. In *Trobairitz: Der Beitrag der Frau in der altokzitanischen höfischen
   Lyrik; Edition des Gesamtkorpus.* Ed. Angelica Rieger, 197. Tübingen: M. Niemeyer,
   1991.

[34] Arnaut de Tintinhac. *Le troubadour Arnaut de Tintinhac: Edition critique des poèmes.*
   Ed. Jean Mouzat. Tulle: Impr. Juglard-Ogier, 1956.

[44] Azar. Transcription in *Die Provenzalische Blumenlese der Chigiana.* Ed. Edmund
   Stengel, 45. Marburg: Elwert, 1878.

[47] Berenguer de Palazol. *Berenguer de Palol.* Ed. Margherita Beretta Spampinato.
   Modena: Mucchi, 1978.

[54.1] Bernart Arnaut d'Armagnac. In *Trobairitz: Der Beitrag der Frau in der altokzitanischen höfischen Lyrik; Edition des Gesamtkorpus.* Ed. Angelica Rieger, 242.
   Tübingen: M. Niemeyer, 1991.

[58.3] Bernart de la Barta. In Adolf Kolsen, "Drei altprovenzalische Dichtungen." In *Mélanges de linguistique et de littérature offerts à Alfred Jeanroy par ses élèves et amis,*
   375–85 (p. 380). Paris: Droz, 1928.

[58.4] Bernart de la Barta. In Frank M. Chambers, "Three Troubadour Poems with Historical Overtones," 51. *Speculum* 54 (1979): 42–54.

[62] Bernart de la Fon. In *Bernart von Ventadorn: Seine Lieder, mit Einleitung und Glossar,*
   301. Ed. Carl Appel. Halle: M. Niemeyer, 1915.

[63] Bernart Marti. *Il trovatore Bernart Marti.* Ed. Fabrizio Beggiato. Modena: Mucchi,
   1984.

[65.1] Bernart de Prades. In *Bernart von Ventadorn: Seine Lieder, mit Einleitung und Glossar.* Ed. Carl Appel, 304. Halle: M. Niemeyer, 1915.

[66.2] Bernart de Rovenac. G. Bosdorff, "Bernard von Rouvenac, ein provenzalischer
   Trobador des XIII. Jahrhunderts." *Romanische Forschungen* 22 (1908): 761–827.

[70] *Bernart de Ventadorn. Bernard de Ventadour, *Chansons d'amour.* Ed. Moshé Lazar.
   Paris: C. Klincksieck, 1966.

———. *Bernart von Ventadorn: Seine Lieder, mit Einleitung und Glossar.* Ed. Carl Appel.
   Halle: M. Niemeyer, 1915

[71] Bernart de Venzac. *Lirica moralistica nell'Occitania del XII secolo.* Ed. Maria Picchio
   Simonelli. Modena: Mucchi, 1974.

[74] Bertolome Zorzi. *Der Troubadour Bertolome Zorzi.* Ed. Emil Levy. Halle: M. Niemeyer, 1883.

[76] Bertran d'Alamanon. *Le Troubadour Bertran d'Alamanon.* Ed. J.-J. Salverda de
   Grave. Toulouse: Privat, 1902.

[80] *Bertran de Born. *The Poems of the Troubadour Bertran de Born.* Ed. William D.
   Paden, Tilde Sankovitch, and Patricia Stäblein. Berkeley: University of California
   Press, 1986.

———. *L'amour et la guerre: L'oeuvre poétique de Bertrand de Born*. Ed. Gérard Gouiran. 2 vols. Aix-en-Provence: Université de Provence; and Marseille: Lafitte, 1985.

[81.1] Bertran de Born lo filhs. In *Los trovadores: Historia literaria y textos*. Ed. Martín de Riquer, 2:952. Barcelona: Planeta, 1975.

[84.1] Bertran de Gordo, with Peire Raimon de Toloza. In *The Troubadour Tensos and Partimens: A Critical Edition*. Ed. Ruth Harvey, Linda Paterson, et al., 1:163. Woodbridge: D. S. Brewer, 2010.

[87] Bertran del Poget. Cesare De Lollis, "Di Bertrand el Pojet trovatore del età angioina." In *Miscellanea di studi critici edita in onore di Arturo Graf*, 691–710. Bergamo: Istituto Italiano de Arti Grafiche, 1903.

[92] Bertran de la Tor. In *Biographies des troubadours*. Ed. Jean Boutière and Alexander Herman Schutz, 289. 2nd ed. Paris: Nizet, 1964.

[95] Lo vesques de Clarmon. Stanley C. Aston, "The Poems of Robert, Bishop of Clermont (1195–1227)." In *Mélanges d'histoire littéraire, de linguistique et de philologie romanes offerts à Charles Rostaing*, 1:25–39. Liège: Association des romanistes de l'Université de Liège, 1974.

[96] Blacasset. Otto Klein, "Der Trobadour Blacassetz." In *Städtische Realschule zu Wiesbaden Jahres-Bericht*, 1886–87. Wiesbaden: Ritter, 1887.

[97.3 and 97.7] Blacatz. In Peire Vidal, *Poesie*. Ed. D'Arco Silvio Avalle, 448, 423. Milan: Ricciardi, 1960.

[97.7] Blacatz. *In *The Troubadour Tensos and Partimen: A Critical Edition*. Ed. Ruth Harvey, Linda Paterson, et al., 1:192. Woodbridge: D. S. Brewer, 2010.

[101.7] Bonifaci Calvo. In *Los trovadores: Historia literaria y textos*. Ed. Martín de Riquer, 3:1426. Barcelona: Planeta, 1975.

[106] Cadenet. *Les poésies du troubadour Cadenet: Édition critique avec introduction, notes et glossaire*. Ed. Josef Zemp. Bern: P. Lang, 1978.

[119] Dalfi d'Alvernha. In *Biographies des troubadours*. Ed. Jean Boutière and Alexander Herman Schutz, 286–92. 2nd Ed. Paris: Nizet, 1964.

[124] Daude de Pradas. *Les poésies de Daude de Pradas*. Ed. Alexander Herman Schutz. Toulouse: E. Privat, 1933.

[132] Elias de Barjols. *Le troubadour Elias de Barjols*. Ed. Stanislas Strónski. Toulouse: E. Privat, 1906.

[133] Elias Cairel. *Il trovatore Elias Cairel*. Ed. Giosuè Lachin. Modena: Mucchi, 2004.

[136] Elias d'Ussel. In *Les poésies des quatre troubadours d'Ussel*. Ed. Jean Audiau. Paris: Delagrave, 1922.

[155] Folquet de Marselha. *Le poesie di Folchetto di Marsiglia*. Ed. Paolo Squillacioti, Biblioteca degli studi mediolatini e volgari. Pisa: Pacini, 1999.

[162.6] Garin d'Apchier. In *Biographies des troubadours*. Ed. Jean Boutière and Alexander Herman Schutz, 343. 2nd ed. Paris: Nizet, 1964.

[163.1] Garin lo Brun. *L'ensenhament alla dama*. Ed. Laura Regina Bruno. Rome: Archivio Guido Izzi, 1996.

[166] Gaucelm Estaca. A. Kolsen, "Die Trobadorlieder Gaucelm Estaca I und Raimon de Miraval 21." *Studi medievali* 13 (1940): 141–48.

[167] Gaucelm Faidit. *Les poèmes de Gaucelm Faidit, troubadour du XIIe siècle.* Ed. Jean Mouzat. Paris: A. G. Nizet, 1965.

[173] Gausbert de Poicibot. *Les poésies de Jausbert de Puycibot, troubadour du XIIIe siècle.* Ed. William Pierce Shepard. Paris: E. Champion, 1924.

[183] Guilhem de Peitieu. *Guglielmo IX d'Aquitania: Poesie.* Ed. Nicolò Pasero. Modena: Mucchi, 1973.

[185] Lo coms de Rodez. In *Poésies de Uc de Saint-Circ.* Ed. Alfred Jeanroy and Jean-Jacques Salverda de Grave, 136. Toulouse: Privat, 1913.

[187] Comtessa de Proensa. In *Trobairitz: Der Beitrag der Frau in der altokzitanischen höfischen Lyrik; Edition des Gesamtkorpus.* Ed. Angelica Rieger, 204. Tübingen: M. Niemeyer, 1991.

[192] Gui de Cavaillo. Saverio Guida, "L'attività poetica di Gui de Cavaillon durante la crociata albigese." *Cultura neolatina* 33 (1973): 235–71.

[192.6] Gui de Cavaillo. In *Trobairitz: Der Beitrag der Frau in der altokzitanischen höfischen Lyrik; Edition des Gesamtkorpus.* Ed. Angelica Rieger, 204. Tübingen: M. Niemeyer, 1991.

[194] Gui d'Ussel. In *Les poésies des quatre troubadours d'Ussel.* Ed. Jean Audiau. Paris: Delagrave, 1922.

[202] Guilhem Ademar. *Poésies du troubadour Guilhem Adémar.* Ed. Kurt Almqvist. Uppsala: Almqvist & Wiksells, 1951.

[205] Guilhem Augier Novella. *Gedichte des Guillem Augier Novella, eines provenzalischen Trobadors aus dem Anfange des XIII. Jahrhunderts.* Ed. Johannes Müller. Halle: Niemeyer, 1899.

[208] Guillem de Balaun. "Le troubadour Guilhem de Balaun." Ed. Jean Boutière. *Annales du Midi* 48 (1936): 225–51.

[210] Guillem de Berguedà. *Les poesies del trobador Guillem de Berguedà.* Ed. Martín de Riquer. Barcelona: Quaderns Crema, 1996.

[213] Guillem de Cabestanh. "Las poesías del trovador Guillem de Cabestany." Ed. M. Cots. *Boletín de la Real Academia de Buenas Letras de Barcelona* 40 (June 1985): 227–330.

[217] Guillem Figueira. *Guillem Figueira, ein provenzalischer Troubadour.* Ed. Emil Levy. Berlin: Liebrecht, 1880.

[223] Guillem Magret. "Der Trobador Guillem Magret." Ed. Fritz Naudieth. *Beihefte zur Zeitschrift für romanische Philologie* 52 (1914): 78–144.

[225] Guillem de Montanhagol. *Les poésies de Guilhem de Montanhagol, troubadour provençal du XIIIe siècle.* Ed. Peter T. Ricketts. Toronto: Pontifical Institute of Mediaeval Studies, 1964.

[227.8] [= 58.2] Guillem Peire de Casals, *tenso* with Bernart de la Barta. In *The Troubadour Tensos and Partimens: A Critical Edition.* Ed. Ruth Harvey, Linda Paterson, et al., 2:603. Woodbridge: D. S. Brewer, 2010.

[231.1a] Guillem Rainol d'At. In Albert Stimming, *Bertran de Born: Sein Leben und seine Werke*, 136. Halle: Niemeyer, 1879.

[233.4] Guillem de Saint Gregori, "Razo e dreyt." In Maurizio Perugi, *Trovatori a Valchiusa: Un frammento della cultura provenzale del Petrarca*, 15. Padua: Antenore, 1985.

[234] Guillem de Sant Leidier. *Poésies du troubadour Guillem de Saint-Didier*. Ed. Aimo Sakari. Mémoires de la Société Néophilologique de Helsinki 19. Helsinki: Société Néophilologique, 1956.

[235.1] Guillem de Salaignac. In *Giraut de Salignac: Ein provenzalischer Trobador*. Ed. Alexander Strempel, 64. Geneva: Slatkine Reprints, 1977.

[236] Guillem de la Tor. *Le liriche del trovatore Guilhem de la Tor*. Ed. Antonella Negri. Soveria Mannelli: Rubettino, 2006.

[240] Guiraudo lo Ros. "Le poesie di Guiraudo lo Ros." Ed. Anna Maria Finoli. *Studi Medievali* ser. 3, vol. 15, no. 2 (1974): 1051–106.

[242] Giraut de Bornelh. *The Cansos and Sirventes of the Troubadour Giraut de Borneil: A Critical Edition*. Ed. Ruth Verity Sharman. Cambridge: Cambridge University Press, 1989.

[244] Guiraut d'Espanha. *Die Lieder des Trobadors Guiraut d'Espanha*. Ed. O. Hoby. Freiburg, Switzerland: St. Paulus–Drückerei, 1915.

[248] Guiraut Riquier. *Guiraut Riquier, las cansos: Kritischer Text und Kommentar*. Ed. Ulrich Mölk. Heidelberg: Carl Winter, 1962.

[249] Guiraut de Salaignac. *Giraut de Salignac: Ein provenzalischer Trobador*. Ed. Alexander Strempel. Geneva: Slatkine Reprints, 1977.

[257.1] Izarn Rizol. In *Provenzalische Inedita aus Pariser Handschriften*. Ed. Carl Appel, 169. Leipzig: O. R. Reisland, 1890.

[262] Jaufre Rudel. *Il canzoniere di Jaufre Rudel*. Ed. Giorgio Chiarini. Rome: Japadre, 1985.

[273.1] Jordan Bonel de Cofolen. In C. A. F. Mahn, *Die Werke der Troubadours in provenzalische Sprache*, 3:311. Geneva: Slatkine Reprints, 1977.

[276.1] Jordan de l'Isla de Venessi. In *Les poèmes de Gaucelm Faidit, troubadour du XIIᵉ siècle*. Ed. Jean Mouzat, 583. Paris: A. G. Nizet, 1965.

[282] Lanfranc Cigala. *Il canzoniere di Lanfranco Cigala*. Ed. Francesco Branciforti. Florence: L. S. Olschki, 1954.

[288] Lombarda. In *Trobairitz: Der Beitrag der Frau in der altokzitanischen höfischen Lyrik; Edition des Gesamtkorpus*. Ed. Angelica Rieger, 242. Tübingen: M. Niemeyer, 1991.

[293] Marcabru. *Marcabru: A Critical Edition*. Ed. Simon Gaunt, Ruth Harvey, and Linda Paterson. Woodbridge: D. S. Brewer, 2000.

[295] Maria de Ventadorn. In *Trobairitz: Der Beitrag der Frau in der altokzitanischen höfischen Lyrik; Edition des Gesamtkorpus*. Ed. Angelica Rieger, 255. Tübingen: M. Niemeyer, 1991.

[297] Matfre Ermengau. Reinhilt Richter and Max Lütolf, "Les poésies lyriques de Matfré Ermengau." *Romania* 98 (1977): 15–33.

[305] Monge de Montaudo. *Les poésies du Moine de Montaudon.* Ed. Michael J. Routledge. Montpellier: Centre d'études occitanes de l'Université Paul Valery, 1977.

[309] At de Mons. *Die Werke des Trobadors N'At de Mons.* Ed. Wilhelm Bernhardt. Heil-
bronn: Henninger, 1887.

[315] Palais. Peter T. Ricketts, "Le troubadour Palais: Edition critique, traduction, et
commentaire." In *Studia Occitanica in Memoriam Paul Remy.* Ed. Hans-Erich
Keller et al., 1:227–40. Kalamazoo: Medieval Institute Publications, Western Michigan University, 1986.

[323] Peire d'Alvernha. *Peire d'Alvernhe: Poesie.* Ed. Aniello Fratta. Rome: Vecchiarelli,
1996.

[330] Peire Bremon Ricas Novas. *Il trovatore Peire Bremon Ricas Novas.* Ed. Paolo Di
Luca. Modena: Mucchi, 2008.

[332] Peire de Bussignac. *In Reinhilt Richter, *Die Troubadourzitate im* Breviari d'amor:
Kritische Ausgabe der provenzalischen Überlieferung, 157–58. Modena: Mucchi, 1976.
———. "Les deux sirventes de Peire de Bussignac (PC 332, 1 et 2)." Ed. P. T. Ricketts.
Rivista di Studi Testuali, forthcoming.

[335] Peire Cardenal. *Poésies complètes du troubadour Peire Cardenal.* Ed. René Lavaud.
Toulouse: E. Privat, 1957.

[337.1] Peire de Cols. In *Rigaut de Barbezilh: Liriche.* Ed. Alberto Vàrvaro, 245. Biblioteca
di filologa romanza 4. Bari: Adriatica, 1960.

[341] Peire Ermengau. In Reinhilt Richter, *Die Troubadourzitate im* Breviari d'amor:
Kritische Ausgabe der provenzalischen Überlieferung, 269–70. Modena: Mucchi, 1976.

[344] Peire Guillem de Luzerna. In Giulio Bertoni, *I trovatori d'Italia.* Modena: Orlandini, 1915.

[345.2] Peire Guilhem de Toloza. In *Poésies provençales inédites tirées des manuscrits
d'Italie.* Ed. Carl Appel, 69. Paris: Welter, 1898.

[353.1] Peire Pelisiers. In *Biographies des troubadours.* Ed. Jean Boutière and Alexander
Herman Schutz, 291. 2nd Ed. Paris: Nizet, 1964.

[355] Peire Raimon de Toloza. *Le poesie di Peire Raimon de Tolosa.* Ed. Alfredo Cavaliere.
Florence: L. S. Olschki, 1935.

[356] Peire Rogier. *The Poems of the Troubadour Peire Rogier.* Ed. Derek E. T. Nicholson.
Manchester: Manchester University Press, 1976.

[361] Peire d'Ussel. In *Les poésies des quatre troubadours d'Ussel.* Ed. Jean Audiau. Paris:
Delagrave, 1922.

[362.1 and 2] Peire de Valeira. In *Poésies provençales inédites tirées des manuscrits d'Italie.*
Ed. Carl Appel, 106. Paris: Welter, 1898.

[364] Peire Vidal. *Poesie.* Ed. D'Arco Silvio Avalle. Milan: Ricciardi, 1960.

[366] Peirol. *Peirol, Troubadour of Auvergne.* Ed. Stanley Collin Aston. Cambridge:
Cambridge University Press, 1953.

[370] Perdigon. *Les chansons de Perdigon.* Ed. H. J Chaytor. Paris: H. Champion, 1926.

[372] Pistoleta. "Der Trobador Pistoleta." Ed. E. Niestroy. *Beihefte zur Zeitschrift für romanische Philologie* 52 (1914): 1–77.

[374] Pons Barba. In *Trovatori minori*. Ed. Saverio Guida. Modena: Mucchi, 2002.

[375] Pons de Capdoill. *Leben und Werke des Trobadors Ponz de Capduoill*. Ed. Max von Napolski. Halle: M. Niemeyer, 1879.

[376.1] Pons Fabre d'Uzes. In "Sept poésies lyriques du troubadour Bertran Carbonel de Marseille." Ed. Giulio Contini. *Annales du Midi* 49 (1937): 1–41, 113–52, 225–40, 237–240 (p. 237).

[377] Pons de la Guardia. István Frank, "Pons de la Guardia, troubadour catalan du XIIe siècle." *Boletín de la Real Academia de Barcelona* 22 (1949): 229–324.

[380] Pons Santolh. In Reinhilt Richter, *Die Troubadourzitate im* Breviari d'amor: *Kritische Ausgabe der provenzalischen Überlieferung*, 381. Modena: Mucchi, 1976.

[384] Prebost de Valensa. In *The Troubadour Tensos and Partimens: A Critical Edition*. Ed. Ruth Harvey, Linda Paterson, et al., 3:1036. Woodbridge: D. S. Brewer, 2010.

[389] Raimbaut d'Aurenga. *The Life and Works of the Troubadour Raimbaut d'Orange*. Ed. Walter Thomas Pattison. Minneapolis: University of Minnesota Press, 1952.

[392] Raimbaut de Vaqueiras. *The Poems of the Troubadour Raimbaut de Vaqueiras*. Ed. Joseph Linskill. The Hague: Mouton, 1964.

[392.26]. In *Poésies du troubadour Aimeric de Belenoi*. Ed. Maria Dumitrescu, 143. Paris: Société des Anciens Textes Français, 1935.

[392.27]. In *Bernard de Ventadour. Chansons d'amour*. Ed. Moshé Lazar, 144 (Song 22). Paris: Klincksieck, 1966.

[397a] Raimon Ermengau. In Reinhilt Richter, *Die Troubadourzitate im* Breviari d'amor: *Kritische Ausgabe der provenzalischen Überlieferung*, 393. Modena: Mucchi, 1976.

[404] *Raimon Jordan. *Il trovatore Raimon Jordan*. Ed. Stefano Asperti. Modena: Mucchi, 1990.

[404.5]. *Le troubadour Raimon-Jordan, Vicomte de Saint-Antonin*. Ed. Hilding Kjellman. Uppsala: Almqvist & Wiksell, 1922.

[406] Raimon de Miraval. *Les poésies du troubadour Raimon de Miraval*. Ed. Leslie T. Topsfield. Paris: Nizet, 1971.

[409] Raimon de las Salas. Frank M. Chambers, "Raimon de las Salas." In *Essays in Honor of Louis Francis Solano*. Ed. Raymond J. Cormier and Urban T. Holmes, 29–51. North Carolina University Studies in the Romance Languages and Literatures 92. Chapel Hill: University of North Carolina Press, 1970.

[411] Raimon Vidal de Besalú. *Raimon Vidal: Il* Castia-Gilos *e i testi lirici*. Ed. Giuseppe Tavani. Milan: Luni, 1999.

[411.III] = Raimon Vidal, *Abril issia* 1162–72. In Raimon Vidal, *Obra poètica*. Ed. Hugh Field, vol. 1. Barcelona: Curial, 1989.

[416] Raimon Bistortz d'Arles. Jean-Claude Rivière, "Raimon Bistortz d'Arles." *L'Astrado* 21 (1986): 29–72.

[420.1] Richard I. In C. A. F. Mahn, *Die Werke der Troubadours in provenzalische Sprache*, 1:129. Geneva: Slatkine Reprints, 1977.

[421] Rigaut de Berbezilh. *Rigaut de Barbezilh: Liriche*. Ed. Alberto Vàrvaro. Biblioteca di filologa romanza 4. Bari: Adriatica, 1960.

[432.2] Savaric de Malleo. In *The Troubadour Tensos and Partimens: A Critical Edition.* Ed. Ruth Harvey, Linda Paterson, et al., 3:1155. Woodbridge: D. S. Brewer, 2010.

[432.3] Savaric de Malleo. In *The Troubadour Tensos and Partimens: A Critical Edition.* Ed. Ruth Harvey, Linda Paterson, et al., 3:1036. Woodbridge: D. S. Brewer, 2010.

[437] Sordello. *The Poetry of Sordello.* Ed. James J. Wilhelm. New York: Garland, 1987.

[440] Tibors. In *Trobairitz: Der Beitrag der Frau in der altokzitanischen höfischen Lyrik; Edition des Gesamtkorpus.* Ed. Angelica Rieger, 641. Tübingen: M. Niemeyer, 1991.

[449.5] Uc de la Bacalaria. Jean Audiau, "Une chanson du troubadour Uc de la Bachelerie." In *Mélanges de philologie et d'histoire offerts à M. Antoine Thomas,* 11–14. Paris: Champion, 1927.

[450] Uc Brunenc. *Il trovatore Uc Brunenc: Edizione critica con commento glossario e rimario.* Ed. Paolo Gresti. Tübingen: M. Niemeyer, 2001.

[454.1] Uc de Mataplana. In *Los trovadores: Historia literaria y textos.* Ed. Martín de Riquer, 3:1090. Barcelona: Planeta, 1975.

[456.1] Uc de Pena. In Adolf Kolsen, *Trobadorgedichte: Dreissig Stücke altprovenzalischer Lyrik,* 66. Halle: Niemeyer, 1925.

[457] Uc de Saint Circ. *Poésies de Uc de Saint-Circ.* Ed. Alfred Jeanroy and Jean-Jacques Salverda de Grave. Toulouse: Privat, 1913.

ANONYMOUS SONGS

[461.21]. In Adolf Kolsen, *Zwei provenzalische Sirventese nebst einer Anzahl Enzelstrophen,* 179. Halle: Niemeyer, 1919.

[461.31a]. In Adolf Kolsen, *Zwei provenzalische Sirventese nebst einer Anzahl Enzelstrophen,* 13. Halle: Niemeyer, 1919.

[461.32]. In Reinhilt Richter, *Die Troubadourzitate im* Breviari d'amor: *Kritische Ausgabe der provenzalischen Überlieferung,* 249. Modena: Mucchi, 1976.

[461.35]. In Pierre Bec, *Burlesque et obscénité chez les troubadours: Pour une approche du contre-texte médiéval,* 170. Paris: Stock, 1984.

[461.48]. In Adolf Kolsen, "25 bisher unedierte provenzalische Anonyma," 287. *Zeitschrift für romanische Philologie* 38 (1917): 281–310.

[461.54] In Adolf Kolsen, "25 bisher unedierte provenzalische Anonyma," 287. *Zeitschrift für romanische Philologie* 38 (1917): 281–310.

[461.57] In Adolf Kolsen, "Zwei provenzalische 'partimen' und zwei 'coblas'," 189. *Studi medievali,* n.s., 12 (1939): 183–91.

[461.75]. In Carl Appel, "Poésies provençales inédites tirées des manuscrits d'Italie," *Revue des Langues Romanes* 40 (1897): 405–26.

[461.76a]. In Peter T. Ricketts, *Contributions à l'étude de l'ancien occitan: Textes lyriques et non-lyriques en vers,* 64. Publications de l'AIEO 9. Birmingham, U.K.: University of Birmingham, 2000.

[461.79]. In *Poésies complètes du troubadour Peire Cardenal.* Ed. René Lavaud, 24. Toulouse: E. Privat, 1957.

[461.79a]. In Adolf Kolsen, *Dichtungen der Trobadors, auf Grund altprovenzalischer Handschriften—teils zume ersten Male kritisch herausgegeben—teils gerichtigt und ergänzt*, 198. Halle: Niemeyer, 1916–19.

[461.82]. In Pierre Bec, *Burlesque et obscénité chez les troubadours: Pour une approche du contre-texte médiéval*, 165. Paris: Stock, 1984.

[461.83]. In Pierre Bec, *Burlesque et obscénité chez les troubadours: Pour une approche du contre-texte médiéval*, 165. Paris: Stock, 1984.

[461.86]. In *Les poésies de Daude de Pradas*. Ed. Alexander Herman Schutz, 96. Toulouse: Privat, 1933.

[461.87]. In Adolf Kolsen, "25 bisher unedierte provenzalische Anonyma," *Zeitschrift für romanische Philologie* 38 (1917): 289.

[461.91]. In Reinhilt Richter, *Die Troubadourzitate im* Breviari d'amor: *Kritische Ausgabe der provenzalischen Überlieferung*, 433. Modena: Mucchi, 1976.

[461.95]. In Adolf Kolsen, "25 bisher unedierte provenzalische Anonyma," 290. *Zeitschrift für romanische Philologie* 38 (1917): 281–310.

[461.98]. In Adolf Kolsen, "25 bisher unedierte provenzalische Anonyma," *Zeitschrift für romanische Philologie* 38 (1917): 287.

[461.101]. In Reinhilt Richter, *Die Troubadourzitate im* Breviari d'amor: *Kritische Ausgabe der provenzalischen Überlieferung*, 434. Modena: Mucchi, 1976.

[461.123]. In Barbara Spaggiari, "La poesía religiosa anonima catalana o occitanica," 314. *Annali della Scuola Normale Superiore di Pisa*, ser. 3, vol. 7 (1977): 117–350.

[461.123b] In Adolf Kolsen, *Zwei provenzalische Sirventese nebst einer Anzahl Enzelstrophen*, 20. Halle: Niemeyer, 1919.

[461.130] In Adolf Kolsen, "25 bisher unedierte provenzalische Anonyma," 292. *Zeitschrift für romanische Philologie* 38 (1917): 281–310.

[461.132]. In Reinhilt Richter, *Die Troubadourzitate im* Breviari d'amor: *Kritische Ausgabe der provenzalischen Überlieferung*, 435. Modena: Mucchi, 1976.

[461.134]. In Reinhilt Richter, *Die Troubadourzitate im* Breviari d'amor: *Kritische Ausgabe der provenzalischen Überlieferung*, 436. Modena: Mucchi, 1976.

[461.135]. In Adolf Kolsen, "25 bisher unedierte provenzalische Anonyma," 292. *Zeitschrift für romanische Philologie* 38 (1917): 281–310.

[461.149] In Adolf Kolsen, "25 bisher unedierte provenzalische Anonyma," 293. *Zeitschrift für romanische Philologie* 38 (1917): 281–310.

[461.154] In Adolf Kolsen, "25 bisher unedierte provenzalische Anonyma," 294. *Zeitschrift für romanische Philologie* 38 (1917): 281–310.

[461.155] In Adolf Kolsen, "25 bisher unedierte provenzalische Anonyma," 294. *Zeitschrift für romanische Philologie* 38 (1917): 281–310.

[461.202]. In Pierre Bec, *Burlesque et obscénité chez les troubadours: Pour une approche du contre-texte médiéval*, 173. Paris: Stock, 1984.

[461.210]. In Reinhilt Richter, *Die Troubadourzitate im* Breviari d'amor: *Kritische Ausgabe der provenzalischen Überlieferung*, 437. Modena: Mucchi, 1976.

[461.213a]. In Adolf Kolsen, "Fünf provenzalische Dichtungen, das Partimen Gr. 350,1 und die Doppelcoblas 158,1, 461,127, [461,]213a, [461,]231," *Neuphilologische Mitteilungen* 39 (1938): 161.

[461.214]. In Adolf Kolsen, "25 bisher unedierte provenzalische Anonyma," *Zeitschrift für romanische Philologie* 38 (1917): 295.

[461.220a]. In Adolf Kolsen, *Zwei provenzalische Sirventese nebst einer Anzahl Enzelstrophen*, 28. Halle: Niemeyer, 1919.

[461.225]. In *Poésies complètes du troubadour Peire Cardenal*. Ed. . René Lavaud, 560. Toulouse: E. Privat, 1957.

[461.227]. In Adolf Kolsen, *Zwei provenzalische Sirventese nebst einer Anzahl Enzelstrophen*, 29. Halle: Niemeyer, 1919.

[461.232]. In Adolf Kolsen, "25 bisher unedierte provenzalische Anonyma," *Zeitschrift für romanische Philologie* 38 (1917): 2295.

[461.237]. In Carl Appel, *Provenzalische inedita aus pariser Handschriften*, 334. Leipzig: Fues's Verlag, 1890.

[461.241]. In Pierre Bec, *Burlesque et obscénité chez les troubadours: Pour une approche du contre-texte médiéval*, 167. Paris: Stock, 1984.

[461.245a] Since identified as a quotation from Raimon Vidal, *Abril issia*. Also in Reinhilt Richter, *Die Troubadourzitate im* Breviari d'amor: *Kritische Ausgabe der provenzalischen Überlieferung*, 232. Modena: Mucchi, 1976.

[461.250]. In Adolf Kolsen, "25 bisher unedierte provenzalische Anonyma," *Zeitschrift für romanische Philologie* 38 (1917): 297.

Editions of Works Containing Troubadour Quotations

[Listed in alphabetical order]

Anon. "An aquest gai son e leugier" [461.104, anonymous *descort*]. In Carl Appel, "Vom Descort," *Zeitschrift für romanische Philologie* 11 (1887): 216.

———. "Jois e chans e solatz" [461.142a, anonymous *descort*]. In *Il trovatore Elias Cairel*. Ed. Giosuè Lachin, 492. Modena: Mucchi, 2004.

Berenguer d'Anoia. *Mirall de trobar* [*Mi*]. Ed. Jaume Vidal i Alcover. Palma: Publacions de l'Abada de Montserrat, 1984.

Bertolome Zorzi. [74.9]. In *Der Troubadour Bertolome Zorzi*. Ed. Emil Levy. Halle: M. Niemeyer, 1883.

Biographies des troubadours [*Biographies*]. Ed. Jean Boutière and Alexander Herman Schutz. 2nd Ed. Paris: Nizet, 1964.

Dante Alighieri. *De vulgari eloquentia*. Ed. and trans. Steven Botterill. Cambridge: Cambridge University Press, 1996.

Francesco da Barberino. *I documenti d'amore, I–II*. Ed. Marco Albertazzi. Lavis: La Finestra, 2008.

Gerbert de Montreuil. *Le roman de la violette*. Ed. Douglas Labaree Buffum. Société des Anciens Textes Français. Paris: Champion, 1928.

Guillelmus de Aragonia. *De nobilitate animi.* Ed. William D. Paden and Mario Trovato. Harvard Studies in Medieval Latin. Cambridge, Mass.: Department of Classics, Harvard University, and Harvard University Press, 2012.

Guillem de Salaignac. [235.2]. In *Giraut de Salignac: Ein provenzalischer Trobadour.* Ed. Alexander Strempel, 59. Geneva: Slatkine Reprints, 1977.

Guiraut d'Espaigna. [244.1a]. In *Die Lieder des Trobadors Guiraut d'Espanha.* Ed. O. Hoby, 38. Freiburg, Switzerland: St. Paulus–Drückerei, 1915.

Jean Renart. **Roman de la rose ou de Guillaume de Dole.* Ed Félix Lecoy. Cahiers Français du Moyen Age. Paris: Champion, 1962.

———. *The Romance of the Rose or of Guillaume de Dole.* Ed. and trans. Regina Psaki. New York: Garland, 1995.

Jofre de Foixà. [304.1]. *In Martín de Riquer, *Los trovadores: Historia literaria y textos,* 3:1648. Barcelona: Planeta, 1975.

———. *Jofre de Foixà: Vers e Regles de trobar.* Ed. Ettore Li Gotti. Modena: Mucchi, 1952. Both 304.1 and the *Regles* are published in this edition.

———. *Las Regles de trobar [ReT].* *In *The "Razos de trobar" of Raimon Vidal and Associated Texts.* Ed. J. H. Marshall. London: Oxford University Press, 1972.

Luquet Gatelus. [290.1a]. In Giulio Bertoni, *I trovatori d'Italia,* 438. Modena: Orlandini, 1915.

Matfre Ermengau of Béziers. *Le breviari d'amor.* Ed. Peter T. Ricketts. 5 vols. Vol. 5, Leiden: Brill, 1976. Vols. 2 and 3, London: Publications de l'AIEO, 1989, 1998. Vol. 4, Turnhout: Brepols, Publications de l'AIEO, 2004. Vol. 5, Turnhout: Brepols, Publications de l'AIEO, 2011.

Molinier, Guilhem. *Las flors del gay saber, estier dichas, Las Leys d'amors.* Ed. A. F. Gatien-Arnoult. 3 vols. Toulouse: Privat, 1841–43.

———. *Las leys d'amors.* Ed. Joseph Anglade. 4 vols. Toulouse: Privat, 1919–20.

Petrarch. Francesco Petrarca, *Canzoniere.* Ed. Rosanna Bettarini. 2 vols. Turin: Einaudi, 2005

Raimon Vidal de Besalú. *[Novas].* In **Obra poètica.* Ed. Hugh Field. 2 vols. Barcelona: Curial, 1989.

———. In *Nouvelles occitanes.* Ed. Jean-Charles Huchet. Paris: Garnier-Flammarion, 1992.

———. *Razos de trobar [RaT].* In *The "Razos de trobar" of Raimon Vidal and Associated Texts.* Ed. J. H. Marshall. London: Oxford University Press, 1972.

Ripoll treatises [Ri]. In *The "Razos de trobar" of Raimon Vidal and Associated Texts.* Ed. J. H. Marshall. London: Oxford University Press, 1972.

Terramagnino da Pisa. *Doctrina d'acort [DA].* In *The "Razos de trobar" of Raimon Vidal and Associated Texts.* Ed. J. H. Marshall. London: Oxford University Press, 1972.

Other Primary Texts

Albertano da Brescia. *Liber consolationis et consilii,* read online at http://www.intratext .com/IXT/LAT0671/__PD.HTM.

————. *Liber de doctrina dicendi et tacendi*. Ed. Paola Navone. Florence: Galuzzo, 1998.

Albertet (de Sestero?) (16.17) and Monge (303.1). In *The Troubadour Tensos and Partimens: A Critical Edition*. Ed. Ruth Harvey, Linda Paterson, et al., 1:99–107. Woodbridge: D. S. Brewer, 2010.

Analecta hymnica medii aevi. Ed. Guido M. Dreves and Clemens Blume. 55 vols. Leipzig: Fues, 1886–1922. Consulted in the digital edition, Augsburg: Erwin Rauner Verlag, http://webserver.erwin-rauner.de/crophius/Analecta_conspectus.htm.

Le bestiaire: Version longue attribuée à Pierre de Beauvais. Ed. Craig Baker. Paris: Champion, 2010.

Dante Alighieri. *Divina commedia. The Divine Comedy of Dante Alighieri*. Ed. and trans. Robert M. Durling, introduction and notes by Ronald L. Martinez and Robert M. Durling. 3 vols. New York: Oxford University Press, 1996–2011.

————. *Rime*. Ed. Domenico de Robertis. Florence: Galluzzo, 2005.

Gace Brulé. *Gace Brulé, trouvère champenois: Edition des chansons et étude historique*. Ed. H. Petersen Dyggve. Helsinki: Société Néophilologique de Helsinki, 1951.

Gilles de Viés-Maisons. In *Fred Marshall, "Blondel de Nesle and His Friends: The Early Tradition of the *Grand Chant* Reviewed," *New Zealand Journal of French Studies* 5 (1984): 10–16.

————. In Holger Petersen Dyggve, "Trouvères et protecteurs des trouvères dans les cours seigneuriales de France," *Annales Academiae Scientiarum Fennicae* 50, no. 2 (1942): 70–72.

Las novas del papagai. In *Nouvelles occitanes du Moyen Age*. Ed. Jean-Charles Huchet. Paris: Garnier-Flammarion, 1992.

————. In *Les troubadours*, vol 2. Ed. René Lavaud and René Nelli. Paris: Desclée de Brouwer, 1966.

Ovid. *Amores*. In *Heroides and Amores*, Trans. Grant Showerman, text revised by G. P. Goold. Loeb Classical Library. Cambridge, Mass.: Harvard University Press, 1963.

————. *Ars amatoria*. In *The Art of Love and Other Poems*. Ed. G. P. Goold, trans. J. H. Mozely. Loeb Classical Library. Cambridge, Mass.: Harvard University Press, 1979.

Uc Faidit. *The "Donatz Proensals" of Uc Faidit*. Ed. J. H. Marshall. London: Oxford University Press, 1969.

Transcriptions and Facsimiles of Manuscripts

BREVIARI

Breviari d'amor de Matfre Ermengaud (Biblioteca Nacional de Rusia, Isp. F.v.XIV.N1). Vol. 1, *Facsimile*. Saint Petersburg: Biblioteca Nacional de Rusia; Madrid: AyN Ediciones, 2007.

NOVAS

[*a¹*]. Alart, B. "Un fragment de poésie provençale du trezième siècle." *Revue des Langues Romanes* 4 (1873): 228–39.

[*a²*]. Moliné i Brasés, E. "Textes catalans-provençals dels segles XIIIè i XIVè." *Buletí de la Reial Acadèmia de Bones Lletres de Barcelona* 6 (1911–12): 457–69.

TROUBADOUR *CHANSONNIERS*

[*Cm*]. Allegri, Laura. "Frammento di antico florilegio provenzale." *Studi medievali*, ser. 3, vol. 27, no. 1 (1986): 319–51.

[*D*]. Avalle, D'Arco Silvio, and Emanuele Casamassima. *Il canzoniere provenzale estense: Riprodotto per il centenario della nascita di Giulio Bertoni.* 2 vols. Modena: Mucchi, 1979–82.

[*Dc*]. Teulié, H., and G. Rossi, "L'anthologie provençale de Maître Ferraro de Ferrara." *Annales du Midi* 13–14 (1901).

[*G*]. Bertoni, G. *Il canzoniere provenzale della Biblioteca Ambrosiana R71.* Gesellschaft für romanischen Literatur 28. Dresden, 1912.

[*Fa*]. Stengel, Edmund. *Die Provenzalische Blumenlese der Chigiana.* Marburg: Elwert, 1978.

[*H*]. Careri, Maria. *Il canzoniere provenzale H (Vat. Lat. 3207): Struttura, contenuto e fonti.* Modena: Mucchi, 1990.

[*I*]. Meliga, Walter. *Bibliothèque nationale de France: I (fr. 854), K (12473).* Vol. 1, part 2 of *"Intavulare": Tavole di canzonieri romanzi,* I.ii. Dir. Anna Ferrari. Modena: Mucchi, 2001.

[*J*]. Stengel, E. "Studi sopra i canzoniere provenzali di Firenze e di Roma." *Rivista di Filologia romanza* 1 (1872): 20–45.

[*K*]. Meliga, Walter. *Bibliothèque nationale de France: I (fr. 854), K (12473).* Vol. 1, part 2 of *"Intavulare": Tavole di canzonieri romanzi,* I.ii. Dir. Anna Ferrari. Modena: Mucchi, 2001.

[*N²*]. Pillet, AlfrEd. "Die altprovenzalische Liederhandschrift *N²*." *Archiv für das Studium der neueren Sprachen und Literaturen* 101 (1898): 265–89; 102 (1899): 179–212.

WORKS OF CRITICISM AND HISTORY

Abulafia, David. "The Kingdom of Sicily Under the Hohenstaufen and Angevins." In *The New Cambridge Medieval History*, vol. 5. Ed. David Abulafia, 497–521. Cambridge: Cambridge University Press, 1999.

Alvar, Carlos. *La poesía trovadoresca en España y Portugal.* Madrid: Cupsa; Barcelona: Planeta, 1977.

Anglade, Joseph. *Etudes, notes, glossaire et index.* Vol. 4 of [Guilhem Molinier], *Las leys d'amors.* Ed. Joseph Anglade. Toulouse: Privat, 1920.

———. "Le troubadour N'At de Mons et les *Leys d'amors.*" *Romania* 51 (1925): 414–22.

Appel, Carl. "Petrarka und Arnaut Daniel." *Archiv für das Studium der neueren Sprachen und Literaturen* 147 (1924): 212–35.

Armstrong, Adrian. *The Virtuoso Circle: Competition, Collaboration and Complexity in Late Medieval French Poetry.* Tempe: Arizona Center for Medieval and Renaissance Studies, 2012.

Armstrong, Adrian, and Sarah Kay, with the participation of Rebecca Dixon, Miranda Griffin, Sylvia Huot, Francesca Nicholson, and Finn Sinclair. *Knowing Poetry: Verse in Medieval France from the Rose to the Rhétoriqueurs.* Ithaca, N.Y.: Cornell University Press, 2011.

Avalle, D'Arco Silvio. *La letteratura medievale in lingua d'oc nella sua tradizione manoscritta.* Turin: Einaudi, 1961.

Baldwin, John W. *Aristocratic Life in Medieval France: The Romances of Jean Renart and Gerbert de Montreuil, 1190–1230.* Baltimore: Johns Hopkins University Press, 2000.

———. " 'Once There Was an Emperor . . .': A Political Reading of the Romances of Jean Renart." In *Jean Renart and the Art of Romance: Essays on Guillaume de Dole.* Ed. Nancy Vine Durling, 45–82. Gainesville: University Press of Florida, 1997.

Barolini, Teodolinda. *Dante's Poets: Textuality and Truth in the "Comedy."* Princeton, N.J.: Princeton University Press, 1984.

Baumgartner, Emmanuèle. "Les citations lyriques dans le *Roman de la Rose* de Jean Renart." *Romance Philology* 35 (1981): 260–66.

Beer, Jeanette. *Beasts of Love: Richard de Fournival's "Bestiaire d'Amour" and a Woman's "Response."* Toronto: University of Toronto Press, 2003.

Beltrami, Pietro G. "Remarques sur Guilhem de Saint Gregori." In *Atti del Secondo Congresso Internazionale della Association International d'Études Occitanes, Torino, 31 agosto–5 settembre 1987.* Ed. G. Gasca Queirazza, 1:31–43. Turin: Dipartimento di Scienze Letterarie e Filologiche, 1993.

Bergin, Thomas G. "Dante's Provençal Gallery." *Speculum* 40 (1965): 15–30.

Bibliografia elettronica dei trovatori [*BEdT*]. Online resource at http://w3.uniroma1.it /bedt/BEdT_03_20/index.aspx.

Billy, Dominique. "Contrafactures de modèles troubadouresques dans la poésie catalane (XIVᵉ siècle)." In *Le rayonnement des troubadours: Actes du colloque de l'AIEO (Association Internationale d'Etudes Occitanes, Amsterdam, 16–18 octobre 1995).* Ed. Anton Touber, 51–74. Amsterdam: Rodopi, 1998.

Boehrer, Bruce Thomas. *Parrot Culture: Our 2,500-Year-Long Fascination with the World's Most Talkative Bird.* Philadelphia: University of Pennsylvania Press, 2004.

Bolduc, Michelle. *The Medieval Poetics of Contraries.* Gainesville: University Press of Florida, 2006.

———. "Naming Names: Matfre Ermengaud's Use of Troubadour Quotations." *Tenso* 22 (2007): 41–74.

———. "A Theological Defense of Courtly Love: Matfre Ermengaud's *Breviari d'Amor*." *Tenso* 20 (2005): 26–47.

Bondanella, Peter E. "Arnaut Daniel and Dante's 'Rime Petrose': A Re-Examination." *Studies in Philology* 68 (1971): 416–34.

Bossy, Michel-André. "L'art belliqueux des troubadours gibelins et guelfes." Unpublished paper presented at the conference "La diaspore occitane au moyen âge," King's College, London, June 5–7, 2008.

Boulton, Maureen McCann. "Lyric Insertions and the Reversal of Romance Conventions in Jean Renart's *Roman de la Rose* or *Guillaume de Dole*." In *Jean Renart and the Art of Romance: Essays on Guillaume de Dole*. Ed. Nancy Vine Durling, 85–104. Gainesville: University Press of Florida, 1997.

———. *The Song in the Story: Lyric Insertions in French Narrative Fiction, 1200–1400.* Philadelphia: University of Pennsylvania Press, 1993.

Boutière, Jean. "Quelques observations sur le texte des *vidas* et des *razos* dans les chansonniers provençaux *AB* et *IK*." In *French and Provençal Lexiciograpy: Essays Presented to Honor Alexander Herman Schutz*. Ed. Urban T. Holmes and Kenneth R. Scholberg, 125–39. Columbus: Ohio State University Press, 1964.

Burgwinkle, William E. "For Love or Money: Uc de Saint Circ and the Rhetoric of Exchange." *Romanic Review* 84 (1993): 347–76.

———. "'The Form of Our Desire': Arnaut Daniel and the Homoerotic Subject in Dante's *Commedia*." *GLQ* 10 (2004): 565–97.

———. *Love for Sale: Materialist Readings of Troubadour Poetry*. New York: Garland, 1997.

———. *Razos and Troubadour Songs*. New York: Garland, 1990.

Butler, Judith. "Imitation and Gender Insubordination." In *Inside/Out: Lesbian Theories, Gay Theories*. Ed. Diana Fuss, 13–32. New York: Routledge, 1991.

Butterfield, Ardis. *Poetry and Music in Medieval France from Jean Renart to Guillaume de Machaut*. Cambridge: Cambridge University Press, 2002.

Cabré, Miriam. "Italian and Catalan Troubadours." In *The Troubadours: An Introduction*. Ed. Simon Gaunt and Sarah Kay, 127–40. Cambridge: Cambridge University Press, 1999.

Caluwé, Jean-Michel. *Du chant à l'enchantement: Contribution à l'étude des rapports entre lyrique et narratif dans la littérature provençale du XIIIᵉ siècle*. Ghent: University of Ghent, 1993.

Carter, Paul. *Parrot*. London: Reaktion Books, 2006.

Castor, Grahame. *Pléiade Poetics: A Study in Sixteenth-Century Thought and Terminology*. Cambridge: Cambridge University Press, 1964.

Cerquiglini, Jacqueline. *"Un engin si soutil": Guillaume de Machaut et l'écriture au XIVᵉ siècle*. Paris: Champion, 1985.

Chaytor, Henry John. *The Troubadours of Dante: Being Selections from the Provençal Poets Quoted by Dante*. Oxford: Oxford University Press, 1902; reprint, New York: AMS Press, 1974.

Chenu, M.-D. "Auctor, Actor, Autor." *Bulletin du Cange: Archivum Latinitatis Medii Ævi* 3 (1927): 81–86.

Cigni, F. "Il trovatore N'At de Mons di Tolosa." *Studi Mediolatini e Volgari* 47 (2001): 251–73.

Compagnon, Antoine. *La seconde main; ou, Le travail de la citation*. Paris: Seuil, 1979.

Corbellari, Alain. *La voix des clercs: Littérature et savoir universitaire autour des dits du XIIIᵉ siècle*. Geneva: Droz, 2005.

Coulet, Jules. "Sur la nouvelle provençale du *Papagai*." *Revue des Langues Romanes* 45 (1902): 289–330.

Dallenbach, Lucien. *Le récit spéculaire: Essai sur la mise en abyme*. Paris: Seuil, 1977.

Dauvois, Nathalie. "L'évolution des formes lyriques dans les pièces primées aux Jeux Floraux toulousains XVᵉ–XVIᵉ siècles." In *Première poésie française de la Renaissance: Autour des Puys poétiques normands*. Ed. Jean-Claude Arnould and Thierry Mantovani, 555–74. Paris: Champion, 2003.

Derrida, Jacques. *Le monolinguisme de l'autre; ou, La prothèse d'origine*. Paris: Galilée, 1996.

———. "Signature événement contexte." In *Marges de la philosophie*, 367–83. Paris: Minuit, 1972.

Dietrich, Jessica S. "Dead Parrots' Society." *American Journal of Philology* 123, no. 1 (Spring 2002): 95–110.

Di Girolamo, Constanzo, and Donatella Siviero. "Da Orange a Beniarjó (passando per Firenze): Un'interpretazione degli *estramps* catalani." *Revue d'études catalanes* 2 (1999): 81–95.

Dragonetti, Roger. *Le mirage des sources: L'art du faux dans le roman médiéval*. Paris: Seuil, 1987.

Dyggve, Holger Petersen. "Trouvères et protecteurs des trouvères dans les cours seigneuriales de France." *Annales Academiae Scientiarum Fennicae* 50, no. 2 (1942) (=*Mélanges Långfors*): 41–247.

Eco, Umberto. "Riflessioni sulle techniche di citazione nel medioevo." In *Ideologie e pratiche del rempiego nell'alto medioevo (16–21 aprile 1998)*, 1:461–84. Spoleto: Presso la sede del Centro Italiano di studi sull'alto medioevo, 1999.

Egan, Margarita. "Commentary, *Vitae Poetae* and *Vida*: Latin and Old Provençal 'Lives of Poets.'" *Romance Philology* 37 (1983–84): 36–48.

Faral, Edmond. "Les chansons de toile ou chansons d'histoire." *Romania* 69 (1946–47): 433–62.

Fasseur, Valérie. "Mort et salut des troubadours: Le *Breviari d'amor* de Matfre Ermengau." In *Eglise et culture en France méridionale (XIIᵉ–XIVᵉ siècles)*. Ed. Jean-Louis Biget, 423–41. Toulouse: Privat, 2000.

———. "Une expérience avec la lyrique: Le *Perilhos tractat d'amor de donas* de Matfre Ermengaud." In *L'expérience lyrique au Moyen Âge: Actes du colloque tenu les 26 et 27 septembre 2002 à l'École normale supérieure lettres et sciences humaines de Lyon*. Ed. Michèle Gally, 169–92. Paris: Société de langue et de littérature médiévales d'oc et d'oïl, 2003.

Ferrando, Antoni. "El *Breviari d'amor*: Autoría, estructura, diffusion." In *Breviari d'amor de Matfre Ermengaud (Biblioteca Nacional de Rusia, Isp. F.v.XIV.N1)*, vol. 2, *Libro de estudios*, 9–29. Saint Petersburg: Biblioteca Nacional de Rusia; Madrid: AyN Ediciones, 2007.

Field, Hugh, Ed. *Obra poètica*. By Raimon Vidal de Besalú. 2 vols. Barcelona: Curial, 1989–91.

Folena, Gianfranco. *Culture e lingue nel Veneto medievale*. Padua: Editoriale Programma, 1990.

Formisano, Luciano. "Troubadours, trouvères, Sicilens." In *Le rayonnement des troubadours: Actes du colloque de l'AIEO (Association Internationale d'Etudes Occitanes, Amsterdam, 16–18 octobre 1995)*. Ed. Anton Touber, 109–24. Amsterdam: Rodopi, 1998.

Francis, Scott. "The *Joglar* as Salesman in Raimon Vidal de Besalú's *Abrils Issi' e Mays Intrava*." *Tenso* 24 (2009): 1–19.

Frank, István. "La chanson 'Lasso me' de Pétrarque et ses prédécesseurs." *Annales du Midi* 66 (1954): 259–68.

———. *Répertoire métrique de la poésie des troubadours*. 2 vols. Paris: Champion, 1953, 1966.

Galvez, Marisa. *Songbook: How Lyrics Became Poetry in Medieval Europe*. Chicago: University of Chicago Press, 2012.

Garber, Marjorie. *Quotation Marks*. London: Routledge, 2003.

Gaunt, Simon. "Linguistic Difference, the Philology of Romance and the Romance of Philology." In *A Sea of Languages: Literature and Culture in the Pre-modern Mediterranean*. Ed. Suzanne Conklin Akbari and Karla Mallette, 43–61. Toronto: Toronto University Press, 2013.

Gennrich, Friedrich. *Bibliographisches Verzeichnis der französischen Refrains des 12. und 13. Jahrhunderts*. Langen bei Frankfurt: [s.n.], 1964.

Gonfroy, Gérard. "Le reflet de la *canso* dans le *De vulgari eloquentia* et dans les *Leys d'amors*." *Cahiers de Civilisation Médiévale* 25 (1982): 187–96.

Grafton, Anthony. *The Footnote: A Curious History*. London: Faber and Faber, 1997.

Greene, Thomas M. *The Light in Troy: Imitation and Discovery in Renaissance Poetry*. New Haven, Conn.: Yale University Press, 1982.

Gruber, Jörn. *Die Dialektik des Trobar: Untersuchungen zur Struktur und Entwicklung des occitanischen und französischen Minnesangs des 12. Jahrhunderts*. Beihefte zur Zeitschrift für romanische Philologie 194. Tübingen: Niemeyer, 1983.

Guida, Saverio. "Ricerche sull'attività biografica di Uc de Sant Circ a Treviso." In *Il medioevo nella Marca: Trovatori, giullari, letterati a Treviso nei secoli XIII e XIV (Atti del Convegno, Treviso, 28–29 settembre 1990)* . Ed. M. L. Meneghetti and F. Zambon, 91–114. Treviso: Premio Comisso, 1991.

Hayes, E. Bruce. "Arnaut Daniel et Dante." In *Le rayonnement des troubadours: Actes du colloque de l'AIEO (Association Internationale d'Etudes Occitanes, Amsterdam, 16–18 octobre 1995)*. Ed. Anton Touber, 125–32. Amsterdam: Rodopi, 1998.

Helgeson, James. *The Lying Mirror: The First-Person Stance and Sixteenth-Century Writing*. Geneva: Droz, 2012.

Heller-Roazen, Daniel. *Echolalias: On the Forgetting of Language*. New York: Zone, 2005.

Hiscoe, David W. "Dante's Poetry, Daedalus's Monster, and Arnaut Daniel's Name." *Italica* 60 (1983): 246–55.

Hunt, Richard W. "The Introductions to the 'Artes' in the Twelfth Century." In *Studia mediaevalia in honorem admodum Reverendi Patris Raymundi Josephi Martin*, 85–112. Bruges: De Tempel, 1948.

Huot, Sylvia. *From Song to Book: The Poetics of Writing in Old French Lyric and Lyrical Narrative Poetry*. Ithaca, N.Y.: Cornell University Press, 1987.

Janzarik, Diether. "Uc de St. Circ—auteur du *Donatz Proensals?*" *Zeitschrift für romanische Philologie* 105 (1989): 264–75.

Jewers, Caroline. "Fabric and Fabrication: Lyric and Narrative in Jean Renart's *Roman de la Rose.*" *Speculum* 71 (1996): 907–24.

Jones, Nancy A. "The Uses of Embroidery in the Romances of Jean Renart: Gender, History, Textuality." In *Jean Renart and the Art of Romance: Essays on Guillaume de Dole*. Ed. Nancy Vine Durling, 3–44. Gainesville: University Press of Florida, 1997.

Kay, Sarah. "How Long Is a Quotation? Quotations from the Troubadours in the Text and Manuscripts of the *Breviari d'amor.*" *Romania* 127 (2009): 140–68.

———. "Knowledge and Truth in Quotations from the Troubadours: Matfre Ermengaud, Compagnon, Lyotard, Lacan." *Australian Journal of French Studies* 46 (2009): 178–90.

———. "La poésie, la vérité, et le sujet supposé savoir: Citations des troubadours et poétique européenne." In *Pourquoi des théories*. Ed. Denis Guénoun and Nicolas Doutey, 87–111. Paris: Les Solitaires Intempestifs, 2009.

———. "L'arbre et la greffe dans le *Breviari d'amor* de Matfre Ermengaud: Temps du savoir et temps de l'amour." In *L'arbre au Moyen Âge*. Ed. Valérie Fasseur, Danièle James-Raoul, and Jean-René Valette, 169–81. Paris: Presses de l'Université Paris-Sorbonne, 2010.

———. "La seconde main et les secondes langues dans la France médiévale." In *Translations médiévales: Cinq siècles de traductions en français au Moyen Âge (XIᵉ–XVᵉ siècles)*. Dir. Claudio Galderisi. 1:461–85. Turnhout: Brepols, 2011.

———. "Occitan Grammar as a Science of Endings." In "Medieval Grammar and the Literary Arts." Ed. Chris Cannon, Rita Copeland, and Nicolette Zeeman, special issue, *New Medieval Literatures* 11 (2009): 39–61.

Kenny, Neil. *The Uses of Curiosity in Early Modern France and Germany*. Oxford: Oxford University Press, 2004.

Krueger, Roberta. *Women Readers and the Ideology of Gender in Old French Verse Romance*. Cambridge: Cambridge University Press, 1993.

Lacan, Jacques. *Le séminaire, livre XV: L'acte psychanalytique*. Online at http://gaogoa.free.fr/.

———. *Le séminaire, livre XVI: D'un Autre à l'autre*. Ed. Jacques-Alain Miller. Paris: Seuil, 2006.

———. *Le séminaire, livre XVII: L'envers de la psychanalyse*. Ed. Jacques-Alain Miller. Paris: Seuil, 1991.

Laske-Fix, Katja. *Der Bildzyklus des Breviari d'Amor.* Munich: Schnell und Steiner, 1973.

Leach, Elizabeth Eva. *Sung Birds: Music, Nature, and Poetry in the Later Middle Ages.* Ithaca, N.Y.: Cornell University Press, 2007.

Lee, Charmaine. "'Versi d'amore e prose di romanzi': The Reception of Occitan Narrative Genres in Italy." *Tenso* (forthcoming).

Léglu, Catherine E. "Languages in Conflict in Toulouse: *Las Leys d'amors.*" *Modern Language Review* 103 (2008): 383–96.

———. *Multilingualism and Mother Tongue in Medieval French, Occitan and Catalan Narratives.* University Park: Pennsylvania State University Press, 2010.

Lemaire, Jacques. *Introduction à la codicologie.* Louvain-la-Neuve: Université catholique de Louvain, Institut d'études médiévales, 1989.

Limentani, Alberto. *L'eccezione narrativa.* Turin: Einaudi, 1977.

Mancini, Mario. "Aimeric de Peguilhan, 'rhétoriqueur' e giullare." In *Il medioevo nella Marca: Trovatori, giullari, letterati a Treviso nei secoli XIII e XIV (Atti del Convegno, Treviso 28–29 settembre 1990)* . Ed. M. L. Meneghetti and F. Zambon, 45–89. Treviso: Premio Comisso, 1991.

Marchesi, Simone. *Dante and Augustine: Linguistics, Poetics, Hermeneutics.* Toronto: Toronto University Press, 2011.

Marnette, Sophie. "La ponctuation du discours rapporté dans quelques manuscrits de romans en prose médiévaux." *Verbum* 28, no. 1 (2008): 29–46.

Marshall, FrEd. "Blondel de Nesle and His Friends: The Early Tradition of the *Grand Chant* ReviewEd. " *New Zealand Journal of French Studies* 5 (1984): 5–32.

Marshall, John H. "La chanson provençale 'Entre·l taur e·l doble signe' (BdT 411,3): une dix-neuvième chanson d'Arnaut Daniel?" *Romania* 90 (1969): 548–58.

———. "Observations on the Sources of the Treatment of Rhetoric in the 'Leys d'Amors.'" *Modern Language Review* 64 (1969): 39–52.

———. "Pour l'étude des contrafacta dans la poésie des troubadours." *Romania* 101 (1980): 289–335.

———, Ed. *The "Razos de Trobar" of Raimon Vidal and Associated Texts.* London: Oxford University Press, 1972.

Massó Torrents, J. "La cançó provençal en la literatura catalana. " In *Miscel·lània Prat de la Riba*, 1:341–460. Barcelona: Institut d'Estudis Catalans, 1923.

———. "A propos d'une pièce inconnue de Jaufré de Foixa." *Annales du Midi* 35–36 (1923–24): 313–18.

Meneghetti, Maria Luisa. "Il florilegio trobadorico de Ferrarino da Ferrara." In *Miscellanea di Studi in onore di Aurelio Roncaglia a cinquant'anni dalla sua laurea*, 3:853–71. Modena: Mucchi, 1989.

———. *Il pubblico dei trovatori.* 2nd Ed. Turin: Einaudi, 1992.

———. "Les florilèges dans la tradition lyrique des troubadours." In *Lyrique romane médiévale: La tradition des chansonniers (Actes du Colloque de Liège, 1989).* Ed. Madeleine Tyssens, 43–56 (discussion, pp. 56–59). Liège: Bibliothèque de la Faculté de Philosophie et Lettres de l'Université de Liège, 1991.

———. "Uc de Saint Circ tra filologia e divulgazione (su data, formazione e fine del Liber Alberici)." In *Il medioevo nella Marca: Trovatori, giullari, letterati a Treviso nei secoli XIII e XIV (Atti del Convegno, Treviso, 28–29 settembre 1990).* Ed. M. L. Meneghetti and F. Zambon, 115–28. Treviso: Premio Comisso, 1991.

Menocal, María Rosa. *Shards of Love: Exile and the Origins of the Lyric.* Durham, N.C.: Duke University Press, 1994.

———. *Writing in Dante's Cult of Truth from Borges to Boccaccio.* Durham, N.C.: Duke University Press, 1991.

Mertens, Volker. "Kontrafaktur als intertextuelles Spiel: Aspekte der Adaptation von Troubadour-Melodien im deutschen Minnesang." In *Le rayonnement des troubadours: Actes du colloque de l'AIEO (Association Internationale d'Etudes Occitanes, Amsterdam, 16–18 octobre 1995).* Ed. Anton Touber, 269–83. Amsterdam: Rodopi, 1998.

Meyer, Herman. *The Poetics of Quotation in the European Novel.* Trans. Theodore Ziolkowski and Yetta Ziolkowski. Princeton, N.J.: Princeton University Press, 1968.

Minnis, A. J., and A. B. Scott, with the assistance of David Wallace. *Medieval Literary Theory and Criticism, c. 1100–1375: The Commentary Tradition.* Revised Ed. Oxford: Clarendon, 1988.

Miranda, José Carlos Ribeiro. "Le surgissement de la culture troubadouresque dans l'occident de la Pénsinsule Ibérique (II): Les genres, les thèmes, et les formes." In *Le rayonnement des troubadours: Actes du colloque de l'AIEO (Association Internationale d'Etudes Occitanes, Amsterdam, 16–18 octobre 1995).* Ed. Anton Touber, 97–105. Amsterdam: Rodopi, 1998.

Monaci, Ernesto. *Poesie in lingua d'oc e in lingua d'oïl allegate da Dante nel "De vulgari eloquentia" premesso il testo della allegazioni dantesche.* Rome: Ermanno Loescher, 1909; reprint, Rome: Libri, 1994.

Monson, Don A. *Les "ensenhamens" occitans: Essai de définition et de délimitation du genre.* Paris: Klincksieck, 1981.

Moreau, John. "Eschatalogical Subjects: Divine and Literary Judgment in Fourteenth-Century French Poetry." Ph.D. dissertation, Princeton, 2011.

Nelli, René. "Arnaut de Carcassès (XIIIᵉ s.): La nouvelle du perroquet." *Cahiers de la pensée française* 2 (1941): 159–77.

Nichols, Stephen G. "Urgent Voices: The Vengeance of Images in Medieval Poetry." In *Text und Kultur: Mittelalterliche Literatur, 1150–1450.* Ed. Ursula Peters, 403–13. Stuttgart: Metzler, 2001.

Nicholson, Francesca M. "Branches of Knowledge: The Purposes of Citation in the *Breviari d'amor* of Matfre Ermengaud." *Neophilologus* 91 (2007): 361–73.

Orr, Mary. *Intertextuality: Debates and Contexts.* Cambridge: Polity, 2003.

O'Sullivan, Daniel E. "Contrafacture from Old Occitan to Old French Song: The Troubadours' Melodic Legacy." Paper presented at the Southeastern Medieval Association Conference, Nashville, Tenn., October 2009.

Paden, William D. "Imaginer Bertran de Born." In *Les cahiers du Carrefour Ventadour*, vol. 17, *Bertran de Born, seigneur et troubadour*. Ed. Luc de Goustine, 97–123. Paris: Carrefour Ventadour, 2010.

———. "Old Occitan as a Literary Language: The Insertions from Occitan in Three Thirteenth-Century French Romances." *Speculum* 68 (1993): 36–63

———. "The Troubadours and the Albigensian Crusade: A Long View." *Romance Philology* 49 (1995): 168–91.

Page, Christopher. *The Owl and the Nightingale: Musical Life and Ideas in France, 1100–1300*. London: Dent, 1989.

Parkes, Malcolm B. *Pause and Effect: An Introduction to the History of Punctuation in the West*. Aldershot: Scolar Press, 1992.

Pasero, Nicola. "Sulle fonti del libro primo delle *Leys d'Amors*." *Studj Romanzi* 34 (1965): 125–85.

Paterson, Linda M. *The World of the Troubadours: Medieval Occitan Society, c. 1100–1300*. Cambridge: Cambridge University Press, 1993.

Peraino, Judith. *Giving Voice to Love: Song and Self-Expression from the Troubadours to Guillaume de Machaut*. New York: Oxford University Press, 2011.

Peirone, Luigi. "Il 'trobar leu' di Arnaut Daniel e un passo del *Purgatorio*." *Giornale Italiano di Filologia* 19 (1964): 154–60.

Perugi, Maurizio. "Arnaut Daniel in Dante." *Studi Danteschi* 51 (1978): 59–152.

———. *Trovatori a Valchiusa: Un frammento della cultura provenzale del Petrarca*. Padua: Antenore, 1985.

Peters, Ursula. *Das Ich im Bild: Die Figur des Autors in volkssprachigen Bilderhandschriften des 13. bis 16. Jahrhunderts*. Cologne: Böhlau, 2008.

Pfeffer, Wendy. *The Change of Philomel: The Nightingale in Medieval Literature*. New York: Lang, 1985.

———." A Note on Dante, *De vulgari eloquentia*, and the Manuscript Tradition," *Romance Notes* 46 (2005): 69–76.

Pillet, Alfred, and Henry Carstens [PC, Pillet-Carstens]. *Bibliographie der Troubadours*. Halle: Niemeyer, 1933. Updated online as *Bibliografia elettronica dei trovatori* [*BEdT*] at http://w3.uniroma1.it/bedt/BEdT_03_20/index.aspx.

Pirot, François. *Recherches sur les connaissances des troubadours occitans et catalans des XIIᵉ et XIIIᵉ siècles*. Barcelona: Real Academia de Buenas Letras, 1972.

Poe, Elizabeth W. "At the Boundary Between *Vida* and *Razo*: The Biography for Raimon Jordan," *Neophilologus* 72 (1986): 316–19.

———. "Cantairitz e Trobairitz: A Forgotten Attestation of Old Provençal Trobairitz." *Romanische Forschungen* 114 (2002): 206–15.

———. *Compilatio: Lyric Texts and Prose Commentaries in Troubadour Manuscript H (Vat. Lat. 3207)*. Armstrong monographs 11. Lexington, Ky.: French Forum, 2000.

———. *From Poetry to Prose in Old Provençal: The Emergence of the* Vidas, *the* Razos, *and the "Razos de trobar."* Birmingham, Ala.: Summa Publications, 1984.

———. "*L'autr' escrit* of Uc de Saint Circ: The *Razos* for Bertran de Born." *Romance Philology* 44 (1990): 123–36.

———. "The Meaning of *Saber* in Raimon Vidal's *Abril issia*." In *Studia Occitanica in Memoriam Paul Rémy*. Ed. Hans-Erich Keller et al., 2:169–72. Kalamazoo: Medieval Institute Publications, Western Michigan University, 1986.

———. "A Re-evaluation of Troubadour Manuscript N². " *Revue Belge de Philologie et d'Histoire* 83 (2005): 19–28.

———. "Teaching Troubadours." Conference paper presented at Mount Holyoke College, South Hadley, Mass., April 20, 2007.

Pontalis, J.-B. *L'amour des commencements.* Paris: Gallimard 1986. *Love of Beginnings*, trans. James Greene with Marie-Christine Réguis. London: Free Association Books, 1993.

Powell, James M. *Albertanus of Brescia: The Pursuit of Happiness in the Early Thirteenth Century.* Philadelphia: University of Pennsyvania Press, 1992.

Ramm, Ben. "A Rose by Any Other Name? Queering Desire in Jean Renart's *Le Roman de la Rose, ou de Guillaume de Dole*." *Exemplaria: A Journal of Theory in Medieval and Renaissance Studies* 19 (2007): 402–19.

Raupach, Manfred, and Margaret Raupach. *Französierte Trobadorlyrik: Zur Überlieferung provenzalischer Lieder in französischen Handschriften.* Tübingen: M. Niemeyer, 1979.

[Raynaud and Spanke.] Hans Spanke, *Gaston Raynauds Bibliographie des altfranzösischen Liedes.* Neu bearbeitet und ergänzt. Leiden: Brill, 1955.

Resende de Oliveira, António. "Le surgissement de la culture troubadouresque dans l'occident de la Péninsule Ibérique (I): Compositeurs et cours." In *Le rayonnement des troubadours: Actes du colloque de l'AIEO (Association Internationale d'Etudes Occitanes, Amsterdam, 16–18 octobre 1995).* Ed. Anton Touber, 85–95. Amsterdam: Rodopi, 1998.

Richter, Reinhilt. *Die Troubadourzitate im* Breviari d'amor: *Kritische Ausgabe der provenzalischen Überlieferung.* Modena: Mucchi, 1976.

Ricketts, Peter T. "Le problème du manuscrit *H* du *Breviari d'amor* de Matfre Ermengaud." *Atti del XXI Congresso Internazionale di Linguistica e Filologia Romanza.* Ed. Giovanni Ruffino, 6:439–44. Tübingen: Niemeyer, 1998.

———. "Une nouvelle citation dans le *Breviari d'amor* de Matfre Ermengaud?" *Revue des Langues Romanes* 104 (2000): 421–25.

Rieger, Angelica. "Relations interculturelles entre troubadours, trouvères e Minnesänger au temps des croisade." In *Le rayonnement des troubadours: Actes du colloque de l'AIEO (Association Internationale d'Etudes Occitanes, Amsterdam, 16–18 octobre 1995).* Ed. Anton Touber, 201–25. Amsterdam: Rodopi, 1998.

Riquer, Martín de. *Los trovadores: Historia literaria y textos.* 3 vols. Barcelona: Planeta, 1975.

Roncaglia, Aurelio. "De quibusdam Provincialibus translatis in lingua nostra." In *Letteratura e critica: Studi in onore di Natalino Sapegno.* Ed. Walter Binni et al., 2:1–36. Rome: Bulzoni, 1975.

Rosenstein, R. "Translation." In *A Handbook of the Troubadours*. Ed. F. R. P. Akehurst and J. M. Davis, 334–48. Berkeley: University of California Press, 1995.

Saïd, Edward W. *Beginnings: Intention and Method*. New York: Columbia University Press, 1985.

Santangelo, Salvatore. *Dante e i trovatori provenzali*. Catania: Giannotti, 1921.

Sayce, Olive. *The Medieval German Lyric, 1150–1300*. Oxford: Clarendon, 1982.

Shapiro, Marianne. *"De vulgari eloquentia": Dante's Book of Exile*. Lincoln: University of Nebraska Press, 1990.

Shepard, William P., and Frank M. Chambers, eds. *The Poems of Aimeric de Peguilhan*. Evanston, Ill.: Northwestern University Press, 1950.

Smith, D. Vance. *The Book of the Incipit: Beginnings in the Fourteenth Century*. Minneapolis: University of Minnestota Press, 2001.

Smith, Nathaniel B. "Arnaut Daniel in the *Purgatorio*: Dante's Ambivalence Toward Provençal." *Dante Studies* 98 (1980): 99–109.

Snow, Joseph T. "The Iberian Pensinsula." In *A Handbook of the Troubadours*. Ed. F. R. P. Akehurst and J. M. Davis, 271–78. Berkeley: University of California Press, 1995.

Stone, Gregory B. *The Death of the Troubadour: The Late Medieval Resistance to the Renaissance*. Philadelphia: University of Pennsylvania Press, 1994.

Swiggers, Pierre. "La plus ancienne grammaire du français." *Medioevo romanzo* 9 (1984): 183–88.

Tavani, Giuseppe, Ed. *Raimon Vidal: Il Castia-Gilos e i testi lirici*. Milan: Luni, 1999.

Taylor, Jane H. "Lyric Insertion: Towards a Functional Model." In *Courtly Literature: Culture and Context*. Ed. Keith Busby and Erik Kooper, 539–48. Amsterdam: Benjamins, 1990.

Thiolier-Méjean, Suzanne. "Le langage du perroquet dans quelques textes d'oc et d'oïl." In *Le plurilinguisme au Moyen Âge: Orient-Occident; de Babel à la langue une*. Ed. Claire Kappler and Suzanne Thiolier-Méjean, 267–99. Paris: Harmattan, 2009.

———. "Le motif du perroquet dans deux nouvelles d'oc." In *Miscellanea mediaevalia: Mélanges offerts à Philippe Ménard*. Ed. Jean-Claude Faucon, Alain Labbé, and Danielle Quéruel, 2:1355–75. Paris: Champion, 1998.

Tischler, Hans. *Trouvère Lyrics with Melodies: Complete Comparative Edition* [= *Tropatorum septemtrionalum poemata cum suis melodiis: Opera omnia*]. 15 vols. Neuhausen: Hänssler Verlag, 1997.

Toch, Michael. "Welfs, Hohenstaufen and Habsburgs." In *The New Cambridge Medieval History*, vol. 5. Ed. David Abulafia, 375–404. Cambridge: Cambridge University Press, 1999.

Topsfield, Leslie T. *Troubadours and Love*. Cambridge: Cambridge University Press, 1975.

Touber, Anton, Ed. *Le rayonnement des troubadours: Actes du colloque de l'AIEO (Association Internationale d'Etudes Occitanes, Amsterdam, 16–18 octobre 1995)*. Amsterdam: Rodopi, 1998.

Tucker, George Hugo, Ed. *Forms of the "Medieval" in the "Renaissance": A Multidisciplinary Exploration of a Cultural Continuum.* Charlottesville, Va.: Rookwood Press, 2000.

Van der Werf, Hendrik. *The Extant Troubadour Melodies: Transcriptions and Essays for Performers and Scholars.* Text Ed. , Gerald A. Bond. Rochester, N.Y.: Published by the author, 1984.

———. "Jean Renart and Medieval Song" and appendices. In *Jean Renart and the Art of Romance: Essays on Guillaume de Dole.* Ed. Nancy Vine Durling, 157–222. Gainesville: University Press of Florida, 1997.

Van Os, J. A. "Structure mélodique et rythme déclamatoire dans la chanson de trouvère." In *Langue et littérature françaises du Moyen Age.* Ed. R. E. V. Stuip, 51–62. Amsterdam: Van Gorcum, 1978.

Washer, Nancy. "Paraphrased and Parodied, Extracted and Inserted: The Changing Meaning of Folquet de Marseille's 'Amors, Merce!' " *Neophilologus* 91 (2007): 565–81.

Wesselofsky, A. "Un nouveau texte des *Novas del papagay.*" *Romania* 7 (1878): 327–29.

Zingesser, Eliza. "French Troubadours: Assimilating Occitan Literature in Northern France (1200–1400)." Ph.D. dissertation, Princeton, 2012.

Zink, Michel. *Belle: Essai sur les chansons de toile.* Paris: Champion, 1978.

———. "Suspension and Fall: The Fragmentation and Linkage of Lyric Insertions in *Le Roman de la rose (Guillaume de Dole)* and *Le roman de la violette.*" In *Jean Renart and the Art of Romance: Essays on Guillaume de Dole.* Ed. Nancy Vine Durling, 105–21. Gainesville: University Press of Florida, 1997.

Zufferey, François. *Bibliographie des poètes provençaux des XIVe et XVe siècles.* Geneva: Droz, 1981.

———. "La partie non-lyrique du chansonnier d'Urfé." *Revue des Langues Romanes* 98 (1994): 1–29.

———. *Recherches linguistiques sur les chansonniers provençaux.* Geneva: Droz, 1987.

INDEX

Acknowledgments

This book was begun as part of the project "Poetic Knowledge in Late Medieval France" which was funded by the United Kingdom's Arts and Humanities Research Council (AHRC) for a total of four and a half years, from January 2005 to June 2009. The funding framework enabled me to work as part of a team, an experience for which I am profoundly grateful. I acknowledge my indebtedness to all my co-researchers on that project, and especially to the Principal Investigator Adrian Armstrong, for their friendship, companionship, and intellectual stimulus. I enjoyed a Visiting Research Professorship at the School of Advanced Study, University of London, in 2008, at the same time as sabbatical leave and research support from Princeton University, which furnished invaluable opportunities for research and interaction with other scholars. The Humanities Initiative at NYU was so gracious as to provide a subvention toward the cost of printing my Appendices, for which I thank them. I have also been fortunate to be able to present my ideas for this book in a number of forums, and have benefited in ways I cannot begin to quantify from the discussions that have resulted. I first began to explore quotations from the troubadours in 2005, in a paper given at Susan Boynton's invitation at Columbia University, and from then on one thing led to another. It is invidious to single out names among so many stimulating interlocutors, but I should at least thank Bill Burgwinkle, Patrick ffrench, Ruth Harvey, Cary Howie, Patti Ingham, Scott Francis, Simon Gaunt, Bill Paden, Peggy McCracken, John Moreau, Steve Nichols, Sara Poor, Ian Short, Vance Smith, and Eliza Zingesser. I am especially grateful to the readers who reported to the Press on an earlier version of this study. The late Peter Ricketts was enormously helpful in all matters relating to the *Breviari* and I am very grateful to him for sharing with me work that was still forthcoming. The same generosity is grounds for thanking Michel-André Bossy, Simon Gaunt, James Helgeson, Charmaine Lee, Daniel O'Sullivan and Elizabeth Poe. Future researchers will join me in paying tribute to Eliza Zingesser for compiling what may be the most important part of this book, Appendix 1, and to my copy-editor, Jennifer Shenk. Finally, I am grateful to my editors at the University of Pennsylvania Press for their continued support and forbearance as what was meant to be a short book grew ineluctably into this one.

Arts & Humanities
Research Council